CORNISH STUDIES

Second Series

NINE

INSTITUTE OF CORNISH STUDIES

Sardinia Pilchardus
(The Pilchard)

EDITOR'S NOTE

Cornish Studies (second series) exists to reflect current research conducted internationally in the inter-disciplinary field of Cornish Studies. It is edited by Professor Philip Payton, Director of the Institute of Cornish Studies at the University of Exeter, and is published by the University of Exeter Press. The opinions expressed in *Cornish Studies* are those of individual authors and are not necessarily those of the editor or publisher. The support of Cornwall County Council is gratefully acknowledged.

Cover illustration: Cornish timbermen underground at the Moonta Mines, South Australia (reproduced courtesy of the Mortlock Library, Adelaide)

CORNISH STUDIES

Second Series

NINE

Edited by

Philip Payton

UNIVERSITY
of
EXETER
PRESS

First published in 2001 by
University of Exeter Press
Reed Hall, Streatham Drive
Exeter, Devon EX4 4QR
UK
www.ex.ac.uk/uep/

British Library Cataloguing in Publication Data
A catalogue record for this book is
available from the British Library

ISBN 0 85989 702 8
ISSN 1352-271X

Typeset in 10/12pt Times by Kestrel Data, Exeter

Printed and bound in Great Britain by
Short Run Press Ltd, Exeter

Contents

INTRODUCTION

Two important features of note in the development of Cornish Studies as an area of academic activity in recent years have been the attempts to encourage a comparative edge and to engage with current debate about the nature and future of Celtic Studies, of which Cornish Studies may (in some of its guises at least) be seen as a component part. Additionally, while taking care to maintain its interest in what might be seen as its 'traditional' spheres of activity, notably the Cornish language, Cornish Studies has expanded its horizons, moving to encompass within its view the condition of modern Cornwall, a focus which has prompted the development of what has been termed a 'new Cornish social science' and allowed the application of new theoretical perspectives.

In this edition of *Cornish Studies*, number nine in the series, there is evidence of each of these trends in a disparate collection of articles which demonstrates the breadth of our subject area and the range of disciplinary specialisms that are now brought to bear in the study of Cornwall and the Cornish. The mere juxtaposition of these articles is calculated to persuade the reader to adopt an interdisciplinary perspective as he/she contemplates and compares the contrasting material and methods presented here, while several of the contributions are themselves interdisciplinary in spirit, the whole pointing to the sophistication that now exists within Cornish Studies.

Manuel Alberro's article on 'Celtic Galicia?' exemplifies a number of these developments, not least in its comparative discussion of what is today called the 'Atlantic Arc' and in its contribution to contemporary Celtic Studies. The position of Galicia (in northern Spain) within the Celtic world has long been the subject of contention, scholars pointing to the region's strong 'Celtiberian' heritage, but with the institutions of Pan-Celticism expressing what has often amounted to overt hostility to Galicia's claim to be a Celtic nation. Indeed, as Alberro notes, in 1987 the Celtic League formally rejected Galicia's application to join that organization, the principal reason being Galicia's failure to meet what Peter Berresford Ellis has called the 'linguistic criterion', the speaking of a Celtic language in modern times. However, as Alberro also shows, this has not prevented an increasingly self-confident and assertive Galicia (now a self-governing region within Spain) from proclaiming a self-defined Celtic identity, an identity that has growing appeal particularly for the younger generation and finds its expression today in a range of festivals and other cultural activities. Moreover, as Alberro goes on to elaborate at length, both popular and academic constructions of Galician Celticity are based on an array of historical comparisons and links between the nations and regions of the 'Atlantic Area' in which Galicia is seen to exhibit numerous similarities with other places, especially Cornwall. Indeed, it is the comparison between Galicia and Cornwall that underscores Alberro's discussion as he attempts to elucidate the case for Galician Celticity. Comprehensive as well as candid, it is a case that sheds considerable light on the nature of contemporary Celticity and the manner in which imaginations of a Celtic past are informing the shaping of new cultural and political identities in north-west Europe.

Celtic comparisons also underpin the work of Paul Cockerham who, drawing together a vast amount of material that has already established his formidable reputation as not only recorder but also analyst of the funeral monuments of Cornwall and other areas of north-west Europe, offers us a detailed examination of models of memorialization in early modern Cornwall, Ireland and Brittany. Unequivocally, he declares that such memoralialization in each of these areas served to signify 'difference', a function of these territories' culturally and politically 'peripheral' relationship with the encroaching English and French states, and that it is this 'difference' that establishes a certain commonality between Cornwall, Ireland and Brittany. However, Cockerham argues, there is in this commonality no real indication of a unifying Celticity in terms of unity of purpose or style, each of the three areas displaying their own highly individual, internal imperatives. Thus, in Cornwall, the memorialization of 'difference' represented the physical assertion of an ethnic identity amongst the lesser gentry that had hitherto been merely oral in its expression, while in Kilkenny (Cockerham's Irish case study) memorialization indicated the construction of a common ethno-religious identity against the background of an ostensibly diverse and potentially mutually antagonistic 'racial' divide. In Brittany, there developed what was a remarkable ethnic alliance across class boundaries in Basse-Bretagne, establishing and maintaining a strong intra-regional distinction between the practices of Basse-Bretagne and those of Haute-Bretagne, that part of Brittany bordering France. And in all of this Cornwall had a special place, the abrupt changes precipitated by the Reformation galvanizing the lesser gentry, in contrast to Ireland and Brittany where religious continuity allowed a more gradual adaption to changing conditions.

Of course, of all the signifiers of 'difference' in early modern Cornwall none was more obvious or more definitive than the Cornish language itself, then still spoken across at least the more western districts beyond Truro, an indisputably Celtic language whose existence has underwritten all subsequent Cornish claims to Celtic nationality. Inevitably, any document in the Cornish language dating from that period, however meagre it might appear at first glance, is of enormous importance—to historians of early modern Cornwall, to students of the Cornish language, and to language planners anxious to reconstruct and propagate Revived Cornish as a contemporary means of communication and identity assertion. For these reasons, Andrew Hawke's discussion of the *Bodewryd Ms. 5* is of considerable significance, examining as it does a Cornish-language document in the National Library of Wales (at Aberystwyth) thought originally to date from 'Circa 1700' but now considered more likely to have sprung from the first half of the seventeenth century. Significantly, the manuscript appears to be unknown outside the National Library of Wales and it is certainly not a copy of any other extant Cornish document. Although only two folios in length, it supplies a number of new words hitherto unknown to modern Cornish language scholarship, though there is still much work to be done to establish their precise etymology, while it also confirms another half dozen previously dubious words or phrases. Thus we find that *beez meas* means 'thumbe', while *Crabanaw* is 'skracching *sic* fingers' and *anclotha* is 'filthiness'. Hawke also postulates an historical link with Wales, suggesting an antiquarian fascination in seventeenth-century Wales with the fate of Cornish, after all the sister language of Welsh. As Hawke rightly concludes, *Bodewryd Ms. 5* 'deserves to be better known'.

If an appreciation of the Cornish language is important to our understanding of the early modern period, then a grasp of the 'myth of Cousin Jack' is equally necessary in assessing the attributes of English-speaking, Protestant, industrialized nineteenth-century Cornwall. Contrary to popular belief, widespread Cornish emigration was not just a reaction to the crash of Cornish copper in the 1860s but was long before then a deeply entrenched social phenomenon, one that had emerged in the immediate aftermath of the Napoleonic Wars. After 1815, and into the 1820s and 1830s and beyond, there were calls for Cornish colonists for emerging British territories in southern Africa, Canada and the Antipodes, but there was, as Sharron Schwartz indicates in her article, a movement of at least equal significance to the newly independent mining states of Latin America. Enticed by the promise of high remuneration for their skills, the Cornish emigrated to these destinations in hope rather than despair, creating in effect a highly mobile labour force for the rapidly developing international mining economy. However, despite this advantageous start, the Cornish—with their traditional disdain for 'booklearned' theorists —were often criticized in Latin America in the early nineteenth century for their lack of scientific knowledge, some observers suggesting that German miners from the Harz Mountains were inherently superior. And yet, with the weight of British informal imperialism behind them, the Cornish miners began to craft their cult of superiority in the New World, working alongside native miners to acquire the necessary knowledge of New World mining skills and geological formations, and applying steam power—their one area of clear advantage—to the problems of deep mining. In this way, as Schwartz argues, the mines of Latin America became a sort of training ground for the production of a new generation of 'super miners', the Cornish nurturing their 'myth of Cousin Jack', the assertion that they were somehow innately qualified above all others as hard-rock miners, a claim they deployed to good effect throughout the mining world in the nineteenth century.

Emigration was, of course, one means by which Cornish people were able to escape the disabilities of life at home, the prospects (for example) of a predictable income dispersed in fixed amounts (as in mining contracts in Latin America) contrasting favourably with the vicissitudes of the tribute system in Cornwall. At the same time, the Methodist movement in nineteenth-century Cornwall embraced emigration enthusiastically as part of its ideology of 'improvement', encouraging individuals to make the most of their God-given talents and the opportunities that presented themselves in life. John Rule, in his article on coping with life and death in the mining districts of nineteenth-century Cornwall, dwells upon both the tribute system and the role of Methodism. As he shows, the nature of tributing encouraged risk-taking. The miner whose faltering candle indicated a dangerous deficiency of oxygen merely moved the candle further back to cleaner air as he continued to work on what he hoped was a promising pitch, ignoring for the moment the threat to his health. The tributer already showing signs of debilitating 'miners' complaint' struggled on in the hope of making one last lucky strike, the tribute system always holding out the tantalizing prospect of striking it rich. But tributing had its 'downs' as well as 'ups', and Rule argues that Methodism played a vital role in offering explanation and consolation in the face of such unpredictability. When things went well, the Lord was to be praised for His abundance but in lean periods He remained as comfort and hope. John Harris, Cornwall's nineteenth-century miner-poet, summed up the fatalism (or faith) that such a view embodied. He loathed his work in the mine, 'Yet I never complained, . . . God had placed me there, and I knew it was right'. Even in the face of death, such belief was sustained, evident in the broadsheet doggerel produced in 1842 to mark a Cornish mining disaster:

Seven beside the youth are dead
His dear father too is fled
Crying with his latest breath,
Jesus is my strength in death.

The salient role of Methodism in moulding Cornish life in the nineteenth century also informs Brian Elvins's article on the newspaper war between the *Royal Cornwall Gazette* and the *West Briton* following the latter's foundation in 1810 as a vehicle for Radical opinion in Cornwall. The formation in 1809 of the Friends of Parliamentary Reform, made up of minor gentry and clergy, including figures such as John Colman Rashleigh and William Lewis Trelawny, heralded the emergence of an organized and determined Reform movement in Cornwall, one outcome of which was the establishment of the *West Briton* with the Friends as its promoters. The newspaper's first editor was Edward Budd, an Irish Protestant who at the time of his appointment was a Liskeard schoolmaster and Wesleyan local preacher. As Elvins notes, although Budd resisted the use of the *West Briton* as merely a mouthpiece for Methodist causes, there was in the newspaper's editorial policy an implicit link between the demands of Nonconformity and the Radical agenda of Reform. As Budd put it, 'Religious and Civil Liberty are inseparable and we are well assured that the only means by which both can be secured . . . is a Reform of the House of Commons'. He championed the 'Independence of Cornwall', by which he meant the freedom of Cornish politics from aristocratic control, and he supported the Cornish farmers in their opposition to the payment of tithes, notably in 1821 when Anthony Geake of Trecarrel was imprisoned for alleged non-payment and again when the issue was raised at the great County Meeting of 1822. In so doing, the *West Briton* raised the political temperature in Cornwall, helping to stimulate political consciousness at a time when the Cornish Radical Tradition, with its enduring Liberal-Nonconformist nexus, was fast developing. When Reform was at last secured in 1832, Budd reflected that 'To us who have had a part in this great contest, to share in the exultation it will excite from the Land's End to the Tamar is ample recompense'.

Emigration was, as noted above, one of the 'improving' causes advocated by Methodism, and amongst Cornwall's many thousands of nineteenth-century emigrants were numerous Methodists and other Nonconformists who, with varying degrees of insight and commitment, saw emigration as a means of seeking religious freedom, civil liberty and socio-economic mobility in new lands overseas. The Cornish Radical Tradition as it developed was thus transplanted abroad, notably in the colony of South Australia (the Antipodes' 'Paradise of Dissent') where the Liberal-Nonconformist nexus was important in shaping Radical politics as they emerged in the mining districts, leading eventually to the formation there of the United Labor Party. In the words of John Verran, a Cornish-Methodist miner and South Australia's first Labor Premier, 'Religion is citizenship, and the relationship between religion and politics is very close'. As the article 'Vote Labor' indicates, however, it has been commonplace for historians to note the apparently contrasting experiences of Cornwall and South Australia. In the former, the crash of Cornish copper, continued emigration, and incipient deindustrialization cut short the development of trade unionism and a wider Labour movement, while in South Australia the continuing prosperity of the Yorke Peninsula copper mines allowed the growth of both trade unionism and an attendant Labor Party. And yet, as is argued here, if the historian's gaze is lifted to bring the twentieth century into view, then new parallels between the Cornish and South Australian experiences appear. For, just as the Cornish experience led to the apparent 'fossilization' of the Liberals as the Radical opponents of the Conservatives at a time when British politics generally were being realigned as a Tory-Labour conflict, so in South Australia the eventual demise of the Peninsula mines in 1923 led to the apparent 'fossilization' of the Cornish-Methodist-mining influence in the Labor Party in the interwar period. At the very least, the suggestion that 'Cornishness' continued to influence the make-up of the South Australian Labor hierarchy in the 1920s and 1930s, together with its beliefs and behaviour, is persuasive, although it is also the case that Labor politicians were drawn increasingly to specifically Australian perspectives and agendas where the Cornish Radical Tradition was hardly relevant.

Indeed, the complex and often paradoxical picture that emerged in South Australia is a reminder, if one were needed, of the complexities of issues of identity, and it may be that the Cornish-South Australian case study presented here has wider theoretical significance for the examination of the experiences of immigrant ethnic groups and their descendents in new lands. Certainly, Cornish Studies as an area of academic activity should be alive to the theoretical possibilities that exist for the elucidation of identity, both in terms of Cornwall and the Cornish providing pertinent case studies *and* with regard to the insights that the application of theoretical approaches to Cornwall and the Cornish might afford. This is the line developed by Cheryl Hayden in her article where she attempts to apply feminist theory to issues of Cornish identity, arguing that Cornwall is a feminized 'other', a region occupying a subordinate place to the England that dominates it: 'And so, we have a situation in which we can argue that Cornwall is to England as woman is to man.' This is a challenging, not to say radical, perspective, one which Hayden presents cogently and persuasively. Thus, for example, she notes that 'numerous writers on Cornish matters . . . demonstrate that Cornwall suffers high unemployment, lower than average wages, poor access to quality housing—similar forms of disadvantage to those experienced by many women'. However, she does caution against uncritical embrace of feminist theory, warning that 'researchers using feminist theory risk doing precisely what they accuse men (or in the Cornish model, England) of doing: categorizing on the basis of difference, constructing stereotypes, and adopting certain behaviours and attitudes accordingly'. Her firm conclusion, though, is that feminist theory does have a place in the elucidation of Cornish identity, in just the same way that it is relevant to research relating to any other marginalized or disadvantaged place or group. Moreover, Hayden insists, 'feminism provides astute campaigners with a range of methodologies that can be used alone or together to weaken and change values and assumptions, argue facts, and ultimately achieve the desired shift of power and focus'.

Cornish identity is also the concern of Philipa Aldous and Malcolm Williams in their article 'A Question of Ethnic Identity', in which they report the results of both quantitative and qualitative research amongst children in selected schools in different parts of Cornwall. Constructed initially as part of a wider research project in 1997 to investigate attitudes towards migration amongst two cohorts of young people aged 15 to 18 in both Cornwall and Devon, the work on identity was developed because it was hypothesized that Cornish ethnicity might be an important factor in any differences in attitude towards migration between young people in Cornwall and those in Devon. As Aldous and Williams found, overall some 29.2 per cent of their sample in Cornwall self-defined as 'Cornish' (in preference to 'English' and other categories ranging from 'Black British' to 'Chinese') in response to questionnaires. As they are quick to point out, this should not be taken as a measure of the number of 'Cornish' in Cornwall but may be seen as a reasonable estimate of the 15-to-18-year-old population prepared to self-define as Cornish. They note that, generally speaking, there was an East-West distance decay in the self-identification as Cornish, and they speculate that if they had been able to include children from schools in West and Mid Cornwall in towns that were not represented in their research (for example, Camborne or St Austell), then the level of self-identification may have been higher. Conversely, if schools in towns in East Cornwall (such as Saltash and Launceston) not represented had been included, the figure might have been lower. In Liskeard, one East Cornwall town that was represented, qualitative research conducted after the questionnaire completion identified hesitancy in self-identification as Cornish as a result of being born in Plymouth, on the 'wrong' side of the Tamar. Place of birth also influenced others' self-identification, although the research revealed a complex situation in which cultural and life-style factors were also seen to be important. Individual youngsters provided comments such as 'Cornwall is more like Wales and Scotland. Cornwall is not English' and 'Cornish is, you know, it is like, almost a breed, a race'. But as Aldous and Williams conclude, while such responses reveal important insights into ethnic self-identification, the data are not comprehensive or conclusive and should be treated with some caution: 'All we know is that around a third of young people in Cornwall choose to be Cornish and not English'.

For David Crowther and Chris Carter, in their article, it is the World Wide Web and the Internet that are likely to be key players in Cornish identity formation in the future: 'The ubiquity of the World Wide Web (WWW) and the Internet provides many opportunities for individuals to combine, to communicate, and to make their respective voices heard.' Drawn to the concept of the 'virtual community', a construct born of postmodernism, globalization and Internet technology, they investigate the subject of 'community', finding it a slippery and elusive concept defying easy definition and shot through with normative assumptions about the idealized 'good life'. However, they do decide that a community of interest does not need to be tied to a specific geographical space or have a separate geographical existence, and they suggest that the 'virtual communities' of the Internet are such communities of interest. Moreover, Crowther and Carter consider that 'The Internet provides the ideal environment for a community of resistance to exist', and they identify in the Cornish Studies group active on the Internet a community of interest and of resistance, one which subscribes to a view that emphasizes Cornwall's difference from England. In conducting a questionnaire on the Internet, they asked members of this 'virtual community' a number of questions relating to their activities on the World Wide Web. The question of self-identification elicited varying responses, from 'I define myself as Cornish only, and perhaps Celtic, never British or UK' to 'I am first of all a US citizen and then a Cornish American', while motives for membership included considerations such as 'exploring Cornish culture', 'communicating with friends sharing a similar identity', and 'a means of research'. However, as Crowther and Carter discovered, 'Cornish' was not the only identity claimed by many of these participants, while for many activity on the Internet was but just one medium for asserting or exploring 'Cornishness', others including traditional geographically based communities such as Cornish Associations. Moreover, those who were active on the Internet were those who were enthusiastic about cyberspace and its possibilities, with many others with an interest in Cornish issues but who were not interested in the World Wide Web being necessarily outside the community. Thus, as Crowther and Carter conclude, it is doubtful whether cyberspace is at present able to provide a comprehensive sense of community in its own right. But they do speculate that, as more and more people are exposed to the Internet, irrespective of their enthusiasm for cyberspace, current perceptions of community may alter and the 'virtual community' may one day establish primacy.

Crowther and Carter note that an important element of Cornish identity for those active on the Internet was the Cornish language, and that facilities existed on the World Wide Web for those who wished to learn and communicate in Revived Cornish. They thought this desire to learn Cornish somewhat paradoxical because, while the Internet users were prepared to embrace the very latest in communication technology, they were at the same time (in Crowther's and Carter's estimation) yearning for an older conception of community, a romantic 'rural idyll' construction within which Revived Cornish was located. Be that as it may, the desire to learn Revived Cornish and to contribute to debates about the language's continuing development shows no signs of abating. Nicholas Williams remains in the vanguard of the process of development and planning, advocating his own 'Unified Cornish Revised' as the preferred model for the future, at the same time offering sustained criticism of the principal rival version—Kernewek Kemmyn or Common Cornish. Thus in his review article he takes to task Ken George's 1993 *Gerlyver Kernewek Kemmyn*, a dictionary of Common Cornish, concluding in characteristic fashion that 'Kernewek Kemmyn is a failed experiment in orthographic reform'. That it has taken Williams the best part of a decade to produce a review of George's dictionary may, at first glance, seem odd, but in fact Williams's article is the result of a painstaking and step-by-step analysis

conducted during precisely the same period that he was also
developing Unified Cornish Revised. For Williams, the unsatisfactory
nature of *Gerlyver Kernewek Kemmyn* is a result not only of what
he considers an illegitimate orthography but of what he insists is
the incomplete and inaccurate state of George's authentication and
frequency codes. Thus, for example, George's dictionary reports that
the Cornish word 'alow', water lily, is attested only in place-names.
Williams disagrees, finding references in works by Lhuyd, Borlase and
Pryce. Similarly, the *Gerlyver Kernewek Kemmyn* indicates that the
word 'golvan' ('sparrow') is confined to one instance each in *The Old
Cornish Vocabulary* and in Lhuyd but Williams discovers several other
occurrences in disparate Cornish sources. George says that 'godra', 'to
milk', is confined to a single occurrence in Lhuyd but Williams thinks
otherwise . . . and so on, and so on.

Neil Kennedy admits that Williams's examination of Revived
Cornish, in its various guises, 'may be regarded by some as unnecessarily abrasive and nit-picking, rather too concerned with
discrediting other approaches . . . he is unlikely to win any prizes for
diplomacy' but he also insists that Williams's 'interrogation of the
language has encouraged rigour and the exchange of ideas'. For, in his
review article devoted to Williams's own English-Cornish dictionary,
the *Gerlyver Sawsnek-Kernowek*, Kennedy adopts a sophisticated
analysis of the processes that lie behind Revived Cornish, offering
insights, reflections, and a degree of self-critical honesty that sometimes eludes the protagonists of the several versions of the language.
As Kennedy notes, with 24,000 headwords Williams's dictionary
is twice the size of Robert Morton Nance's *An English-Cornish
Dictionary*, and offers Cornish equivalents for objects and concepts
from air-terminal and alliteration to calculator and communist. This, as
Kennedy also observes, is the result of hundreds of neologisms devised
by Williams himself, in effect a personal exercise in language planning,
'the product of conscious verbal hygiene'. Kennedy is uncomfortable
with this process, wondering whether it is really necessary to coin neat
neologisms that translate English equivalents, and he worries that
Cornish is being reconstructed in the shadow of English, with English
providing the template against which Cornish words must be either
found from historical sources or constructed as neologisms. In other
respects, however, Kennedy welcomes Williams's approach, especially
'his acceptance of historical vocabulary from all sources and his evident
rejection of the extreme "Celtic" purisms that have characterized
Revived Cornish', the latter practice (the desire for 'Celtic purity' and
the determination to eradicate all traces of 'English influence' and
'corruption') a cause of anxiety for Kennedy who sees within it a form

of linguistic ethnic cleansing. More generally, Kennedy welcomes the fact that in appearance, vocabulary, grammar and even pronunciation, Williams's Unified Cornish Revived is much closer to Revived Late/ Modern Cornish (Kennedy's preferred form) than either Kernewek Kemmyn or Nance's 'original' Unified, a middle course which, given the plurality inherent in the Cornish language movement, makes all forms of the language more viable by aiding mutual intelligibility.

Actually, notwithstanding the herculean efforts of Nicholas Williams, Richard Gendall, Ken George and others, perhaps the most remarkable feature of the Cornish language today is simply that it has survived at all. While there are relatively few fluent speakers of any of the forms of Revived Cornish, there is widespread knowledge of the existence of the language, together with an equally widespread appreciation of its significance as an icon of identity, a marker of 'difference'. Given the continuing reluctance of central government to recognize let alone support the existence of Cornish, the popular status of Cornish in Cornwall is a tribute to its advocates but also speaks volumes about the enduring but changing nature of identity in modern Cornwall.

But if the survival of the Cornish language says something about both the tenacity of the Cornish identity and its ability to reinvent itself in the face of change, then the same must be true of Cornwall's distinctive political culture, something that was observable in the years before 1832 and is still apparent today, no analysis of contemporary Cornish voting behaviour, parliamentary representation, or the composition of Cornwall County Council being complete without the customary reference to Cornwall marching to a different drum. As Garry Tregidga remarks in the third of our review articles, Edwin Jaggard has done much to illuminate this distinctive politics, his unsurpassed knowledge of the sources for nineteenth-century Cornish political history matched by his powers of narrative and analysis, his detailed understanding of Cornwall made all the more remarkable given that he lives and works in Western Australia. But, as Tregidga also observes, despite the intense interest in recent years in modern Cornish politics, there are still gaps in our knowledge and opportunities for further research.

Most pressing is the need for a thoroughgoing history of the relationship between religion and politics in Cornwall, especially the oft-alluded to Liberal-Nonconformist nexus, while it is time that the often privileged attention afforded the politics of the mining communities be replaced at least in part by a new focus on the farmers. In the nineteenth century, Cornish farmers, especially in the east and north of Cornwall, embraced Radicalism (including hostility to the payment of tithes) with considerable effect, and Tregidga wonders whether this 'independent activism' in the farming community was still a dominant determinism of electoral contestation in the eastern constituencies of Bodmin and North Cornwall after 1945, when the Liberals were still the principal opponents of the Tories. Since 1945, this independent activism seems to have influenced the emergence of an anti-metropolitan strand in Cornish politics, not least in the quintessentially farming constituency of North Cornwall where in the 2001 General Election the Liberal Democrat, Paul Tyler MP, was returned with an impressive majority. Indeed, the politics of anti-metropolitanism itself needs further attention, from the dogged persistence of Mebyon Kernow over the last half century and the deployment of Cornish issues by the mainstream parties (principally, but by no means exclusively, the Liberal Democrats) to attempts to revive Cornwall's ancient Stannary Parliament and the 50,000 plus signatures collected on a petition calling for a Cornish Assembly. As the constitutional make-up of the United Kingdom continues to develop, with a Parliament in Scotland and Assemblies in Wales and Northern Ireland (and London), it is fascinating to observe Cornwall's participation in the on-going devolution debate, not least the assertion of its historic territorial identity. Here, surely, is an important and fruitful area of research for those concerned to understand the condition of modern Cornwall.

Philip Payton,
Professor of Cornish Studies and
Director,
Institute of Cornish Studies,
University of Exeter.

CELTIC GALICIA? ANCIENT CONNECTIONS AND SIMILARITIES IN THE TRADITIONS, SUPERSTITIONS AND FOLKLORE OF THE CORNISH PENINSULA AND GALICIA IN SPAIN

Manuel Alberro

INTRODUCTION

It is commonplace now to note that the term 'Celtic' is problematic and often ambiguous. To begin with, the strictly linguistic definition devised originally by the academic world of Celtic Studies was driven as much by nineteenth-century romantic ideas of language as the basis of national identity as it was by the scientific analysis of European language groups. Moreover, the term moved swiftly in both academic and popular usage to encompass literature as well as language, together with many other aspects of non-material and material culture, in effect identifying or even creating a 'Celtic' ethnic identity and expanding the scope of Celtic Studies to that of an interdisciplinary 'area studies'. Additionally, there has been of late an explosion of self-asserting 'Celtic identities', ranging from the practice of 'Celtic spirituality' (both Christian and Pagan) to the performance of 'Celtic music' and other art forms.[1]

Part of this complexity has been Pan-Celticism, the notion that the several Celtic lands have much in common (not only in linguistic affinity but in terms of their wider cultural, historical and political experiences), a commonality that organizations today such as the Celtic Congress and Celtic League believe should be fostered and given further expression in the creation of new cultural or political ties. Such organizations have tended to set themselves up as the custodians of Celticity, guarding their self-appointed right to adjudicate as to who or what might legitimately be labelled 'Celtic'. At the same time, activists and enthusiasts within the several self-defining 'Celtic nations' have sought to claim common cause with one another, creating or joining Pan-Celtic organizations to promote such contact and exchange. But this process has not been without difficulty. The resistance at the beginning of the twentieth century to recognition of Cornwall's status as a Celtic nation has been discussed elsewhere in this series,[2] while the more recent attempts by the boundary-keepers of Celticity to resist the claims of Galicia and other self-defining 'Celtic' areas of the Iberian peninsula have been documented in part in Berresford Ellis' unsympathetic discussion of the issue.[3]

Indeed, it is this issue, the claims of Galicia, that concerns us in this article. The idea that the Iberian peninsula is possessed of an ancient Celtic heritage is not new but the concept was given renewed currency and impetus in the radical restructuring of post-Franco Spain, a process which revealed (or exaggerated?) a complex pattern of ethnic and territorial aspirations and led to the explicit recognition in the 1978 Constitution of *España de Las Autonomias*.[4] Galicia was one of the autonomous regions created under the Constitution, lending a new political legitimacy to Galician expressions of separate identity, which in turn led to ever more insistent expression by many Galicians of a self-defined Celtic identity. However, such expression was resisted by the institutions of Pan-Celticism, not least by the Celtic League which in 1987 asserted its 'linguistic criterion' to deal with what was dubbed 'the Galician crisis', declaring that Galicia could not be considered a Celtic nation (and was therefore ineligible to join the League) because no Celtic language was spoken there today or had been spoken in modern times. Berresford Ellis admitted that 'It is true that a number of Celtic loan words are now found in Galician [Galego]' and, departing for a moment from the linguistic criterion, went on to also admit 'a few identifiable folk customs—and local traditional music has a distinct echo of Celtic roots'.[5] However, the Celtic League decided that 'in no way could the Galician claim meet the linguistic criterion', and so the claim was denied.[6]

And yet, this repudiation has not prevented the continuing assertion of a Galician Celtic identity by both popular and academic practitioners, and one feature of the last decade or so has been increased scholarly interest in Iberia's Celtic connections, observable most recently in Raftery's 2001 *Atlas of the Celts*.[7] This interest was also reflected in no fewer than nine of the papers presented at the 10th

International Congress of Celtic Studies at the University of Edinburgh in 1995, including such subjects as 'Some Literary Testimonials to the Celtic Tradition in Spain' and 'Celtiberians: "Cumulative Celticity" in South-west Europe?' Especially interesting was the paper 'Celtiberian Studies and Spanish Celtic Historiography in the 19th Century' which sought to 'trace the origin of the main ideas about Celts, Celtiberians, druidism and Celtic languages in Spanish romantic historiography' and, crucially, to examine:

> The construction of a so-called 'mythological history' in which Celts were to play an important part . . . [in the] romantic nationalist historiography of Spain, mainly in Galicia and the Basque Country, and supplied in the former, at the turn of the [twentieth] century, a kind of 'Celtic Renaissance' with its ideological frame.[8]

It is this 'Celtic Renaissance' and its 'ideological frame' that have informed the more recent and popular assertions of a Galician Celtic identity, while the attendant 'historiography' has continued to guide many scholars with a Galician allegiance or sympathy. The aim of this article, therefore, is to elucidate and articulate the arguments advanced by such scholars in substantiating their claims to Galician Celticity, not with a view to deciding whether such claims are 'correct' or even admissible but rather to promote understanding of how those claims are constructed in the first place.

CORNWALL AND IBERIA COMPARED

A major feature of the articulation of a Galician Celtic identity is its comparative element, the attempt to locate Galicia as an integral part of an Atlantic-edged Celtic world and to identify archaeological, historical, folkloric and other similarities with the other Celtic lands. For our purposes here, a particular comparison with Cornwall is both relevant and instructive. Indeed, Cornwall and the north-west of the Iberian Peninsula (in which contemporary Galicia is located) have, it can be argued, very old and well-established connections that go back to prehistoric times, based on tin extraction and trade, and this is the starting point for constructing our comparisons. The argument runs like this:

These ancient connections between Cornwall (and the wider 'Cornish Peninsula', running up into Devon and western Somerset and Dorset) and north-west Iberia continued during the Bronze Age, when the two geographical regions were both elements of what scholars call the Atlantic Area, a well-defined socio-cultural and commercial zone which included Ireland, the Isle of Man, Scotland, Wales, the Cornish Peninsula, Armorica (today's Brittany) and the north-west of the Iberian Peninsula. This Atlantic Area lasted for at least three millennia.[9] The most recent discussion of this zone is Cunliffe's 2001 volume *Facing the Ocean: The Atlantic and Its Peoples*, where he writes:

> I have become convinced that the peoples of the long Atlantic facade of Europe have shared common beliefs and values over thousands of years, conditioned largely by their unique habitat on the edge of the continent facing the ocean. They lived in a resource-rich zone, in many ways remote from neighbours by land yet easily linked to others by sea.[10]

Moreover, Cunliffe affords north-west Iberia a particular importance within the zone, noting how the complex confluence of western seaways converged 'around the isolated yet reassuring stepping-stone of Galicia',[11] a role not unlike that of Cornwall with its own stepping-stone function in movements between Ireland and Wales and Brittany.

All these Atlantic Area regions were, it is argued, pre- or 'proto'-Celtic, and all of them emerged soon thereafter as integral elements of the Pan-European Celtic culture that had by then embraced the continent. Both north-west Iberia and Cornwall 'lost' their Celtic language, the former due to the Roman occupation and later political developments, the latter much later during the eighteen or nineteenth century, (though Cornish was soon the subject of a vigorous Revivalist movement). However—and this a key part of the argument—this loss did not mean that these regions surrendered all vestiges of their Celticity, the many old traditions, superstitions and folklore which have been recorded or are still present in both Galicia and Cornwall often showing marked similarity and hinting at common Celtic origins and evidencing a shared contemporary Celtic identity.

SOME PREHISTORY

The above is a general summary of the 'Celtic Galicia' thesis; what follows is explanation in greater detail. As noted above, social and commercial relations between the populations of north-west Iberia and those of Armorica, the Cornish Peninsula, Wales, Scotland and Ireland date from prehistoric times. Hencken has made a study of the tin trade; quoting Diodorus Siculus, this author describes the sea-route from the Cornish Peninsula to Corbilo at the mouth of the Loire.[12] The later period, the Bronze Age, owes its name to the widespread extension of copper-alloy metallurgy, which first appeared in the Near East, and reached the West by *c.*2000 BC when many European regions adopted copper-tin alloys, or bronze. The success of bronze metallurgy is thus linked to the availability of both copper and tin ores, especially the latter. Prehistoric copper mines have been found in many European regions, especially in the Balkans, Austria, the Iberian Peninsula, Britain and Ireland.[13] Tin, on the other hand, is a very rare and scarce metal, only available in a few geographical locations, among them the Cornish Peninsula, Brittany, the north-west of the Iberian Peninsula and perhaps (on a minor scale) also in Ireland.[14] The copper and tin lodes of Cornwall and Devon have a very long history of mining: probably exploited since prehistoric times, they are known to have been in existence in the Roman period.[15] The importance of tin-mining in Cornwall is described by Carew as late as the seventeenth century when he says that 'In times paft, the *Cornifh* people gaue themfelues principally, (and in a maner wholly) to the feeking of Tynne, and neglected husbandry: fo as the neighbours of *Deuon* and *Sommerfet* fhires, hired their paftures at a rent, and ftored them with theyr owne cattell'.[16]

The tin trade had already been described by classic authors. The sixth-century BC *Massilliote Periplous* contains references to islands in the North Atlantic called the Oestrymnides which were rich in tin, together with a description of native boats made of leather hides. This source locates these islands at two days' sailing distance from Ireland, which would indicate that the Oestrymnides may be the Cassiterides, possibly Cornwall, (considering that early writers were not aware of the fact that the latter is a peninsula).[17] This 'tin route' is also described by a later navigator, Pytheas, in *c.*320 BC, quoted by Polybius, Strabo, and Avienus in his *Ora Maritima*.[18] The latter describes how the merchants buy the tin from the natives and carry it in small ships made of leather hides (*curraghs*, still used in the Aran Islands) to continental Europe. Diodorus Siculus describes merchants sailing from Cornwall to Brittany, then to the Mediterranean[19]; Julius Caesar indicates the role played in this trade by the Veneti, a powerful seafaring Celtic tribe which occupied Armorica in the last century BC.[20]

The early seafarers, who navigated along these sea-routes from the south, followed the Atlantic coasts of Portugal and north-west Spain, then crossed the Bay of Biscay to Brittany. The first and most important port of call in Britain was somewhere in Cornwall; from there this main sea-route split into three directions, one to southern Ireland, one into St George's Channel (and from there to Wales, northern Ireland, the Isle of Man and Scotland) and a third one into the Severn Sea Basin.[21] Maritime traffic along these routes could date from the Mesolithic at least, and helped to unite all the Atlantic fringes of western Europe from Caithness in northern Scotland to Galicia in north-west Spain. This Atlantic or, as some Galicians prefer to call it, 'Celtic' Area was used extensively before the Christian era and even in early Christian times, during the so-called 'Age of the Saints'.[22]

The Mediterranean connection with the Atlantic Area was mainly focused on the tin-producing areas of Armorica and Cornwall, besides the tin, copper and gold of the south-west and the north-west of the Iberian Peninsula and the gold of Ireland. The tin-producing areas of the Cornish Peninsula were in close contact with the Iberian and Mediterranean world from the fifth century onwards, following trading traditions dating from very ancient times. Avienus says that the Tartessians traded with the Atlantic Region, as did later the Phoenicians, the Carthaginians and the Greeks, from their bases in the Iberian Peninsula. The Atlantic–Mediterranean interaction took place in Tartessus, located in the south-west of Atlantic Spain, in or near present-day Huelva. When this ancient kingdom decayed (for unknown reasons) and disappeared from the international scene, contact with the Mediterranean world continued through the Phoenician commercial port of Gades or Gadir (present day Cádiz), on the Atlantic coast, west of Gibraltar. The extent and importance of this linkage between these two networks, the Atlantic and the Mediterranean, in the south-west of Spain, has been recently researched by María Teresa Ruíz-Gálvez and Catriona Gibson.[23]

THE BRONZE AGE ATLANTIC AREA

Just as the prehistoric period was important in building the background relationships that were to underpin 'Celtic Galicia', so too was the Bronze Age. In the Bronze Age, the Atlantic Area constituted a cultural entity that was united by maritime routes. It was quite different from the Central zone of the European continent and also from the Mediterranean zone, although there were clear contact points linking the three. To the east, the great navigable rivers, the Rhine, the Seine, the Loire and the Gironde provided lines of communication with Central Europe. To the west, the Atlantic Area was mainly made up of peninsulas—the south of Ireland, Wales, Cornwall and the south-west of England, Armorica and the north-western corner of the Iberian Peninsula. All of them were damp, temperate regions facing the Atlantic, with a great wealth of minerals. Contact probably developed between them because of this abundance of minerals, mainly tin, copper and gold, and the trading contacts also extended onto a social, cultural, religious and technological plane. The Celtic language(s) became a *lingua franca* for the whole area, as well as in a large part of central and western Europe at that time. Contact between the communities of the Atlantic Area, which extended approximately 3,000 km from Gibraltar to the Shetland Islands, north of Scotland, lasted in all about three millennia.[24]

Indeed, reliable testimony exists to the effect that relations between the different Atlantic regions, and maritime communication and trade between Ireland and the areas farther south, go back to prehistoric times: there was trading in tin between Ireland and the Iberian Peninsula in the Neolithic Era.[25] Some authors maintain that this contact dates from the Megalithic. From the fourth millennium BC, megalithic tombs of the type known as 'passage graves' were to be found all along the Atlantic seaboard from Portugal to Ireland,[26] and common symbols have been found to be repeated in the orthostates of the graves.[27] This Atlantic Area, it has been argued, remained a clear and distinct cultural entity throughout the Bronze Age.[28] Koch has analysed the social bases for the so-called 'Celticisation' of the zone, presenting a model in which an important role is played by the consolidation of a proto-Celtic language that took place during the Late Bronze Age (*c.*1300–600 BC). He describes the period as one of 'economic bonanza, when the Atlantic Zone was in continuous and close contact with the cultural course of the Urnfield Culture and then with that of the Hallstatt C period in Central Western Europe'. The author also refers to the model of trade and linguistic links proposed by Colin Renfrew, who suggests 'a trade chain in which Ireland was the *terminus* of long distance routes which reached as far as the Iberian Peninsula'.[29]

Thus, it is argued, the Celtic populations of the Atlantic coastal regions were in regular contact from very remote times,[30] a contact which was facilitated by their audacity, their navigational skill and their ability and efficiency in the use of their peculiar kind of seagoing craft, the *curragh*. Furthermore, Breton and Irish ships of larger size are known to have travelled along the Atlantic sea-routes during the final stages of the prehistoric period.[31] The seafaring experience of the ancient Celts has been analysed by several authors. The Celts had accurate knowledge of the physical background of winds, currents and regular tide tables, and could make use of this knowledge to travel at a speed of five knots (nine nautical km per hour).[32] It was then possible for them to have travelled the approximately 1,000 km between the south of Ireland and the north-west of Spain in a *curragh* in the nine days mentioned in the Leabhar Gabhála. The nature and characteristics of this maritime means of transport, including the navigation techniques of the ancient Celts, have been researched by McGrail.[33]

These Atlantic connections can be detected again after the Iron Age by means of archaeological and historical data on the emigration

of Brythonic Celts to Brittany and Galicia in Spain in the fifth century
AD (another key event in the construction of 'Celtic Galicia'), along
with the importation of Mediterranean pottery and other commodities
to Cornwall, Ireland, Wales and Scotland.[34] Trade and commerce,
which continued to exist during this period between the various regions
of this Atlantic Area, seemed to be concentrated in two main subjects:
the export of Cornish tin to the Mediterranean world,[35] and importation of wine in amphorae.[36] There is, therefore, sufficient testimony
pointing to the integration of the north-west of the Iberian Peninsula
within the Atlantic world several centuries before the Christian era.[37]
Such contact between Galicia and the Celtic communities of Armorica,
the Cornish Peninsula, Wales, Scotland and Ireland would continue up
to the middle of the first century AD.[38]

ARCHAEOLOGICAL EVIDENCE: SOCIAL AND CULTURAL INTERCHANGE BETWEEN THE REGIONS OF THE ATLANTIC AREA

Archaeological evidence informs much of the construction of 'Celtic
Galicia'. The following archaeological evidence has been deployed to
bear witness to the social, trading and cultural contacts and exchange
between the Atlantic regions. The discovery of the skull of a Barbary
Ape in Ireland in 1986 suggests the existence of extensive maritime
contacts between this country and regions as far away geographically
as the western Mediterranean.[39] The similarity between the rock
engravings of Mogor, near Marín, Pontevedra, Spain, and those of
Sess Kilgreen in Ireland is notable,[40] as is the similarity between the
symbols and marks on petroglyphs and stones bearing passage-tomb
art found in the Megalithic passage graves of Loughcrew, County
Meath, Ireland and others in the Iberian Peninsula.[41] The stone slab
found in Cluain Fionn-loche, County Offaly, Ireland, has apparent
analogies to other Neolithic ones found in Spain.[42] The are also the
burial monuments called 'Linkardstown cists' of Late Neolithic or
Early Bronze Age Ireland; some authors consider that the indigenous
traditions of the period did not develop this kind of burial and suggest
they may have been inspired or constructed by individuals from the
Iberian Peninsula.[43] Then there are the similarities between leaf-
shaped flint javelin heads found in chambered tombs and settlement
sites of southern Spain and Portugal and those of approximately the
same period found in Ireland,[44] which are even more visible in the
javelins found in Vila Nova de San Pedro in present-day Portugal.[45]
Such parallels between Ireland and the Iberian Peninsula were first
traced by W. Bremer, who believed them to be very important[46]; later
archaeologists have used this example of the flint javelin to place due

emphasis on the importance of the Atlantic route for the circulation and movement of people towards Ireland.[47]

The similarities between the early hill-forts of Ireland and Atlantic Scotland and the *castros* (Celtic hill-forts) of the Atlantic seaboard of the north-west of the Iberian peninsula have also been a cause for comment, each having widely spaced multi-vallation and protecting *chevaux de frise*; in fact, the 'Castro culture' of the north-west of Spain, with its stone-built round houses and numerous *castros* has been used to stress the cultural links between Galicia and the northernmost areas of the Atlantic province.[48] The similarity of structural and defence elements of the Irish hill-forts with those of the Atlantic zone of the Iberian Peninsula has also extended to artefacts found within them: among these are two-link iron horse bits, disc querns, especially those typical of Atlantic Scotland, and iron penannular brooches (such as those discovered at Cahercommaun), which have been found both in Ireland and the Iberian Peninsula. All this leads to the conjecture that part of the inspiration for the prehistoric Iron Age of the south of Ireland and also for that of Atlantic Scotland came from the Iberian Peninsula.[49] The similarity between *fibulae* found at Mount Batten in Devon and at Harlyn Bay in Cornwall and those found in Spain and the French region of Aquitaine is also deemed significant.[50] Two bronze figurines, one found in Sligo in Ireland and the other in Aust, on the estuary of the River Severn, which were probably imported from the south of Spain, are further evidence.[51] So too are the relatively large number of Greek and Carthaginian coins found on the Armorica Peninsula and in the south of England.[52] Several spearheads possibly made in Ireland which were found in a large hoard discovered at the bottom of Huelva Bay in south-western Spain may be significant evidence.[53] There is also the spearhead found in Castleconnel, County Limerick, which Rynne believes could be an import from Spain.[54] Then there is the stamped pottery with similar motifs and designs typical of the Hallstatt D and the early La Tène periods, found in Brittany, Cornwall and central and north-western regions of Spain.[55] There are the large number of Irish cauldrons found in France and northern Spain,[56] and those leather shields preserved in Irish bogs which have a V-shaped notch on one side, similar to the ones found in the Iberian Peninsula.[57]

Regarding the specific references to the Cornish Peninsula, the two *fibulae* found in the cemetery at Harlyn Bay on the north coast of Cornwall, two of bronze and one of iron, are according to Cunliffe characterized 'by a knob-ended cross piece for the pin to pivot on, a high bow and an upturned foot ornamented with a large disc head . . . They belong to a well-recognized class of fifth-century brooches found in Spain.'[58] With respect to the stamped wares found in Cornwall, Leeds has expressed his view that stamped ware was introduced into that area by way of the Atlantic sea-ways, probably from the Iberian Peninsula.[59] The regional style of pottery made in the Cornish Peninsula during the Middle Iron Age period (400/300-100 BC), shows a free curvilinear style very similar to that produced in Armorica, a region which was closely connected with the north-west of the Iberian Peninsula.[60]

The Celtic tribes of the Dumnonii and the Durotriges had been settled in the Cornish Peninsula from very ancient times. Overseas trade throughout the Bronze and Iron Ages was carried through the ancient harbours of Hengistbury (near Christchurch) and Poole, directly to Brittany.[61] The ceramic development of this region shows two very distinctive styles. The earlier one, the 'Glastonbury wares', probably originated in the fourth century BC under inspiration from Brittany. The second style, known as cordoned ware, was the result of the close connections and shared cultural traditions that took place between the two peninsulas, Cornwall and Brittany, long before the Roman occupation.[62] The typical Iron Age stamped pottery studied by Júdice Gamito only appears in six well-defined areas of Europe, all of them 'Celtic' territories. Among them are the Cornish Peninsula, Brittany, the north-west and other 'Celtic' areas of the Iberian Peninsula such as those of the Celtiberians and the Celtici of the south-west, and 'Celtic' territories in central Europe and northern Italy. The vases' shapes differ in the different regions, but the stamped motifs (spiral or geometric patterns, squares, triangles, zig-zags, lozenges, crosses, or various combinations of these) predominate and are very similar in all of them. They are typical of the period from the late phase of Early Iron Age until the beginning of Late Iron Age.[63]

Many Iron Age 'cliff castles' are found on the coasts of Cornwall and north Devon, mainly on promontories projecting into the sea.[64] These cliff castles have long been hailed as a 'Celtic' phenomenon, and for those asserting a Galician Celtic identity it is important to note that they are also to be found in Ireland, Brittany and Galicia. The cliff castles of the Scilly Isles and the Cornish Peninsula are fortified by multiple defenses. The structure of the defensive elements of the cliff-castle at Gurnards Head, Penwith, western Cornwall, highly resembles that of the small fortresses of Kerkaradoc and Penhars near Quimper, in Brittany, and the cliff-castles of Castel Coz and Castel Mow on the Finistère coast between Douarnenez and Ponte du Rez are very similar to those of Cornwall.[65]

Traditional Celtic historiography, though increasingly challenged by new archaeological perspectives which cast doubt on the extent of early migrations, postulates that in the beginning of the fourth century there was an invasion by La Tène Celts from Spain, the French Atlantic coasts and Brittany, which made their way into Cornwall first, then Devon, Somerset, Dorset and the Cotswolds. They, according to Hawkes, absorbed or drove out the so-called Iron Age A people living in those territories and took over their settlements.[66] This was an idea which had already been proposed by Leeds in 1927, after his excavation at Chun Castle in Cornwall.[67] These are the Celts who were to be called the Iron Age B people, a view supported by Spanish La Tène *fibulae*, typical decorated pottery and historical contacts connected with the tin trade, and their putative existence is yet further evidence in the hands of those wishing to emphasize the apparent Celtic connections of Cornwall, Brittany and Galicia.[68]

THE ATLANTIC SEA-WAYS DURING THE AGE OF THE SAINTS

Traditional historiography has also argued that the Roman invasion and conquest of Gaul, the Iberian Peninsula and a large part of Britain during the last century BC and the first century AD was to have detrimental effects upon the Atlantic sea-routes. A very serious blow was that of Caesar's smashing the power (and the fleet) of the Veneti. As a consequence of the spreading of Roman power, the Atlantic sea-ways would not recover their former strength until the invasion of Britain by Anglo-Saxon peoples and the rise and spread of what has been dubbed 'Celtic Christianity' which produced, among other things, the so-called 'Age of the Saints'.

Again, this is powerful material in the hands of those who would assert Galicia's place in the Celtic world. Indeed, some historians today speak of a 'Celtic Thalassocracy' which, they argue, extended in the first centuries of the Christian era from the kingdom of Dalriada to Galicia in Spain.[69] The considerable activity along the Atlantic sea-routes during this 'Age of the Saints' in the fifth and sixth centuries AD was studied by Radford by analysing the archaeological material recovered at the Celtic settlement at Tintagel in Cornwall, and although his interpretation of the site has been supplanted by later work many of his detailed observations still hold good. Radford detected there various types of pottery, Roman in character, and the remains of amphorae used for imported wine and oil. Some of the Tintagel sherds show parallels with similar pieces from southern Gaul, Tunisia and Egypt, something which suggests the extent of the Western sea-routes at this time: trade was once more flowing northwards along the Atlantic seaways.[70]

Throughout the Middle Ages, the influence of highly respected Spanish authors such as Isidore and Orosius can be detected in several of the Celtic countries, including the Cornish Peninsula and adjacent areas. According to Hillgarth, who has researched this subject, during the seventh century the relations between the Spanish and Irish churches were close, in part a function of Isidore's works,[71] and it has been further argued that Irish monks travelled to the north-west of Spain, via Cornwall and Brittany, to help the newly set-up Celtic colonies in that region.[72] Conner has recently assembled a list of surviving manuscripts written before the twelfth century and kept at Exeter Cathedral. In his list of the 67 extant manuscripts, no. 4 contains the *Historiae aduersus paganos*, by Orosius; no. 15 *De natura rerum* by Isidorus; no. 18 several fragments by Orosius and no. 43 the *Etymologiae* of Isidorus. Both Isidore and Orosius are further mentioned and/or commented upon in a large number of pages of Conner's work.[73] The links between Spain and Ireland during this time are also evident. Orosius mentions in the early fifth century a city in Galicia called Brigantia (exactly as in the *Leabhar Gabhála*), which has, according to him, a direct relationship with Ireland.[74] Furthermore, specific art motifs present in Ireland at this time, such as the characteristic Visigothic marigold design, which is found all over the Iberian Peninsula, probably reached Ireland from Galicia.[75]

The Age of the Saints is characterized by the hundreds of *peregrini* whose names and records have survived, and the hundreds more who vanished when propagating the Christian faith over the rough countryside or on the wide seas when following the ancient sea-routes which linked Ireland, Wales, Cornwall, Brittany and Galicia. Doble recorded the names of a series of saints revered in the Newquay, Padstow and Bodmin area of Mid Cornwall. The most prominent are Brioc, Carantoc and Petroc, who have churches dedicated to them not only in Cornwall (mainly in the Camel estuary) but also in Wales, England and especially in Brittany, just one example of how these saints—or at least their reputations or 'Lives'—travelled the Atlantic sea-ways.[76] The expansion of this 'Celtic Church' into north-west Spain is an historically attested fact and a further key element in the construction of 'Celtic Galicia'.[77] For reasons that are not yet clear, somewhere around the fifth century Celtic-speaking peoples began to emigrate from the Cornish Peninsula to Armorica and even farther, to the north-west of the Iberian Peninsula, where they landed between the provinces of Asturias and Lugo in Galicia.[78] These Celtic colonies, it is argued, managed to maintain their own culture, identity and peculiar religious structures, and were recognized as such in the Council of Lugo which took place in the year 567 AD. They were granted their own Christian see, Britonia or Bretoña, with headquarters in a monastery of their own, whose bishop Mahiloc or Mailoc (*prelado de la Britonensis Ecclesia*) signed the acts of the II Council Bracarense which took place in Braga in the year 572 AD.[79] These Celtic colonies continued to expand, and contributed to the fact that that whole region retained its Roman name of *Gallaecia* (today's Galicia). The see of Bretoña was ravaged in AD 830 by the Moors, but it continued to exist at least until the Council of Oviedo in AD 900. This Britonensis Ecclesia was located in the present-day Santa María de Bretoña, province of Lugo. Relatively recent archaeological excavations have uncovered remains of this church, which was found inside a large *castro*.[80]

According to Irish legends from the eighth century, a bishop had led a group of Britons in their migration to that area. Some of these legends describe these contacts between the north-west of Spain and Britain and Ireland, as well as the various expeditions by Celtic-Irish monks who arrived in Galicia during the first centuries of the Christian Era.[81] One example of these, collected in *The Book of Leinster*, is the *Immram Curaig Ua Corra* or The Voyage of the 'Uí Corra boat' with nine men aboard, among them a bishop. This *curragh* landed at 'the corner of Spain' (the north-west), where its passengers founded a church.[82] Another religious factor which is held to have united the Celtic peoples of the Atlantic throughout the early Middle Ages was the widespread extension of Priscilianism, considered a heresy by the Roman Catholic Church. Priscilian had great prestige, and Priscilianism was common and even prevalent in early British Christianity, as it was in Ireland, Wales, Cornwall and the Iberian Peninsula.[83]

To summarize, then, the main Atlantic sea-routes brought the north-west of the Iberian Peninsula into contact with Brittany, the Cornish Peninsula, Wales, Scotland, the Isle of Man and Ireland from prehistoric times. These contacts reached their zenith during the Bronze Age Atlantic Area but grew again during the so-called Age of the Saints. Together, these contacts provide much of the material from which the idea of 'Celtic Galicia' is constructed.

SIMILARITIES IN TRADITIONS, SUPERSTITIONS AND FOLKLORE

To the archaeological, historical and other evidence of the Atlantic Area is added popular traditions, superstitions and folklore, the argument being that there are common 'Celtic' folk-narratives shared by each of the Celtic countries, including Galicia. Indeed, the existence of such folk-narratives within Galicia is taken to be yet further evidence of the region's Celtic identity. In the Finisterre region of Galicia, for example, the raven is considered as a bad omen and a herald of bad news;[84] in many Celtic fairy tales the crow is a bird of ill omen connected with death.[85] In Cornwall, a raven on the roof of a house was a harbinger of the death of one of its inhabitants.[86] The same would happen when a cock was heard crowing at midnight.[87] In Penzance, in the mid nineteenth century, there were supposedly some who believed that a chough (a relative of the raven) should never be killed under any circumstances, since King Arthur's spirit was re-incarnated within this bird. This belief must have extended to some degree along the Atlantic Area countries described above: even the famous Spanish writer Miguel de Cervantes knew it. In his *Don Quixote*, Book I, Chap. XIII he narrates how 'King Arthur did not die, but turned into a raven; in due time he will come back and take over his crown and reign'. This is the origin of the reluctance to kill a raven still present these days in many Celtic and British regions.[88] Both in Cornwall[89] and Finisterre, Galicia, the mournful barking of a dog presaged an imminent death. To avoid this distressing omen, the person who heard this kind of barking had to set under his or her bed an old shoe, with the sole facing upwards. If the barking was heard when a person was walking along a road, he or she had to take one shoe off and place it upside down on the ground until the dog stopped barking.[90]

Almost all the villages of Galicia had a so-called *vedoiro* (a man) or *vedoira* (a woman), who could foresee a neighbour's death.[91] These *vedoiros* had intuitive visions where the person who was supposed to die appeared to them. In the folklore of Ireland a *taise* is a sudden apparition of a person whom one knows, but that person is not the real one but a look-alike. This is what is called in English a *fetch* or a *wraith*. If one meets a *taise*, this means that the person represented by it is either going to die or to suffer a great misfortune. In Galicia the most common announcer of death was the *rolda*, 'the one who walks in the night'.[92] When an adult met a *rolda*, the best thing he or she could do was to draw a circle on the ground and place him/herself inside it to avoid being taken away. Another kind of apparition is the 'Santa Compaña', or procession of death, which occurs in Galicia and the north of Portugal,[93] and also exists in the folklore of the Celtic countries which once made up the Atlantic Area. The 'Santa Compaña' of Finisterre, and many other areas of Galicia, appeared in front of a house where somebody was going to die, or left a coffin by the door.[94] In the adjacent province of Asturias, people also believed in this 'Santa Compaña', called here 'güestia', which according to Gómez Tabanera was in the past a common myth in the whole north-west of Spain and northern Portugal.[95] The equivalent of the 'Santa Compaña' in northern Scotland is the *Sluagh*.[96] In Ireland, this 'Santa Compaña' is 'The Host' from the 'Otherworld' who behaved like humans when dwelling among the mortals, clearly represented in one of the most famous Irish tales, 'The Adventure of Nera', where a curious reference is found to a host of ghosts who return to the 'Otherworld' after a visit to the mortals' world: when Nera returned to Ráth Cruachan, the palace of Medb and Ailill, he saw it in flames, and the heads of Ailill and his warriors were being taken away by Otherworld dwellers.[97] The 'Santa Compaña' often appears during the night, surrounded by a dazzling light;[98] brilliant lights are also common in many Celtic folk-tales and stories.[99]

Also common in the region of Galicia was the extreme fear of having a corpse nearby, which was widespread among the fishermen,[100] as it was, too, among the fishermen of western Cornwall: they always tried not to sail during the night by a shoal or rocks where a shipwreck causing human losses had taken place, with the corpses of the drowned floating on the sea. It was thought that the souls of those dead victims were wandering around the area and often dared to call the names of the persons they could see passing by. These happenings occurred more often during stormy nights. On some occasions, according to legend, a voice from the sea was heard saying: 'The hour is come, but not the man!'[101] Rhys describes two almost identical stories he heard himself in Wales. In one of them, a strange man utters from the waters of Lake Llyn Gwernen to a passer-by: 'Daeth yr awr ni daeth y dyn!' In the second story, a person is seen walking by the shore of Cynnwch Lake and crying out: 'Mae'r awr wedi dyfod a'r dyn heb dyfod!'[102] Both these utterances echo strongly the voice from the Cornish sea described above.

In the region of Finisterre and some other places around Galicia, a solitary soul, a death-messenger similar to the Irish Banshee, often wandered around the countryside. She was a 'fairy woman' or 'woman of the Otherworld',[103] often appearing as an old hag with long white hair;[104] she also resembled the *Glaisrig* or Green Dam of the Scottish Highlands, since some times she wore a long green cape. In Wales, according to Rhys, she appeared as a 'spectral female [who] used to be oftener heard than seen', uttering cries that 'meant the approaching death of the hearer's husband, wife, or child . . . [or] the hearer himself'. She is compared by Rhys to the Irish hag Cailleach Bhéara, or Caillech Bérre, 'the Old Woman of Beare'.[105] In Galicia, as in the south-east of Ireland, the Banshee could also appear as a beautiful maiden, combing her long blonde hair with a golden comb.[106] This is a story (among many others which were almost identical to those

preserved in Ireland and other Celtic countries) that the present author
has more than once heard himself from the 'official' story-teller of the
small village in the remote and isolated region between Asturias and
Lugo where he has his roots.[107] González Reboredo reports several
instances of this legend still being preserved in certain villages of
Galicia; one of them is Santiago de Tortoreos, township of Las Nieves,
province of Pontevedra, where a fairy still appears combing her hair by
a spring, located inside a *castro* (Celtic hill-fort).[108] In the *Leabhar
Gabhála*, the *Tuatha Dé Danaan* are said to be the *sídhe* (*shee*) or
spirits, known in Welsh as the *Tylwyth Teg*, in Old Cornish as *cor*, in
Breton as *korr* or *korrigan*[110] and in English as fairies, who inhabit
ancient *síde* and interfere occasionally in human affairs—for either
good or evil.[111]

González Reboredo reports the existence in Galicia of mythical
creatures known by the common folk as *mouras*, which are also found
in the adjacent region of Asturias under the name of *xanas*. These
feminine beings, who are supposed to live underground, occasionally
appear by springs, fountains, lakes or rivers combing their blonde long
hair.[112] They are similar to the ones described in Ireland as spirit folk
living close to human beings, but normally unseen or concealed from
them, dwelling underneath certain hills (*aos síde or 'people of the
sídhe'*).[113] They are also described by the scholar Julio Caro Baroja.[114]
Slightly different from the *mouras* or the *xanas* are the *xacios* who live
underwater in the fords of the River Miño, and show up sometimes in
human shape near *castros*. They are reported as having been seen near
the *castro* of Marce (Saviñao, province of Lugo), where villagers who
were fishing in the river have seen in the past beautiful (feminine)
xacias who addressed them before disappearing.[115] Thus, these *mouras,
xanas* and *xacias* offer clear similarities with the feminine beings of the
Aos Sídhe, 'Race of the Fairy Mounds', commonly shortened to 'the
Sídhe' (*Shee*), described in the mythology of ancient Ireland,[116] and the
korrigan who dwell by springs near the ancient dolmens of Brittany.
The *bean-sídhe* (dweller of a *síd*), *ben síde*, or *banshee* (anglicised form)
of Ireland, is then another form of the 'fairy woman' described in
various Celtic countries, and the existence of such 'fairy women' in
Galicia and Asturias in Spain is often presented as yet further evidence
of those regions' Celticity.[117] Furthermore, these fairies of north-west
Spain, like their Celtic counterparts elsewhere, could present themselves as either benevolent or extremely evil.[118] Additionally, that
rivers were often associated in Ireland with 'Otherworld women' is well
known. Many are thought to be the old 'river goddesses' of Irish
primeval religion like Boand (Boyne) and Sinnan (Shannon).[119] Thus it
is no coincidence, supporters of 'Celtic Galicia' would argue, that one

of the main rivers in the north-west region of Spain is still called by the name of a famous Celtic goddess, the Navia.[120]

In Cornwall, it was thought by some people that the soul of a person who had died in an accident or committed suicide wanders around the vicinities of the nearest parish.[121] The inhabitants of Mousehole were thought to believe in the existence of such ghosts in the not too distant past.[122] In Ireland, a common belief was that if somebody died a sudden death, he or she would become a ghost, or that the fairies could sometimes get hold of the souls of those who had just died and take them with them. That is why people would never throw water into the street or onto the ground (if in the countryside), without shouting 'Take care of the water!', or 'Away with yourself from the water!' This practice was intended to avoid soaking the invisible souls that could be passing by the house at that moment. Even more, in Ireland, and also in Galicia, it was believed that the souls of the dead took the shape of butterflies in order to ascend to heaven.[123] In the so-called Celtic regions of Portugal, they avoided crying when a young child died, for they believed that the tears could soak its wings, thus preventing it flying to heaven.[124]

Another common belief among the Celtic peoples is that of the *Dallahan* of Ireland, a decapitated ghost who carried his head under his arm. The *Dallahan* strolling by a house meant death to somebody inside it. This horrible-looking character also appeared driving the hearse of the Banshee, carrying the reins in one hand and his head in the other. In a similar way, there are legends in Cornwall of riders who carry their own heads under one of their arms, driving in the vicinities of a megalithic dolmen. This legend is also common in the southern English counties of Hampshire, Wiltshire and Gloucestershire, and again there are echoes of the belief in Galicia, suggesting once more for those who care to pronounce it a common Celticity.[125]

Similarly, people living in the countryside of Galicia and Asturias are said to have a highly unusual belief in dreams, and faith in what they see in them. This peculiar characteristic was also common in the country-folk of Cornwall. Richard Carew, writing in 1602, describes how 'some haue found Tynne-workes of great vallew, through meanes no leffe ftrange, then extraordinarie, to wit, by dreams'. He continues, saying how 'a Gentlewoman, heire to one Trefculierd, and wife to Lauyue', and 'one Taprel lately liuing, & dwelling in the Parifh of the hundred of Weft, called S. Niot', had dreams which became true about discovering a 'great ftore of Tynnne, as would ferue to inrich' them and their 'pofteritie'.[126] The witches of Galicia, too, are very similar to those in Cornwall, Brittany, Scotland and Ireland. They could manage to escape through the chimneys and take the shape of diverse animals,

especially hares. For many Galician fishermen certain words are still
taboo: they never talk or mention hares when they are on board a
vessel, a peculiarity shared by fishermen of various parts of Britain and
Ireland.[127] Not long ago, people in Cornwall believed that young girls
who die of sorrow and melancholy after having been abandoned or
rejected by their sweethearts become white hares which suddenly
appear in front of the disloyal boyfriends or lovers to distract them.[128]
Witches in the Isle of Man have the power to change themselves into
the shape of hares, and to meet during Beltain (the First of May) to
plan their deeds. These witches are called in Manx butches.[129] Caesar
included the hare as one of the beasts held in awe by the early Britons,
suggesting its religious significance.[130] This is corroborated by the fact
that the famous queen of the Iceni, Boudicca, released a hare and
invoked her goddess, Andraste, before setting out on their historical
wide-scale campaign against the Romans.[131]

Galician witches, like their counterparts in Ireland, liked to sit by
the hearth to plan their future deeds.[132] They had a predilection for
rocky cliffs and promontories, something they had in common with
their 'sisters' in St Levan, in the south of Penwith, Cornwall. From
those high cliffs they enjoyed creating terrific storms, which caused
many ships to sink into the seas with their entire crews.[133] Their usual
abode was located at Castle Peak, a rocky hill near St Levan, where all
the witches of Penwith used to meet during the summer solstice in
alternate years. They had another dwelling in an old tin mine in Trewa,
near Zennor, around a huge rock locally known as 'The Witches'
Rock'. Many of them, it is said, used to fly from there directly to
Spain.[134] Even in modern times, the belief in the existence of witches
was highly extended among people of all social levels in both Cornwall
and Galicia. Reports of this type of superstition in Galicia are clear
and multiple.[135] Sharpe reports how widespread these beliefs were in
the Cornish Peninsula, both among the common people and also in the
political élite. In 1426, for example, the House of Commons appointed
a commission to investigate witchcraft allegations in Somerset, Dorset
and Cornwall.[136]

In the past, a great feat in Cornwall was to dare to go out at
midnight and touch the 'Witches' Rock' nine consecutive times. This
was thought to protect the one who did it and at the same time showed
that he or she was brave and fearless. However, there was a belief
in the region of Penwith that a woman who touched a Logan Stone
(an oscillating or rocking stone) nine times at midnight would become
a witch. A woman could also get transformed into a witch if she
managed to climb onto a Logan Stone nine times without causing
the stone to swing.[137] The various rituals and beliefs based on these

oscillating stones were also very common in Galicia, suggesting once more a 'Celtic connection'.[138] Taboada Chivite researched this interesting subject and found out that in both Galicia and Asturias, as in other Celtic regions and countries, oscillating stones are often used in divination practices, something which has been confirmed in Brittany.[139] An oscillating stone located in Nancledra, near St Ives, Cornwall, could only be made to swing at midnight. It was supposed to cure rickets in children, if they were set upon the stone and could make it oscillate.[140] In Treryn, Land's End, Cornwall, there used to be located a stone of this type that was utilized in these or similar practices.[141] In Galicia, in the not too distant past, these oscillating stones were customarily used in trials, and served to prove a person guilty if he or she could not manage to climb up and make the stone move.[142]

The cult of 'the stone', in general, existed in ancient times in Galicia.[143] Oscillating stones were believed to have fertility-propitiatory properties, and could help women who were infertile or had difficulties in getting pregnant,[144] a belief which was also common in other Celtic countries.[145] The deployment of stones as cult objects is recorded in Galicia in the vicinity of various *castros*, for instance the one at Baixada de San José, near the township of Verín in the province of Ourense,[146] and often involved use of megalithic dolmens.[147] In the valley of the Conway, Wales, many couples promised each other everlasting love by such stones.[148] In Brittany, maidens climbed on oscillating stones to prove their virginity. If a girl managed to make a stone move, she was a virgin.[149] Legends associated with stones with hollows or holes in them are also seen by some commentators as distinctly 'Celtic', and once again there is a strong Pan-Celtic dimension to such belief. In a recent work, Ken Dowden expresses his view that in ancient times, 'stones, like trees and groves, called for recognition and respect'.[150] Rolleston describes how stone-worship was particularly common among the ancient Celts, a practice which endured in many regions till recent times.[151] In the parish of Madron in Cornwall there is the large perforated stone called Mên-an-Tol. People seeking a remedy for rheumatism and other illnesses used to crawl through the hole. This practice was also supposed to help children afflicted with rickets.[152] In Minchinhampton (Gloucestershire) there is a 'Long Stone' with a hole in the bottom, 'through which children used to be passed for the cure or prevention of measles, whooping-cough and other ailments'.[153] In Ireland and Wales they used to collect rainwater from hollow stones, to be used for its supposed healing properties.[154] These stones were also thought to have symbolic fertility properties: infertile women in the region of Rennes in Brittany were encouraged to rub themselves against hollow stones.[155] In the Isle of Mull, Scotland, people suffering from various ailments used to go to the seaside to walk across natural holes that the erosion produced by the waves had made through some rocks. However, before they performed this curative ritual they had to immerse their heads in sea-water from the ninth wave, which they carefully collected in a pail.[156]

This rite of the ninth wave has a particular connection with the ancient Celtic world.[157] The number nine had a very special significance for the ancient Celts.[158] There were nine hazels of wisdom that grew at the heads of the main rivers of Ireland;[159] companies of nine are common in Irish literature; Queen Medb rode with nine chariots; Bicriu's hall had nine rooms; CúChulainn owned nine different kinds of weapons;[160] nine were the maidens who kindled the Cauldron of the Head of Annwfn in Wales with their breath; the 'Curse of Macha on the Ulstermen' was for nine times nine generations; nine was connected with the Beltain fire in Scotland; in Wales the Beltain fire 'was made with nine sticks collected by nine men from nine different trees'.[161] As late as the twentieth century, Rhys described how a lady living at Peel, in the Isle of Man, related to him how she was cured of a swelling in her neck by a lady 'charmer' who used for the purpose 'nine pieces of iron'.[162] The number nine was very influential in divinations and in folk remedies, and people believed that the waves of the sea broke in a sequence of nine, the ninth being larger than the rest and having a considerable importance for its curative, beneficial and fortune-giving properties.[163] In the *Leabhar Gabhála*, when the Milesians from Galicia in Spain landed in Ireland, the three kings of the Tuatha Dé Danaan, Mac Cuill, Mac Cecht, and Mac Greine 'adjudged' that 'they should have possession of the island to the end of nine days'. Finally, they accepted the judgement given by the Milesians' poet, the druid Aimirgin, who asked his companions to go back to their ships and retire into the sea to the distance of nine waves.[164] In an old Irish folktale, 'The Tale of the Ordeals', the beneficial effects of the ninth wave are described, and in Wales the ninth wave is sinonymous with happiness and well-being.[165] In another folktale, this time in Ireland, the crew of a ship energetically hurried to reach and pass the ninth wave, in order to avoid a deadly epidemic infection which pervaded the island. They were convinced that the pest could not possibly pass beyond that ninth wave.[166]

The symbolic importance of the ninth wave for the ancient Celts can be still observed to this day in the north-west of the Iberian Peninsula, a significant survival in the iconography of 'Celtic Galicia'. In the 4 km long beach of Lanzada, located in the townships of Ogrobe and Sansenxo in the province of Pontevedra in Galicia, a very old fertility ritual has been held year after year since time immemorial and is still being observed: infertile women, or women having difficulties in getting pregnant, dip into the sea semi-naked just before midnight till they are covered by the ninth wave.[167] Some scholars believe that this practice of walking into the sea till reaching the ninth wave was in old times a generalized custom all along the coastal regions of Galicia.[168] Furthermore, at a promontory located above that beach of Lanzada, archaic fertility and religious rites connected with the Celtic goddess of fertility, and the Land of Forever Young (*Tir na nÓg*) were held until the site was 'Christianised' by the Spanish Church in the thirteenth century.[169]

To obtain some kind of protection against black witchcraft, a series of different kinds of amulets were used in Galicia. One of the most common and powerful charms was a wild-boar tusk, something again common in other Celtic countries.[170] In general, the rites and magic objects which were used by Galician fishermen for protection against witches and stormy seas are very similar to the ones common with their counterparts in the rest of the Celtic regions of the European Atlantic Area.' And again this is evidence deployed in support of the 'Celtic Galicia' thesis.[171] For example, in Galicia, not long ago, when a mother took a baby to the church to be baptized, she always placed a piece of bread on its neck in order to protect it against any bad spell, sorcery or witch's curse.[172] This was also practised in both Galicia and parts of Portugal when a mother was taking a baby to another house for a visit.[173] Bread was also used in Galicia to get rid of the spells casted by the mythical beings who lived underground (Otherworld dwellings, something like the Irish *sídhe*),[174] generally located in or near the *castros*[175]. In Cornwall, when a baby was taken to be baptized, the mother also took with her a piece of bread; if she met somebody on the way to the church, she had to give him or her a little piece of that bread.[176]

A very curious ritual used to be practised in western Cornwall in the past: whenever a man or a woman sensed an imminent hazard or peril they repeatedly bumped their head against the mantelpiece several times. This practice, known as 'touching the cravel', was followed by throwing a handful of straw or a little dry stick into the fire to make it sparkle.[177] A curious remnant of this pagan ritual, again thought to be 'Celtic', has been adopted (like many others) by the Spanish Christian Church: it is customarily performed by the pilgrims arriving at the Cathedral of Santiago (Saint James) de Compostela in Galicia, by bumping their heads several times against an effigy of the *Santo dos croques*.[178] Moroever, as Celtic enthusiasts readily attest, the pilgrim routes to Santiago de Compostela, still very much in use today, reflect those old Atlantic Area sea-ways, with pilgrims regularly journeying to Galicia from places such as Ireland, Cornwall and Brittany.

'CELTIC GALICIA' TODAY
In today's Galicia, the notion of a 'Celtic heritage' is receiving increasingly serious attention. A number of *castros* ('Celtic' hill-forts) which have been recovered by local archaeologists are presented now for all to see, together with many gold torques, diadems, tiaras, amulets, charms, ear-rings, necklaces and bracelets which have been found within them. Alonso Romero describes a yearly folk pilgrimage to San Andrés de Teixido, where the pilgrims decorate their houses with green branches and wild flowers in a manner which resembles that of May Day in Padstow, on the north coast of Cornwall.[179] Furthermore, the branches used in Galicia for adorning the houses are unfailingly from a yew, which is described by many authors as one of the most sacred trees of the ancient Celts.[180]

Celts and Celticity are now attracting an enormous interest in many villages in Galicia where the inhabitants, especially the young, are anxious to reintroduce archaic festivals, rites and traditions as a way of proclaiming what they consider their Celtic identity. Amongst the principal events of this kind is the 'Festa dos fachóns da Vila do castro', in Castro Caldelas in the province of Ourense, during San Sebastian Day. The villagers perform a nocturnal parade brandishing large torches made of straw, proceeding through the village's streets until they reach the central square, where they light a large bonfire.[181] The 'Fiesta Castrexa', in Xunqueira de Ambía, again in the province of Ourense, was reinitiated in 1994 to celebrate a feast similar to one that used to be held in this village by the River Arnoya during pagan times to honour a local nymph called Tanitaco who is deemed to be 'Celtic'. The festival of 'Lugnasada' is held in Bretoña in the province of Lugo, a town which is very proud of its Celtic connection (it was the religious capital of the migrants from Britain who arrived to the area during the fourth and fifth centuries AD). The local young boys and girls revere Lug in a forest locally considered by some to be enchanted. Lugnasad is held on August 1, with Celtic music, bag-pipe bands, harps and flutes. After dark, the villagers go to the forest and hold certain ceremonies, dance and sing around fires. 'Fiesta de Las Fachas', in Taboada, province of Lugo, which takes place every year on the top of a *castro*, in order to celebrate once more an almost forgotten festival dating from time immemorial that is now repackaged as 'Celtic'. The burning of the 'fachas' (long torches), is presented as having been a means of communication between the various *castros* of the region during Celtic times, a sort of illumination for nocturnal events, or perhaps part of now forgotten magic-religious rituals.[182]

CONCLUSION

For both scholars and popular enthusiasts, the 'Celtic heritage' in the north-west of the Iberian Peninsula, an area which includes the whole four provinces of Galicia, the region of Asturias, the adjacent geographical zones in Spain, and the north of Portugal as far as the River Douro, is located in and 'proved' by an array of comparative historical, archaeological, linguistic, religious, mythological and cultural evidence, much of which has been presented above, where there are alleged to be compelling similarities with Cornwall and the rest of the Celtic world. All these Iberian regions formed part of an Atlantic Area which, it is asserted, united the Celtic world over three millennia. Present-day Galicians show a keen interest in this Celtic heritage and display great confidence in its continuing value and relevance in contemporary Galacia. Folk-tales and rituals from the pre-Christian past, often concerned with the 'Otherworld' and echoing those of the Celtic world, have continued to be narrated down to our own times. Ancient fertility rituals continue to be held year after year by the sea. The old Pagan religion can still be discerned in many elements which consciously or unconsciously have been embedded in the peculiar rites and rituals of the adopted (or enforced) Christianity. Popular religion is now composed of a colourful amalgam of magic, prayers, charms, legends, and pilgrimages, which incorporate Christian doctrine and remnants of what many like to see as a 'Celtic Paganism'. All of this makes for a heady mix which appeals to many people, especially the young, as Galicia asserts its separate identity as an Autonomous Region within Spain and plays an increasing role within the Atlantic Arc and the wider European Union as one of the historic regions of Europe. Whether external observers like it or not, this increasingly confident, visible and vocal Galicia has no difficulty in viewing its identity as essentially 'Celtic'.

ACKNOWLEDGEMENTS

The author wishes to thank Professor Fernando Alonso Romero for his most valuable help, also my daughter Anne Louise, and Helen Hodgkinson.

NOTES AND REFERENCES

1. For a sceptical assessment see M. Chapman, *The Celts: The Construction of a Myth*, Macmillan, 1992; for a more positive approach to the complexity of contemporary Celtic Studies see A. Hale and P. Payton (eds), *New Directions in Celtic Studies*, University of Exeter Press, 2000.
2. A. Hale, 'Rethinking Celtic Cornwall: An Ethnographic Approach' and 'Genesis of the Celto-Cornish Revival? L.C. Duncombe-Jewell and the Cowethas Kelto-Kernuak', in P. Payton (ed.), *Cornish Studies: Five*, University of Exeter Press, 1997, pp. 85–111.
3. P. Berresford Ellis, *The Celtic Dawn: A History of Pan Celticism*, Constable, London, 1993, pp. 19–27.
4. P. Payton, 'Ethnicity in Western Europe Today', in Karl Cordell (ed.), *Ethnicity and Democratisation in the New Europe*, Routledge, London, 1999, pp. 26–7.
5. Berresford Ellis, 1993, p. 24.
6. Berresford Ellis, 1993, p. 25.
7. B. Raftery (ed.), *Atlas of the Celts*, Philip's, London, 2001; see especially pp. 48–9 and p. 113.
8. J. Renales and V. Renero-Arribas, Abstract: 'Celtiberian Studies and Spanish Historiography in the 19th Century', in *Programme of the 10th International Congress of Celtic Studies*, Edinburgh, 1995, p. 106.
9. B. Cunliffe, *The Ancient Celts*, Oxford, 1997, p. 148.
10. B. Cunliffe, *Facing the Ocean: The Atlantic and Its People*, Oxford, 2001.
11. Cunliffe, 2001, p. 60.
12. H.O.N. Hencken, *The Prehistoric Tin Trade*, Chap. V—'Cornwall and Scilly', London, 1932, pp. 174–5.
13. W. O'Brien, *Bronze Age Copper Mining in Britain and Ireland*, Princes Risborough, 1996, p. 5.
14. K. Kristiansen, *Europe before History*, Cambridge, 1998, p. 144.
15. O'Brien, 1996, p. 9.
16. R. Carew, *The Survey of Cornwall*, London, 1602, facsimile edition, Amsterdam and New York, 1969, p. 19.
17. D. Rankin, *Celts and the Classical World*, London and New York, 1996, p. 5.
18. T.G.E. Powell, *The Celts*, London, 1991, p. 22.
19. Diodorus Siculus, V, 22, 38.
20. Julius Caesar, *De Bello Gallico*, III, 8. See also Strabo, *Geog.*, IV, 4, 1.
21. E.G. Bowen, *Saints, Seaways and Settlements in the Celtic Lands*, Cardiff, 1977, p. 6.
22. A.R. Lewis, *The Northern Seas*, Princeton, 1958, p. 64.
23. M. Ruíz-Gálvez, 'El Occidente de la Península Ibérica, punto de encuentro entre el Mediterráneo y el Atlántico a fines de la Edad del broncé', *Complutum* 4, 1993, pp. 41–68; C. Gibson, 'Plain sailing? Later Bronze Age Western Iberia at the Cross-Roads of the Atlantic and Mediterranean', in J.C. Henderson (ed.), *The Prehistory and Early History of Altantic Europe*, BAR International Series 861, 2000, pp. 73–97.

24. Cunliffe, 1997, pp. 148–56; F. Alonso Romero, *Relaciones Atlánticas Prehistóricas entre Galica y las Islas Británicas*, Vigo, 1976; M. Ruíz-Gálvez, *La Península Ibérica y sus Relaciones con el Circulo Cultural Atlántico*, (2 vols), Madrid, 1984; C. Meijide, 'Atlantic Relations in the North-west of the Iberian Peninsula during the Bronze Age', *Spal* 3, 1994, pp. 197–223.

25. R.A.S. Macalister, *Ireland in pre-Celtic Times*, Dublin, 1921, p. 116.

26. G. Eogan, 'The Prehistoric Foundations of the Celtic West: Passage Tombs and Early Settled Life in West Europe', in R. O'Driscoll (ed.), *The Celtic Consciousness*, Portlaoise, 1982, pp. 95–117; L. de Paor, *The Peoples of Ireland—From Prehistory to Modern Times*, Notre Dame (Indiana), 1986, pp. 20–5.

27. Cunliffe 1997, p. 147.

28. T.D. Kendrick, *The Druids—A Study in Keltic Prehistory*, London, 1996, p. 34.

29. J.T. Koch, 'Ériu, Alba, and Letha', *Emania* 9, 1991, pp. 17–27 (at 18–19).

30. V.G. Childe, *The Bronze Age*, Cambridge, 1930, p. 52.

31. H.O.N. Hencken, *The Archaeology of Cornwall and Scilly*, London, 1932, pp. 184–5.

32. J. Waddell, 'The Question of the Celticisation of Ireland', *Emania* 9, 1991, pp. 5–16, at p. 12.

33. S. McGrail, 'Cross-channel Seamanship and Navigation in the Last Millenium BC', *Oxford Journal of Archaeology* 2(3), 1983, pp. 229–337; S. McGrail, 'Assessing the Performance of an Ancient Boat. The Hasholme Logboat', *Oxford Journal of Archaeology* 7(1), 1988, pp. 35–46.

34. J.M. Wooding, *Communication and Commerce along the Western Sealanes AD 400–800*, BAR International Series 654, Oxford, 1996.

35. S. Piggot, 'A Glance at Cornish Tin', in V. Markovic (ed.), *Ancient People and the Mediterranean*, 1978, pp. 141–5; I.S. Maxwell, *Occupation Sites on a Chiltern Ridge*, BAR British Series 29, Oxford, 1976; S. Mitchell, 'Cornish Tin, Julius Caesar and the Invasion of Britain', *Latomas* 180, 1983, pp. 80–99; B. Cunliffe, 'Ictis: Is it Here?', *Oxford Journal of Archaeology* 2(1), 1983, pp. 123–6; C.F.C. Hawkes, 'Ictis Disentangled, and the British Tin Trade', *Oxford Journal of Archaeology* 3(2), 1984, pp. 211–33; B. Cunliffe, *Iron Age Communities in Britain*, London and New York, 1991, p. 443.

36. G. Williams, 'Survey and Excavation on Pembrey Mountain', *Transactions of the Carmarthenshire Antiquaries Society* 17, 1981, pp. 3–33; D.P.S. Peacock, 'Amphorae in Iron Age Britain: A Reassessment', in: S. MacReady and F.H. Thompson (eds), *Cross-channel Trade between Gaul and Britain in the pre-Roman Iron Age*, Society of Antiquaries Occasional Paper 4, London, 1984, pp. 37–42; P.R. Sealey, *Amphoras from the 1970 Excavations at Colchester Sheepen*, BAR British Series 142, Oxford, 1985.

37. A. Tranoy, *La Galice Romaine*, Paris, 1981, p. 103; Ruíz-Gálvez, 1984.

38. F. Alonso Romero, 'Tradition and Innovation in a Galician Pilgrimage of

Celtic Origins: The Pilgrimage to San Andrés de Teixido', *8th International Congress of Celtic Studies at Swansea, 1987*, Cardiff, 1990; Bowen, 1977.

39. C.J. Lynn, 'Navat Fort: A Draft Summary Account of D.M. Waterman's Excavations', *Emania* 1, 1986, pp. 11–19.
40. H. Savory, *Spain and Portugal. The Prehistory of the Iberian Peninsula —Ancient Peoples and Places*, London, 1968, pp. 211, 222.
41. E. Mac White, 'A New View on Irish Bronze Rock-scribings', *Journal of the Royal Society of Antiquaries of Ireland* 76, 1946, pp. 59–80; P. Harbison, *Pre-Christian Ireland—From the First Settlers to the Early Celts*, London, 1988, p. 119.
42. Macalister, 1921, pp. 223–4.
43. H.E. Kilbride-Jones, 'The Excavation of a Composite Tumulus at Drimmagh, Co. Dublin', *Journal of the Royal Society of Antiquaries of Ireland* 69, 1939, pp. 130–220 (at pp. 205–7, 215); H. Savory, 'Some Iberian Influences on the Copper Age Pottery of the Irish Channel Area', Univ. de Valladolid, *Boletín del Seminario de Estudios de Arte y Arquelogía* 44, 1978, pp. 5–13 (at p. 6). Cf. M. Ryan, 'Some Burial Monuments of the Later Neolithic', *Carloviana* 2, 1972, pp. 18–21; M. Ryan, 'The Excavation of a Neolithic Burial Mound at Jerpoint West, Co. Kilkenny', *Proceedings of the Royal Irish Academy* C 73, 1973, pp. 107–27; J. Raftery, 'A Neolithic Burial at Ballintruermore, Co. Carlow', *Journal of the Royal Society of Antiquaries of Ireland* 74, 1944, pp. 61–2.
44. G. Leisner and V. Leisner, *Die Megalithgräber der Iberischen Halbinsel*, Erster Teil, Der Süden, Berlin, 1943; A.E.P. Collins, 'Flint Javelin Heads', in Donnchadh O'Corrin (ed.), *Irish Antiquity*, Dublin, 1994, pp. 111–33 (at pp. 124–5).
45. E. Jalhay and A. do Paço, *El Castro Vilanova de San Pedro*, Madrid, 1945, pp. 33–4.
46. W. Bremer, *Ireland's Place in Prehistoric and Early Historic Europe*, Dublin, 1928, p. 17.
47. J. Raftery, *Prehistoric Ireland*, London, 1951, p. 134.
48. Cunliffe, 1997, pp. 165–6.
49. S. Caulfield, 'Celtic Problems in the Irish Iron Age', in O'Corráin (ed.), 1994, pp. 205–15 (at p. 211); Cunliffe 1997, pp. 165–6.
50. Cunliffe, 1991, p. 431.
51. Cunliffe, 1997, p. 150.
52. Cunliffe, 1997, p. 150.
53. Harbison, 1988, p. 139.
54. B. Rynne, 'An Early Celtic Spanish–North Munster Connection', *North. Munster Antiquarian Journal* 21, pp. 7–10. Cf. B. Raftery, 'The Celtic Iron Age in Ireland.' *Emania* 9, 1991, pp. 28–32.
55. T. Júdice Gamito, 'The Celts in Iberia', Actes du Congrès International d' Études Celtiques, Paris, 8–11 Juillet, *Études Celtiques* XXVIII, 1991, pp. 173–93 (at p. 185).
56. Harbison, 1988, pp. 137–88.
57. Harbison, 1988, p. 90.

58. Cunliffe, 1991, p. 431.
59. E.T. Leeds, 'Excavations at Chun Castle in Penwith, Cornwall', *Archaeologia* 76, 1927, pp. 205–40.
60. Cunliffe, 1991, p. 93.
61. Cunliffe, 1991, pp. 159–60 and Fig. 8.1 on p. 160.
62. Cunliffe, 1991, p. 182.
63. Júdice Gamito, 1991, pp. 183–5.
64. Cunliffe, 1991, p. 184.
65. R.E.M. Wheeler, 'Hill Forts of Northern France—a Note on the Expedition to Normandy', *Antiquaries Journal XXI, 1939, p. 268.*
66. C.F. Hawkes, 'Hill Forts', *Antiquity* 5, 1931, p. 77.
67. Leeds, 1927, pp. 205–40.
68. Cunliffe, 1991, p. 9.
69. Lewis, 1958, Chap. II, *passim.*
70. C.A.R. Radford, 'Imported Pottery found at Tintagel, Cornwall', in D.B. Harden (ed.), *Dark Age Britain*, London, 1956, pp. 59–70.
71. J.N. Hillgarth, 'Ireland and Spain in the Seventh Century', *Peritia*, Journal of the Medieval Academy of Ireland, 3, 1984, pp. 1–16.
72. F. Alonso Romero, *Santos e Barcos de Pedra*, Vigo, Ed. Xeraix, 1991, p. 58.
73. P.W. Conner, *Anglo-Saxon Exeter: A Tenth-century Cultural History*, Woodbridge, 1993, pp. 2–8. Isidore is furtherly mentioned on pp. 33–4, 37, 52–3, 65, 80, 84, 86, 95, 242 and Orosius on 28, 53, 149–50.
74. Orosius, *Operae*, Book I, Chap. ii.
75. A.W. Clapham, 'The Origins of Hiberno-Saxon Art', *Antiquity* VIII, 1934, p. 50; J.N. Hillgarth, 'Visigothic Spain and Early Christian Ireland', *Proceedings of the Royal Irish Academy* 62, 1962, pp. 190–1.
76. G.H. Doble, 'St Carantoc', *Cornish Saints Series*, No. 20, 1937. p. 25 (cited by Bowen, 1977, p. 70).
77. P. David, *Études Historiques sur la Galice et le Portugal du VIe au XIII siècle*, Paris, 1947, p. 44.
78. J. Orlandis, *Historia Social y Económica de la España Visigoda*, Madrid, 1975, pp. 48–9; A. García y García, 'Ecclesia Britoniensis', *Estudios Mondonienses* 2, pp. 121–34; P. Berresford Ellis, *The Celtic Empire* London, 1993, pp. 56–7.
79. García y García 1986, p. 124.
80. M. Chamoso Lamas, 'Las Primitivas Diócesis de Britonia y de San Martín de Mondoñedo a la Luz de Recientes Descubrimientos', *Bracara Augusta* 21, 1967, pp. 351–9; M. Chamoso Lamas, 'Avance Informativo Sobre las Excavaciones Arqueológicas Realizadas en Bretoña (Lugo) durante las Campañas de 1970 y 1971', *Noticiario Arqueológico Hispánico, Prehistoria* 4, pp. 268–71.
81. M. Dillon and N. Chadwick, *The Celtic Realms*, London, 1973, p. 61.
82. *Leabhar Laignech* (The Book of Leinster), facsimile reprod., London, 1880; W. Stokes, 'The Vogage of the Hui Corra', *Revue Celtique* XIV, 1893, pp. 22–69; R.I. Best and M.A. O'Brien, (eds), *The Book of Leinster, formerly Lebar na Núachongbála* II, Dublin, 1956.

83. Alonso Romero, 1991, p. 76.
84. X.M. Gonzáalez Fernández, *Tradicións e Costumes Populares da Fisterra*, Concello de Corcubión, RP Edicións, 1989, pp. 20–1.
85. E.B. Gose, Jr., *The World of the Irish Wonder Tale—An Introduction to the Study of Fairy Tales*, Toronto, 1985, p. 90.
86. R. Hunt, *The Drolls, Traditions and Superstitions of Old Cornwall*, 1881, p. 431.
87. C. Hardwick, *Traditions, Superstitions and Folklore*, Manchester, 1973 (first edition in 1872), p. 133.
88. Hunt, 1881, pp. 308–9.
89. Hunt, 1881, p. 380.
90. F. Alonso Romero, 'Animas y Brujas de Finisterre, Cornulles e Irlanda', *Anuario Brigantino* 22, 1999, pp. 91–104, at p. 92.
91. J. Rodríguez López, *Supersticiones de Galicia y Preocupaciones Vulgares*, Lugo, Editorial Celta, 1974, p. 196.
92. C. Lisón Tolosana, *La Santa Compaña*, Madrid, Ed. Akal, 1998, p. 94.
93. Alonso Romero, 1991, p. 120.
94. F. Alonso Romero, *Creencias y Tradiciones de los Pescadores Gallegos, Británicos y Bretones*, Santiago de Compostela, Xunta de Galicia, 1996, pp. 147–51.
95. J.M. Gómez Tabanera, *Prehistoria de Asturias*, Oviedo, 1974, p. 86.
96. Alonso Romero, 1996, p. 152.
97. Dillon and Chadwick, 1973, p. 185. For 'The Adventures of Neru' see T.P. Cross and C.H. Slover (eds), *Ancient Irish Tales*, New York, 1996, pp. 248–53 (first edition 1936).
98. Alonso Romero, 1996, p. 149.
99. J. Rhys, *Celtic Folklore—Welsh and Manx*, 2 vols, Oxford, 1901, vol. 1, p. 244; Gose, 1985, pp. 88, 96, 155, 183.
100. Alonso Romero, 1999, pp. 91–104, at p. 93.
101. Hunt, 1881, p. 366.
102. Rhys, 1901, vol. 1, pp. 243–4.
103. T. O'Cathasaigh, 'The Semantics of "Sid"', *Éigse* 17, 1977–8, pp. 137–55. Cf. J. Carey, 'Notes on the Irish War-Goddess', *Éigse* 19, 1983, pp. 263–75.
104. González Fernández, 1989, p. 55.
105. Rhys, 1901, vol. I, pp. 393–4, vol. III, pp. 453–4. According to Rhys, the name Béara, or Bérre, suggests identification with that of Bera, daughter of Eibhear, king of Spain, and wife of Eoghan Taidhleach, which appear in the story of 'The Courtship of Moméra' edited by E. O'Curry, *The Battle of Maghleana, and The Courtship of Momera*, Dublin, 1855.
106. T.C. Croker, *Researches in the South of Ireland 1812–1822*, Dublin, 1981, p. 91; P. Lysaght, *The Banshee. The Irish Supernatural Death-Messenger*, Dublin, 1986, p. 126.
107. A large corpus of folk beliefs about the Banshee are kept in the archives of the Department of Irish Folklore, University College of Dublin. See also P. Lysaght, 1986, especially pp. 321–64; P. Lysaght, 'Aspects of the Earth-Goddess in the Traditions of the Banshee in Ireland', in S.

Billington and M. Green (eds), *The Concept of the Goddess*, London and New York, 1996.

108. J.M. González Reboredo, *El Folklore en Los Castros Gallegos*, Santiago de Compostela, Monografías de la Univ. de Santiago 5, 1971, p. 32–4, 38.

109. R.A.S. Macalister, and J. MacNeill, tr. and eds, *Leabhar Gabhála* (The Recension of Mícheál Ó Cléirigh), Dublin, 1916; R.A.S. Macalister, 1938–1956, *Lebor Gabála Erenn*, 5 vols.

110. Rhys, 1901, vol. II, p. 671 and *passim*.

111. D. Hyde, *A Literary History of Ireland—From Earliest Times to the Present Day*, London, 1901, p. 284.

112. González Reboredo, 1971, pp. 32–4, 38, 39, 43.

113. E. Knott and G. Murphy, *Early Irish Literature*, London, 1966, p. 104.

114. J. Caro Baroja, *Algunos Mitos Españoles* Madrid, 1944, Chap. I, *passim*.

115. González Reboredo, 1971, p. 40.

116. S.H. O'Grady, ed. and tr., *Silva Godelica*, London, 1892, p. 370.

117. C. Squire, *The Mythology of Ancient Britain and Ireland*, London, 1906, p. 41.

118. González Reboredo, 1971, pp. 39, 42; Rhys, vol. 1, p. 82.

119. M. Low, *Celtic Christianity and Nature—Early Irish and Hebridean Traditions*, Edinburgh, 1996, pp. 66–9.

120. There is also a large city called Navia.

121. Hamilton A.K. Jenkin, *Cornwall and its People*, London, 1946, p. 238.

122. W. Bottrell, *Traditions and Hearthside Stories of West Cornwall*, I, 1870, facsimile reprod., Felinfach, 1996, p. 179.

123. W.B. Yeats (ed.), *Fairy and Folk Tales of Ireland*, London, 1981 (first edition in 1888), p. 117.

124. C. Pedroso, *Contribuçoes Para Uma Mitología Popular Portuguesa e Outros Escritos Etnográficos*, Lisbon, 1988, p. 283.

125. L.V. Grinsell, *Folklore of Prehistoric Sites in Britain*, London, 1976, p. 36.

126. Carew, *The Survey of Cornwall*, London, 1602 (1969).

127. F. Alonso Romero, 'Palabras Tabú y Eufemismos de los Pescadores Británicos: Paralelos Gallegos', Coloquio Manuel de Boaventura 1885–1985, *Esposende* 1987, pp. 381–96, at p. 389; Alonso Romero, 1996; P. Waring, *A Dictionary of Omens and Superstitions*, London, 1978, p. 117.

128. E. and M.A. Radford, *Superstitions of the Countryside*, London, 1978, p. 57.

129. Rhys, 1901, vol. I, pp. 294–5.

130. Julius Caesar, *Bel. Gallic.* V, p. 12.

131. A. Ross, *Pagan Celtic Britain*, London, 1967, p. 350.

132. F. de Ramón y Ballesteros, *Oscurantismo Finisterrano*, Santiago de Compostela, 1970, p. 97.

133. K. Harris, *Heva!*, Redruth, 1983, p. 70.

134. Hunt, 1881, pp. 321, 328, 330–31; F. Alonso Romero, 'El Folklore Sobre el Monto 'Casa da Joana' (macizo del Pinto)', *Cuadernos de Estudios Gallegos* XXXV, 1984, pp. 569–74 (at p. 569).

135. F. Alonso, 'Galician Legends about Miraculous Sea-voyages in

Stone-boats: Some Irish and Breton Parallels', Actes du IXe Contrès International D'Études Celtiques, Paris 7–12 juillet, *Études Celtiques XXIX*, 1992, pp. 89–95; F. Alonso Romero, *Relaciones Atlánticas Prehistóricas entre Galicia y las Islas Británicas, y Medios de Communicación*, Vigo, 1976; F. Alonso Romero, 'As nove Ondas da Mar Sagrada: Ritos y Mitos Galaicos Sobre las Olas del Mar', *Cuadernos de Estudios Gallegos* 98, 1982, pp. 589–605; Alonso Romero, 1990, Alonso Romero, 1991, Alonso Romero, 1999, pp. 91–104.

136. J. Sharpe, *Instruments of Darkness—Witchcraft in England 1550–1750*, London, 1996, pp. 24–5.

137. Hunt, 1881, pp. 321, 328. See also R. Hunt, *Cornish Folk-Lore*, 1871; reprinted by Truro, 1969.

138. M. Murguía, *Galicia*, Vigo, Ed. Xeraix, 1982; J.A. Castro Fernández, 'Las Piedras Vacilantes en Galicia y la Vision del Celtismo Decimonónico', *O Museo de Pontevedra* 36, 1982, pp. 480–96.

139. S. Taboada Chivite, 'O Culto das Pedras no Noroeste Peninsular', in *Ritos y Creencias Gallegas*, Á Coruña, Ed. Sálvora, 1980, pp. 167–8.

140. Radford, 1978, p. 74.

141. T. Deane and R. Shaw, *The Folklore of Cornwall*, London, 1975, p. 140.

142. Alonso Romero, 1991, p. 15.

143. González Reboredo, 1971, p. 91.

144. Castro Fernandez, 1982, pp. 480–96 (at p. 493); J.E. Carro Otero, and M.C. Masa Vázquez, ' "Santuarios" Impetratorios de la Fecundidad Humanan', *I Coloquio Galaico-Minhoto*, Ponte de Lima, 1981, vol. II, pp. 233–47.

145. C. and J. Bord, *Earth Rites*, London, 1982, pp. 31–67.

146. J. Taboada, 'Carta Arqueológica de la Comarca de Verín, III Congreso Nacional de Arqueología, Editorial Institución Fernando el Católico, Zaragoza, 1956, p. 337.

147. F.L. Cuevillas, A. Fraguas y P. Lorenzana, 'As Mámoas do Saviñao', *Arquivos do Seminario de Estudos Galegos*, Tomo V, p. 91.

148. T. Gwyn Jones, *Welsh Folklore and Folk-Custom*, Cambridge, 1979, p. 29.

149. R. Barros Silvelo, *Antigüedades de Galicia*, ÁCoruña, 1875, p. 81.

150. K. Dowden, *European Paganism—The Realities of Cult from Antiquity to the Middle Ages*, London and New York, 2000, p. 64.

151. T.W. Rolleston, *Myths and Legends of the Celtic Race*, London, 1911, p. 66.

152. W. Borlase, *Antiquites, Historical and Monumental, of the Country of Cornwall*, London, 1769, p. 177.

153. E.A. Philippson, *Germanische Heidentum bei den Angelsachsen*, Leipzig, 1929, p. 49.

154. N. Pennick, *Celtic Sacred Landscapes*, London, 1996, pp. 41–3.

155. S. Reinach, 'Les Monuments de Pierre brute dans le Lenguage et les Croyances Populaires', in *Cultes Mythes et Religions*, vol. 3, Paris, 1908, pp. 364–433, at p. 407.

156. J.G. Frazer, 'Balder the Beautiful', vol. II, in *The Golden Bough, A*

Study in Comparative Religion, London, 1966, p. 168 (facsimile reprint, London, 1890).

157. Alonso Romero, 1982, pp. 589–605.
158. A Rees and B. Rees, *Celtic Heritage*, London, 1990, p. 192.
159. Rhys, 1901, vol. II, p. 392.
160. J. Dunn, tr., *The Ancient Irish Epic Tale Aáin Bó Cúalnge*, London, 1914, p. 189.
161. G. Storms, *Anglo-Saxon Magic*, The Hague, 1948, pp. 96–8, 195–7; P. MacCana, *Celtic Mythology*, London, 1983, p. 11; P. Berresford Ellis, *A Dictionary of Irish Mythology*, Santa Barbara, 1987, p. 184; M.J. Green, *Dictionary of Celtic Myth and Legend*, London, 1992, pp. 50–1.
162. Rhys, 1901, vol. I, pp. 296–7.
163. Rees and Rees, 1961, p. 194; J.G. Frazer, 'Balder the Beautiful', vol. II, in the *Golden Bough*, London, 1966, p. 168.
164. Macalister and MacNeill, 1916, pp. 252–5.
165. J. Loth, 'L'année Celtique d'après les textes Irlandais, Gallois, Bretons, et le Calendrier de Coligny', *Revenue Celtique*, 25, 1904, pp. 153–4 and 156.
166. W. Stones, 'Mythological Notes', *Revenue Celtique* III, 1873, p. 201.
167. V. Lis Queiben, *La Medicina Popular en Galicia*, Pontevedra, 1949, p. 292; J. Rodríguez López, *Supersticiones de Galicia*, Lugo, 1974, p. 144; Alonso Romero, 1982, pp. 589–605.
168. F. Bouza Brey Trillo, *La Mitología del Agua en el Noroeste Hispánico*, Artes Gráficas de Galicia, 1973, p. 34; E. Alonso, *Bajo Miño y Costa Sur*, La Guardia, 1980, p. 300; E. Becoña Iglesias, *La Actual Medicina Popular Gallega*, La Coruña, 1982, p. 252.
169. A. Blanco Ferijeiro, 'Punta da Muller Mariña', in *Homaxe a R. Otero Pedrayo*, Vigo, 1958, p. 301; Alonso Romero, 1982, pp. 580–605, at p. 595.
170. F. Alonso Romero, 'El Significado Mágico del Colmillo de Jabalí entre los Celtas y los Germanos: Testimonios Literarios, Arqueológicos y Etnográficos', en *Filología Alemana y Didáctica del Alemán*, Universidad de Valladolid, 1989, pp. 515–30.
171. Alonso Romero, 1996, *passim*.
172. V. Lis Queiben, 1449, p. 269.
173. F. Martins Sarmiento, *Antiqua: Tradiçoes e Contos Populares*, Guimaraes, 1998, p. 65.
174. C. Squire, 1906, p. 41.
175. F.L. Cuevillas, 'Prehistoria de Melide', in *Terra de Melide*, various authors, published by Seminario de Estudos Galegos, Santiago de Compostela, 1933, pp. 99–100.
176. Hunt 1881, p. 428, R. and V. Radford, *West Country Folklore*, Newton Abbot, 1958.
177. Bottrell, 1996, p. 17.
178. Alonso Romero, 1999, p. 101.
179. Alonso Romero, 1990, Alonso Romero, 1991, p. 118; E. Gill, 'News from Cornwall', *Dalriada* 15, Lughnasadh 2000, No. 3, pp. 19–21, at p. 20.

180. Green, 1992, p. 213.
181. Prof. Fernando Alonso Romero, University of Santiago, personal communication.
182. Information provided by: The Department of Culture, Xunta de Galicia, Santiago de Compostela, which is the elected government of this autonomous region; 'Associación Cultural M. Celtas', Cartagena, Murcia.

MODELS OF MEMORIALIZATION: CORNWALL, IRELAND AND BRITTANY COMPARED

Paul Cockerham

INTRODUCTION

Recently, I presented a case for the large-scale appraisal of late medieval to early modern Cornish church monuments.[1] Although the study of such artefacts has, historiographically, been tarred with both a romantic antiquarianism and/or a clinical art historical classification into style periods, the fact that these monuments relate to specific persons and are unique contemporary documents in their own right is frequently overlooked. Collectively, therefore, a study of their form, iconography, distribution and patronage contributes handsomely to an understanding of society in both parish and regional history.

Prior to the Reformation, tombs in Cornish churches were generally made in Devon or further afield and patronized by the clergy and greater gentry. The great majority who could not afford a monument were remembered via the corporate structures of parish bede-rolls or gild-rolls, such that prayer for the departed was ensured in one form or another, no matter about the status or wealth of the dead. The Reformation abruptly terminated this equanimity, simultaneously effecting a change in the function of a monument from soliciting intercessory prayer to acting as a highly visual symbol of lineage continuity and status, stressing the maintenance of social hierarchical regularity.[2] The greater gentry continued to memorialize themselves, therefore, although the role tombs played in the death ritual had changed. The lesser Cornish gentry, languishing suddenly in a commemorative vacuum, responded to an urgency to demonstrate their own Cornishness by erecting highly individual Cornish-made slate tombs which contrasted acutely with monuments imported from elsewhere. I argued that cultural and socio-economic subtleties were visually magnified in this distinction between tomb types, such that the popularity of slate monuments became one sign of a growing ethnic tension in Cornwall, between 'us'—the traditional Cornish lesser gentry Royalists, and 'them'—the increasingly cosmopolitan Puritan county gentry and aristocracy and their inherent Parliamentarianism. Such sweeping historiographic judgements are dangerous, but the monuments are symptomatic of the fact that while these ethnicities differed in terms of politics, marriage habits, wealth and power, they practised the same religion in the same parish churches and lived cheek-by-jowl in Cornwall.[3] A thriving slate monument industry developed in Cornwall, the output of which I compared with that from monumental workshops in Devon, Norfolk and Caernarvonshire. Although the overall trends are similar post-1630, prior to that time the Cornish statistics demonstrate a passion for physical memorialization which one hesitates to say is unique, but at the very least must be considered highly unusual. Gillespie's assessment that funeral monuments 'document over time both the secular and sacred concerns of contemporaries' is particularly apt, such that even the most hardened sceptic might accept in this instance that the Cornish were 'different'.[4]

'Different', though, from whom? My comparative models were selected not just for their geographical disparity and their partial involvement in the Centre–Periphery framework (as part of the 'Inner Periphery' regions of Cornwall, Wales and northern England),[5] but also because inventories of these areas' monuments could be compiled from documentary sources for an easy match. An element of subjectiveness must be admitted. But moving away from the mainland, comparisons with Brittany or Ireland look attractive in order to test this Cornish paradigm of differential ethnic memorialization against a wider framework—the 'Outer Periphery'. The peripherality of Cornwall and its cultural distinctiveness from the Centre, and thereby the practical 'Celtic' similarities with Brittany to the south and Ireland to the north-west, offers a new, objective set of comparisons. This is particularly enticing during the (rarely discussed) early modern period, when the geographical and ethnic isolation of Cornwall was, paradoxically, firmly subjected to Tudor government machinery. The ethnic and governmental tensions of the Cornish, together with the geographical limitations and opportunities of Cornwall, contribute to a potentially exciting mix of comparative interpretation. Moreover, the spatial dimension opened up by these comparisons is the third of a three-stage research model for the Cornish Studies project proposed by

Malcolm Williams. As Deacon identifies this stage as 'less well' represented than the first—'overall constructions of "Cornwall" '—there is a value in pursuing this line of enquiry as an exercise in itself.[6]

In summary, were Cornish monuments and the Cornish need for memorialization a 'constant of peripherality'[7] mimicked by trends in Brittany and Ireland? Or was it a truly unique case, hence one of 'Cornishness' rather than 'Celticity'?

CORNISH AND IRISH MEMORIALIZATION

The Irish had long settled in Cornwall.[8] By the sixteenth century they had a distinct pattern of integration to the west of Cornwall[9] and although they appear to have been accepted into the working element of the social community, Leland observed that 'The town of Padestow is ful of Irisch men',[10] so they were still acknowledged as a separate ethnicity. Later on, as the Irish troubles became more enduring, there was a problematic tide of emigrants, denigrated by Carew as 'these crooked slips':[11] stray soldiers, beggars, refugees, and perhaps minor tradesmen, left their country using the smaller boats and headed for Cornwall. Their impact was at parish level with these wanderers benefiting from alms donated by the churchwardens;[12] as regards any cultural contribution to Cornwall this seems remote.

Is there any value then in comparing Irish memorialization with the Cornish pattern, other than to strengthen (or otherwise) a concept of outer peripheralism, when links between the two countries were insignificant at this time? The response is based not on an assessment of the monuments of the whole country, as losses have been acute, widespread and almost impossible to account for satisfactorily, but on those of County Kilkenny. A large number of sixteenth- and seventeenth-century monuments survive in the county which provide a solid basis for a statistical and analytical study.[13] Secondly, the city of Kilkenny was a centre of monument production.[14] Thirdly, the county was in the thick of the political turbulence which characterized early modern Ireland: there were changes in land ownership, a growing mercantile prosperity, religious uncertainty and the devastating military campaigns of Queen Elizabeth roundabout. Add to that the religious unrest leading up to the Confederacy of 1642–9, Cromwell's ruinous wars in 1650 and the slow rebuilding processes thereafter. Then, superimpose on this hothouse of social, religious and economic activity an increasing awareness of changes in artistic and cultural representation inherent in the Renaissance, and, so one might think, the comparison with Cornwall was slight. Paradoxically, however, these changes resounded in Kilkenny in almost complete isolation, as the city and county were strongly and continuously buffered against the

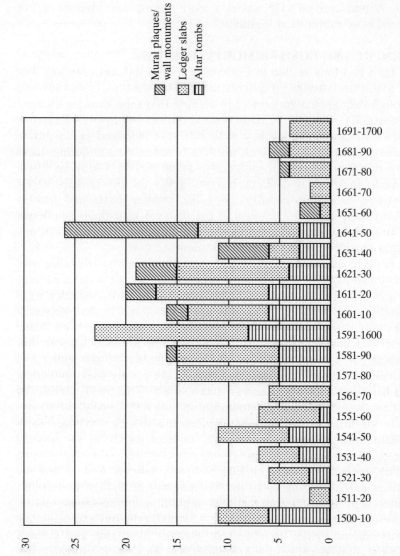

Figure 1: Chronology of Kilkenny monuments 1500–1700

extremes of warfare, political meltdown and intermittent economic privation (the Cromwellian campaign excepted) by the complete domination of the Earls of Ormond. They ruled Kilkenny very much as their own kingdom throughout the sixteenth and seventeenth centuries, one of the most pivotal men during this period being Thomas Butler tenth earl of Ormond (1546–1614).[15] A favourite of the London court, in Kilkenny the tenth earl displayed in his own demesne a religious ambivalence so exceptionally tolerant that the town could easily be held up as the recusant capital of the south,[16] but this easygoing equilibrium amongst his fellows gave way later to a determined Catholic loyalty culminating in the Confederacy of the 1640s. There is a tripartite tension in the county, therefore, between the aspirations of 'New English' opportunist settlers, the 'Old English' residents who had colonized the country some 400 or so years earlier, and the native 'Gaelic Irish'. This ethnic interaction was fuelled by the religious and social changes induced by Elizabethan government and the Reformation, counterpoised by religious conservatism, the comparative failure of the introduction of the Church of Ireland and the determinism of the Counter-Reformation.[17] These distinctive features—an ethnic incompatibility within a clearly defined insularity; a tradition of aristocratic memorialization; and the religious conservatism of the people— are surprisingly similar to the background against which Cornish memorialization was practised.

The statistics of monument erection in the county demonstrate a moderate output during the whole of the sixteenth century. It increased steadily towards the end and continued up to 1650, but was decimated thereafter (Figure 1). The devastating local impact of the Cromwellian campaigns was acutely transferred to monument erection, and yet in the wider Irish context there was not so great a drop in monument production as revealed in Kilkenny, emphasizing even more this county's insularity.[18] Furthermore, the period shows a continuous flux in the enthusiasm of the three main ethnicities in erecting funeral monuments in Kilkenny[19] (Figures 2 and 3). Before the 1555–65 hiatus[20] monuments were favoured by Old English families, primarily the Ormonds and their relatives, followers and the more important of the clergy.[21] The Old English manorial lords were anxious to follow the tenets of their religious Catholic upbringing in expressing a desire for the salvation of their souls via a funerary monument. This was duly erected in the parish church of their settlement, the centre of the parochial system which they themselves—as Anglo-Normans—had imposed upon the country.[22] Hence, as well as an intercessory instruction such a monument served its secondary function as a tangible bolster to the prestige, power and local influence of the manorial

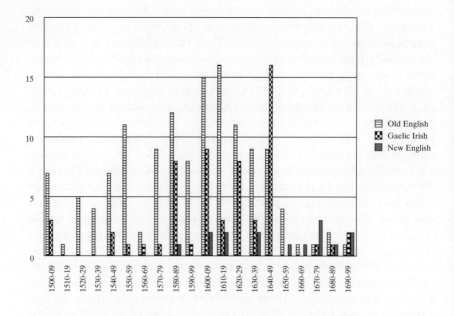

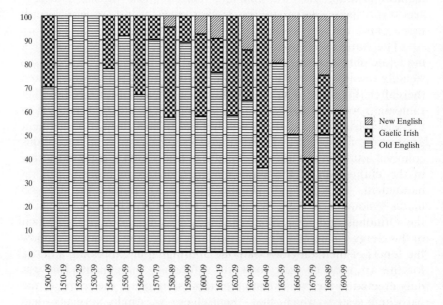

Figures 2 and 3: Ethnic identity of tomb patronage in Kilkenny 1500–1700

family. Later on, well into the seventeenth century, the growing number of monuments suggests that a wealthy generation was developing, or successive generations were becoming increasingly prosperous, but as much concentrated in the town as in the country.[23] A Catholic mercantile patronage focused in the towns was beginning to emerge, with the means as well as the desire for memorialization, in addition to the traditional Old English minor esquire in his manorial demesne.[24]

By the turn of the century there was a noticeable change in memorialized family status, from lineage dominance (the Ormonds, their court, and the rural manorial lords), to urban financial power. The erection of a tomb was becoming less family-orientated (in the sense of pedigree), and more an act of self-glorification, as a nuclear family or even an individual. Apart from the request for intercessory prayer being maintained, the motive—status—was the same; for the 'nouveaux-riches' businessmen the monument itself was a simple tool, being a fashionable and necessary novelty by which their new wealth might be demonstrated comparable to the awe-inspiring dominance of the Ormond tombs.[25]

Gaelic Irish families were also increasingly keen on physical memorialization. Family tombs had customarily been used with successive generations buried at the same site, obviating the need for repeated monumental structures to the same family. Often these tombs were in monasteries as 'to be buried near the saints . . . in Ireland [this] was a particularly potent force because of the literal kinship connections between the ruling elites and certain specific saints and regions'.[26] These monastic sites, post-Dissolution, were frequently redeployed or destroyed, so forcing Gaelic Irish families to re-establish a burial place with a new monumental structure. By the end of the century this led to either some disintegration of ethnic identity or perhaps an increased appreciation of Old English burial customs.[27] Although the funeral ceremonies appeared to retain their differences the two groups of Gaelic Irish and Old English monuments at one time so distinctive[28] now tend to coalesce in the forms adopted. The ethnic need to be seen to be different and, moreover, to maintain that difference in competing for dominance numerically, socially and culturally, was diminished.[29] The iconography of their tombs was similar, employing a complex of overt Catholic symbols—typically the Cross and Symbols of the Passion (Figure 4). These themes swayed under pressure from the Counter-Reformation teachings to become less prominent visually, with more importance attached to the individual penitent and his nuclear family than hitherto. Moving on from conservative tomb formats of the early seventeenth century, new styles—largely

*Figure 4: Ledger slab of William O'Donoghou (1597),
St Canice's Cathedral, Kilkenny*

architectural—of memorials were produced with long eulogies reflecting upon the honour and virtue of the commemorated.[30]

New English tombs were slow to become established, analogous to the difficulties these families experienced in settling in the county.[31] Kilkenny's recusant status, bolstered by the return of priests trained in the spirit of the Counter-Reformation, was stony ground in many ways for the New English Protestants. The Old English were concerned with preserving their positions against New English government innovations and protecting their faith against New English Protestantism, antagonized simultaneously by economic and political grievances. By 1630–9 New English tombs comprised only 15 per cent of the total and although after 1650 the proportion had increased to 40-50 per cent, this was of a very reduced number of monuments.[32] As Smyth has observed:

Figure 5: Wall plaque of Diana Woodlefe (1604), St Canice's Cathedral, Kilkenny

The New English were a varied group: some were early seventeenth century New English government officials, many others were soldiers and officers of the Cromwellian army, others were essentially adventurers and speculators in land and money and others were simple ordinary people probing for a better home. They had no sense of their region's past histories; they were concerned with creating their own futures and the existing landscapes, peoples and placenames they encountered were simply the instruments towards that achievement.[33]

They needed kudos, with visible symbols of authority, power and standing at the heart of their newly acquired estates. A monument was just such an authoritative symbol and the iconography was equally distinctive[34] (Figure 5).

CORNWALL AND KILKENNY COMPARED: RELATED OR PARALLEL DEVELOPMENT?

The Kilkenny and Cornish monumental workshops were relatively isolated from mainstream cultural attitudes so that their differential assimilation of various pressures, whether artistic, religious or purely business, are directly comparable. Kilkenny was shielded from the New English influence of the Pale—yet aware of continental influence;[35] and Cornwall was remote from Court fashions but open to influences imported from maritime trade and mining.[36] Workshops in the two regions were small, flimsy, artistically conservative concerns, which stresses the case that on the one hand the intricacies and direction of Cornish and Kilkenny tombs were slow to evolve artistically, and on the other, that the wider issue of memorialization imposes a reactivity on Cornish and Kilkenny workshops rather than the sculptors proactively forcing the pace. The tombs reveal the motives of the patrons, therefore, rather than those of the sculptors.

In Cornwall the monumental tension between the tombs of the greater gentry and those of the lesser Cornish gentry and yeomanry was sharpened not just by what they showed but that these latter tombs were locally made and of a distinct Cornish material—slate. The ethnicity relating to Cornish tomb patronage is socially orientated, therefore, concentrated in east Cornwall where the contrast between the lesser gentry and the congregation of Puritan 'anglicized' gentry was most blurred. The language was dying out here and the regional folklore poorly remembered,[37] particularly by the greater gentry in their regional government positions. Their out-of-county made tombs of alabaster, freestone or other foreign materials, signify the power of a class spread authoritatively over the Hundreds. But they are mimicked —and countered—by Cornish-made slate monuments which impose a visual and social cohesion of the lesser gentry across village and town boundaries.

Merging with this is the assumed desire of the Cornish to demonstrate a sense of social regularity in the late sixteenth century. At all levels of society, from upper gentry to husbandman, they seemed content to put their mid-century rebelliousness behind them, and, albeit in the isolated fashion that came naturally, form an ordered, locally governed, civil society. Carew's account of Cornwall is not only symptomatic of such a feeling, appearing when it did as a celebration of this regional sense of self-satisfaction, but his direct, step-by-step analysis of Cornish society, its customs and government, and his appraisal of their mutuality, suggest a recognition of a settled hierarchy at a time when things were just starting to change.[38] Naturally, the social activities associated with differential status were keenly adopted: new house-building for instance, was notable amongst all types of gentry, so memorialization could be construed as a similar facet, particularly as it was demonstrated with intensity after 1600. Kilkenny too, in 1598, had 'the most shew of civilitie of any other of the border Counties, in respect of the fayre seats of Howses, the number of Castles and Inglysh manner of Inclosure of their Grounds'.[39] What more reason than this supposition of 'Inglysh'ness than to continue their own practices of physical memorialization, increase their sophistication and ultimately use them as a device for rejecting New English religious and government advances.

In Kilkenny, where tombs to the aristocracy and the local gentry were all made of local stone, their materialism was unremarkable; it was their iconography which was crucial. As monument patronage broadened out at the turn of the sixteenth to seventeenth centuries so an expression of adherence to the tradition of the Catholic religion became commonplace on Kilkenny tombs, as a response to the attempted imposition of the new liturgy. Overt artistic religiosity was at a highpoint demonstrating the Catholicism common to the Old English gentry and their tenants, and the Gaelic Irish families and their clans, which linked the commemorated over an ethnic divide.

The seed of Cornish tomb iconography was also germinating at this time when the 'Cornishness' of a monument was signalled not only by the fact that it was there at all, or made of slate, but also by using its own iconographical system to indicate the parochiality and social limits of the commemorated. Heraldry was a powerfully employed sign and inscriptions frequently aid the identification of the families represented by it. But the genealogical detail is in excess of what is necessary for a

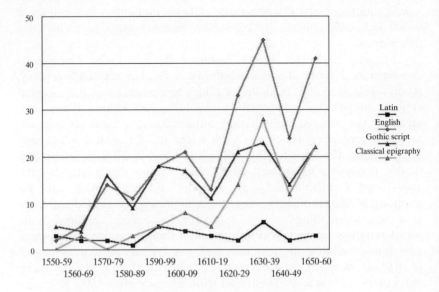

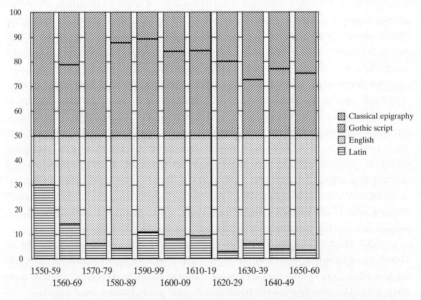

Figures 6 and 7: Inscription comparison, Cornwall 1560–1660

simple understanding of lineage, and the armorial significance is explained verbatim for the lower classes to whom it might not have been instantly comprehensible. There is an element of making a link with the commoners in the parish amidst the panoply of the monuments and hence extending the social relevance of the Cornish tombs.

Why were these traits so forcibly conspicuous at this period? Were the visual signs of heraldry and religion a kind of common symbolism which emerged as a reaction to prevailing socio-economic conditions in the two regions? Both were increasing in prosperity after the various internal and external military and naval campaigns had lost their weight. Social structures, also, were more stable, and those benefiting tended to attach some importance to a demonstration of their relative success. Even now, for instance, a mark of social, economic and hierarchical distinction is to buy oneself a coat of arms. This kind of reaction, using funerary monuments, was an analogous display of 'success'—in Cornwall of the Cornish, retaining their identity against the Tudor government machine; and in Kilkenny as symbolic of a new prosperity in the face of attempts at religious and governmental reform.

The establishment of this broad parallel between Cornwall and Kilkenny in regard to memorialization can be tested again in later aspects of tomb design. For example, in the first quarter of the seventeenth century certain traditional elements are retained in Kilkenny—notably the Cross and the ecclesiastical language of Latin in its conservative Gothic letter-form—which jar with artistic innovations.[40] In Cornwall too, although English was used on monuments well before the end of the sixteenth century, Gothic script was retained long after it had been abandoned elsewhere (Figures 6–7).[41] That said, from the second quarter of the seventeenth century a growing number of inscriptions were engraved using Classical epigraphy when the Royalist loyalties of the Cornish found themselves under intensive governmental pressure.[42] Remarkably, the same kind of changes were taking place concurrently in Kilkenny with a rise in English inscriptions using Classical epigraphy (Figures 8–9). Perhaps it can be hypothesized that external and oppressive government influence (in Cornwall) and religious influence (in Kilkenny) forced a reduction in the intensity of traditional exhibitionism on their isolated tomb-making industries, such that new, educated influences, which were religiously more bland, were encouraged instead. The regional similarity persists but with different causes it is merely a parallelism.

Essentially, therefore, Cornish monumental iconography was an expression of place (parish) and of traditionalism (Cornishness). It was not symbolic of a particular kind of religion but of the Cornish native

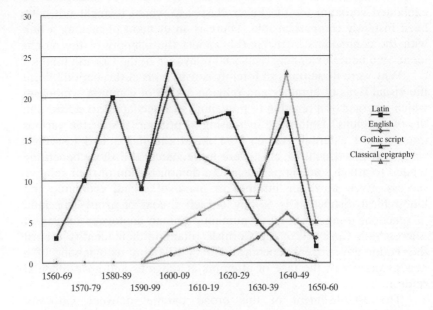

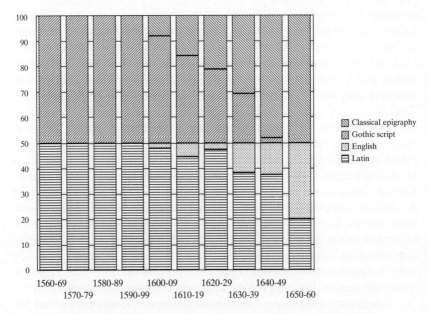

Figures 8 and 9: Inscription comparison, Kilkenny 1560–1660

population revelling in their opportunity to commemorate themselves, such that their tombs were competing with—almost grating against—those of the 'Anglicised' gentry.[43] By the second quarter of the seventeenth century this aspect of memorialization symbolized Cornish support for the King against the Parliamentary tendencies of the Puritan greater gentry. And in Kilkenny a similar sense also evolved. Unlike Cornwall, where monuments indicate a social dichotomy, in Kilkenny it was only the wealthy and landed gentry who were physically memorialized. It was a religious ethnic divide which their tombs displayed: the long-established Catholic landowners (whether Old English or Gaelic Irish) conflicted with the Protestant New English acquisitors. Moreover, although passionately recusant, loyalty to the Crown was crucial among the 'old-fashioned catholics', who 'still protested their loyalty to the crown and hoped for compromise and the preservation of their Catholic religion', even up to the Confederacy.[44] Thereafter, the irreconcilability of the two beliefs conflicted; 'the needs of Royalism sat very uneasily with the Catholic confederation, forcing the pace of political negotiations there'[45] and, taking the link between Kilkenny and Cornwall still further, perhaps the desperation of the King for support in the Civil War might have opened up the possibility of a Catholic-Royalist coalition in Ireland. Would this necessarily have been anathema to the Cornish?[46]

The two groups of monuments harmonize in their wider significance, with Kilkenny patronage accelerating in advance of Cornish commissions. However, although the latter accentuate social division and ethnicity, and the former a significant and increasingly urgent religious message, overall, there is an element of orthodoxy in support of what they knew, valued and desired—a degree of independence and government, secularly, by the King. Clearly though, on close analysis there is little similarity in Kilkenny to what went on in Cornwall. Physical memorialization in Kilkenny was an extension of what the aristocracy had practised for centuries, affordable to the rich merchants and gentry who made up the Kilkenny oligarchy, conservative in government, religion and loyalty. Virtually nobody of the lower social orders was memorialized; for them both pre- and post-Reformation individual commemoration was achieved only in the (sometimes excessive) funeral ceremonies, but thereafter no marker was erected. In Cornwall the slate memorials directly replaced organized pre-Reformation corporate remembrance. They aped the sustained tomb-erecting habit of the greater gentry and formed a nucleus of 'Cornishness' among the lesser gentry, cultivating a rural parochial sense of status and place and conflicted with the county gentry's wider influence and status. Crucially, the paradigm of Cornish memorialization retains its unique motivation in this comparison. Parallels there might have been, but aspirations were quite different.

Whilst this model of a (governmentally isolated) community proves disappointing in establishing an 'Older Periphery' connection, Brittany offers an enticing prospect. Geographical separation is clear, such that, 'Even to the most casual visitor gazing across the land-scapes first of Brittany and then of Devon and Cornwall, the essential similarities between the regions are obvious. Their resemblance springs not just from geology and topography, but from human geography too.'[47]

CORNISH AND BRETON MEMORIALIZATION

During the first half of the sixteenth century Bretons, like the Irish, were commonly recorded living in Cornwall[48] and trade was brisk,[49] although culturally and artistically the links between Brittany and Cornwall, as between Ireland and Cornwall, were hardly promoted by this exchange in basic commodities.[50] 'There are many Bretons with smaul shippes to resorte to Padestow with commodities of their country and to by fische', John Leland observed sometime between 1535 and 1540.[51] The types of persons frequenting each others' ports, and those Bretons settling in Cornwall in hope of better pay, were of the lower social classes. Bretons working in Cornwall on church fittings seem to have been itinerants and although skilled they 'were generally encouraged to copy Cornish models rather than to introduce new ideas of their own.'[52] Whatever forms of memorialization were used in the two regions prior to the Reformation, one can expect liturgical similarities to have forged something of a bond. But the development of post-Reformation Cornish memorialization makes comparison with Brittany a tantalizing opportunity. Links between the two regions began to disintegrate and 'a rift appeared between Protestant Cornwall and Catholic Brittany, made all the more apparent now that the English and French states were religiously and politically antagonistic to each other'.[53] But did a distinct relationship between memoriali-zation practices of the two 'Older Peripheral' regions persist post-Reformation? In other words, did one facet of peripherality survive to extend across politico-religious boundaries, or, like Kilkenny, was there merely a parallel development of this ritual practice?

One problem in comparing like with like, Cornish and Breton monuments, is the lack of any comprehensive record of tombs in the four modern departments of Brittany. Copy's work on the socio-political background to the erection of late medieval tombs concentrates on that one form of monument only in Haute-Bretagne.[54] Local topographical studies in the historiographical manner of the grand antiquarian English county histories do not exist, such that the tombs and ledgers assessed here have been trawled from a variety of documentary sources, concentrating on the most westerly department of Finistère.[55] Their number is disappointingly low[56] and compared to Cornish statistics there is nothing initially to imply that they shared any memorialization trends. But these very small numbers also suggest that losses have been great; or that most Bretons were commemorated in other ways, without monuments; or both. Faced with this apparent lack of material evidence an appreciation of Breton memorialization and its comparison with the 'Older Peripheral' region of Cornwall poses its own challenge.

SIXTEENTH-CENTURY MEMORIALIZATION IN BRITTANY

At a time when commerce between the two regions was intimate, local languages predominated and Catholicism was universal, there were similarities in the ways in which the two populations memorialized themselves. The upper gentry of both Basse-Bretagne and Cornwall ordered ostentatious, free-standing tombs (or brasses) with effigies, while the lower social orders were commemorated corporately or with simple graveslabs. The motives of these unequal levels of society were different—but they were the same between Brittany and Cornwall across the class structures as they were throughout much of 'mainland' England and France among the élites. The upper classes needed a demonstration of their hold over their place and over their people as a status symbol and one of lineage continuity;[57] the solicitation of prayer was just as important, but visually was relegated almost to a secondary function. On the other hand the lesser classes looked just for prayers for their souls and a swift passage through Purgatory, using the corporate strength of, in Brittany the parish, and in Cornwall, the gild system, which actively maintained these commemorative rituals. Family graves in churches were sometimes marked with tombstones engraved with crosses or personal marks, more so in Brittany than in Cornwall, suggesting the rise of rural élites among the parish populations; or, as Collins notes, they were of the 'insider' families to the gentry.[58]

During the fifteenth century in Brittany, as the Duchy was pushed westwards in regression into a Basse-Bretagne sanctuary, where legends, rites and traditions were cemented by the retention of the language, the Duchy stimulated its own social court and its own artistic patronage.[59] As just one sign of this isolation, for instance, 'Brittany constituted an heraldic March and the duke had his own kings of arms, heralds and poursuivants'.[60] Essentially, the Dukes went 'native'.

Churches and chapels were newly built or rebuilt, they were lavishly fitted out and the veneration of local saints and their cults was given more substance by activities such as erecting personalized saintly tombs, putting up their images in churches and building their fountains.[61] An assured touch of lordly patronage is manifest in conjunction with the parish 'fabricquiers' therefore,[62] suggesting a neat amalgam of Duchy influence with parishioners in the western Breton-speaking regions and furthering even more their traditional beliefs and customs. The nobles of Basse-Bretagne ordered their monuments from local workshops, to a relatively homogeneous, traditional Gothic set of standards and employing local stone, tombs being just one sculptural end-product of an otherwise booming trade in religious statuary. This nucleus of sculptural patronage in the far west was distinct from tomb manufacture in Haute-Bretagne, where a cohesive development never came about as a result of the regional north-south topographical divide. Granite was used in Finistère initially,[63] progressing to the more workable 'kersanton' stone by the end of the sixteenth century,[64] but by then the work being imported into Haute-Bretagne was effectively revitalizing the sculptural output of that region, in contrast to the west, where conception was stagnating.[65] This difference reinforced the progressive split between the two regions maintaining the sculptural insularity of Basse-Bretagne and its people from the rest of France as there was generally no need at all to import stone—or ideas—either for building or sculptural use.[66]

The sixteenth-century influence of the Breton Duchy was in two directions. The one encouraged individual lordly commemoration with a chantry, tomb or other similar structural means; the other furthered the overall religiosity of the Basse-Breton village, invigorating individual village identity, independence and verbal self-commemoration.[67] The critical result was that the aristocracy reinforced Catholicism across the social strata particularly where the 'Breton seigneurial regime was harshest'.[68] A broadly similar effect occurred pre-Reformation in Cornwall but to a much lesser degree, and in terms of buildings and monuments, hardly as a result of *widespread* aristocratic patronage. The tombs of the Cornish gentry were fewer in number and provided less of a social presence than their Breton counterparts; local government was by no means as autonomous as in Brittany, and there was little of the sense of individuality of Breton parishes. Although the intensity of the faith of the commoners in each Cornish parish cannot be doubted, it was virtually interchangeable from village to village and on homogeneous, traditionally organized lines. The low number of pre-Reformation Cornish tombs provoked only a weak contrast to the widespread system of corporate commemoration, in itself gild-based and which divided up the parish—losing its identity—even further. This conflict between territorially based (parish manorial lordships) and socially based (gilds) institutions contributed greatly to the split between the social classes.[69] Religiously, they were all Catholics but the lower classes' Cornish-speaking ethnic identity grated with the developing gentry classes—who were losing touch with their roots by their growing wealth and cosmopolitanism. The Breton comparison, of a social hierarchy within a parochial or more regional basis and welded by a common religiosity, tends to dull the ethnicity of the divide between the noblesse and the lower classes. This contrast should not, however, be pushed too keenly. Like the Cornish gentry, the Basse-Breton élite developed a sense of their own particular identity, defined as the provincial possession of legal, fiscal and judicial privileges, held under contract with the King of France by the Edict of Union of 1532. They were free to assume multiple identities, therefore, whether parochial, regional or national, depending on the context of their activities and relationships. But importantly, on a parochial level they sponsored their church, and liturgically they shared their Catholicism in their church with the *paysans*.[70] They were all Catholics together, and in their parish they were all Basse-Bretons together; not quite the same, perhaps, as the Bretons in the adjoining parishes (with their own social hierarchies) but Bretons nevertheless—in language, culture and religion.

SEVENTEENTH-CENTURY MEMORIALIZATION IN BRITTANY

As France emerged out of the 1540s depression, mercantile and financial new wealth increased as Duchy traditions waned[71] and there was a greater interest in physical memorialization by these new social classes. Coincidentally, there was an increasing awareness of death as a central feature of Basse-Breton culture by the emphasis of Counter-Reformation doctrine in an area where reformed Catholicism and Breton folklore merged, that is the cult of the dead.[72] By the seventeenth century mass corporate commemoration continued but it was increasingly followed by laying down a burial marker to the individual as a gesture of respect for the personalty of death and the dead body. All social types were involved, 'from the lowest ranks of society to the highest',[73] and at this period of increasing population mobility in Brittany such a want encouraged those that could afford it to employ a family gravestone. It satisfied their religious needs, demonstrated a healthy respect of 'L'Ankou' (as the real time personification of 'Death') and broadcast the family status in their

*Figure 10: Ledger slab to the Quellen family (16th century), Runan,
Côtes-d'Armor*

parish at one stroke.[74] Its presence served adroitly to maintain a remembrance of that family even if its members died out or moved on.

During this period graveslabs were relatively crude, sometimes retaining an archaic, tapering coffin shape, but more often they were a thin rectangle in form (Figure 10). Frequently they are anonymous for an individual whilst properly retaining a family identification such as heraldry or that of a profession or trade of the deceased.[75] Hence they do not represent *an individual's* burial place as such—how could they when they were uninscribed?—and neither, moreover, do they solicit a prayer for the individual's soul but more for the corporate body of the entire family. A priest might be distinguished by having a chalice or Bible as symbols, and a very few are effigial,[76] but whatever the precise symbolism the function of the great majority of these graveslabs is unmistakable, marking the burial site of a family. Even if the ground beneath the slab was ritually emptied to enable new family interments to take place and the bones of the deceased transferred to the parish ossuaries, the commemoration of these individuals collectively as a family was never overlooked.[77] A functional dualism of these grave-slabs emerges, combining family (the marker) with individual motives (the ritual transfer of bones).[78] This individualism is also evident in the rising number of free-standing tombs with gisants which were erected by the Basse-Bretagne noblesse in the second and third quarters of the seventeenth century. They were ordered from local workshops and made from local stone, and although the forms are still amazingly retentive of Gothic they are now just tinged with Renaissance features. The gisant, typically, is represented as if asleep with his head on a pillow and feet resting on an animal and with his hands at prayer, on top of a three-dimensional tomb with either open Renaissance-style sides, as a catafalque, or with closed sides ornamented with heraldic shields held frequently by angels.[79] Inscriptions were sometimes in Roman capitals but most betray their traditionalism and retain a Gothic script, matching what was frequently the case in Kilkenny and Cornwall. The sense of the individual, not the dynastic nature of the families, is more prominent for these aristocratic tombs than the graveslabs of the lower social orders, as they bear precise, prominent inscriptions relating the details of the deceased. This evolving Christian humanism is also signified by the lack of saints' effigies memorialized by gisants after 1600. The idea of an effigy representing a mortal individual, invoking memory rather than lineage status, is hardly now the ideal suitable for the portrayal of the everlasting, almost dynastic, influence of a saint.

By the end of the seventeenth century commemoration in Basse-

Bretagne had evolved into a regular tripartite phenomenon. Firstly, there was the celebration of the *individual*, the funeral being a significant social event in the village.[80] Secondly, the person was buried in the *family* grave, which was used for the wider genealogical family —not just the nuclear one. Lastly, there was a fully *corporate* means of remembrance of previous inhabitants of the grave when their remains were transferred to the parish ossuary accompanied by requiem masses, and which simultaneously embraced the concept of their individuality. There was an idea of a continued remembrance for what and who you were, but it was locally orientated with physical monuments produced by one's own countrymen and verbal commemoration uttered by one's neighbours.[81] This ritualization was symptomatic of a delineation of sacred and funerary space, seen not only in the location of graveslabs inside the church—which in itself was subject to a high degree of control, but also in the establishment of the parish *enclos* and the ossuary. All of these were material changes indicative of adjustments to death and religious awareness—changes in the wider need of memorialization—throughout the whole parish.[82] An analysis of these dated features in Finistère during the sixteenth and seventeenth centuries shows how sparse monuments are compared with the picture painted earlier of village churches like mausolea, stuffed full of gravestones. Contemporary accounts reveal, however, that this was indeed the case:

> In 1677 the King's Commissioner charged with reporting on the aristocracy in the village of Plougasnou [F.] noted 'We have made only a description of the gravestones which are notable for different reasons; as the said church is paved with nothing other than these gravestones, the task of making their record has taken a very long time.'[83]

More recently, de Fréminville, in his account of Tréguier cathedral, found that

> in the nave and side aisles . . . there are lots of gravestones on which can be made out figures sculpted in light relief, others engraved simply with a cross; but these tombs serve as the pavement, and the wear and tear by walking has nearly entirely effaced the figures they carry.[84]

Losses have been immense[85] but a chronology of what remains demonstrates two waves of tomb popularity which coincide with the erection of monumental gateways to the *enclos*, calvaries and

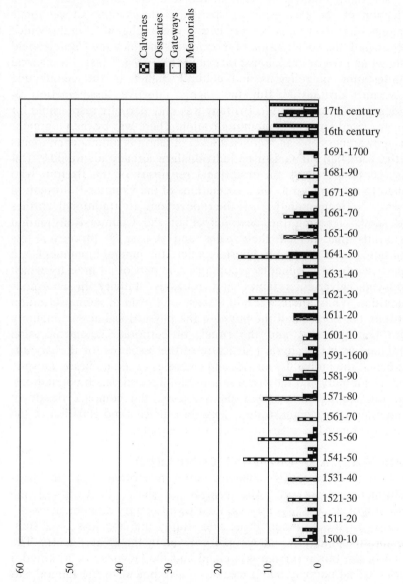

Figure 11: Chronological comparison of memorialization artifacts, Finistère 1500–1700

ossuaries[86] (Figure 11). Funeral monuments in Brittany are one aspect of a much wider spectrum of physical evidence concerned with death and commemoration.

The mild enthusiasm seen in the mid sixteenth century was a reflection of the increasing prosperity of the region; an economic stimulus was involved. A century later it was a religious stimulus which encouraged 'the construction of monuments in which the Church could conduct and control religious practice in rural area . . [as] . . a physical manifestation of religious and cultural change in the countryside of western Brittany'.[87] But the highly effective dissemination of Tridentine Catholicism into Brittany was only partially responsible for this increased interest in memorialization. There was by then a greater social awareness and an increased level of learning among commoners as the Christian humanism or individualism already identified.[88] But this was tempered by the traditional religiosity of the Bretons who 'failed to measure up to the expectations of the Counter-Reformation elites . . . [continuing] . . . their devotions to traditional shrines and saints, ignoring the new heroes of the Counter-Reformation for saints that healed their pains and disease'.[89] Moreover this traditionalism is marked in Finistère where the funeral monuments are a particularly homogeneous group, just one part of an industry which produced calvaries, retables and religious statuary in enormous quantities. Whilst there was still a sense of élitism of memorialization between the nobles and the *paysans*, the physical artifacts of memory were homogeneous, and the rituals of corporate commemoration combined with the physical structure of the ossuaries for the *paysans* paralleled the individual masses and chantries of the noblesse. Despite peasant mobility and the disruption to families and parish populations, and the cosmopolitanism of the noblesse, the complex rituals of memorialization demonstrate a sense of ethnicity and isolation of the entire region of Basse-Bretagne across its society.

CORNWALL AND BRITTANY COMPARED

How does this thesis compare with memorialization in post-Reformation Cornwall? The contrast is sharp. In Cornwall the assertion of the lesser gentry via their own funerary monuments was a reaction to the enforced Protestant liturgy and the loss of a commemorative practice which was still enjoyed by the greater gentry. The ritual of the burial service was bland and the language demystified.[90] Ecclesiastical panoply had gone, social attachment to the funeral was discouraged, and their tombs as memorials—as an entity in themselves —became crucial symbols of an intra-regional ethnic identity which signified a dehiscence in Cornish society. At the end of the sixteenth century a Cornish slate tomb broadcast a sense of status, lineage continuity of a certain family and class and a narrow, parochial sense of place; in short, a sense of Cornishness. A century later the same sense of Cornishness existed but tempered by an individualism and an epitaph which referred not to a genealogical descent but to a person's virtuous character. The Cornish slate monument even evolved into a commemorative mural plaque, such that the marker was no longer a marker but a true memorial,[91] recording an individual's death, certainly, but also celebrating his or her life and achievements in a eulogistic epitaph. The separation of the living from the dead was complete. Death, *per se*, had lost its 'sting'; and at the same time an individual or humanist appreciation of life and death crept in. This would have been anathema to the Basse-Bretons. Maintaining their cultural and religious traditionalism, although the physical evidence of memorialization also reveals a change from a broad family significance to an individualism, the continued tripartite commemoration of death was crucial to their firmly held Catholic beliefs.

There was no contemplation of any kind of communal or corporate remembrance in post-Reformation Cornwall, except, perhaps, in the very region where physical memorialization was least practised, that is in Penwith.[92] There, folklore traditions and rituals and their own distinct hagiography were strongest; second, the general giving of individuals within their community to their own parish churches was disproportionate to the comparative poverty of the region; and last, the language and ethnicity of the Cornish was strongest here.[93] In this cultural context I have argued that the dearth of Cornish-made monuments was because they would have been redundant amongst a population whose 'topographical and cultural sense of isolation . . . extended even into the inhabitants' preparations for death'.[94] There is an ethos of commemoration which shares something of the rituals of Basse-Bretagne such that as Basse-Bretagne was to the entire province of Brittany, so Penwith was to Cornwall.

A COMMON CELTICITY?

Clearly, the regions possessed their own distinctive monument and memorialization trends, so an attempt to trace a 'communal Celticity' by identifying a common denominator of the three models is challenging. The foundation laid in the early Church lacks promise, however. Not only is it 'not yet feasible to build up a reassuring context of Irish saint-cults in Cornwall',[95] but also 'there is little to show that venerating a Brittonic saint in Cornwall differed from worshipping an international one elsewhere . . . Cornish saints and their devotees showed much in common with saints and their worshippers every-

where.[96'] Also, despite the active trading links between Cornwall,
Ireland and Brittany, cultural and artistic similarities between the
regions seems hardly to exist because of the almost exclusively low-
grade commodity trading basis.[97]

Philip Payton has suggested that:

> The Celtic identity was . . . perpetuated through Cornwall's
> continuing links with Brittany which endured as strong as ever
> *until as late as the sixteenth century* [my italics]. Of all the
> Celtic tongues, Cornish and Breton are the closest cousins,
> in that period mutually intelligible and giving the monoglot
> Cornishman a much closer feeling of affinity with his Breton
> counterpart than with an English speaker of neighbouring
> Devon. Like Cornwall, Brittany had survived the encroach-
> ment of the Norman, French and English states, retaining her
> status as an independent Duchy until the Treaty of Union
> with France in 1532.[98]

The ties up to the Reformation were close. Thereafter, naturally,
they lessened, but following increased English settlement in Ireland in
the early seventeenth century there was considerable in-migration from
Ireland to Brittany. 'Hundreds if not thousands of Irish appear in
Brittany from 1603 on . . . [and] . . . stray soldiers, beggars and small
tradesmen dominate in the first 50 years.'[99] Although Irish traces in
Brittany from this period are numerous—in archives, print and
in genealogy, 'the migration left no major mark on Brittany'.[100]

The fallowness of this communal 'Celtic' ground is further confirmed by an assessment of monuments with inscriptions in Cornish,
Gaelic and Breton as a reflection of contemporary ethnicity. Although
language is 'not always an accurate marker of ethnicity', it is often
asserted that 'having a spoken Celtic language was the prime identifier
of a "genuine" Celtic identity'.[101] But even though the spoken
languages were more widely practised, there are no Cornish language
monumental inscriptions in the early modern period; only a handful of
tombs in the whole of Ireland have Gaelic inscriptions; and Breton
inscriptions are equally rare.[102] Other elements of 'Celtic style'
on monuments are difficult to identify,[103] so one is left to regard a
traditionalism, identified concurrently in all three regions, as something
like a kindred spirit, or as Payton identifies, 'more a reaction to
peripheral status—to being not quite within the law's writ',[104] but to
push the parallel further would be presumptive. The Cornish, for
instance, allied themselves to a traditional culture and ethnicity, or
as Coate has it, 'natural conservatism, family tradition, [and] long

association with the Crown and religious sentiment';[105] the Irish, in the form of the Old English and the Gaelic Irish, adhered to a traditional religion; and the Basse-Bretons retained their religious symbiosis with 'L'Ankou'—Death.

There is also the trait of individualism which builds up during the first half of the seventeenth century in all three regions, broadly revealed by a change in commemorative motive from a nuclear family to a single person.[106] This is fuelled primarily by a Christian humanism reinforced by the Counter-Reformation in Brittany, the Counter-Reformation and the threat of New English government in Ireland, and an unrelated—or was it?—Laudinian Protestantism in Cornwall.[107] But behind the sense of responsibility of the individual for their own sins/salvation and the encouragement of stricter personal conduct of morality and discipline, the theological justifications differed sharply. That they shared similar concepts and ideals is, however, quite obvious when assessing the regions' memorialization customs and material evidence. The stimulus was different in Cornwall, but the result was the same.

A deeper analysis of this theme by Alan Macfarlane proposed that an embryonic English individualism existed at a much earlier period than the early seventeenth century.[108] At first sight this looks poorly supported by the evidence of Cornish memorialization, neither does it seem to fit the other two comparative models. Late medieval Gaelic Irish families were typically buried in their own vault in a regular religious house, a custom fractured by the monastic dissolution, which denied them their genealogical, wider family burial place. Religious and cultural education stimulated a new interest in personal commemoration much later. Similarly, there was a change in the concept of Basse-Bretagne memorialization from the artefact of a traditional family tomb (as in the Gaelic Irish tradition) to the transfer of an individual's remains to an ossuary. In both Kilkenny and Basse-Bretagne, therefore, during the late sixteenth to early seventeenth centuries the genealogical, wider family unit slowly metamorphosed into a strong sense of individual commemoration. At the same time, the Cornish slate tombs display an iconography representing status and lineage continuity of the genealogical family which softens to an embodiment of the nuclear family, thence to individuals' memorials. Yet as Macfarlane relates, an Englishman, 'symbolised and shaped by his ego-centred kinship system . . . stood in the centre of his world'. The intra-regional social dichotomy shown up in Cornwall from west to east by the distinctiveness of the Cornish slate tombs—their Cornishness —can thus be taken as symptomatic of an individualism. But the kin were not a genealogical family, they were his Cornish fellows.

Cornishness, therefore, in this context of an individual ethnic identity, is much older than the 'Renaissance, Reformation and the Enlightenment, as the period of great transition'.[109]

CONCLUSION

Memorialization served, emphatically, to signify a difference. In Cornwall a new expression of physical memorialization was established by a section of society which had previously only enjoyed oral corporate commemoration. The lesser gentry promoted an ethnic identity independent of their upper-class governors, such that there was a difference inside Cornwall—as an intra-regional distinction of Cornishness.

In Basse-Bretagne, memorialization demonstrated a cohesion between the upper and lower classes. They adhered to a profound similarity of rituals, and memorials to both were sculpted from the same local materials by the same local schools of workmen. In both the sixteenth and seventeenth centuries, these same classes of Breton society enjoyed an evolving expression of commemoration together. An ethnicity developed, and was maintained between Basse-Bretagne and Haute-Bretagne as an inter-regional distinction.

Kilkenny monuments, erected in a region of relative stability inside a politico-religious cauldron, show a common religious ethnic identity across racial ethnic tensions. The tombs of the Old English and Gaelic Irish Catholics coalesce in their symbolism, contrasting acutely with those of the opportunist Protestant New English settlers. There was an expansion of physical memorialization into the 'nouveaux-riches' of Kilkenny, and across the social and ethnic differences the adoption of a common, new, Catholic iconography signified the maintenance of a traditionalism, not just of religious liturgy but embracing regional government as well.

At a time when there is a dearth of overt 'Celtic' evidence to link these 'Older Peripheral' regions together, even the common individualism of the early seventeenth century can be explained by simultaneous pan-European culturo-religious advances, albeit with a different foundation in Cornwall to Ireland and Brittany. And therein lies the nub of this article and a validation of the spatial dimension of Cornish Studies. The more gradual religious changes in Ireland and Brittany provoked a response in memorialization rituals which were less an exhibition of something reactionary than an adaptation of pre-existing customs to specific purposes. In Cornwall, the abrupt religious changes stimulated a response from those lesser elements of society which were suddenly denied the chance of commemoration. The speed and enthusiasm with which they patronized their own

funeral monument industry, thereby developing their own Cornish
ethnicity, was unique.

NOTES AND REFERENCES

1. P. Cockerham, ' "On my grave a marble stone"': Early Modern Cornish
   Memorialization', in P. Payton (ed.), *Cornish Studies: Eight*, Exeter, 2000,
   pp. 9–39.
2. N. Llewellyn, *The Art of Death*, London, 1991, pp. 101–20. Llewellyn has
   expanded his thesis on the social contextualization of monuments and
   their use to display a social differentiation in *Funeral Monuments in
   Post-Reformation England*, Cambridge, 2000, pp. 272–362.
3. A. Duffin, *Faction and Faith—Politics and Religion of the Cornish Gentry
   Before the Civil War*, Exeter, 1996, pp. 7–37.
4. R. Gillespie, 'Irish Funeral Monuments and Social Change 1500–1700:
   Perceptions of Death', in B.P. Kennedy and R. Gillespie (eds), *Ireland
   —Art into History*, Dublin, 1994, p. 168.
5. P. Payton, *The Making of Modern Cornwall*, Redruth, 1992, p. 18.
6. B. Deacon, 'In Search of the Missing "Turn"': the Spatial Dimension and
   Cornish Studies', in Payton (ed.), 2000, pp. 213–30.
7. Payton, 1992, p. 65.
8. This is not the place to enter the archaeo-historical debate on early
   medieval settlement patterns in Cornwall, but Charles Thomas convincingly demonstrates the spread of a people from Ireland to west
   Wales, their subsequent conversion to Christianity and its spread
   down the peninsula to Cornwall using medieval memorial stones. See C.
   Thomas, *And Shall These Mute Stones Speak? Post-Roman Inscriptions
   in Western Britain*, Cardiff, 1994.
9. From the lists compiled by T.L. Stoate, *Cornwall Subsidies in the Reign of
   Henry VIII*, Bristol, 1985, then the distribution of individuals by Hundred
   with the surname 'Irishe' or variations thereof, is as follows: Penwith—6;
   Kerrier—8; Powder—5; Pydar—3; Trigg—4; East—2; and Lesnewth,
   Stratton and West have none. These returns as analysed by Stoate are
   admittedly incomplete, but even so the distribution pattern is marked.
10. L. Toulmin Smith (ed.), *The Itinerary of John Leland in or about the year
    1535–1543*, 5 vols, Oxford, 1964, I, p. 179.
11. Francis, Lord de Dunstanville (ed.), *Carew's Survey of Cornwall*,
    London, 1811, p. 184.
12. For example the St Neot's Churchwardens' Accounts record that in 1626,
    2d. was paid to 'three Irish people' and in 1657 1s. was donated to a
    'poore Irish woman' and 2s.6d. to 'poore people yt came out of Ireland';
    Cornwall Record Office ref. P/162/5/1.
13. For example, P. Shee (ed.), *Epitaphs on the Tombs in the Cathedral
    Church of St. Canice, Kilkenny, collected by John O'Phelan*, Dublin, 1813;
    J. Graves and J.G.A. Prim, *The History, Architecture and Antiquities of
    the Cathedral Church of St. Canice, Kilkenny*, Dublin, 1857; W. Carrigan,
    The History and Antiquities of the Diocese of Ossory, 4 vols, Dublin,

1905; J. Hunt, *Irish Medieval Figure Sculpture*, 2 vols, Dublin and London, 1974; J. Bradley, 'The Medieval Tombs of St. Canice's Cathedral', in S. Barry et al. (eds), *A Worthy Foundation—the Cathedral Church of St Canice, Kilkenny*, Portlaoise, 1985; and P. Cockerham and A.L. Harris, 'Kilkenny Funeral Monuments 1500–1600: A Statistical and Analytical Account', *Proceedings of the Royal Irish Academy*, forthcoming. There are also numerous short but informative accounts of Kilkenny tombs in the thirteen thick volumes of the *Journal of the Society for the Preservation of the Memorials of the Dead in Ireland*, 1888–1937.

14. D. Tietzsch-Tyler, *Building Stones of St Canice's Cathedral, Kilkenny*, Geological Survey of Ireland, n.d.; and E.C. Rae, 'Irish Sepulchral Monuments of the Later Middle Ages—I', *Journal of the Royal Society of Antiquaries of Ireland* 100, 1970, pp. 1–38.

15. See W.G. Neely, 'The Ormond Butlers of County Kilkenny 1515–1715', in W. Nolan and K. Whelan (eds) *Kilkenny—History and Society*, Dublin, 1990, pp. 107–26.

16. W.G. Neely, *Kilkenny, An Urban History, 1391–1843*, Belfast, 1989, pp. 43–4.

17. For a general summary see A. Clarke, 'Varieties of Uniformity: The First Century of the Church of Ireland', in W.J. Shiels and D. Wood (eds), *The Churches, Ireland and the Irish—Studies in Church History* 25, Oxford, 1989, pp. 105–22; also A. Ford et al. (eds), *As by Law Established—the Church of Ireland since the Reformation*, Dublin, 1995.

18. For example, in Dublin the decade 1650–59 saw the same number of monuments laid down as in 1640–49, and although nationwide the number of tombs was depressed in 1640–49, recovery in the following decades was much swifter than in Kilkenny. See A.L. Harris, 'The Funerary Monuments of County Dublin 1560–1660', M.A. thesis, University College, Dublin, 1994, Fig. 3—chronology chart; and R. Loeber, 'Sculptured Monuments to the Dead in Early Seventeenth-Century Ireland: a Survey from *Monumenta Eblanae* and other sources', *Proceedings of the Royal Irish Academy*, 81.C.11, 1981.

19. For an explanation and contextualization of these three groups of peoples see William J. Smyth, 'Ireland a Colony—Settlement implications of the revolution in military-administrative, urban and ecclesiastical structures, c. 1550 to c. 1730', in T. Barry (ed.), *A History of Settlement in Ireland*, London, 2000, pp. 158–86.

20. This was caused by the demise of the dominant sculptural workshop providing for Kilkenny in the sixteenth century; see Cockerham and Harris, *Proceedings of the Royal Irish Academy*, forthcoming.

21. Of the forty monuments ethnically attributable from this period, only six (2.5%) are to Gaelic Irish families, whereas between 1565 and 1600, out of fifty-one monuments, fourteen are to the Gaelic Irish, thirty-six to the Old English and a single plaque to the New English (27:71:2). The proportion to Gaelic Irish families nearly doubled in this latter period therefore.

22. C.A. Empey, 'County Kilkenny in the Anglo-Norman Period', in Nolan and Whelan (eds), *Kilkenny: History and Society*, pp. 75–95; and for a general overview see K. Whelan, 'Towns and Villages', in F.H.A. Aalen et al. (eds), *Atlas of the Irish Rural Landscape*, Cork, 1997, pp. 180–96; and T. Barry, 'Rural Settlement in Medieval Ireland', in Barry (ed.), 2000, pp. 110–23; and S. Duffy et al. (eds), *Atlas of Irish History*, Dublin, 1997, pp. 38–40.

23. Statistically 50/89 tombs in the sixteenth century were in the city of Kilkenny (56%). In the seventeenth century then the figures are 70/128 (55%). In the first half of the sixteenth century however, up to the 1555–65 hiatus, then only 20/45 tombs were in Kilkenny city (44%) pointing to the dominance of the tomb at that time in the rural parish rather than an urban setting.

24. See J. Bradley, *Kilkenny—Irish Historic Towns Atlas 10*, Dublin, Royal Irish Academy, 2000, pp. 5–6.

25. For example in St Johns Priory, Kilkenny, is an altar tomb topped by a palimpsest slab which bears a fourteenth-century inscription to a burgess of Kilkenny. This was later appropriated to another burgess who died in 1571. Here is a newly erected tomb to a burgess of Kilkenny city using a memorial to a much earlier local government officer with the probable intent of emphasizing the antiquity of his position in life. See Carrigan, op. cit., III, pp. 255–6.

26. S.A. Meigs, *The Reformations in Ireland*, Dublin, 1997, p. 13. See also S.L. Fry, *Burial in Medieval Ireland 900–1500*, Dublin, 1999, pp. 153–63; and C.J. Tait, 'Harnessing Corpses: Death, Burial, Disinterment and Commemoration in Ireland, c. 1530–1655', Ph.D. thesis, National University of Ireland, Cork, 1999, ch. 4.

27. R. Gillespie, 'Funerals and Society in Medieval Ireland', *Journal of the Royal Society of Antiquaries of Ireland* 115, 1985, pp. 86–91.

28. This is a subject which requires greater analysis, but see R. Gillespie, 'The Image of Death, 1500–1700', *Archaeology Ireland*, 6.1, Spring 1992, pp. 8–9; and T.E. McNeill, 'The Archaeology of Gaelic Lordships East and West of the Foyle', in P.J. Duffy et al. (eds), *Gaelic Ireland—Land, Lordship and Settlement c.1250–c.1650*, Dublin, 2001, pp. 346–56.

29. This was not necessarily true of the rest of the country (stressing Kilkenny's relative isolation) as a post-Tridentine friction grew between the traditionalist, kin-orientated and deeply superstitious loyalties of the Gaelic Irish compared with the urban humanization of the Old English families. See R. Po-Chia Hsia, *The World of Catholic Renewal 1540–1770*, Cambridge, 1998, pp. 90–1.

30. H. Potterton, *Irish Church Monuments 1570–1880*, Ulster Architectural Society, 1976, pp. 8–9; see also P. Cockerham, 'A Butler Tomb at Aharney, County Kilkenny, *Old Kilkenny Review* 50, 1998, pp. 83–98. A symptom of this growing individualism manifested itself in the management of land in the county, such that 'Kilkenny urban societies helped to sustain the population densities and more complete rural settlement hierarchies in their hinterlands'. Hence, the enlarging

materialist/individualist merchant classes in urban Kilkenny dictated land ownership and its associated prestige and sense of independence. See W.J. Smyth, 'Territorial, Social and Settlement Hierarchies in Seventeenth Century Kilkenny', in Nolan and Whelan (eds), pp. 127–60.

31. R. Loeber, *The Geography and Practice of English Colonisation in Ireland from 1534 to 1609*, Group for the Study of Irish Historical Settlement 1991, pp. 38–40, 57–60; and Duffy et al. (eds), *Atlas*, pp. 58–63.

32. For example, in Dublin between 1560 and 1660 Harris analysed the ethnic identities of those commemorated on funeral monuments as 35 New English: 20 Old English: 3 Gaelic Irish; hence over 60% of monuments were to New English families. See Harris, 'Dublin', Fig. 6.

33. Smyth, p. 151. See also K. Bottigheim, *English Money and Irish Land— The Adventurers in the Cromwellian Settlement of Ireland*, Oxford, 1971; and A.F. O'Brien, 'Ireland—Conquest, Settlement and Colonisation', in D. O'Ceallaigh, *New Perspectives on Ireland*, Dublin, 1998, pp. 9–51.

34. The prime example of this kind of exhibitionism is provided by Richard Boyle, 1st earl of Cork, who erected four tombs in Ireland and England in celebration of his lineage (by marriage) and his newly found social, economic and political status. See A.L. Harris, 'The Funerary Monuments of Richard Boyle, Earl of Cork', *Church Monuments* XIII, 1998, pp. 70–86; and for a comparison between Catholic and Protestant funeral monument iconography see Loeber, 'Sculptured Monuments', pp. 276–7; also R.J. Hunter, 'Style and Form in Gravestone and Monumental Sculpture in County Tyrone in the Seventeenth and Eighteenth Centuries', in C. Dillon and H.A. Jefferies (eds), *Tyrone: History and Society*, Dublin, 2000, pp. 291–325.

35. For example in the return of priests to Kilkenny from their training abroad and in the patronage by the Ormonds and their court of Renaissance building styles; see P.J. Cornish, *The Catholic Community in the Seventeenth and Eighteenth Centuries*, Dublin, 1981, pp. 24–8; F. O'Fearghail, 'The Catholic Church in County Kilkenny 1600–1800', in Nolan and Whelan (eds), *Kilkenny*, pp. 197–249; J. Fenlon, *Ormond Castle*, Dublin, 1996, pp. 26–47, and J. Bradley, *Discover Kilkenny*, Dublin, 2000, pp. 35–6.

36. The pronounced influence of prints by the Renaissance Dutch artist Jan Vriedeman de Vries on the designs of several Cornish slate tombs of the late-sixteenth/early seventeenth centuries, has been convincingly identified by A. Wells-Cole, *Art and Decoration in Elizabethan and Jacobean England*, New Haven and London, 1997, pp. 76–7. The adaptation of these designs specifically by a Cornish tomb workshop suggests a highly restricted circulation of such prints. Their importation into the gentry circles of the county was perhaps via German mining engineers, for which see A.L. Rowse, *Tudor Cornwall*, London, 1941, pp. 56–8. For a general appraisal of port trade see W.B. Stephens, 'The Foreign Trade of Plymouth and the Cornish Ports in the early 17th Century', *Transactions of the Devonshire Association* 101, 1969, pp.

125–37; and T. Gray, 'Fisheries, Exploration, Shipping and Mariners in the Sixteenth and Seventeenth Centuries', in R. Kain and W. Ravenhill, *Historical Atlas of South-West England*, Exeter, 1999, pp. 377–83.

37. Duffin, 1996, pp. 38–71.

38. Dunstanville, *Carew*, pp. 178–86.

39. E. Hogan (ed.), *The Description of Ireland, and the State thereof, as it is at this present in Anno 1598*, Dublin and London, 1878, p. 65.

40. See P. Cockerham, ' "Its pieces now lie scattered around": the Brennache tomb at Pollrone, County Kilkenny, reconstructed', *Old Kilkenny Review* 53, 2001, forthcoming.

41. F.A. Greenhill, *Incised Effigial Slabs*, 2 vols, London, 1976, I, p. 315. He notes also that 'black-letter' script continued in extensive use in the northern parts of the Scottish Lowlands. A contrary view, with which I would concur, however, suggests that Gothic script was the exception during the seventeenth century in Scotland (and thereby isolating Cornwall even more in this respect) is proposed by B. Willsher, *Understanding Scottish Graveyards*, Edinburgh, 1995, pp. 38–9; and understood from surveys such as those by D. Christison, 'The Carvings and Inscriptions on the Kirkyard Monuments of the Scottish Lowlands . . .', *Proceedings of the Society of Antiquaries of Scotland*, 36, 1901, pp. 280–457.

42. Such conformity was rejected during the Commonwealth when inscriptions in Gothic script were more popular.

43. See Duffin, 1996, pp. 41–57; and N. Llewellyn, 'Claims to Status through Visual Codes: Heraldry on post-Reformation Funeral Monuments', in S. Anglo (ed.), *Chivalry in the Renaissance*, Woodbridge, 1990, pp. 145–60.

44. Smyth, 'Ormond Butlers', p. 116.

45. M. Bennett, *The Civil Wars in Britain and Ireland 1638–1651*, Oxford, 1997, p. 230.

46. M. Mullett, *Catholics in Britain and Ireland, 1558–1829*, Basingstoke, 1998, p. 124. There were also occasional attempts to claim adherence to Catholicism in Cornwall by using their monuments, such as on the brass inscriptions to the Arundells at St Mawgan. These were isolated cases, however, not just because of the low official level of recusancy and its patchy distribution in the county, albeit tending to be centred around St Mawgan (for which see the *Recusant Rolls* published by the Catholic Record Society—Vols 18, 57, 61 (1916–70), but also because the London manufacturers of these brasses would have avoided conspicuous iconographic or lexical controversy. The sort of wording on these Arundell brasses was purely a family influence however; it was not, nor could it ever have been, part of a more general attempt at promoting a deeper Cornish Catholic identity. It is a tantalizing hypothesis therefore, as to whether the Arundells, seeking perhaps more specifically to Catholic imagery on their tombs, would have been better served by Cornishmen rather than London craftsmen. See M. Stephenson and R.H. Pearson, 'Brasses to the Arundell Family at Mawgan-in-Pyder, Cornwall', *Transactions of the Monumental Brass Society 7*, 1940, pp. 303–21.

47. M.A. Havinden et al., (eds), *Centre et Pérephérie: Bretagne, Cornouailles—Devon: étude comparée*, Exeter, 1991, p. 13.

48. J. Mattingly, 'A Note on Breton-Cornish Links', *Institute of Cornish Studies, Associates Newsletter*, 2nd Series No. 4, May 1995, pp. 16–8; see also P. Payton, *Cornwall*, Fowey, 1996, pp. 115–17.

49. See Skol Vreizh, *Histoire de la Bretagne et des Pays Celtiques 1532 à 1789*, Morlaix, 1986, pp. 28–34; H. Poisson and J.-P. Le Met, *Histoire de Bretagne*, Spézet, 1995 edn, pp. 198–203; and for a succinct account of Breton maritime trade and its wider context see A. Croix, *L'âge d'or de la Bretagne 1532–1675*, Rennes, 1993, pp. 177–91.

50. J.C.A. Whetter, 'Cornish Trade in the 17th Century: an Analysis of the Port Books', *Journal of the Royal Institution of Cornwall*, New Series IV part 4, 1964, pp. 388–413, highlights the significance of Breton trade. In summarizing the commodities traded through Cornish ports, between 1608 and 1641 the total number of vessels entering/leaving Cornish ports to/from Brittany was 203 (27%) compared with 267 (33%) for the whole of western France, 136 (18%) for Ireland, 72 (10%) for Spain and Portugal and 65 (9%) for the rest of the world. The importance of Breton trade is clearer still when considering the statistics for vessels entering/leaving Cornish ports for trade along the English coast. A total of 251, just one or two more boats *per year* were trading with the whole of England than with Brittany.

51. Toulmin Smith (ed.), I, p. 179.

52. Mattingly, 1995, p. 17.

53. Payton, 1992, p. 60.

54. J-Y. Copy, *Art Société et Politique au temps des Ducs de Bretagne—Les Gisants Hauts-Bretons*, Paris, 1986.

55. Sources include M. Le Chevalier de Fréminville, *Antiquités de la Bretagne—Finistère*, 2 vols, Brest, 1832–3; J. Taylor et al., *Voyages Pittoresques et Romantiques dans l'Ancienne France – Bretagne*, 2 vols, 1845, Paris; H. Waquet, *Vieilles Pierres Bretonnes*, Quimper, 1920, pp. 121–49; R. Couffon and A. le Bars, *Répertoire des Églises et Chapelles du Diocèse de Quimper et de Léon*, Saint-Brieuc, 1959; J. Brosse (ed.), *Dictionnaire des Églises de France—Bretagne*, vol. 4a, Paris, 1968; J.-L. Flohic (ed.), *Le Patrimoine des Communes de Finistère*, 2 vols, Charenton-le-Pont, 1998.

56. For example, the detailed inventory of the canton of *Carhaix-Plouger, Finistère*, produced by the Inventaire Général des Monuments et des Richesses Artistiques de la France, 2 vols, Paris, 1969, covers eight cantons in which not a single funerary monument from the period 1500–1700 is identified.

57. For a description of the social hierarchy and the interaction between the different strata see J.B. Collins, *Classes, Estates, and Order in Early Modern Brittany*, Cambridge, 1994, pp. 60–70; 78–9.

58. Collins, 1994, p. 81.

59. See P. Galliou and M. Jones, *The Peoples of Europe—The Bretons*, Oxford, 1991, pp. 247–52; also Vreizh, pp. 74–5; and Poisson, pp. 144–70.

60. Galliou and Jones, p. 246. See also Abbaye de Daoulas, *1491–1991—la Bretagne au temps des Ducs*, Daoulas, 1991, pp. 114–58. There were weaknesses in this ducal stance however, for which see M. Jones, *The Creation of Brittany—a Late Medieval State*, London, 1988, pp. 283–307.

61. See C. Prigant, *Pouvoir ducal, religion et production artistique en Basse-Bretagne, 1350–1575*, Paris, 1992, pp. 457–527; and J. Charpy (ed.), *Patrimoine Religieux en Bretagne*, Rennes, 1998.

62. See especially M. Dilasser, 'L'église de Locronan et le mécénat des ducs de Bretagne', in X. Barral I Altet et al (eds), *Artistes, Artisans et Production Artistique en Bretagne au Moyan Age*, Rennes, 1983, pp. 111–19; also C. Prigent, 'Le rôle des classes sociales dans la production des statues en Basse Bretagne', pp. 129–32.

63. Such as the gisants of Hervé de Saint-Alouarn and his wife (late 15th century) at Guengat (F.), or that of Jacques de Tournemine (late 15th century) at Tréflaouenau (F.); see Flohic, *Finistère*, I, p. 416; II, p. 1092.

64. See R. Couffon, 'L'évolution de la Statuaire en Kersanton', *Mémoires de la Société d'Émulation des Côtes-du-Nord* 89, 1961, pp. 76–106; C. Prigent, 'Le tombeau en calcaire de l'evêque de Quimper Gatien de Monceaux', in *Bulletin de la Société Archéologique du Finistère* 113, 1984, pp. 339–45.

65. The apogee of Basse-Bretagne sculpture is reached in the famous tombs of Troilus de Moudragon (*c.*1540) at Quimper, which is, 'despite this late date, entirely gothic'. See H. Waquet, *Art Breton*, Paris, 1960, pp. 63–4, pl. 84.

66. Exceptions are traced by C. Prigent, 'Étude de quelques sculptures bretonnes influencées par les modes venues des pays nordiques', in *Bulletin de la Société Archéologique de Finistère* 108, 1980, pp. 269–88.

67. Galliou and Jones, op. cit., pp. 267–79.

68. Collins, op. cit., p. 79.

69. N.J.G. Pounds, *A History of the English Parish*, Cambridge, 2000, p. 111; see also K. Farnhill, *Guilds and the Parish Community in Late Medieval East Englia, c.1470–1550*, York, 2001, pp. 154–65.

70. It would be an interesting exercise to assess which noblesse families adopted truly Basse-Breton funeral monuments and which more 'French' styles. From an analysis of Finistère tombs the ecclesiastic and the aristocracy around Quimper were celebrated by tombs reminiscent more of mainland activity, whereas tombs of saints and aristocracy in the heartland of Basse-Bretagne adopted their own idiosyncratic style.

71. D. Potter, *A History of France, 1460–1560*, Basingstoke, 1995, pp. 232–3.

72. E. Musgrave, 'Memento Mori: The Function and Memory of Breton Ossuaries 1450–1750', in P.C. Jupp and G. Howarth (eds), *The Changing Face of Death—Historical Accounts of Death and Disposal*, Basingstoke, 1997, pp. 62–75. For a full appreciation of death contextualized within the beliefs of early modern Brittany, the standard work is A. Croix, *La Bretagne aux 16e et 17e siècles—La vie, la mort, le foi*, 2 vols, Paris, 1981; which more recently appeared in summary form as *Cultures et Religion en Bretagne aux 16e et 17e siècles*, Rennes, 1995. See also C. Prigent,

'L'empreinte de la mort sur le paysage en Bretagne aux XVe et XVIe siècles', in G. De Boe and F. Verhaeghe (eds), *Death and Burial in Medieval Europe—Papers of the 'Medieval Europe Brugge 1997' Conference*, 2 vols, Zellik, 1997, II, pp. 67–70. The wars of religion and the threat of Protestantism with the associated mortality, iconoclasm and destruction, might also have focussed the minds of the people towards the cult of the dead and dying. See P. Benedict, 'Settlement: France', in T.A. Brady Jr. et al. (eds), *Late Middle Ages, Renaissance, and Reformation*, 2 vols, Leiden, 1995, II, pp. 417–54.

73. Collins, p. 80. See also J. Collins, 'Geographic and Social Mobility in Early-Modern France', *Journal of Social History* 24.3, 1990, pp. 563–77.

74. Croix, *La Bretagne*, II, pp. 1024–36, who analyses in detail using probate evidence the growing desire of family members to be buried within the same grave as their ancestors.

75. For example the sixteenth-century slabs at Loctudy (F.) and Prat (C.) comprise a cross and shield under an arch and a shield of arms respectively.

76. For example the slab at Gouesnou (F.) to Guillaume Tpouronce (1620), canon of Vannes, shows him in full ecclesiastical garb and with a marginal inscription in Gothic script. See Flohic, *Finistère*, I, p. 113.

77. See J.M. Abgrall, 'Les ossuaires bretons', in *Congrès archéologique de France, 81e Session à Brest et Vannes*, Paris, 1914, pp. 529–41; R. le Deunff, *Les ossuaires bretons*, Guingamp, 1999.

78. A neat example of this concurrent remembrance is cited by Croix, *Cultures et Religion*, p. 124. The undated gravestone of a siegneur of Landjuan (I.) is inscribed 'Stop, passer-by—pray for a poor fisherman who was yesterday as you will be tomorrow', a variation on the doggerel, 'As I am now so you will be'. The inference is just that of, say, the tomb of the Unknown Soldier in Westminster Abbey. A specific type of person is commemorated by a single person but within that type the individual is anonymous, extending the commemorative sense to the whole. See also E. Badone, *The Appointed Hour: Death, World View and Social Change in Brittany*, Berkeley, 1989, p. 135ff.

79. For example see the kersanton tomb of Thibaul de Tanouarn (1655) at Plérin (C.), see J.-L. Flohic, *Le Patrimoine des Côtes-d'Armor*, 2 vols, Charenton-le-Pont, II, p. 905.

80. Croix, *La Bretagne*, II, pp. 955–1000. Several nineteenth-century accounts of Breton funeral customs are given by A. le Braz, *Magies de la Bretagne*, Paris, 1994 edn, pp. 210–3; 222–5.

81. This was not necessarily representative of Brittany as Anjou tombs were also locally produced—but it does suggest an active rejection of the post-Tridentine Italian schools of artistic influence. See F. Lebrun, *Les Hommes et la Mort en Anjou aux 17e et 18e siècles*, Paris, 1971, p. 474.

82. For an analysis of the liturgical and cultural influences on church fittings and decoration see R. Barrié, 'Mobilier cultuel et décor intérieur dans l'église de Basse-Bretagne aux XVIIe et XVIIIe siècles', *Annales de*

Bretagne, 90, 1983, pp. 377–86. For an account of mainline French tomb sculpture and its assimiliation of Italian influence with Counter-Reformation doctrine, hence emphasizing a reliance on locally produced rather than imported tombs, see E. Mâle, *L'Art Religieux de la Fin du XVIe siècle, du XVIIe siècle et du XVIIIe siècle*, Paris, 1972 edn, pp. 206–27.

83. Prigent, *Pouvoir ducal*, p. 362.
84. Le Chevalier de Fréminville, *Antiquités de la Bretagne—Côtes-du-Nord*, Brest, 1837, p. 55.
85. Although not specific to Brittany for a full account of the destruction of French monumental artefacts within which Breton monuments might be contextualized, see L. Réau, *Les Monuments Détruits de l'Art Française*, 2 vols, Paris, 1959, I, pp. 65–106.
86. See Y. Pelletier, *Les enclos paroissiaux*, Rennes, 1981; P. Chamard-Bois et al. (eds), *Enclos Paroissiaux—Livres de bois, livres de pierre*, Rennes, 1994.
87. Musgrave, p. 67.
88. Y.-M. Bercé, *The Birth of Absolutism—A History of France, 1598–1661*, Basingstoke, 1996, pp. 211–12.
89. Hsia, p. 73.
90. J. Maltby, *Prayer Book and People in Elizabethan and Early Stuart England*, Cambridge, 1998, p. 59.
91. This returns almost to the medieval concept of the 'ex-voto' mural monument, so common in fourteenth and fifteenth-century France and Belgium; there are many examples described and illustrated by F. Guilhermy, *Inscriptions de la France . . . ancien Diocèse de Paris*, 5 vols, Paris, 1873–83, *passim*.
92. See Cockerham, 'Cornish Memorialization', pp. 26–8.
93. Hence the Parliamentary iconoclasm from 1646–9 was particularly acute in Penwith; see M. Stoyle, ' "Pagans or Paragons?" Images of the Cornish during the Civil War', *English Historical Review* CXI, April 1996, pp. 322–3; and Stoyle, 'Dissidence of Despair', pp. 439–40. A valuable overview of Stoyle's research, contextualizing his construction of ethnic identities in Cornwall is given by Deacon, 2000, pp. 215–19.
94. Cockerham, 'Cornish Memorialization', p. 27.
95. N. Orme, *The Saints of Cornwall*, Oxford, 2000, p. 28.
96. Orme, 2000.
97. Some early sixteenth-century sculptural similarities between the three regions have been identified, see E.C. Rae, 'Irish Sepulchral Monuments of the Later Middle Ages—II', *Journal of the Royal Society of Antiquaries of Ireland* 101 (1971), pp. 8–15.
98. Payton, 1992, p. 55.
99. E. O'Ciosain, 'Les Irlandais en Bretagne 1603–1780: "invasion", acceuil, intégration', in C. Laurent and H. Davis (eds), *Irelande et Bretagne—vingt siècles d'histoire*, Rennes, 1994, p. 152.
100. O'Ciosain, p. 152. See also A. Lespagnol, 'Les relations commercials entre l'Irlande et al Bretagne aux temps modernes (XVe et XVIIIe

siècles) Complémentarité ou concurrence?' in Laurent and Davis, pp. 168–77.

101. A. Hale, 'Rethinking Celtic Cornwall: An Ethnographic Approach', in P. Payton (ed.), *Cornish Studies: Five*, Exeter, 1997, p. 92.

102. For example in Ireland that at Kilmore, Co. Meath (1575) for which see P. Harbison, *The Crucifixion in Irish Art*, Blackrock, 2000, pp. 54–5; for Breton inscriptions see J.-M. Abgrall, 'Inscriptions gravées et sculptées sur les églises et monuments du Finistère', *Congrès Archéologique de France, à Morlaix et à Brest*, Paris, 1898, pp. 113–59; also Prigent, *Pouvoir ducal*, pp. 612–25.

103. Characteristic Irish dress was occasionally represented on effigal tombs, particularly in Kilkenny on the work of Rory O'Tunney, that 'most individualistic and "Irish-minded" of the Ossory sculptors of the sixteenth century'; see Hunt, op. cit., I, p. 96.

104. Payton, 1992, p. 56.

105. M. Coate, *Cornwall in the Great Civil War and Interregnum, 1642–1660*, Truro, 1963 edn., p. 31.

106. See C. Gittings, *Death, Burial and the Individual in Early Modern England*, London, 1984, *passim*; and R. Houlbrooke, *Death, Religion and the Family in England 1480–1750*, Oxford, 1998, pp. 380–4. For a European overview see P. Ariès' seminal work, *The Hour of Our Death*, New York, 1981 edn, pp. 260–93.

107. Coate, pp. 322–30; Duffin, 1996, pp. 38–71; and see N. Tyacke, 'Puritanism, Arminianism and Counter-Revolution', in M. Todd (ed.), *Reformation to Revolution—Politics and Religion in Early Modern England*, London 1995, pp. 53–70.

108. A. Macfarlane, *The Origins of English Individualism*, Oxford, 1979 edn, p. 196.

109. Macfarlane, 1979, p. 196.

A REDISCOVERED CORNISH–ENGLISH VOCABULARY

Andrew Hawke

INTRODUCTION

The National Library of Wales has a number of Cornish manuscripts in its collections of which the most important is undoubtedly Peniarth 105, a play of the life of Meryasek copied in 1504, and uniquely important as the only local saint's play to have survived in Britain. The other Cornish manuscripts in the Library's collections, being almost without exception copies of other earlier manuscripts preserved elsewhere, have understandably received far less attention. One manuscript that certainly does deserve to be edited is Llanstephan 84, Edward Lhuyd's notebook vocabulary of Cornish which he and his Oxford helpers used in Cornwall during their fieldwork in 1700. There is much material in Llst. 84 which Lhuyd did not publish in his *Archæologia Britannica* (vol. I., Oxford, 1707), although he had promised it for the second volume which unfortunately never appeared. Morton Nance did examine it, presumably in the 1930s, since his 1938 dictionary refers to it frequently.[1]

A booklet entitled *Cornish Manuscripts in the National Library of Wales* was printed and published in 1939 by the National Library of Wales.[2] This was compiled by the National Librarian, William Llewelyn Davies as an address to the Celtic Congress at its meeting held at Truro on 12–17 September, 1939. Davies lists in all sixteen manuscripts in Cornish, both ancient and modern. To it has been appended an undated typewritten sheet adding a further three manuscripts, including the following:

XIX.

BODEWRYD MS. 5.

A fragment (2 pages on 2 folios) of a Cornish–English
Vocabulary. Circa 1700.

A brief description appears in the *Schedule of Bodewryd Manuscripts*,
dated October, 1932.[3] On the second page of this typescript, the
manuscript is listed:

> 5. VOCABULARY. Two sheets only of a Cornish–English
> vocabulary. The words are not in alphabetical order and the
> first sheet is practically confined to parts of the body.

To this has been added in pencil, 'C17' and 'Connexion betw. Wynne
family & Bodewryd?'

This manuscript appears to be unknown outside the National
Library, probably because no one at the time that it was catalogued
realized that the scarcity of Cornish manuscripts renders each surviving
example very significant. Nor is this manuscript a copy of any other
extant Cornish manuscript.

PHYSICAL DESCRIPTION OF THE MANUSCRIPT
The manuscript is a folio volume consisting of two paper folios (unfortunately lacking watermarks) approximately 29 cm by 19 cm, each
written on one side only. This has been rebound, repaired and strengthened at the National Library to include a number of blank sheets to
lend some bulk to the volume. It appears to be part of a commonplace
book, with Latin quotations from Cicero heading both pages in a
contemporary (or near contemporary) italic hand.

It has been double-ruled in two columns in red or pale brown
ink, which the copyist has subsequently subdivided into two columns,
one for the Cornish words, and one for their English glosses, on the
first, but not the second, folio. It appears to have been written in some
haste as there are several deletions and corrections and some of the
entries have been transposed. There is some blank space at the end of
the first folio (listing parts of the body), whilst the text on the second
folio runs right to the end, and could conceivably have been followed
by one or more further folios, as there is no apparent order to the
entries.

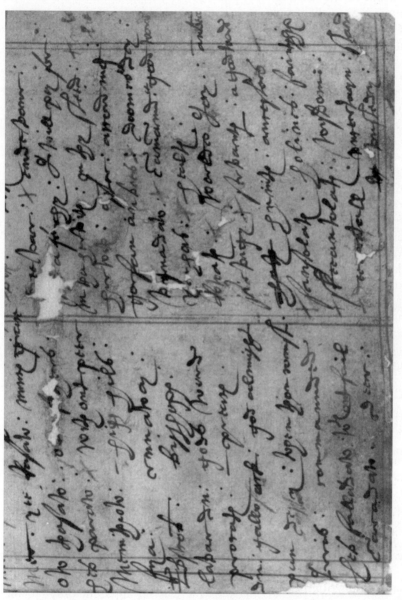

Figure 1: The lower part of page 2 of NLW Bodewryd 5 (reduced), by permission of the National Library of Wales

THE HAND
The vocabulary is written in a rapid secretary hand, with characteristic
swashes to the tails of *h*, *k*, and *y*,[4] and the initial stroke of *n*. The
letters have a slight rightwards slope, characteristic of the later period
of this type of hand, but the hand is otherwise free of later influences
and exhibits a number of early features, such as the flat-topped *g*.

DATING
The manuscript contains no internal evidence for dating, other than the
form and orthography of the Cornish words. Mr Daniel Huws, a former
Keeper of Manuscripts at the National Library of Wales and an
acknowledged expert on dating Welsh manuscripts, very kindly agreed
to examine the manuscript in May 1995 and suggested that it may have
been written at any time between about 1575 at the very earliest and
1625 to 1650 at the latest. Mrs Susan Davies, an expert on palaeo-
graphy, also generously examined a copy of the manuscript at the
writer's request and suggested dating the hand to the first half of the
seventeenth century, whilst acknowledging that the secretary hand in
Wales and Cornwall did survive even into the eighteenth century. This
places it probably rather earlier than the 'circa 1700' of the typewritten
addition to the list of Cornish manuscripts mentioned above, and
agrees more closely with the 'C17' of the Bodewryd *Schedule*. Some
internal evidence, particularly in the realization of geminate -*nn*- and
-*mm*- (which became -*dn*-/-*bm*- or just -*d*-/-*b*-),[5] and especially the
widespread use of the plural termination -*aw* point however to a later
rather than an earlier date.

AUTHORSHIP AND PROVENANCE
There is no colophon nor any other mention of the compiler or copyist.
It is natural to look among the Cornish antiquarians of the seventeenth
and eighteenth centuries for the writer of this vocabulary, but comparison with the known hands has provided no identification, although
more work needs to be done on this. The hand is closest in appearance
to that of William Jordan CW (1611), although Bodewryd 5 is
definitely not in his hand. Presumably the list would have been written
by a Cornish speaker. Although apparently written in haste, there are
no obvious scribal errors that could be accounted for by miscopying or
writing by a non-native speaker, and the remarks *lavar teag* (99) and *a
good word* (108, 111) suggest a Cornish speaker. However it could
have been written by an English or Welsh scribe, and it is impossible to
determine whether it was written in Cornwall, Wales, or elsewhere.
There are at least two English words which appear now to have
become dialectal, namely *nuddock* which glosses p*o*lkeel ('nape of the

neck') and *armwrist*. According to Wright, *nuddock* only occurs in Cornwall, Devon and Somerset, and in Pembrokeshire.[6] However, in Pembrokeshire it only occurs in the form *niddick* and *nedack*. It is interesting to note that John Keigwyn[7] uses *nuddock* to gloss *kylban* (same meaning) in his transcription and translation of the *Creacon of the World*. Similarly, *armwrist* occurs only in Cornwall, Devon and Somerset.[8] This tends to suggest a Cornish provenance for the manuscript or at least for the copyist.

DESCRIPTION OF CONTENTS

Folio 1
The first folio lists the parts of the body, in the traditional order from the crown of the head to the soles of the feet (although the 'teates' (i.e. breasts) have been left until the end), and there is a small supplementary list such as 'fatt' and 'bones' which must have been considered more general. The list is quite exhaustive, even listing various colours of beards, and the names of all the fingers. However, the list in the well-known 'Old Cornish Vocabulary' (VC) is far more extensive.

Generally the Cornish forms are listed first, with English glosses following. However the first entry in the first column (1) and both the second and third entries in the second column (39, 40) have been transposed. The writer evidently noticed this, as he has tried to correct the headings 'English' and 'Cornish', and then, no doubt in desperation, has crossed them out.

There are sixty entries in total on this folio, two of which have been deleted before writing the English glosses. Ten entries list singular and plural forms in both Cornish and English. The Cornish word *gerne* appears to have been added by a different hand alongside the English 'chin'. There is nothing particularly remarkable about the list, except that it is not a copy of any other extant list of this kind, and supplies a number of previously unrecorded or otherwise dubious forms.

The most notable aspect of this folio is that the vocabularly is very definitely Modern Cornish in form, and very reminiscent of that recorded by Edward Lhuyd on his visit to Cornwall in 1700, although much of what Lhuyd recorded would have been the speech of elderly speakers, and therefore representative of the language spoken around the middle of the century. There is little here to suggest that the list has been copied from any existing source, except for the confusion between the two columns and the deletions, although these may simply result from the speed of writing.

Folio 2

The second folio contains a strange mixture of words and phrases in no particular order, except that the Cornish is given first. In all there are fifty-four entries. There is a strong religious flavour to the vocabulary, as can be seen from a few of the English glosses: 'an Evill one', 'excommunicat', 'devils, evil ones', 'bisshopp', 'gods word', 'preach', 'god almight', 'bishops crosse', 'did worship', 'doomesday', 'holines, saintship'.

Many of the Cornish words occur in the Middle Cornish texts, although not in the form presented here, which is reminiscent of the Modern Cornish texts, as far as the orthography and (presumed) phonology are concerned. Mention has already been made of the characteristic geminate *-nn-* and *-mm-* development to *-dn-* and *-d-* (as in *pen > pedn > ped*) and *-bm-* (as in *worthibmen*). However, some of the verbal forms appear to be comparatively old, such as the 3rd pers. sing. pret. *-as* endings in *mee resettias ow holan*, glossed 'I purpose', but literally meaning 'I have set my heart', *recommaundias* 'did commaund' and *worthias* 'did worship', and note the perfective *re* in two of these forms corresponding to Middle Welsh *ry*.

Overall, it is tempting to see the second folio as a set of glosses on a text or texts. Perhaps it was written to facilitate the study of a particular text. Many of the phrases and words do indeed occur in some of the extant Middle Cornish texts, but there are additional words in the vocabulary and in no text do the correspondences occur in this order, nor together in the same text. If these are glosses on a single text, then that text must have disappeared.

There is evidence for a number of missing texts, the most certain of which is a missing life of St Columb (a female saint, not Colum Cille) mentioned by Nicholas Roscarrock who wrote to William Camden in 1607 to correct Camden's derivation of the names of St Columb Minor and Major from the male saint, 'whereas in truthe yt taketh name of Columba, a woman St who was a vyrgine and martyre whose lyfe I have in my handes translated owt of Cornyshe'.[9] Some of the Cornish manuscripts remained in Cornwall until comparatively recently, such as the fifteenth-century BL Harleian 1782, the 'Passion Poem', said to have been discovered in Sancreed Church in the eighteenth century.[10]

NEW VOCABULARY

A number of new words or combinations appear in this manuscript, including the following:

1. *gerne* 'Chin' (16): possibly = W. *cern* (fem.) 'cheek bone, side of the head', unless it is a spelling of *gên* 'chin' (cf. AB 89a), with

the *-r-* emphasizing the length of the preceding *-e-*, as in Co.
dialect *ayrth* for *eath* 'eight'.[11]

2. *beez meas* 'thumbe' (33) (in this combination): see below on
   meas.
3. *beez nessa beean* 'middle finger' (37) (in this combination).
   Lhuyd's term for this is *Bez nessa dhan bez krêz* which he
   glosses 'modrwyvŷs' ('middle finger'), NLW Llst. 84, 20.
4. *creeb an gar* 'the shinne' (47) (in this combination).
5. *burnvghall* 'instepp' (49): might include *vghall* 'high' (cf. AB
   42b), but cf. W. *mwnwgl, mynygl* 'neck; instep', and *mwnwgl*
   (*mynygl*) (*y*) *troed*, also meaning 'instep' (see GPC s.v.).[12] Initial
   b- and *m-* are frequently confused, cf. *belin/melin*, but the
   intrusive *-r-* is difficult to explain.
6. *Craban*aw 'skracching fingers' (62): Possibly related to W.
   crafangau 'claws, talons', but Richard Gendall suggests a
   connection with Thomas Tonkin's *crab(aliaz)* 'to creep' and the
   dialect word *crabalorgin* 'spider crab'.[13]
7. *Crowwelder* 'cruelty' (67): presumably a borrowing from English
   cruel+-der/-dar, cf. *cruell* TH 15a, 24a, 47a, etc.

DUBIOUS WORDS

Some of the words are a total mystery, occasionally because of the
holes in the folios which have deleted some letters, but even some that
are perfectly legible seem not to be recorded elsewhere, and lack
readily apparent cognates in Welsh or Breton:

1. *stroneak* 'breast' (25): This word is unknown, but presumably
   includes the adjectival ending *-ak* (Ml.Co. *-ek*, O.Co. *-oc*).
2. *asaw* 'liver' (39) does not occur in any other text in this meaning.
   AB 67a gives *Avy*, 'The liver of man or beast'. As the English
   and Cornish in this entry are reversed, perhaps the writer had
   lost his place and confused this word with *azan* 'a ribb' or *azaw*
   'ribbs' which occur a little further on, out of order, and following
   two deletions. *azan* is well attested in Old, Middle and Modern
   Cornish.
3. *œezeelee* 'loynes & sides' (56) (first letter could possibly be
   a ligature such as *œ* or a misformed *d*.): cf. *Yssilli* 'Limbs,
   members' AB 242c, *eyssely* TH 19a, *Sely*, 'Arms' Borlase2 454;
   esely 'limbs, members' occurs in OM 2735, BM 541, 3048, TH
   35a, etc.; *ysyly* occurs in OM 1797, PC 1733, etc. but the meaning
   does not suit particularly well here.
4. *kirthen* 'about the loyns' (61): ?some borrowed form from ME.
   gerth(e) 'to gird'. Richard Gendall[14] suggests taking this and the

preceding line together: *bl[o]nacke kirthen* 'fatt: about the
loyns', taking *kirthen* as *kerghyn* in *an queth a fue yn kerghyn
ihesu* 'the garment that has been about Jesus' RD 1936–7.

5. *prensa* 'deer byys it' (64): presumably the conditional of *prena*:
   'would buy', although the English gloss suggests that something
   may have been omitted in the Cornish, cf. *caid prinid* gl. *emptius*
   'purchased slave', VC 102; Ml.Co. has forms in *pren(ne), perna*.

6. *anclotha* 'filthines' (68): Could this be miscopied (and mis-
   interpreted) from PC 1545, rag *an clathva* crystunyon 'for a
   burial-place of Christians' (Nance)? This seems rather unlikely.

7. *desonowes* 'fore prophesied' (70): possibly containing *sowyny*
   'prosper, succeed, thrive, flourish', although the meaning does
   not fit.[15]

8. *frappis: frappigy* 'shreid torns' (74): Since *frappis* appears to be a
   past participle and *frappigy* appears to be a plural (although
   usually applied to persons), Richard Gendall suggests that
   'shreid' should be taken with the former, and 'torns' with the
   latter.[16] *frape* occurs in Co. dialect meaning 'to bind, wrap' and
   frappia occurs in the sense 'to strike' (e.g. BM 961). Both
   frappigy and English *torns* are unknown.

9. *bith* 'both' (102): *bith* is attested in various meanings: 'will
   be' (CW 99), '(n)ever' (TH 7a), but the meaning 'both' is a
   mystery.

10. *--eevar* 'endevour' (103): Pryce has *devar*, 'owing, due' (Pryce
    sig. N1va), but the meaning does not fit.[17]

11. *--- a sorhy* 'I will pay for' (104): Probably *Mi a . . .*, but the verb is
    unknown.

12. *hunith* 'ancestors' (102): a related meaning is found in Mn.Co.
    heeneth 'generation, descendants, age' (William Rowe), *thort
    heenneth da heenneth* 'from generation to generation' CWBF 39;
    heenath Old Cornwall viii. 559, *heeneth* 'Genaration' Gwavas
    MS., ff. 123r; *henath* (Thomas Boson, 1710) CWBF 41: possibly
    from the stem of *hanvos* = W. *hanfod*, or = W. *hen* 'old, ancient'.
    hvnythe CW 2247.

CONFIRMATION OF DUBIOUS WORDS OR MEANINGS

A handful of words do help to confirm some otherwise dubious words
or forms:

1. *beez meas* 'thumbe' (33): *meas* would be a regular development
   from O.Co. *möd*, cf. W. (*bys*) *bawd* 'thumb', but the only other
   possible example occurs in the word *misne* (*recte misue*)[18] 'an
   inch' of 1599.

2. *beez Rage* 'for finger' (36): This combination was previously only known from Lhuyd's *Bêz râg* which he glosses 'rhagvŷs' ('forefinger'), NLW Llst. 84, 20. See below on *Rage*.

3. *bell angarr* 'calf of the legg' (45): Previously only known in *belgar* 'the calf of the Leg' (Borlase2) and *bil an gar* 'krôth y goes' [= 'calf of the leg'], Lhuyd, NLW Llst. 84, 20b.

4. *goobiddar* 'ankels' (46): cf. AB 84b, *gybeddern* . . . '*the ankle or ankle-bone*' under *Malleolus*; Borlase2 435c, *Gybeddern*, a little Hammer (probably from Lhuyd). The first two forms would appear to be independent, but the etymology of this word remains unclear. Comparison with W. *bigwrn* (from an original *migwrn*) is probably misleading.

5. *(ne) veath* 'dareth not' (65): ?Cf. *na veth*, BM 3470 and *methaf* 'I dare', CW 1352 with characteristic *b-/m-* confusion.[19]

6. *(pan) deffry* 'when thou comst' (85): 2 s. pres.-fut. subj. *devos, devones* (long form of *dos, dones*) *dyffy* (Nance, 208). Neither *deffry* nor *deffy* occurs in the texts, but *deffe* is quite common, e.g. *pan deffe thy wlascor ef* 'when He came to His Kingdom', RD 273. The *-r-* is probably erroneously inserted under the influence of the extremely common adv. *deffry* 'indeed, verily, etc.'.

7. *gotha* 'suffer' (95): Cf. *gothe*, BM 890, 1753, 1765, 2245, which seem to be the only examples of the verb-noun.

8. *keeren anpedn* 'crown of head' (in this combination) (3): cf. *in guryn po an top an pen* translating 'very crowne, or topp of the head', TH 46. *curun, curon* occurs frequently in the ordinary sense of 'crown', but is *keeren* cognate with W. *corun* 'crown of head' (< Lat. *corona*), or W. *coron* 'crown' (< ME *corone*)?

INTERESTING FORMS

Some of the forms are interesting for various reasons, showing features not previously noted, or having a certain correspondence with particular existing texts.

1. *polkeel* 'nuddock' (6): Previously the only other example was *Pol kîl* 'The hinder part of the head', AB 104c; cf. also 'Nuddic, the hinder Part of the Head', Borlase2 447c. *kyl* also occurs in O.Co. *chil* gl. *cervix*, VC 41, and Mn.Co. *kylban* (with *pen*), CW 1112, with the same meaning. Cf. Ml.Br. *quil*, W. *cil*.

2. *geelin* 'elbowe' (29): Cf. *Gelen* 'An elbow; a cubit', AB 52c. The *g-* is inorganic, cf. O.Co. *elin* gl. *ulna*, VC 56, Ml.Br. *elin* 'cubitus', Mn.Br. *ilin*; the following word shows the same development.

3. *gweenas* 'nails' (32): With inorganic *g-*, cf. O.Co. *euuin* gl. *unguis* and *euynoc* in *kenin euynoc* gl. *algium* (VC 58, 271) and Mn.Co. *Winaz* 'Nails', AB 28a. Modern northern dialectal Welsh exhibits the same feature: *gwinadd* for *ewinedd*, exactly cognate with *gweenas*.

4. *Rage* 'for' (36): (= 'fore-'); for the adjectival use of *rag* cf. *Darras rag*, 'The Fore-door' and *Danz rag* 'A fore-tooth' (both AB 13b), and cf. O.Co. *flurrag* gl. *prora*, VC 130.[20]

5. *pedgleen* 'knee' (43): (< *pednglin* < *penglin*). Cf. *penclin* gl. *genu*, VC 61; *pedn glín* 'A knee' AB 63a.

6. *bl[o]nacke* 'fatt' (60): *blonec* gl. *adeps* VC 52; other later glossaries (Pryce, Borlase2, AB) all derive from the O.Co. form, as this may well do.

7. *obskommineiis* 'excommunicat' (66): Cf. the verb-nouns *omskemenegy* and *omskumenesa* (TH 39r), the shortened form *skemyna*, CW 1212, and the past participles *omskemynes*, *omskemnys* 'cursed', CW 1205, 1211, *skemynys* 'cursed one', CW 212). *ob-* from *om-* is a late development, but cf. *obma* 'here', CW 2524 as early as 1611, later becoming *obba*, e.g. CWBF 15 (*c*.1670).

8. *re* (75, 93): Perfective particle, in *mee resettias ow holan* 'I purpose' and *re commaundias* 'did commaund', Gendall states that this was 'not normally used after 1611', PDMC under *re* (1).

9. *worthibmen* 'commandment' (89): < Ml.Co. *gorhemmyn*, cf. *goribmyn*, CW 402, *karebma*, CWBF 46 (John Boson).

10. *ompleg* 'well liking' (98): cf. Lhuyd's *Amplek, mar thym amplek* 'I am much pleased', NLW Llst. 84, f. 8a, the unique example, although copied in other vocabularies, and ?cf. *(th)om pleg(adow)* 'to my satisfaction', CW 2411 (*tham plegadow*, Stokes 2410), which could conceivably have been mis-interpreted.

11. *mi dor askarn* '*lavar teag*' (99): This presumably means 'I shall break a bone', but why is it described as '*lavar teag*' ('a fair expression/saying')? Is *mi dor askarn* some sort of oath or ejaculation, or could *lavar teag* imply 'good (idiomatic) Cornish', cf. 'a good word', below (108, 111)?

Furthermore there is a another group, which, despite being small in number, suggest something rather interesting:

1. *kehar clave* 'soar sides' (59): Cf. *keher claff* 'sore muscles' (Nance's translation), BM 3291 (a hapax in this combination).

2. *mer yee Rasaw* 'much grace' (76): Cf. BM 486, *mur o rasow*, the only example of *mur* with the plural of *ras* (*ras* = W. *rhad* (not *gras*)).

3. *gotha* 'suffer' (95): Cf. *gothe*, BM 890, 1753, 1765, 2245, which seem to be the only examples of the verb-noun, as noted above.

4. *bagill* 'bishops crosse' (90): Cf. *Sens the vagyl in the leff*, BM 3007; = W. *bagl* < Late Latin *bac'lus* < *baculus* 'staff, crosier, crook' (but cf. following stage direction in English: *bagyll of syluer & myter aredy*: so it could be an English borrowing from *bagle* OED (obsolete)). Nance under *bagyl* refers to 'Pryce MS.', but the writer cannot find the word in BL Add. 43409.

5. *Rowath . . . anbeis* 'worldes Yoy' (110): Cf. *roweth an beys*, BM 357 (a hapax in this combination).

6. *sanstolath* 'holines: saintship' (113): Cf. *sansoleth*, BM 137—a hapax?

And these should possibly be included as well:

1. *barve* 'beard' (17–21): Occurs in O.Co. as *barf* gl. *barba* and *baref* gl. *barbam*, both VC 48; but it does not occur in Ml.Co. apart from the form *barvov* in BM 2309, 2313, 3450, 3529. It is, however, attested in later sources such as *bar*, 'A Beard', AB 11c, *Bar, †barev*, 'A Beard', 44c. However, this word occurs in the list of parts of the body, and the BM evidence is probably coincidental.

2. *v_nadaw* 'Cammand. a good word' (108): Cf. *gothvos ynweth descernya / omma ynter drok ha da yv ov ewnadow pup vr '. . .* is my desire always',[21] BM 30: a hapax? On 'a good word' in this and the following note, cf. *lavar teag*, above, p. 92.

3. *sirvigy* 'servants: a good word' (111): Cf. *servysy*, BM 3262, 3373, 3801, 4275; but it is also quite common in the other texts: *servysy*, OM 235; *servisi*, PC 167; and *Ser-vidzhi* 'Servants', AB 242c.

A POSSIBLE CONNECTION

As the surviving evidence for Cornish is relatively sparse, one might expect to find a large number of unique occurrences of particular words or phrases. However, this particular group all seem to come from a single manuscript, *Beunans Meriasek* mentioned at the start of this paper, preserved in Aberystwyth at the National Library of Wales.

Whitley Stokes, the great nineteenth-century philologist, has often been credited with discovering *Beunans Meriasek* in the Hengwrt Library of W.W.E. Wynne in 1869.[22] *Beunans Meriasek* is a two-day saint's play of some 4,500 lines written, according to the colophon, in 1504. William Llywelyn Davies quotes from a number of letters by Canon Robert Williams of Rhydycroesau, the compiler of the *Lexicon Cornu-Britannicum*, to Mr Wynne, which make it clear that Wynne made the initial discovery, contacted Williams, whose dictionary had only recently been published in 1865, and that Williams approached Stokes as a possible editor—a job which Stokes apparently relished, publishing his edition in 1872. However, both Nance (as recorded in his manuscript introduction to his unpublished edition of *Beunans Meriasek* now in the Nance Bequest at the Royal Institution of Cornwall in Truro) and before him Henry Jenner, the first of the modern Cornish scholars, had already noticed an intriguing entry in Edward Lhuyd's catalogue of 'British' manuscripts[23]:

> Llyvyr yn iaith Kernyu 4*to*. Modv. a hanner o drûχ. Vaugh. W.
> *M*. h. *e*. *Codex dialecto Cornubiensi scriptus, sesquidigitum crassus.*

No other Cornish manuscript is known to have been a part of the Hengwrt Library, but it would appear to be too thick to be Peniarth 105 at an inch and a half. Nance suggested it could originally have had thick covers, but the present binding is under an inch thick. However, Mr Daniel Huws[24] has pointed out that Lhuyd's thicknesses for manuscripts are notoriously inaccurate, and that this is not a problem. The inevitable question is, why did Lhuyd subsequently ignore this manuscript? Every other Cornish manuscript he could find he had transcribed, and indeed some of these have found their way to the National Library (e.g. NLW Llst. 97 (a transcription amd translation of the *Ordinalia* trilogy, translated by John Keigwyn of Mousehole[25]) and NLW Peniarth 428, another transcription of the *Ordinalia* made *c*.1695–1700, this time without the translation, and almost certainly once in Lhuyd's possession[26] and with the name Izabel Keigwyn on the first folio).

John Keigwyn (1641–1716) was commissioned by Sir Jonathan Trelawny, the Cornish Bishop of Exeter (whose diocese extended throughout Cornwall at that time), to translate some of the major texts.[27] Bishop Trelawny (by then Lord Bishop of Winchester) is also thanked by Lhuyd in his *Archæologia* for making a contribution towards his travelling costs in Cornwall, and directing him to knowledgeable people (including, presumably, John Keigwyn).[28] Lhuyd rather vaguely states that there are 'not above three or four Books (that we know of) extant in writing' in Cornish.[29] He elaborates in his Cornish preface to his Cornish grammar where he states:

I got the best part of my knowledge from three Cornish manuscripts, placed in my hands by . . . Sir Jonathan Trelawny, Bishop of Exeter, and . . . John Anstis Esq., . . . and the aforementioned Mr. Keigwyn, who by command of the previously named bishop translated these books into English, and who is unanimously judged to be the most knowledgeable in the Cornish dialect in our time.[30]

John Anstis provided a copy of the Passion Poem, Trelawny provided the *Ordinalia*, and Keigwyn supplied the *Creacon of the World*.

It seems most strange that Lhuyd could have overlooked the unique exemplar of *Beunans Meriasek*, having catalogued it at Hengwrt. Lhuyd even mentions Cynan Meiriadog in his Cornicized spelling *Kenan Meriazhek* in the Cornish preface to his Cornish grammar,[31] where one feels that he would surely have mentioned *Beunans Meriasek* had he been aware of the contents of the manuscript he catalogued at Hengwrt.

However it appears that Lhuyd spent but a single day at Hengwrt, and used that in numbering and cataloguing the vellum manuscripts, hoping to return later to examine them more fully.[32] *Beunans Meriasek* is written on paper, so presumably he only glanced at it and was never able to return. Lhuyd did not use *Beunans Meriasek* in any of his writings on Cornish, and seems otherwise to have been completely unaware of its existence. The evidence of Bodewryd 5, however, suggests that someone did consult it, and understood enough of it to gloss some of the vocabulary, and even make such comments as 'a good word', suggesting a Cornish speaker who was confident in his use of the language. This person, whoever it was, evidently had access to other Cornish texts (or copies of them), as evidenced by the vocabulary which does not occur in *Beunans Meriasek*, and he presumably supplied the list of body parts from his own personal knowledge or that of his contemporaries, as they are exclusively Modern in form and orthography, whilst the remainder of the vocabulary belongs to a number of different periods.

It is not known how *Beunans Meriasek* reached Hengwrt. If it was there in about 1700 when Lhuyd was doing his research, where was it for the preceding 200 years? It appears in Robert Vaughan's list of manuscripts in NLW MS 9095B of 1659.[33] He lists it simply as 'llyfr o iaith Cernyw' ('a book in Cornish'), sandwiched between two volumes of *cywyddau*.[34] The note written in the *Schedule*,[35] 'Connexion betw. Wynne family & Bodewryd?' presumably refers to a possible connection between the Wynnes of Peniarth who aquired the Hengwrt manuscripts and the Wynnes of Bodewryd and the Bodowyr estate (both in Anglesey) and also of the Plas Einion estate in Denbigh-shire.[36] If there was indeed a connection, that might explain how the glossator saw the manuscript itself or a now lost copy of it. If he did see a copy, it must have been a copy of the entire work, as the examples he quotes come from throughout the play.

Of course, this could all be coincidental. There are probably more hapaxes in Cornish than in Welsh because of the paucity of the written records. That confirmation of some of them should be found in a 'new' manuscript should not, perhaps, be surprising. What is striking about Bodewryd 5 is that it supplies the only other example of five or six of them out of a total word-count of only 176 items. If the manuscript was written in Wales, how did the writer come to see other Cornish material? Many of the other glosses do not occur in NLW Peniarth 105, but they do occur in other Middle Cornish manuscripts (such as, perhaps, *gans can* glossed 'with singing' which would seem to be from the *Ordinalia*, *gans can ha mur a eleth*[37] 'with song and many angels' (Nance[38]). It is interesting also, of course, that Bodewryd 5 should have turned up in Anglesey not so far from the Merionethshire home of *Beunans Meriasek*. Could it be that a Cornish speaker in Wales in the latter half of the seventeenth century used *Beunans Meriasek* to help draw up a Cornish word-list? That there was interest in Wales at this time in the Cornish language is demonstrated by the fact that John Davies[39] included an appendix containing Cornish versions of the Lord's Prayer and the Creed in his *Llyfr y Resolusion*, first published in 1632.[40]

SIGNIFICANCE FOR CORNISH LANGUAGE STUDIES

Despite being only two folios in length, this manuscript holds considerable importance for Cornish studies. It supplies a number of new words from an apparently dependable source, although the etymology of some of them evidently requires more work. It also confirms another half dozen previously dubious words or phrases. Of course, it also poses rather more questions than it answers, giving us another ten or so dubious words, and the hurried handwriting is also quite a hindrance.

If the hypothesis about *Beunans Meriasek* is correct, Bodewryd 5 also provides a tantalizing glimpse of some sort of antiquarian interest in Cornish in Wales in the seventeenth century. Bodewryd 5 evidently deserves to be better known.

Appendix: Aberystwyth NLW Bodewryd MS 5D

Key
<u>underline</u> = uncertain reading
superscript = superscript in original
italics = expanded contraction
[ ] = hole in manuscript
~~strike through~~ = deletion
~~?~~ = deletion (deleted letter unclear)
sans serif type = Cornish words

[*folio 1ʳ; left column*]

	de Prudentia.
Ciceronis	Prudentia est inuestigatio <u>reg</u>.
]infinitio	
~~inglish~~	Cornish:
a Man:	Dean:

	pedn:	a head.
	keeren anpedn:	crown of head
	~~b?~~[1] bleaw:	heare:
5	codntall	forhead.
	p<u>o</u>lkeel	nuddock:
	pidnian:	braynes
	lagas: lagasaw.	eye: eyes
	abranz. abran<del>z</del>aw[2]:	eylid. eilidds
10	freegaw: freeg:	nose~~t~~: nostrils[3]
	ganaw:	mouth:
	gwelve. gwelvaw:	lip: lips
	tavas. tavos<u>a</u>w:	tongue: tongues
	skovarn: skovornow:	eare: eares.
15	boah: bohaw:	Cheek: cheeks
	gerne[4]:	Chin:
	barve	beard:
	barve looz:	gray berd
	barve velin:	yellow beard
20	barve deew.	black beard
	barve widne	whitbeard
	Codna:	necke:
	brensan:	Throat:
	skooth. skothow:	shoulder. shoulders
25	stron<u>e</u>ak:	breast:

Tor: bellye:
kine   backe
breah: arme:
geelin: elbowe:
30   Codna breah.   armwrist.
beez   finger
gweenas   naile:
beez meas   thumbe:
beez beean   litell finger
35   beez creese   middle finger
beez Rage.   for finger
beez nessa beea*n*   next to littel

[*right column*]

~~inglishCor~~   ~~Cornish~~
Colan   ha̱rt
liver   asaw
40   light.   skephanz
patchan: buttocke.
morrhas   hip or thigh
pedgleen.   knee:
garr: legg.
45   bell angarr: calf of the legg
goobiddar: ankels
c̱reeb an gar: the shinne~~s~~[5]
goolas an trooz: sole of the foot
burnv̱ghall: instepp:
50   brodn:: brodnaw: teat. teates
trooz tra̱z   foott. feet:
~~a Rib~~[6]
~~a??????~~
azan: a ribb
55   azaw: ribbs:
œ̱ezeelee[7]   loynes & sides
yskar̲ne: bones:
oskarne   a bone:
ke̱har clave: soar sides
60   bl[ ]nacke   fatt:
kirthen: about the loyns

[*folio 2ʳ; see end for key; glossary entries only are numbered*]
De Agitatione.
Agitatio in mentix, quæ nunqua*m* acquiescit, potest nox in Ludijs
rogitationis etiam suie opera*m* nostra*m* continere. Cicero. lib. 1.

[*left column*]

	Crabanaw:	skracching fingers
	Meligas:	an Evill one:
	prensa:	deer byys it
65	Ne veath:	dareth not:
	obskommineiis:	excommunicat
	in Crowwelder:	in crueltye:
	anclotha:.	filthines
	in Yeeselder:	Vnder: lowe.
70	desonowes[8]:	fore pʳºhesied
	ogas:	near.
	aban .reis:	as need must:
	Tebelas:	devils: evil ones
	frappis: frappigy:	shreid torns
75	mee resettias ow holan:	I purpose
	mer yee Rasaw:	much grace
	ow thasaw:.	o[ ] f[ ]hers.
	heb parow: x	without peer
	menithiow:	high hils:
80	fya:	runaway:
	Ebscob:	bisshopp:
	lavar du:	gods word
	procath:	preach
	du: gallosack:	god almight
85	pan deffry:	when thou comst.
	Irris:	commaunded[9]
	heb falladaw:	Wᵗʰout fail
	Caradaw:	deer:

[*right column*]

	worthibmen:	com*m*andment.
90	bagill:	bishops crosse:
	gans can:	with singing.
	mittin a brees:	to morow early
	recommaundias[10]:	did com*a*und
	worthias:	did worship
95	gotha:	suffer.

lorall:		Rag in all:: Rogue:
Cadnas:		messenger:
ompleg:	x	well liking:
mi̱ dor askarn:		lavar teag:
100 worthebaw:	x	answears
the weath:	x	the worse:
bith:		both:
[ ]eevar:	x	endevour:
[ ] a sorhy:		I will pay for:
105 in tha hervith:		in thy steed: x <u>mle</u>
herwith:		after: attending: <u>lea</u>[11]
gorfan an bees:	x	doomesday:
v_n̶adaw[12]:		Camm̱and. ᵃ good wor<u>d</u>
yechas:	x	health:
110 Ro̱wath:	x	worldes Yoy: anbeis
sirvigy:	x	servants: a good word
h̶u̶t̶h̶[13] hunith:		ancestors
x sanstolath:		holines: saintship
x skeeantolath:		wisdome:
115x dee[ ]ntall		vncertayn: stand[
		v̶n̶ vnstedy:

NOTES

1. Two letters deleted, beginning *b-*.
2. *s* and *z* written over one another.
3. *nose* altered to *nost<ril>*; final *s* deleted.
4. *gerne* added later in a different hand with lighter ink.
5. Final *s* deleted.
6. Two deletions, both beginning with *a-*.
7. Possibly a malformed initial *d*, otherwise a ligature, possible *æ*.
8. Could be *n* or *u*.
9. Could be *n* or *u*.
10. Could be *n* or *u*.
11. Added in margin in a very light hand.
12. *n* deleted.
13. *huth* deleted.

ABBREVIATIONS

AB	Edward Lhuyd, *Archæologia Britannica* I., Oxford, 1707.
BL	A manuscript in the British Library, London.
BM	Whitley Stokes, *The Life of St Meriasek, Bishop and Confessor. A Cornish Drama [Beunans Meriasek]*, London, 1872.
Bodl.	A manuscript in the Bodleian Library, Oxford.
Borlase2	William Borlase, *Antiquities Historical and Monumental of . . .*

	Cornwall, second edition, London, 1769 (the Cornish vocabulary is on pp. 415–64).
Br.	Breton.
Co.	Cornish.
CW	Paula Neuss, *The Creacion of the World. A Critical Edition and Translation*, New York and London, 1983. (Previously edited by Whitley Stokes, *Gwreans an bys. The Creation of the World*, London and Edinburgh, 1864. The lineation used by Neuss and Stokes differs slightly: the former is used here unless otherwise stated.)
CWBF	Oliver J. Padel, *The Cornish Writings of the Boson Family*, Redruth, 1973.
GPC	*Geiriadur Prifysgol Cymru*, Cardiff, 1950–.
Llst.	A manuscript in the Llanstephan collection at the National Library of Wales, Aberystwyth.
MC	Whitley Stokes, 'The Passion. A Middle Cornish Poem', *Transactions of the Philological Society* (1860–1), Appendix, 1–100.
ME	Middle English.
Ml.Br.	Middle Breton.
Ml.Co.	Middle Cornish.
Mn.Br.	Modern Breton.
Mn.Co.	Modern Cornish.
Nance	R. Morton Nance, *Gerlyver Noweth Kernewek ha Sawsnek: A New Cornish–English Dictionary* [St Ives, Cornwall], 1938.
NLW	A manuscript in the National Library of Wales, Aberystwyth.
O.Co.	Old Cornish.
OM	'Origo Mundi', first play of the *Ordinalia*. References are to lines.
Ordinalia	The cycle of three plays found in Bodl. 791, published by Edwin Norris, *The Ancient Cornish Drama*, 2 vols, Oxford, 1859.
PC	'Passio Christi', second play of the *Ordinalia*. References are to lines.
PDMC	Richard Gendall, *A Practical Dictionary of Modern Cornish*, Part One, Menheniot, 1997.
Pryce	William Pryce, *Archæologia Cornu-Britannica*, Sherborne, 1790.
RD	'Resurrexio Domini', third play of the *Ordinalia*. References are to lines.
TH	The 'Tregear Homilies' from BL Add. 46397 (from an unpublished transcription by Andrew Hawke).
VC	'Vocabularium Cornicum', the O.Co. vocabulary in BL Cotton Vespasian A XIV, as edited by Eugene van Tassel Graves, *The Old Cornish Vocabulary* (Ph.D. dissertation, Columbia, 1962; published Ann Arbor, 1962). References are to page numbers in Graves.
W.	Welsh.

Andrew Hawke would welcome any comments, corrections, or conjectures (at ach@aber.ac.uk).

ACKNOWLEDGEMENTS

I am indebted to a number of people who have assisted in various ways with the preparation of this article: Dr Oliver Padel and Mr Patrick Donovan checked my initial transcription and made many valuable comments. Mrs Susan Davies of the department of History, University of Wales, Aberystwyth, kindly gave much palaeological assistance and advice on dating, as did Mr Daniel Huws; Mr C.F. Bice identified a number of the words and provided a number of valuable insights. My greatest debt, however, is to Mr Richard Gendall who very kindly provided extensive comparative notes on all the words found in the text, together with many interpretative suggestions. Individual identifications or suggestions of his are noted in the text.

NOTES AND REFERENCES

1. R. Morton Nance, *Gerlyver Noweth Kernewek ha Sawsnek: A New Cornish–English Dictionary*, St Ives, 1938.
2. W.Ll. Davies, *Cornish Manuscripts in the National Library of Wales*, Aberystwyth, 1939.
3. *Schedule of Bodewyrd Manuscripts and Documents deposited in the National Library of Wales by Alfred F. Sotheby, London, October, 1932*, Aberystwyth, 1932.
4. Compare plate 20 (dated 1587) in Giles E. Dawson and Laetitia Kennedy-Skipton, *English Handwriting 1500–1650*, Chichester, 1981.
5. The only possible example in the 'Tregear Homilies' (*c.*1555–8) is *mamb* 'mother' whereas Bodewyrd 5 has *pedn, codntall, pidnian, widne* (< *(g)wyn*), *Codna, pedgleen, brodn(aw), worthibmen* (<*(g)orhemmyn*), and *Cadnas*. The change is quite common in Jordan's *Creacon* (1611), and place-name evidence points to a change in the mid to late sixteenth century.
6. Joseph Wright, *The English Dialect Dictionary*, 4 vols, Oxford, 1896–1905, s.v. *niddock*. See also *Oxford English Dictionary* s.v. *nuddock*, which gives *nuddock* as a sixteenth-century spelling, suggesting that the editors did not consider it to be a dialectal form at that time.
7. John Keigwyn (1641–1716) lived in Mousehole in West Penwith, one of the last strongholds of the Cornish language, and was responsible for translating a number of Cornish texts.
8. Wright, 1896–1905, s.v. *arm-wrist*.
9. Quoted in Brian Murdoch, *Cornish Literature*, Woodbridge, 1993, p. 8. See also, Nicholas Orme, *Nicholas Roscarrock's Lives of the Saints: Cornwall and Devon*, Exeter, 1992, p. 68, where Roscarrock (*c.*1546–50–1633/4) claims, 'This I haue taken out of an olde Cornish Rymthe containing her Legend, translated by one Mr Williams, a Phis[it]ion there, but howe Autentick it is I dare not saye, being loath to comptrowle that which I cannot correct.'
10. Murdoch, 1993, p. 19.

11. I am indebted to Mr Richard Gendall for this suggestion. He also compares *mener/menar*, Borlase2 445, for Mn.Co. *mena* (< *meneth*) 'mountain, hill'.

12. I am indebted to Mr Richard Gendall for this suggestion. Note also the French *cou-de-pied*.

13. Personal correspondence.

14. Personal correspondence. *-gh-* > *-th-* in Modern Cornish, cf. *marth* (< *margh*), *mirth* (< *myrgh*).

15. The MS. reading *-so-* is difficult, but cf. *sole of the foot* (48). Richard Gendall postulates a form *dar+aswonys/aswones* (past participle) = 'reknown', but this would require contraction and metathesis.

16. Personal correspondence.

17. I am indebted to Mr Richard Gendall for this suggestion.

18. Printed in 'On the Antiquity, Variety, and Etimology of Measuring Land in Cornwayl' by 'Anonymous' in Thomas Hearne, *Collection of Curious Discourses*, second edn, 1773 (Vol. I, 195–7) from BL Cott. Faustina E V which has Richard Carew's name. (Ref. in F.E. Halliday, *Richard Carew of Antony: The Survey of Cornwall*, London, 1953, p. 323.)

19. I am indebted to Oliver Padel for this reference.

20. Richard Gendall, personal correspondence.

21. Nance's translation.

22. Although the Preface to his edition of BM, p. v, does make this clear.

23. Ab 262a.

24. Personal correspondence.

25. Davies, 1939, pp. 8–9.

26. Ibid., p. 11; see also R. Morton Nance, 'Cornish Manuscripts in the National Library of Wales', *Journal of the Royal Institution of Cornwall* xxv (1937), p. 3 and *Welsh History Review* vii (1974/5), p. 173 which suggests that it was originally 'Rug No. 2', and, if so, that it was purchased by Griffith Howel Vaughan of Hengwrt and Rug from Evan Williams (bookseller), who purchased it in 1807 from the Sebright Manuscripts.

27. Murdoch, 1993, p. 131.

28. AB [x].

29. AB 225a.

30. AB 222, my translation, the original reads: 'me a gavas an Radn guella a 'm Dyskaz dhort trei levar skrefyz Kernûak, gorryz en ma dhûla gen . . . *Sr. Jonathan Trelauny* Ispak *Kar-êsk*; ha . . . *John Anstis Esq*; . . . ha 'n raglaveryz *Mr. Keiguyn*, neb dre Orphennyaz an raghanuyz Ispak a 'ryg traylia an levrouma dhan Zouznak; hag yu heb paro vêth, barnyz an skientèka a 'n ûz nei en Tavazeth *Kernûak*.'

31. AB 224.

32. I am indebted to Mr Daniel Huws for this information.

33. On Robert Vaughan, *c*.1592–1667, see E.D. Jones, *Journal of the Merioneth Historical and Record Society*, i (1949) pp. 21–30 and Richard Morgan, ibid. viii (1980) pp. 397–408.

34. NLW MS 9095B, 83. Vaughan also had a copy of Richard Carew's *Survey of Cornwall* (1602), which he lists on p. 86. Carew's work contains some

remarks about the Cornish dramas, and some words in Cornish, but none of these occur in Bodewryd 5.

35. See above.
36. See *Guide to the Department of Manuscripts and Records*, National Library of Wales, Aberystwyth, 1994, p. 54 and p. 171, which also mentions the connection with Edward Wynne (d. 1755), Chancellor of Hereford and with Humphrey Humphreys (1648–1712), bishop of Bangor and later of Hereford, one of Lhuyd's benefactors.
37. RD 515.
38. Nance Bequest (uncatalogued), Royal Institution of Cornwall, Truro.
39. John Davies of Mallwyd, *c.*1567–1644, one of the leading Welsh scholars of the Renaissance, best known as a lexicographer, grammarian, and translator of the Bible.
40. A translation of *The First Book of the Christian Exercise Appertayning to Resolusion*, by Robert Parsons.

THE MAKING OF A MYTH: CORNISH MINERS IN THE NEW WORLD IN THE EARLY NINETEENTH CENTURY

Sharron P. Schwartz

INTRODUCTION

outside the rock-ribbed peninsula of Cornwall, all over the world, he [the Cornishman] has taught men how to dig the ore.[1]

One might be forgiven for suspecting more than a hint of filio-pietism in the above words of Dr T.A. Rickard, a prominent geologist and mining expert, who spent many years in Northern America in the late nineteenth and early twentieth centuries. He was, after all, of Cornish extraction. Yet Rickard is not alone in his observation of the Cornish contribution to the international metalliferous mining industry. Writing about the inter-relationship between British capital investment and the expansion of the mining in Western America, Clarke Spence articulates the prominent role the Cornish came to occupy, as deep lode mining took off in the decade following the gold-rush of 1848–9: 'It was the Cornish "expert", self-trained and uninhibited, who formed the backbone of practical mine management during the entire period [the 1860s to the early twentieth century] and was foremost in promoting, inspecting, and publicizing western mines.'[2]

Moreover, in this development Cornish engineering prowess made no small contribution. 'Outlandish, huge, awkward, expensive to install, and very complex, requiring constant inspection and management', the Cornish beam engine epitomized 'backyard engineering' according to Roger Lescohier.[3] However, he concedes that there was, in the 1850s and 60s, no comparable pump and without it the development of deep lode metalliferous mining in California might have been delayed for nearly half a century.

By the 1860s the Cornish appeared to have achieved something of a cult status in mining fields across North America and beyond. In the recent 'new Cornish historiography' this has been dubbed the 'myth of "Cousin Jack" ',[4] the Cornishman having gone down in mining lore world-wide as the hard rock miner *par excellence*. Yet to date, little attention has been paid to how the Cornish achieved this following and there has been scant critical analysis examining whether or not it was an accolade that was truly deserved.[5] The mines of Cornwall were predominantly of tin and copper. But contemporary accounts of the Cornish miners arriving in the Western United States in the 1850s suggest that as well as being accomplished hard rock miners, able to bore and blast through difficult ground, many were already well versed in the extraction and dressing of complex ores of gold and silver.[6] Such skills could not have evolved from their industrial experience in Cornwall alone.

This article will chart and attempt to explain the rise to world-wide prominence of the Cornish miner by exploring the genesis of the international, integrated, modern mining economy in the early nineteenth century, with its attendant fluid, complex labour market. The birthplace of this phenomenon, this paper contends, was the New World. In the ancient mining regions across South and Central America, the right to the title of best hard rock miner in the world was bitterly contested, as the Cornish were forced to compete in the expanding metalliferous mining labour market with miners imported from Continental Europe and with Ibero-Americans. The mines of the New World therefore acted as a training ground for the Cornish, where their skills as miners and engineers were rigorously questioned and tested. Having emerged apparently strengthened from their industrial experience in the mines of Latin America in the early nineteenth century, Cornish miners and engineers played on their growing cult status to ensure that they secured the best jobs in the expanding global mining labour market. But whether or not they deserved their legendary status continued to be contested, as this article will reveal.

A NEW WORLD ORDER: THE BRITISH CAPITALIZATION OF LATIN AMERICAN MINING

Before proceeding further, it is necessary to explain the background to the Cornish arrival on Latin American mines in the early nineteenth century. The post-Napoleonic period had witnessed the collapse of Iberian hegemony in South and Central America, creating a power vacuum that had provided the opportunity for the peoples of Latin America to attain a degree of self-determination. Inspired by heroic figures such as Simon Bolívar, *El Libertador*, Latin America was gripped by revolutionary fervour, and battles raged for many years as the people fought for emancipation from Iberian rule. Britain had long cast a covetous eye on Latin America, the markets of which the Spanish and Portuguese had jealously guarded, and numerous British subjects fought alongside the Latin Americans during the Wars of Emancipation. With the opening of Brazilian ports to foreign trade in 1808, and for Britain, the highly advantageous Treaty of Navigation and Commerce two years later with Brazil, local newspapers had been following events in Latin America closely. The *Royal Cornwall Gazette* commented in 1825 that 'trade with the South American states is in itself a subject of the greatest interest in England . . . we view it therefore as opening a wide field for commercial enterprise and extensive commerce'.[7]

But the long years of war had devastating consequences for the economies of the fledgling democracies of Latin America, particularly the mining sector. Mines that had once been the envy of the world lay derelict, their workings flooded and their equipment plundered, the mining towns and villages depopulated, and to compound matters further, Hispanic financiers fearing for their lives had fled to Europe with their capital. Latin American mine owners, alarmed at the decline of their once great industry, and believing the resumption of mining to be the cornerstone of rebuilding their countries' economies, requested financial aid from Britain, relaxing restrictions that had previously barred 'foreigners' from involvement in the mining sector.[8] Britain, enjoying considerable prosperity as a result of the industrial revolution, was the only country with a capital surplus capable of financing such costly enterprises, as the Directors and shareholders of the Franco-Mexican Company discovered. Realizing that they had little hope of completing arrangements in France they turned their attention to England, where 'a greater abundance of money, and unrestrained intercourse with the New World, would induce capitalists to become interested in a concern which promised the most brilliant success'.[9]

In Britain, the end of the Napoleonic Wars had witnessed deflation and depression compounded by a lack of specie. A dwindling stock of precious metals, caused primarily by the collapse of mining in the New World, created a downward spiral of prices that had worrying implications for British domestic and foreign trade.[10] However, it was widely believed that this trend could be reversed by a resumption of production in precious metals, and Britain seized the opportunity of gaining a legitimate commercial foothold in Latin America. The British stock market went wild in 1824–5, as people raced to buy shares in Latin American Government bonds and in joint stock companies, their cupidity matched only by their gullibility. Of the 127 new companies added to the London Stock Exchange, 44 were mining companies; a significant fact, as practically none had existed before. Moreover, over 50 per cent of these new companies were formed to work mines in Latin America. This period can be said to mark the real commencement of British investments in independent and semi-independent foreign nations.[11]

Yet the prospectuses of many of the proposed mining enterprises were based not on scientific grounds, but on dubious and highly embroidered reports of, for example, the German, Baron Von Humboldt, who travelled widely in Latin America and was, therefore, considered something of an expert. Such reports contained two basic points. First, that the once rich mines of Latin America would be so again, with the aid of British capital. Second, and more importantly, through the introduction of new technology such as existed in the 'work shop of the world', combined with skilled labour and scientific know-how, a modern metalliferous mining industry could be developed.

In order to acquire the skilled labour to revitalize derelict mines across South and Central America, the British-backed companies looked primarily to Cornwall. Here centuries of deep lode mining had resulted in the adaptation, acceleration and perfection of European mining and engineering methods. Cornwall as an industrial region probably possessed the best European mining technology known at the time. Nothing epitomized this more than the remarkable genesis of the steam engine, used to dewater Cornwall's deep mines. The expiry of the Boulton and Watt patent in 1801 had ushered in a period of creativity, when engineers, most famously Richard Trevithick, had pushed the frontiers of steam engine technology beyond what contemporary physics said was theoretically possible. The result was the high-pressure Cornish engine, which importantly, had already proved itself in the Peruvian Cordilleras, when in 1816 several engines were set to work at the Cerro de Pasco Mines by the Pasco Mining Company, and overseen by Richard Trevithick.[12] This transatlantic venture, the first of its kind in the New World, was initially successful, Caldcleugh noting that the Pasco Mining Company saw a dramatic rise in silver production figures for Cerro de Pasco as soon as the Cornish engines came into operation.[13] People in Britain were conversant with the Cornish system of mining and its attendant technology, and, with this allied to large amounts of British capital, they could see no reason for the failure of the proposed transatlantic ventures, a feeling captured in the prospectus of the Guanaxuato Mining Association: 'But for want of Capital, proper Machinery, and Implements for Mining, as well as the Cornish Science, [the trustees in Mexico] have been unable to work them to the extent to which they are capable.'[14]

While the mines of Latin America were in decline, by contrast, those of Cornwall were booming as the copper mining industry approached its zenith. Here there appears to be an apparent paradox. Why would Cornish miners and artisans be enticed overseas at a time when the mines of Cornwall were doing so well? Historically, Cornish miners had shown a propensity to migrate in search of better wages and conditions, a phenomenon that Brooke has traced back to the mid eighteenth century, with miners from the western mining districts moving eastwards within Cornwall and onto the mines of neighbouring Devonshire.[15] At the turn of the nineteenth century Cornish miners were to be found in several metalliferous mining regions across the British Isles.[16] When advertisements and offers of work in the mines of Latin America began to occur in the early 1820s, Cornish miners and artisans, previously used to travelling within Britain in search of the best wages and conditions, found work offers for Latin American mines hugely attractive.

First, they were attracted because the wages advertised were in many cases far higher than anything that could have been earned in Cornwall, or indeed, in many other metalliferous mining regions of Britain. For example, the average mine captain's annual wage in Cornwall would have been in the region of £300, but the Bolivar Mining Association offered the fabulous sum of £1,200 to a captain to manage their Aroa Mines in modern-day Venezuela. Second, because the system of payment—for a fixed salary with regular quarterly disbursements paid directly to a Cornish bank for the maintenance of their families—offered the prospect of financial security for perhaps the first time, for work as a 'tributer' was notoriously responsible for great variations in wages. Third, the development of mines across Latin America held out the prospect to ambitious men the opportunity of being able to climb far higher up the mining hierarchy than they could have done had they remained in Cornwall. Last, almost a third of the mining companies established in 1824–5 had Cornish Directors, representatives from some of the most powerful industrial families in Cornwall, including those of Williams and Fox. To this list must be added mining doyen, John Taylor. Although not of Cornish extraction, his name was synonymous with Cornish mining after his incredible success with Consolidated Mines in Gwennap, which he turned from a failure into bonanza. These men were responsible for hand-picking the mining captains and engineers who were to manage the mines of Latin

America, and they in turn were given considerable licence to select the most skilled and reliable men known to them.

Thus the early 1820s witnessed the transatlantic migration of the industrial revolution and the birth of the modern, integrated, international mining economy with its attendant capital and labour markets, in which the Cornish played a high profile role from the very beginning.[17] It also heralded the genesis of the remittance phenomenon that assumed great importance in Cornwall as the nineteenth century wore on, and also the beginning of the much-discussed 'Cousin Jack Network'. This informal system of recommendation famously enabled the Cornish to edge out rival ethnic groups and to dominate the international mining scene for much of the nineteenth and early twentieth centuries.

FIASCOS AND FAILURES: INITIAL SETBACKS
The birth of the modern international mining economy was less than auspicious. Many of the fledgling mining companies set up at the height of the speculation boom lasted only briefly. The main reason for their sudden decline was the collapse of the London Stock Market in early 1826. The root cause of this debacle was the flotation process of the Latin American Government bonds that allowed merchant bankers and swindlers to rig the market.[18] When irregularities came to light, capital was suddenly withdrawn. This resulted in only a fraction of the authorized capital for the mining companies ever being paid in. Rippy estimates total losses probably amounted to over £3 million sterling.[19] With the industry starved of capital, casualties among the mining companies were numerous.

But other explanatory factors have also to be considered. The very nature of the enterprises, involving the movement of men and complicated machinery half-way around the world, created logistical problems. Many of the mines were situated in inaccessible and remote regions, poorly served by roads or even navigable rivers. In Colombia for example, there was a shortage of wheeled vehicles to carry equipment, and miners arriving in Mexico in 1825 had to build a road over which the imported steam engines could be transported from the coast inland to the mines of Real del Monte. Moreover, information contained in the mining prospectuses was, in many cases, revealed to be little more than humbug. Mines often situated at incredible distances apart were purchased at exorbitant prices by European Commissioners who knew little about their true geology. Agents and workmen were dispatched even before the ink was dry on contracts granting British companies mining rights. Misinformation abounded and was merely compounded by doing business in the cavalier atmosphere of Latin

Table 1: British mining companies which were known to have been formed to operate in Latin America in the years 1824–1825

Name of Company	Country of operation	Capital		Cornish directors	Failed before 1830
		£ authorized	£ paid up		
Anglo-Chilean	Chile	1,500,000	120,000		x
Anglo-Colombrian	Colombia	1,500,000	75,000		x
Anglo-Mexican	Mexico	1,000,000	750,000		
Anglo-Peruvian	Peru	600,000	30,000		x
Bolaños	Mexico	200,000	87,500	✓	
Bolívar	Venezuela*	500,000	50,000		
Brazilian	Brazil	2,000,000	20,000	✓	
Castello	Brazil	1,000,000	50,000		x
Chilian	Chile	1,000,000	75,000	✓	x
Chilian and Peruvian	Chile & Peru	1,000,000	50,000	✓	x
Colombian	Colombia	1,000,000	150,000	✓	
Famatina	Argentina	250,000	50,000		x
General South American	Primarily Brazil	2,000,000	100,000		
Guanajuato	Mexico	400,000	6,000		x
Haytian	Haiti	1,000,000	50,000	✓	x
Imperial Brazilian	Brazil	1,000,000	200,000	✓	
Mexican	Mexico	1,000,000	150,000		x
Pasco-Peruvian	Peru	1,000,000	150,000	✓	x
Potosí-La Paz & Peruvian	Peru & Bolivia	1,000,000	50,000		x
Real del Monte	Mexico	400,000	325,000	✓	
Río de la Plata	Argentina	1,000,000	75,000	✓	x
Tarma	Peru	200,000	5,000		
Tlalpuxahua	Mexico	400,000	120,000		
United Chilian	Chile	500,000	50,000	✓	x
United Mexico	Mexico	1,240,000	775,000		
United Provinces	Central America*	1,500,000	15,000		x
Total		**24,190,000**	**3,508,500**		

Source: Main details extracted from Henry English, *A General Guide to the Companies formed for Working Foreign Mines*, (London, 1825).

*Venezuela was then a part of the state of Gran Colombia; the activities of the United Provinces company were focused on the Princias Unidas del Centro América: Guatemala, Honduras, El Salvador, Nicaragua and Costa Rica. In addition to the above was the highly disorganized Catorce Company, Mexico, which also failed.

America, where corrupt local officials were apt to prevaricate, as the Río de la Plata Mining Association discovered. Upon arrival in Argentina, its workforce of Cornish miners was sent back home because it had failed to secure the mines it had planned to work, due to a volte-face by the local government.[20]

Yet another reason must also be considered—one that is explicit enough in the mining reports and contemporary literature—and that is the suitability of the labour force selected by the companies both before and after the crash. Although miners from the North of England, Scotland, Wales, Ireland, France, Spain, Germany, Hungary and America were recruited, the Cornish were numerically stronger than these ethnic labour groups and therefore came in for much criticism.[21] But was this deserved?

THE CORNISH MINER CRITICIZED

For those companies that survived the stock market crash, or were created in the aftermath, caution was the byword. Since so many shareholders had lost or seen no return on their capital when the bubble burst in 1826, reports in the *Mining Journal* thereafter reveal a constant suspicion of managerial and/or company impropriety. This included fears of bogus assays, the issuing of inflated or misleading reports of the mineral potential of a mine, or managerial attempts to misinform shareholders by concealing the truth about the working of the mine or of the competence and behaviour of its workforce. As many of the mine managers and senior staff were Cornish, they bore the brunt of the criticism.

One of the most vociferous opponents of the Cornish was former Royal Engineers officer, Captain Francis Bond Head, who had been sent out to Argentina by the Río de la Plata Mining Association in 1825, an enterprise that ended in failure. Referring in 1827 to the debacles of 1825–6 when many of the fledgling mining companies collapsed, he sarcastically questioned the wisdom of bringing Cornishmen to Latin America. For as well as being unsuited to a tropical climate, he considered the Cornish to be insufficiently qualified. '[W]hile the natives were smiling at the Cornish *tinners*, who were standing on the sunny sides of the street, devoured by mosquitoes, and cutting water-melons the wrong way', he remarked, 'the governments began to ask for *loans!*'[22] And this apprehension was echoed by Strasbourg-born Charles Lambert in his letter to the directors of the Chilian Mining Association in London in 1825. He noted that he considered the Cornish of little use until they had been in Chile for some time, commenting that 'they are still misled by the different mineral deposits in this country'.[23] Moreover, one of the mining captains, Tregonning, presented specimens which he thought contained tin ores, such as were found in Cornwall, only to discover he was in error.[24]

Here Lambert, educated at the École Polytechnique in Paris, where he acquired an excellent knowledge of mining, metallurgy and geology, had put his finger on the basic limitation of the Cornish miner. They were beyond doubt, good practical miners, but few had obtained any specific schooling in the principles of geology, physics, engineering or chemistry which would have provided them with an underlying theoretical knowledge that would have enabled them to adapt to new circumstances such as were encountered in Latin America.[25] Moreover, reports of their poor temperament, propensity to insubordination and lawlessness were commented upon on numerous occasions. Former officer and Scotsman, Captain James Vetch, of the Real Del Monte Mining Company, Mexico, came to dislike the Cornish intensely, and even proposed replacing them by drafting in labourers from Ireland, Scotland and Northern England. In his estimation the Cornish were not the 'steady and submissive' workers he had hoped for, but 'the most difficult we have to manage . . . and the most ungrateful'.[26] More damning still were the comments of yet another military man, Captain Andrews, of the Chilian and Peruvian Mining Association who wrote scathingly of the Cornish. In the light of their constant squabbling with a group of London labourers and Welsh miners, he too wished to replace the Cornish miners with Germans, whom he considered to be:

> more hardy, patient, and enduring, and far less nice and punctilious about trifles. Cornishmen are intractable if put the least out of their way. They harmonize together 'one and all', but not with strangers; and their dispositions and habits by no means correspond with the tried, placid tempers and dispositions of the South Americans.[27]

At the Zacatecas and Fresnillo Company's operations at Fresnillo, Mexico, the Cornish labour force had caused much trouble, as the mining Captain, Edward Roberts of Breage, was forced to admit in a letter to Nicholas Harvey, of Harvey's Foundry, Hayle in 1839. 'In the last group of men sent out by the company', he remarked, 'there were but four steady men . . . the remainder of the party has been drunk, fighting and discontented and pay no regard to there [*sic*] duty'.[28]

Centuries of successfully working the mines in Cornwall on a system akin to self employment had conspired to give the Cornish miner the 'frank and blunt manners' quoted in the 1842 Children's Employment Commission, often mistaken for insolence. A 'character of independence—something American' therefore existed amongst the Cornish population.[29] Used to working under their own terms in their native land, and in ways that had been handed down from father to son over generations, Cornish miners did not react well to having the hours and nature of their work strictly regulated in the mines of Latin America. And especially not by military men who often knew very little about mining. Traditionally their own bosses, many were accused of acquiring ideas above their station. This attitude was only reinforced as they were usually given jobs supervising natives or Negro slaves, as Captain Munday of the National Brazilian Mining Association observed in 1830:

> I would recommend in future, if any more [men] are sent out to this country, that there should be a little discrimination between men, in consequence of some of the last party not being so civil as could be wished for. In fact some come out under the wrong ideas, expecting to be captains instead of workmen.[30]

Yet more damning was their failure to deviate greatly from the traditional Cornish *modus operandi* which had, according to Mr Debercken of the National Brazilian Mining Association, contributed to the failure of the Coaces Mine in Brazil:

> The reason why [the company] had not been rich and made fortunes like the former proprietors was [because] the English miners were too proud to take a lesson from the Brazilians, who were used to work the gold mines. They [the 'English'] worked the Brazilian mines as if they were tin [or] copper.[31]

Indeed, the sudden introduction of the Cornish 'tribute' system of mining caused periodic mayhem in Mexican mines in the 1820s and 30s, as native miners struck and even rioted in defence of their customary rights and for the reintroduction of the age-old 'partido' system.[32] This provided a stark reminder to the Cornish management at the mines of Real del Monte, Zacatecas and Guanajuato of the dangers of trying to graft Cornish mining methods onto an industry as old and equally as proud as their own.

By the 1850s doubts were being raised periodically in the *Mining Journal* as to the competence of Cornish miners and geologists. Lying next to the Island of Cuba, where fabulously rich copper mines had been developed, Jamaica provides a perfect example. Shareholders in Britain were hopeful that the same mineral wealth would be discovered there, but the beginning of mining in Jamaica was not altogether auspicious and the role played by the Cornish thereafter constantly questioned. A scheme to work copper mines contiguous to Kingston in 1842 foundered after a sum of around £3,000 had been expended sending miners and tools from Cornwall to the Mount Vernon area. Behind the ill-fated scheme was John Drew, a native of Cornwall, who, by his own admission 'was not a professed miner'.[33] In 1853 Philip Lawrence, Chairman of the Jamaica Mining Association, commented in the *Mining Journal*: 'If we may venture an opinion, we would say that some time must elapse . . . before the English miners will have obtained sufficient knowledge of the geological features of this island to work our mines to the best advantage.'[34] Moreover, the Metcalfe Mining Company's failure was in no small part attributed to the incompetence of its Cornish mining captains. The mine reports were found to be inaccurate and the appointment of Captain Henry Clemes was stated to have been 'money thrown away'. Captain Thomas Lean, initially suspected of deliberately trying to deceive the shareholders, was later exonerated, but his mine management capabilities were found to be sorely lacking.[35]

Consequently, the reports and surveys of Cornish mining captains and even distinguished geologists such as W.J. Henwood were questioned.[36] Henwood examined several mining setts in Jamaica in 1854, none of which he considered very promising. Yet the directors saw fit to question his judgement, contemporary opinion reported to have been that 'Cornish captains do not understand the nature of mining operations in that colony'. 'I hope to refute the calumnies which have been heaped promiscuously upon the West Indian mines', wrote Englishman Thomas Austin, a Bristol-based geologist in 1854:

> I am quite cognisant of the fact that mining captains from Cornwall have been *prejudiced* in their *opinions*, from their not finding lodes . . . similar to their own country, and have condemned . . . [Jamaica] wholesale on that account.
>
> A similar instance of bigoted prejudice was perpetrated upon the Irish mines, *en masse*, by Cornish captains. The best and most practical illustration of the fallacy of judging from analogy, and refutation of their opinions, lies in the inspection of the present returns from Irish mines.[37]

And Jamaica was not an isolated case. In 1853 the Directors of the Veraguas [West Granada] Gold and Silver Mining Company had mining captain, James Eddy, and a staff of Cornish miners reputedly highly experienced in the mines of South America, recommended to them. But Eddy's appointment at the company's mines on the Isthmus of Panama was reported to have been a disaster. He and his Cornish mining captain were accused of incompetent management which resulted in the death from fever or intemperance of many of the workforce, as well as submitting bogus assays and false reports. 'Mr Eddy, either from apprehension of the climate, or other causes, stated that the ores were too poor to pay, and recommended abandonment of the undertaking.' Eddy and his staff of Cornishmen found themselves dismissed and replaced by miners from Freiberg, Germany, who, scientifically educated, were considered to be vastly superior miners.[38]

Yet considerable controversy persisted over this affair; the editor of the *Mining Journal* had eventually to call a halt to the correspondence. Doubts were cast on the integrity of the company, and the officers—English and Americans—were accused of having a vendetta against the Cornish miners because of Eddy's unfavourable report of the Fort Bowen Mine.[39] This is a direct contrast to the accusation regarding the tendency of Cornish mining captains to submit reports which were engineered to suit their employer's views, the so-called 'London schemer', as voiced in the *Mining Journal* in 1853. Inaccurate reports would not trouble the Cornish mine captain, noted the London writer with the pseudonym *Fair Play*, 'for he is well aware that as soon as the present bubble bursts there is always some scheme afloat in which they can row together'.[40] On the payroll of companies, many of whose shareholders were eternal optimists when it came to the prospect of foreign mining fields, Cornish mine managers often found themselves in unenviable positions. The truth about the potential of some overseas mines was often not what the shareholders or board of directors wished to hear, particularly when thousands of pounds had been expended on a venture condemned as worthless. Reports by individuals like *Fair Play* provide evidence of the intent to discredit the international integrity of the Cornish miner.

The passage of time proved the accuracy of the Cornish reports of both the Panamanian mines and those of Jamaica, none of which ever yielded the much-hyped and hoped-for riches. Such episodes reveal how bitterly contested was the Cornish right to be considered the most experienced and accomplished hard rock miners in the emerging international mining labour market.

THE MAKING OF A MYTH
Much evidence can be provided to challenge the adverse reports of Cornish miners' skills, attitude and competency, outlined above. It is true that at the beginning of the mining enterprises in the New World, the Cornish came across geology, such as the alien 'jagotinga'

formations found in the gold fields of Minas Gerais, Brazil, which were particularly challenging. However, although initially deficient in knowledge of gold or silver mining, there was much the Cornish miner could offer the redundant mining industry of Latin America. The first was steam technology, harnessed to dewater workings hundreds of fathoms deep, or to operate machinery that dispensed with human or animal labour—effecting huge financial savings. The second was their ability to sink shafts deep below the surface, blast and bore miles of tunnels through solid rock, timber difficult ground, and organize such workings on a massive scale, both safely and efficiently.

The introduction of steam technology revolutionized mining in some Latin America mining fields, but not all. The fuel-hungry engines were not suitable in areas where there was difficulty in obtaining coal, or a shortage of alternative fuel such as timber or peat. Here age-old Ibero-American techniques persisted, with ores being raised on labourers' backs, dewatering effected by *malacates*, and the crushing of ores carried out by *arrastres*.[41] Mexico provides a classic example, where steam technology was received on its deep and flooded mines with mixed results. At the Bolaños mines, 44 *malacates* employing 2,000 mules (50 to each) overseen by 384 drivers, stable boys and others, had cost, between 1791 and 1798, £79,552 each year. By the late 1820s the mine was being drained by one steam engine and one waterwheel. At Real del Monte, the expense of drainage by steam was about £8,000 a year, effecting an annual saving of £62,000 over that of *malacates*, although the mine was being worked at far greater depths.[42] The companies of Tlalpujahua, Anglo-Mexican and Mexican followed that of Real del Monte in importing steam engines. In fact Duport maintained that had it not been for steam, the mines of Fresnillo could not have been worked at all.[43] However, after installing steam engines in 1825 at their Guanajuato mines when there was a shortage of mules to work *malacates*, the Anglo-Mexican Company was forced by a lack of good timber to become primarily dependent on Mexican methods.[44]

The mines of Cuba utilized steam on a large scale, the engines for the copper mines of the Cobre Mining Association and Royal Santiago Mining Company being cast at Harvey's Foundry, Hayle, and the Fox-Williams Foundry at Perranwell, respectively, and the coal imported from South Wales. But in Chile, steam engines never made a huge impact; only one mine in twenty-three was worked by steam in the 1870s, it being far cheaper to use *apires* (workmen hired to convey the ore) in fairly dry mines worked on shallow copper deposits.[45] When Cornishmen introduced this technology to Bolivian mines in the 1870s, they encountered considerable logistical problems in obtaining and transporting water across the Atacama Desert to maintain the engines' boilers.

In Brazil and Colombia steam technology also made very little impact, as much of the dewatering, stamping and amalgamation was effected through a sophisticated system of waterwheels. However, harnessing the power of water to dewater mine workings and operate surface machinery had also been perfected over centuries in Cornwall, and coexisted with steam engines on many mines in the early nineteenth century. Cornish carpenters and blacksmiths were employed in great numbers to design, make and install the huge waterwheels across Latin America. For as Eakin reminds us, it was the British who employed waterwheel technology on an unprecedented 'rational, large-scale and systematic basis' on for example, the gold mines of Brazil.[46]

The Cornish, therefore, achieved a very visible presence at the surface of Latin American mines. The steam engines, some attaining cylinder sizes of 80 inches, accommodated in their characteristic engine houses were a very visible sign of British industrial prowess and must have left quite an impression on Latin American miners.[47] Moreover, the workmen to erect, install, and thereafter maintain these monstrous engines were usually Cornish and with mystagogic zeal they jealously guarded them, arguing that only they had the necessary skills to operate such complex and complicated machines. In this way the Cornish created and then perpetuated the myth of their engineering genius, kept the best-paid, most highly skilled and responsible engineering positions for themselves, and were able to keep out rival ethnic groups.

But in the field of amalgamation and smelting of silver ores, the Cornish had rather less success. The traditional Cornish mode of dressing had failed with the silver ores at Real del Monte, Mexico, where they could not improve on the 'patio' system of silver amalgamation. This remained the preserve of Ibero-American miners who had perfected the technology introduced by the Spanish centuries before.[48] It was not until the introduction of the cyanide treatment of ores at the turn of the twentieth century by American companies that significant advances in the refining of silver ores were made. As noted earlier, German miners were to be found in many mining regions across South and Central America in the early nineteenth century where they mounted a strong challenge to the Cornish for the right to be considered the best hard rock miners. In Mexico in particular the Cornish encountered stiff opposition from German refiners and smelters who were experienced in the metallurgy of silver ores. The Germans introduced many incremental changes in the smelting of silver ores that improved methods that were found to be 'superior to those before practised in Mexico'.[49] Consequently, Germans were engaged in most of the silver concentration departments in Mexico. For example, the United Mexican Mining Association mentions that Thomas Widder, who had received a regular education in Germany as a miner and metallurgist, had been appointed to a managerial position overseeing the reduction of silver ores at the company's hacienda.[50]

The Cornish failing with silver ore dressing was somewhat compensated by their successful innovations in gold and copper refining. In the Colombian gold mines in the 1830s for instance, Captain John Carthew had introduced a new system of dressing in a Cornish *tye* (a long trough to separate roughs from slimes by washing). This had 'succeeded beyond expectation', resulting in a reduction of gold loss from 60–70 per cent to approximately 37 per cent. 'It is now certain that dressing in Cornish *tyes* offers decided advantages over every other method hitherto employed', commented manager, Mr Bodmer, 'and that it must be introduced without delay.'[51] And in the Aroa copper mines of the Bolívar Mining Company, Venezuela, Cornishmen in the reduction department made significant advances in the calcination process of copper ore.[52]

But it was their overall knowledge and great experience of deep lode mining, immortalized in the names of countless shafts, winzes, lodes, adits and cross cuts on Latin American mining plans, which made the Cornish stand out above their ethnic rivals. 'English labourers are less expensive in proportion to the work performed', commented Captain Cotesworth of the Cata Branca Mine in Brazil, 'and preferable in every respect to other nations or Negroes.'[53] Echoing this sentiment was the mine manager of the Colombian Mining Association. He had introduced the tribute system, finding that the Cornish miners could work hard and difficult stopes far more cheaply and efficiently than native labourers, who were 'but inferior miners, being but little accustomed to blast and break the ground'.[54] At the Imperial Brazilian Mining Association's mines at Gongo Soco, G.V. Duval agreed that the native workforce 'cannot supersede the necessity of a supply of good miners from England'.[55] He was later forced to admit to the board of directors: 'I am afraid that it would never be possible to render you entirely independent of English labour and of home engagement.'[56] Indeed, the general policy of this and other Brazilian companies gradually became to encourage miners' wives and families to migrate from Cornwall to settle in the mining villages of Minas Gerais, thus breeding the next generation of Cornish miners *in situ*. Thriving 'little Cornwalls' were created where a way of life reminiscent of Cornwall was carried on.[57]

Captain Sampson Waters of the Copiapó Mining Company was constantly frustrated in his efforts to increase productivity in his mines in Chile. 'We have several places in this mine [El Chico] where good ore could be broken out to advantage with proper hands', he grumbled to the board of directors in London, 'but, if taken out by the native miners, there will be a great sacrifice; they appear to have no idea or care in anything, which is the chief thing wanted in extracting rich and soft ore.'[58] Consequently, he regularly requested fresh and experienced hands from Cornwall. By 1854, following the discovery of gold in California and the development of mines elsewhere and with these new enterprises holding out very inviting prospects for would-be workers, it was becoming harder to recruit Cornish miners. For they were said to be in great demand, as the Royal Santiago Mining Company found when it required fresh hands to develop its property in Cobre, Cuba.[59] It appears that the myth of Cousin Jack, hard rock miner, *par excellence*, had by this time begun to take hold. This was a tremendous coup for the Cornish who were not slow to see the global benefits of creating their mythological status in the mines of Latin America and then perpetuating this as the international mining labour market expanded.

CONCLUSION
There can be little doubt that upon their arrival in Latin America in the early 1820s, the limitations of the 'practical' Cornish miner were exposed. 'While as practical men, the miners of England have everywhere shown themselves the first in the world, yet their scientific attainments are undoubtedly deficient', noted the *Mining Journal*, adding that it was not wise to be blind to the value of science. Gold working in particular, as it was then carried out, was a new study, the writer stated, and mere adherence to the rule of thumb, or reliance on age-old tradition derived from practice and experience alone, so cherished in Cornwall, was not enough.[60] In the emerging, highly competitive international mining labour market, the Cornish miner encountered stiff opposition from the German, whose aptitude, skill and practical ability, coupled with his superior scientific knowledge, made him a candidate for the accolade of the best hard rock miner in the world. But however deficient the Cornish were in the underlying theoretical knowledge of science and geology, working alongside native miners they soon became conversant with New World mining methods and new geological formations, acquiring fresh skills which they then blended with their own considerable mining knowledge. The mines of Latin America acted, therefore, as a training ground for the Cornish that bred a new generation of super miners, able to understand

and work the most complex mineral bodies anywhere in the world. 'Whatever might be the predilection for foreigners, the English miner has not only held his own against foreigners at home, but has successfully exerted himself in Spain, in Norway, and in various points of Europe', sounded the *Mining Journal* in 1853. 'If the Spaniard began the exploration of the Americas, the Englishman and his tribe have now carried it out. In our mining districts; Cuba, Jamaica, Mexico, Colombia, California, Brazil, Peru and Chili, are now as familiar as Redruth, Swansea or Alston.'[61]

But the Cornish were not blind to the benefits of marketing themselves as the world's best miners. This was achieved by virtue of the initial set-up of the international mining economy, when Britain financed the majority of the mining enterprises in Latin America. There in large numbers, the Cornish thereafter appointed themselves to the best-paid and high-profile jobs in the emerging mining labour market using what is known as the 'Cousin Jack' network.[62] By 1853, even mining companies in Germany were importing Cornish miners who were considered vastly superior to the Germans themselves.[63] By the mid 1850s most mining concerns across the New World were staffed by Cornish mining captains, agents, engineers and foremen, as Clark Spence's observation reminded us at the beginning of this article. Yet this informal system of recommendation was open to abuse and did not always result in the appointment of sufficiently qualified men, which perhaps accounts for at least some of the criticism that continued to be levelled at the Cornish. Captain Roberts of Breage, manager at the mines of Zacatecas and Fresnillo, Mexico, had brought this fact to the attention of Nicholas Harvey in 1839. He implored Harvey to enlist a group of men from Cornwall whom he knew to be reliable, adding that it was not the best policy to 'take [men] in through the interest of others'.[64] Indeed, forged letters of recommendation were not unheard of, particularly when generous wages were in the offing. James Reynolds of Redruth, acting as agent in Cornwall for the Cuban Cobre Mining Company, refused two references of a young engineer who had come to him 'strongly recommending himself', and saying that he could get 'good testimonials from his employers'. However, he brought only two papers, which Reynolds was 'disposed to think were complete forgeries'.[65] Hence some of the criticism the Cornish received was probably deserved. There were very many excellent Cornish mining captains and engineers whose skill and capabilities were beyond reproach, and many became legendary in their lifetimes—Captain Thomas Treloar, 'the Brazilian Gold King', Francisco Rule, 'el Rey de la Plata', of Mexico, and Don Sampson Waters of Chile. Yet, it has to be conceded that there were equally as many that were at best mediocre and perhaps should never have been appointed to positions of such responsibility.

The modern, integrated mining economy that had taken root in Latin America in the early nineteenth century spanned the globe by the twentieth century. As the most visible migrant labour group at the commencement of the international mining economy, the Cornish worked their way into a virtually unassailable position during the nineteenth century and attracted much resentment and jealously from competing ethnic labour-groups as a result. As this article has focused on deep lode, hard rock mining technology, further research is needed to examine the validity of the myth in other places where the technology required was minimal. However, the right of the Cornish to be considered the best hard rock miners and engineers in the world, able to command and demand correct practice in the mining and milling of metals throughout the world, continued to be a contentious issue. And by the early twentieth century the myth of Cousin Jack looked less certain, as the following extract from the American *Mining Magazine* of 1909 illustrates:

> Is it for a coterie of Englishmen to dictate to the 25,000 mining engineers and metallurgists in the English speaking countries as to what is good form and what is bad form? We think not. It is time to drop this distinction between American and English engineers . . . the profession of mining is neither insular or provincial, it is cosmopolitan.[66]

This was a warning to the Cornish that they could no longer rely on the mythological status they had in part created, and thereafter enjoyed for almost a century, keeping out rival ethnic groups and thus enabling them to retain the coveted crown of excellence in mining.

ACKNOWLEDGEMENTS

This article was first presented as a paper at the annual conference of the California Cornish Cousins at Mariposa, California, May 2001. I am indebted to the organizers and attendees for their valuable comments and observations, many of which have been included in this version.

NOTES AND REFERENCES

1. T.A. Rickard, *A History of American Mining*, New York, 1932, p. 246. Thomas Arthur Rickard was born in Italy in 1864, educated in England and Russia, and was said to have arrived in the United States when aged 21, to work in the mining fields of Colorado, where he attained a top mining job. He died in Victoria, British Colombia, in 1953. See James M.

Nesbitt, 'A Prominent Victorian, Dr T.A. Rickard, Dead', *The Daily Colonist*, Victoria, 18 August 1953.
2. Clark C. Spence, *British Investments and the American Mining Frontier, 1860–1901*, New York, 1958, p. 13.
3. Roger P. Lescohier, *The Cornish Pump in the Californian Gold Mines*, Grass Valley, 1992, pp. 7, 13.
4. See for example, Philip Payton, *The Cornish Overseas*, Fowey, 1999, p. 34. There is no clear consensus on how the Cornish acquired this name, but evidence seems to point to the mines of Devonshire in the eighteenth century, where Cornish miners sought work. The term 'Cornish Jack' is also thought to have been used to express an 'otherness', the Cornish considering themselves a distinct people with specific mining skills that they jealously guarded.
5. For more on this see Sharron Schwartz, 'Creating the Cult of Cousin Jack: Cornish Miners in Latin America 1815–1848 and the Development of an International Mining Labour Market', in Robert D. Aguirre and Ross G. Forman (eds), *Connecting Continents: Britain and Latin America 1780–1900*, forthcoming 2002.
6. A.C. Todd, *The Search for Silver: Cornish Miners in Mexico 1826–1947*, Padstow, 1977, repub. Cornish Hillside, St Austell, 2000, p. 131.
7. *Royal Cornwall Gazette*, 21 May 1825.
8. Other countries did put capital into Latin America mining ventures but at nowhere near the level of investment of the British. For example, the Germans formed mining ventures in Mexico, as did the Americans.
9. Henry English, *A General Guide to the Companies Formed for Working Foreign Mines*, London, 1825, p. 30.
10. Leyland Hamilton Jenks, *The Migration of British Capital to 1875*, New York, 1927, p. 28.
11. J. Fred Rippy, 'Latin America and the British Investment "Boom" of the 1820s', *The Journal of Modern History*, 1947, pp. 122–9.
12. Sharron Schwartz, 'Exporting the Industrial Revolution: Trevithick and the Migration of British Steam-Engineering Technology to Latin America', *Journal of the Trevithick Society*, 2001.
13. Henry English, 1825, quoting Caldcleugh, p. 91.
14. Henry English, 1825, p. 36.
15. Justin Brooke, 'Henric Kalmeter's Account of Mining and Smelting in the South West in 1724–25', unpublished M.Phil. thesis, University of Exeter, 1997.
16. Such movement within the British Isles is summarized in Payton, 1999, pp. 30–2.
17. Sharron Schwartz, 'Exporting the Industrial Revolution: The Migration of Cornish Mining Technology to Latin America in the Early Nineteenth Century', in Will Kaufman and Heidi Macpherson (eds), *Translantic Studies: New Perspectives*, forthcoming 2002.
18. See M.J. Fenn, 'British Investment in South America and the Financial Crisis of 1825–26', unpublished M.Phil. thesis, University of Durham, 1969.

19. Rippy, 1947, p. 129.
20. *Quarterly Mining Review*, 1830, pp. 81–106.
21. For example, see Desmond Gregory, *Brute New World: The Rediscovery of Latin America in the Early Nineteenth Century*, British Academic Press, London, 1992.
22. *Quarterly Mining Review*, 1830, p. 101.
23. John Mayo and Simon Collier, *Mining in Chile's Norte Chico: Journal of Charles Lambert, 1825–1830*, Oxford, 1998, p. 15.
24. Claudio Veliz, 'Egaña, Lambert, and the Chilean Mining Associations of 1825', *Hispanic American Historical Review*, 55, 1975, 637–63.
25. Cornwall was later than its European or even Latin American counterparts in developing schools to help develop mining-related theory. A mining school was inaugurated in Mexico in the late eighteenth-century and the Germans had founded the Academy of Freiberg in 1765 that reached its celebrity in 1775 under the famous Werner. Pupils came from as far afield as Brazil, Spain and Russia to take advantage of the classes for mine managers, as well as those on arithmetic, geometry, art of mining, elementary mineralogy, grammar and drawing. Mining schools were formed at Liège and Paris, France, in 1810. Although Cornwall formed the Royal Cornwall Geological Society (1814), the Royal Institution of Cornwall (1818), and the Royal Cornwall Polytechnic Society (1833), the learned societies' membership, structure and cost made it difficult for a miner or even a mine captain to join. It was not until Sir Charles Lemon's efforts to inaugurate a mining school at Truro in 1838 that the lack of mining schools was truly acknowledged.
26. Todd, 1977, p. 36.
27. Captain Andrews, *Journey from Beunos Ayres through the Provinces of Cordova, Tucuman and Salta, to Potosi, thence by the Deserts of Caranja to Arica, and subsequently, to Santiago de Chili and Coquimbo, undertaken on behalf of the Chilian and Peruvian Mining Association 1825–26*, 2 vols, London, 1827, vol. 1, pp. 209–10.
28. Edward Roberts' letter from Fresnillo, Mexico, to Nicholas Harvey, Hayle, 14 February 1839, CRO, H/1/20/171.
29. Charles Barham, 'Report on the Employment of Children and Young Persons in the Mines of Cornwall and Devonshire, and on the State, Condition and Treatment of Such Children and Young Persons to the Royal Commission on Children's Employment', *BPP*, 1842, xvi, p. 759.
30. *Quarterly Mining Review*, 1830, p. 356.
31. *Mining Journal*, 22 August 1841.
32. Cornish *tributers* contracted to work a *pitch*—an area in the mine that had been examined by the mine captain—for a previously agreed price. They received a proportion of the value of the ores raised. The Mexican mining system was ancient and complex. Put simply, *buscones* mined the ore wherever it looked promising, and hired *tenateros* to carry it to the surface. Mexican miners received half the ore raised in this way—the *partido*. The *ad hoc* methods of working under the *partido* system often resulted in a maze of unstable galleries and tunnels, a matter that greatly concerned the

British management of Mexican miners, who considered it militated against mine safety and correct management.

33. *Mining Journal*, 25 February 1843.
34. *Mining Journal*, 17 December 1853.
35. *Mining Journal*, 19 November 1853.
36. Henwood had previously been the agent at the gold mines of the National Brazilian Mining Company, Minas Gerais, Brazil.
37. *Mining Journal*, 27 May 1854. Henwood advised the abandonment of the Sue River Company's mines, but his report did not please the shareholders who dismissed it as a 'sweeping condemnation' and demanded a further and more complete inspection. Captains Jehu Hitchins and John Maynard, both highly experienced in the copper mines of neighbouring Cuba, inspected the properties of the Clarendon Mining Company and the latter with Captain Bennetts, those of the Liguanea and General Mining Company of Jamaica in 1853–4, with similear pessimistic results. See *Mining Journal*, 11 March and 25 March 1854. This was reported to have 'cast a gloom' over other mining ventures in Jamaica.
38. *Mining Journal*, 3 December 1853; 24 December 1853.
39. *Mining Journal*, 1 July 1854.
40. *Mining Journal*, 10 September 1853.
41. *Malacates* resembled horse whims. *Arrastres* were primitive grinding mills operated by horses dragging large boulders over ore fragments. In Cornwall, this task was performed mechanically by the stamps.
42. *Quarterly Mining Review* 1836, p. 359.
43. Saint Clair Duport, *De la production des métaux précieux au Mexique*, Paris, 1843, pp. 387–8.
44. Margaret E. Rankaine, 'The Mexican Mining Industry in the Nineteenth Century with Special Reference to Guanajuato', *Bulletin of Latin American Research*, 2(1) 1992, pp. 29–48, p. 29. Newton R. Gillmore, 'British Mining Ventures in Early National Mexico', unpublished Ph.D. thesis, University of California, 1956, p. 80.
45. Leland R. Pederson, *The Mining Industry of the Norte Chico, Chile*, Evanston, 1966, pp. 191–2.
46. Marshall Eakin, 'The Role of British Capital in the Development of Brazilian Gold Mining', *Miners and Mining in the Americas*, (eds) Thomas Greaves and William Culver, Manchester: Manchester UP, 1985, p. 13.
47. Through superstition and fear the Otomi Indians in Mexico actually destroyed one of the first engines installed at the Real del Monte mines in the early 1820s.
48. For a detailed report of the patio process, see the *Quarterly Mining Review*, 1830, pp. 393–402.
49. *Quarterly Mining Review*, 1830, p. 477.
50. *Quarterly Mining Review*, 1830, p. 319.
51. *Quarterly Mining Review*, 1830, p. 516.
52. HJ/1/17, Royal Institution of Cornwall.
53. *Mining Journal*, 22 July 1837.
54. *Mining Journal*, 22 April 1837.

55. *Mining Journal*, 24 June 1837.
56. *Mining Journal*, 29 July 1837.
57. See Sharron Schwartz, ' "Joining hands across the main": Cornish labour migration and evolution of transatlantic transnationalism', unpublished paper presented at the Mining: Communities and Culture Conference, Cornish History Network, University of Exeter, Newquay, January 2001.
58. *Mining Journal*, 4 May 1844.
59. *Mining Journal*, 15 July 1854.
60. *Mining Journal*, 4 June 1853.
61. *Mining Journal*, 4 June 1853.
62. For a discussion of the way the Cousin Jack network was viewed in the USA, see Sharron Schwartz 'Bridging "the Great Divide": Cornish Labour Migration to America and the Evolution of Transnational Identity', paper presented at the Race, Ethnicity and Migration: the United States in a Global Perspective Conference, University of Minnesota, USA, November, 2000.
63. *Mining Journal*, 23 July 1853. The Obernhof Mining Company considered Cornish miners to be superior to its native Germans, and saw fit to import several practical miners from Cornwall in 1853 who were said to have blasted in a few minutes one ton of ore from a place that would have occupied the Germans for some hours.
64. Edwards Roberts' letter from Fresnillo, Mexico, to Nicholas Harvey, Hayle, 14 February 1839, CRO, H/1/20/171.
65. Letter of James Reynolds to Harvey's Foundry, Hayle, 13 February 1840, CRO, H/1/25 (85).
66. *Mining Magazine*, vol. 1, Sept–Dec., 1909, p. 17.

THE MISFORTUNES OF THE MINE: COPING WITH LIFE AND DEATH IN NINETEENTH-CENTURY CORNWALL

John Rule

INTRODUCTION

A poem by John Harris the Cornish poet contains this verse:

> A month was nearly ended,
> And he severe had wrought
> Day after day in darkness,
> And it was all for nought
> The mineral vein had faded
> And now all hope was fled,
> Tomorrow should be pay day
> His children have no bread.[1]

Harris had worked many years as a miner and well knew the vicissitudes of the tribute system of wage payment used in the Cornish mines. Indeed, the verse could be considered autobiographical. Harris had married in 1845 and recalled almost a year of privation as a tributer before a remarkable upturn in his fortune:

> For the first ten months of my married life, fortune was against me so that my earnings amounted to no more than tenpence a day. Then the tide turned, providence blessed my labours, and I soon became the owner of two hundred pounds.[2]

Harris had managed to live on around 5s a week; managed because his poor run had happened before the household was enlarged by children. In 1840 the local newspaper carried a report from a mining district that a farmer had caught a tributer stealing swill from his pig trough to feed his family. Taking pity he loaned the miner money, which the man was able to repay with ease on the next pay day. The episode is instructive. A visitor to the district in 1788, by which time the system was already general, described it as 'the merest lottery in the world'. Miners could earn as much as £20 a month, a week or even a day or as little as 20 farthings: 'Thus we find the generality of these inhabitants wafted from time to time on the variable waves of prosperity and adversity.'[3]

Under the tribute system small groups of men undertook to work a measured section of the mine known as a 'pitch'. They contracted for a rate in £1 of the value of the ore raised from it. According to the expectation from it, a pitch might be taken for as little as the equivalent of 5p or as much as 75p. It needed experienced judgement. If a tributer estimated more accurately than the mine agent, he might be getting a high tribute rate for larger quantities of better-quality ore than the pitch had been judged by the agent to contain. If on the other hand he had overestimated the potential and accepted a low rate in £1, then he could hardly make wages. In extreme cases mineral lodes could disappear, due to rock faulting, and a tributer could find himself working for a month or even two months for nothing. Periodically after inspection by the miners and the mine management pitches were put up at a 'setting'; a form of Dutch auction at which the tributers offering to work for the lowest rate secured the 'bargain'. A report in 1849 accepted the view that although miners earned typically 14s or 15s a week, they could not be considered as 'so well off as an agricultural labourer with constant work at 10 shillings'.[4]

That was in fact a pessimistic view. For the middle decades of the nineteenth century when the Cornish industry was at its peak, £3 a month was constantly cited as an *average* wage for a steady competent tributer. That is that taking the highs with the lows a miner earned perhaps 50 per cent more than an agricultural labourer, and further had perhaps once or twice in an earning lifetime the good fortune to enjoy a considerable windfall. Harris's £200 in a matter of weeks was not a far-fetched hope, for as William Pryce, the writer in 1778 of the first treatise on the industry, put it: 'A tinner is never broke until his neck is broke.'[5]

The survival strategies of Cornish mining families were not, then, those driven by a need to manage in conditions of extreme and persistent poverty, nor of periods of deprivation resulting from seasonal employment patterns. This article is not concerned either with periods of exceptional general distress, such as the grain crises of 1795/6 and 1800/01, or with the widespread distress associated with the potato famine of the late 1840s.[6] Nor is it concerned with the decline of Cornish mining after the 1860s. Its purpose is to examine the 'mixed economy of welfare' among families dependent on a particular industry, that is with endemic situations which could happen in any mining household in normal times and with the means and methods through which available resources could be managed to the best effect.[7]

In general terms some groups in the nineteenth-century working class fared better, but many fared worse. However, the management of the fluctuations of the tribute system needed from time to time a fall-back to other sources of household income and onto considerable skills of domestic management. As well as this, for a miner to obtain the best outcome from the tribute system he needed to work that system in a particular way in which a satisfactory relationship with the mine management was paramount. Consider this evidence from a mine captain (manager) in 1864:

> We have a first rate old man at North Roskear, a first rate old man, who has been working here for thirty years; the last two years he has always been speculating, and has done badly. I said to him the other day, 'You are doing badly'. 'Yes' said he, 'I never had such a long run before, but I will make it up again soon'. I said 'You have not done badly on the whole, you have been here from a boy.' He is worth £200 or £300 probably; he has one or two cottages, and keeps a cow and so on; we never let him go on less than £2. 5s a month, though for a long time he has not earned any money.[8]

Several things stand out here (apart from the fact that someone who was probably in his later forties is described without any sense of misuse as an old man!) (1) the importance of being a long-serving and well-regarded workman (2) the fact that the mine was paying the man close to the average wage even though he was raising little copper ore (3) the probability of several 'starts' (windfalls) which had allowed the accumulation of savings and the acquisition of a cottage. Tributers who were established and trusted to work to good effect in winning copper or tin ores were usually paid an advance for subsistence, a payment known as 'subsist'. At the end of the pay period, usually a month in the mid nineteenth century, any balancing amount was paid over, while if total earnings did not cover subsist and other deductions, then the debt was carried forward. Clearly this practice went for a considerable section of the workforce a long way towards ironing out the fluctuations in the system. It was, however, not a right but a favour and there was clearly a limit to the debt a mine would allow to build, and it could be used with discrimination, as on one occasion in 1838 when it was refused to miners known to spend time in alehouses.[9]

It was important to get established in a well-run and generally prosperous mine: 'It is seldom there is any indiscriminate bidding, or any great scamble at the settings. Men who have gained a footing in the mine have generally the preference over strangers.'[10] The practice of sons first going underground with their fathers was a main route to 'natural' or hereditary establishment as it was in many other occupations, but there also developed a strategy by the 1840s of securing a footing known as taking 'farthing pitches'. This was the taking of tribute bargains at almost nominal rates with no expectation of making sound wages, and it depended on the convention that, having proved themselves effective miners, the pare would be offered the pitch again the following month, this time at a paying rate.

For those who were unable or unwilling to carry on after a poor run of tributing, there was an alternative employment strategy. They could seek work in the mine on *tutwork*. Tutworkers worked in the 'dead ground', that is, did not excavate the ore, but prepared the access by sinking shafts or driving levels. They 'bargained' according to the hardness of the rock on the time it took to drive a measured distance at a rate per fathom. There were fluctuations but wages were much more steady, so that in the mid nineteenth century few mines found it necessary to pay subsist to tutworkers. The average earnings of tutworkers were lower, but not by very much. In 1841, for instance, in the main mining Redruth district tributers earned from £2.15s to £3.2s a month while tutworkmen from £2.12s to £3.0. In normal times it is clear that the preference of most miners was for tributing, its much greater risks notwithstanding. Significantly, though, there is evidence that miners' wives might have preferred the steadier income from tutwork.[11] In the first place it was a matter of status: 'He was a tributer, and tributers look with as great a contempt upon the tutmen, as the latter do upon the surface labourers.'[12] A tributer, according to one account in 1849 would have to be on the point of starvation before he undertook tutwork. That is perhaps an exaggeration. Most miners had probably worked at both over their working lives. That was not surprising. The amount of work available of each kind varied. For example, during a period of optimism and high expectations the opening of new ventures and the extension of old ones would bring at first a large demand for tutworkers, while even in a time of normal activity, as suggested by an estimate made in 1838, out of 100 employees 50 would be underground miners and of these 30 would be tributers and 20 tutworkers. In the second place the tributer was strongly attracted to the possibility of a 'start'. Attached to this hope was what one witness described as the miner's 'grand desideratum' to own a cottage. When John Harris's luck changed after ten poor months he acquired a lease and built himself a home, just as his father had once done: 'If they have managed to live without getting into debt, when they get this start, the first thing they do is to build a house.'[13]

Estimated costs, expecting that a miner was usually his own builder, in the mid nineteenth century were around £50 and, given that a plot of land could usually be leased cheaply on a three-life tenancy from landowners in the mining districts, where the value of the land for commercial agriculture was low, then for many tributers aspiration to a cottage and plot can be regarded as central to their living strategies. For many it remained an ideal, but as such it probably had a powerful role to play in the preference for tributing over more steadily remunerated forms of mine labour.

COLLATERAL AIDS TO LIVING

This raises the question of how important non-mining sources of support were for mining households. John Harris describes himself as growing up in the 1820s in a cottage built by his grandfather on a small farm of 7 or 8 acres, then being worked by his father: 'He followed his daily avocation underground, and performed his farm work in the evenings and mornings and on holidays and leisureable opportunities.'[14] In fact the farmwork was input by the family rather than by the father singularly. The double description 'tinner and husbandman' occurs often in parish registers of the early eighteenth century and probably describes a genuine dual occupation. It occurs rarely later and the miners who produced some at least of their family food from small plots thereafter are better considered as pursuing a supplementary activity. From the late eighteenth century it was common for local landowners to lease portions of downland and wastes to miners in plots of 3 to 6 acres. Sir Francis Bassett, the dominant owner in the important mining parish of Illogan, estimated in 1795 that over the previous few years fifty miners had built cottages on such plots on his lands, while the steward for a neighbouring estate in 1802 was even more of an enthusiast. Remarking on the temptation of the alehouse which faced the miner in his spare time, he continued:

> To guard against an evil of such extensive magnitude, I have often wished that the proprietors of wastelands would

endeavour to direct and guide the industry of these people to such efforts as would soon lessen these evils [by leasing small plots] . . . When ever this has been tried . . . you may now see them busily employed in enclosing and cultivating their little fields.[15]

He continued to describe how beginning with a crop of potatoes to break and clear the ground, over a few years the miners were able to grow a small amount of corn, using the ashes from the turf they used as fuel as manure. With hard work within six years the poor ground could be improved to the extent of allowing the pasturing of a cow and overall to make a very substantial contribution to the family food supply, as well as having become 'careful and thrifty', self-respecting and better fathers and husbands.

The practice continued into the nineteenth century, a landowner telling an enquiry in 1842 that he and others leased such small plots in and near the mining villages, but that it was hardly possible for the increasing numbers of miners who lived in towns like Redruth or Camborne to all have access to such plots. In 1841 it was estimated that a quarter of all miners lived in such cottage allotments. Of the rest many, but not all, had gardens. Even more important was the practice which seems to have become widespread in the nineteenth century of potato allotments under which farmers allowed miners to take plots rent-free under condition that they dressed the ground in cultivating their potatoes in readiness for the farmer to take a corn crop from it the following year. Charles Barham in his authoritative account of 1842 did not use the term 'small farm' at all. He regarded the plots as 'collateral aids', that is as a distinctly secondary employment. Indeed by then attempts to combine significant farming activity with mining were no longer meeting with unqualified approval. Barham himself considered attempts to work more than a very few acres were rarely successful, while the manager of a large mine stated that he preferred employing men with small plots to those with large ones, since the latter could not be depended on to work as fully at the mine. Keeping in good standing with the major mines, was as we have noted, an important condition for tributers.[16]

In parts of Cornwall fishing offered 'collateral aid'. Around St Ives ten or so miners sometimes combined to share an inshore fishing boat. Perhaps one in ten of miner heads of household there were involved in such ventures. However, the object was to secure a supply of fish for family consumption rather than for sale. Pig keeping was an activity of practically any miner who had the small amount of space needed.[17]

FAMILY INCOME

Once children began to grow up they began to contribute increasingly to family income. The report of 1842 gives a detailed example of the family earning structure of a miner:

> Miner aged 47, wife 45, married 26 years, 12 children—4 dead, 1 married. Highest wages have been 55s per month. Whole gettings of family are now:

Constance	-21 earns	15. 0d
John	-19	£2 .0s 0d
Richard	-17	£1 6s 0d
James	-14	16s 0d
Elizabeth	-12	2s 0d
Total with his own wages		£7 10s 0d a month

Another miner earning £3 a month depended upon his children for an additional £1.[18]

On the basis of the detailed example it is possible to make adjustments to ages and earnings and some for marriage of older children and construct a possible history of the family's income over time.

Year	No. in family	Earnings per head in new pence per month
1827	6	46
1832	8	38
1837	10	52.5
1842	9	83
1847	7	117

The effect of the family cycle is clear. Family *per capita* income at its lowest point was less than a third of its highest level.

Miners' wives, although many of them would have worked before marriage at the mines as surface workers, do not seem to have done so after marriage and bridal pregnancy was in any case common, even usual.[19] Pre-marriage employment was frequently blamed for a supposed lack of domestic skills, while the importance of a wife's management of the household was clearly recognised:

> You will find two men, and one has got a clean, decent, wholesome industrious wife, and that man's children will be kept as clean and comfortable as possible. You will then see one of the same 'pare' who has got a dirty careless wife, and that family will be in rags, and yet that man will make the

same earnings. One man will be well off and the other always in misery.[20]

The heavy tones of the Victorian domestic ideology are apparent here. But the importance of wives to household functioning is clear enough. Among other things they had to cope with the problem of the erratic remunerations of the tribute system. Few sought their opinion of it. Further, in a region where salted fish and potatoes had become dietary staples, wives had to manage the storage and preservation of food as well as its purchase. The extent to which wives might have worked from home still needs research. One miner described his wife as having a fish-hawking round, and further, spoke of his intention of leaving the mine to join her as soon as he could afford a donkey and cart. In the meantime she presumably was bearing the fish on her back in a cowal.[21] Cornwall offered few opportunities in domestic textiles, although the spinning needs of the Devonshire serge manufacture had reached into its eastern parts during its eighteenth-century boom period.

DEATH, INJURY AND SICKNESS

Miners' wives too frequently became their widows. Cornwall had the highest proportion of widows to its total female population of any county in 1851. Some of these had been made so from deaths in mine accidents and frequently in early life. But more were widowed later in middle age by the toll taken by the lung disease which overcame the miners typically in late middle age. Accidental death was a risk: a lingering decline from miners' phthisis almost inevitable for those who continued working in the mine. Around 1850 miners in the age range 45 to 55 had a death rate two and a quarter times that of non-miners in the same sample of six parishes. Between 55 and 65 it was more than two and a half times. The contribution to widow-making is clear. In the mining parish of Gwennap in 1837 the average age of death in persons dying over 30 years of age was 46 for miners, 60 for non-mining males and 64 for women. This was not something which the mining community could put out of mind. Death or injury from accident might be considered a risk, albeit a high one: a survey made in the early years after civil registration began in 1837 indicated that as a percentage of male deaths above 10 years of age in four populous mining parishes, accidents accounted for 14.1 per cent for miners compared with 5.4 for non-miners. Diseases of the chest accounted respectively for 61.1 per cent and 36.1 per cent. It was the latter that a working miner had in mind when he replied simply to an inquiry in 1864: 'You cannot expect miners to live as long as other men.'[22]

Given that miners consciously pursued an occupation with a shorter working life but higher total earnings, compared with available alternatives, then becoming a miner in the first place could be considered a strategy for economic survival.[23] But was there any strategy which could minimize the effect on life and earnings of the onset of phthisis or other lung conditions brought on by working in dust-laden or oxygen-deficient air? Since local medical opinion was generally agreed that the final crippling and killing stages came on quite suddenly, but after giving some preliminary indications, a life-employment strategy which suggests itself is to leave underground work at an appropriate age, say around 40, and move to another employment. Mine doctors constantly advised this, but it would seem very few adopted it. A doctor retained by a large mine, Fowey Consols, which at the time employed more than 1,600 persons of whom more than 1,000 were adult males, explained his situation in 1841:

> I have frequently felt it my duty to point out to a patient in the strongest terms, the necessity of his leaving off working underground, and what has been the reply? 'I have a wife and a large family of young children to support, how can I keep them on nine or ten shillings a week . . . when I can barely manage on twelve or thirteen shillings a week; I will try it on a little longer.' That little longer renders the case soon hopeless.[24]

He added a further consideration, which was that so long as a miner worked at the mine he would be entitled to receive 7s a week from the 'sick club' when disabled for the rest of his life. In this important respect the decision of putting by something from each pay for a fund to cover some disability either permanent or short-term was not a strategy left up to the miner. From well back into the eighteenth century compulsory deductions were made at most mines for the retention of a doctor and for the sick club. But in what circumstances was relief from this fund allowed? From the evidence just cited it would seem that at Fowey Consols a weekly relief was payable in cases where disease had resulted in the inability to continue working underground, although it is also clear that that point would only be reached once the disease had become fatally advanced. It did nothing to allow a miner to quit in time, but worked the other way. In fact payment from the club in cases of disease rather than accidental injury does not seem to have been the norm. In many mines only 'hurt pay' was given for visible injuries. As a manager pointed out in 1864, sometimes men were taken on in whom the disease had already commenced its ravages

unseen, and that to allow pay from the fund would take too much out
of it at the expense of those who did suffer injury. But Fowey Consols
was probably representative of other large mines, for example
East Crofty, employing around 450 adult males. The manager there
indicated a significant area of discretion allowed by the larger funds
built up in sizeable enterprises. The rule was still visible hurt only, but
it was often overlooked: 'We have many men home for years who have
been fairly worn out in the mine, because miners do not live to be very
old.' While another mine stated that it had always been liberal: 'We
apply it to pensioning off old men who are unable to work any longer
on the mine, who have been there for many years and whose money is
spent. We always make them some allowance . . . We treat an illness
brought on by working in the mine as a visible hurt.' Here as in the
matter of wages it seems that the best economic survival strategy for a
miner was to become established in one of the larger enterprises. In
1838 ten copper mines employing more than 500 persons accounted for
43 per cent of the total labour force, but while this is a significant
proportion, it still suggests that for the majority of the workforce relief
when disease ended their working lives was obtainable only from the
Poor Law, or from any private provision they might have been able to
make.[25]

Did many make some provision of this nature? Here the necessary
research has yet to be done, but there are some indications that it
might have been more common than has been assumed. Gorsky's
figures for friendly society membership in the early nineteenth century
place Cornwall twelfth among the 42 English counties.[26] The two
mining parishes sampled by Eden in his classic inquiry of 1797 are
suggestive of an early and significant role. In Gwennap he found three
societies with 400 members and in Kenwyn four with 400. In both cases
that is one in ten of the total population, suggesting that a high
proportion of the adult male population did belong, although the
nature of the benefits covered is not specified.[27] Illogan in 1803 had a
friendly society to population ratio of 1:5.[28] Overall in 1831, Cornwall
was in a small group of counties where total society membership was in
excess of 10 per cent of the population.[29] Nor were friendly societies
the only means of making a measure of provision. Barham's report of
1842 suggested that of £282,541 deposited in Cornish savings banks,
two-thirds probably belonged to miners.[30]

When all this is taken into account, however, there is still little
doubt that to a partial or total extent sick or injured miners and their
families were likely to fall into dependence on official poor relief. After
a miner's death, whether lingering or sudden, that was even more likely
to become the fate of widows and orphaned children.[31] The Union

Workhouse at Redruth at Christmas 1843 contained 120 women, 150 children, but only 33 men. Redruth Union covered the most densely populated of the mining parishes, so the small number of men among its inmates is worth noting.[32] It seems clear that despite the Act of 1834 workhouse-based relief had not become the usual final destination of worn-out miners. The parish of Gwennap was part of that union and in one quarter of 1848 miners made up 200 of 240 families receiving relief. Of the fathers of these mining families, 15 had been killed in accidents; 40 had been injured or blinded; 65 had died; and 15 others, who had between them 80 children, were dying from miners' consumption.[33] It is important to note the structure of Poor-Law relieved poverty in the mining districts. Overall levels of poor-rate expenditure were low at times when there was no food or employment crisis. The overall figure for county expenditure in 1838 was 23p a head of the 1841 population. In the Redruth Union it was 17p and for the districts of Gwennap and St Day within it 21p. The mining parish of St Just in Penwith had a rate of only 7p against an overall figure for the Penzance Union of 17p. In the non-industrial Stratton Union, on the other hand, the per capita rate was 34p. There is certainly a suggestion here that the poor-rate cost of relieving the poverty situations which arose in mining households in the middle years of the nineteenth century was less than that of relieving the structural problems of low rural wages and unemployment.[34]

However, an important qualification needs to be made. Cornwall may have been a low-spending county in overall terms, but in one respect it was well above the average for England and Wales. In 1851–6 its ratio of female to male paupers at 2.82 to 1 was exceeded only by Northumberland at 3.09. Cornwall was almost matched by Durham at 2.79, South Wales at 2.8 and the West Riding at 2.75. There is a strong suggestion of a link between mining and proportionately high female to male pauper ratios.[35]

When miners died or were crippled in accidents it created in the immediate term a larger problem of relief simply because they were much more likely to leave families including young children. We noted above the significance of the family cycle in determining household income generally. Using the example family from 1842 (see above), it can be shown how significant it was for the impact of a loss of a mining father's earnings. The miner was 47 and had he died in that year with five children between the ages of 12 and 21 at work, family per capita income would have fallen from 83p to 59.4p a significant fall, but one which would hardly have brought the family to destitution. Had, however, his death happened ten years earlier in 1832, the fall would have been from 38p to 4p, a total family income of 29p: less than 6s in old money. In short the references to the destitution of widows and children are real enough. Fifteen of the forty miners who perished in the flooding disaster at East Wheal Rose Mine in 1846 were married and together left sixty children orphaned. Relief subscriptions were collected and they were often done so for individual cases, but while they met immediate expenses they provided for little more than short-term relief.[36]

THE ROLE OF CHARITY
Special subscriptions following particular episodes of distress were a reactive form of charity. What needs fuller consideration is the role of charity generally. It is said by historians of many groups of 'proud' workmen such as the Cornish miners that their pride and independence stood between them and the willing receipt of charity. This may have been more true after the mid nineteenth century than before. Victorian attitudes, symbolized by the awesome authoritarianism shown by organizations like London's Charity Organization Society, perhaps represented a cultural shift on the part of the providers which was reciprocated by a change in attitude from potential recipients. There is certainly evidence that the Cornish lower classes of the eighteenth and earlier nineteenth centuries, as elsewhere, could exhibit in certain circumstances expectations from charity which could even be expressed in a language of entitlement. In particular charity expectations were part of the network of social relations which existed between the mining community and the mine and land-owning elite. This charity typically operated through the mediation of estate stewards. One wrote to his employer during the food crisis of 1847:

> Wheal Prosper is not your property neither are you at present receiving any dues of consequence, but merely on Halvana . . . I do not think you can be expected to subscribe to anything more than the relief fund of the Parish which I consider they are in great want of.

On another occasion he wrote that he had not forwarded his employer's agreed donation because he had heard that some of the other landowners, 'had not come forward on the occasion'.[37]

The language here is one of calculation and instrumentality as well as sympathy and expectation. Solicitations came on behalf of individuals as well as for parish funds. In 1799 another steward had written to his employer:

There was a poor man unfortunately killed in Herland Mine
. . . he has left a widow and several small children. The man
bore a good character . . . a neighbouring gentleman and one
of the Lords of the mine was so kind as to send the poor
woman a guinea. I took the liberty of doing the like on your
behalf.[38]

The man 'bore a good character': clearly such a bearing and conduct
was an important consideration for those who might one day need
charity. When Lady Bassett's 'venerable' steward died in 1841, the
local press praised his concern over fifty years for the miners of Illogan,
especially his care in bringing 'deserving persons' to the notice of his
employers.[39] William Jenkin brought a general need to the attention of
his employer in 1799, reminding him of 'some little assistance to the
poor families of Illogan' which he had given in the previous year, and
advising him that: 'the poor creatures are enquiring whether anything
of that sort is to be expected this year', while in 1845 another landowner was also reminded of the nature of the poor's expectations from
him:

A subscription of two guineas has generally been given to the
poor of Probus and the like at Grampound for purchasing
coals . . . if it is your wish to give £5 had it not better be
divided between them? . . . as the poor of Grampound in
consequence of living in your houses and your paying a large
part of the poor's rates consider they have similar claims on
you to those of Probus.[40]

These are indicative examples. A full account of the working of charity
is as wanting for Cornwall as it is for other areas. It is an important
subject. At some point in their history many families had recourse to it.
Its total impact may well have been hardly less than that of official
poor relief.

CONSOLATION

Concern with a community with such a distinct mortality profile, with
death and bereavement at such high levels, raises questions not only
over strategies for economic survival, but also for emotional survival:
ways of dealing with death, injury and illness. So far as the mining
villages of Cornwall were concerned consolation came overwhelmingly
in a religious idiom. Contemporary descriptions and the evidence
of the religious census of 1851 indicate that the religiosity of these
communities was perhaps their most striking cultural characteristic.

It took the form of Methodism, mostly in the form of the parent Wesleyanism, and was extremely revivalist in its nature. I have written elsewhere in detail on the relationship of Methodism to the risks of mining life.[41] But what I have in mind is the kind of sentiment expressed in some of the verses in a broadsheet published in 1842 after an explosion killed eight miners:

> Seven beside the youth are dead
> His dear father too is fled
> Crying with his latest breath,
> Jesus is my strength in death.

> O what solace thus to see
> Christ had set his spirit free,
> Born on angel wings away
> To the realms of endless day.

> Some have shouting crossed the flood,
> They were washed in Jesus blood,
> Now before the throne they shine,
> Clothed with victory divine

> Widow, dry the falling tear.
> God will be thy husband here,
> Orphan cease they accents wild,
> God will be thy Father, child.

> Now on him your griefs repose,
> He will listen to your woes,
> Feed you, guide you with his hand,
> To that holy, happy land.

Or from another example after seven were killed in 1858:

> Ah, no! they cannot come again;
> No more their voice you'll hear;
> But may we hope in heaven they rest,
> And may we meet them there.

> Widows and orphans now are left,
> Their sad bereave to mourn
> May David's God their father be,
> And serve him in return

Funerals of mine victims were hugely attended:

> Then borne unto the silent tomb,
> What thousands gathered there,
> To mingle with the relatives
> Sorrow's lingering tear.

The *Mining Journal* described the funeral of one of mining's victims at the end of the 1850s as being attended by a 'black mass of several thousands' who processed several miles to the churchyard.[42]

CONCLUSION

There are links which can be made and conflicts which can be noted. Pursuit of short-term economic strategies may at times have contributed to the onset of disease. For example, tributers knew well enough that the failure of a candle to burn as a level end indicated that the air was too deficient in oxygen to be safely breathed. But if their gettings were proving good, then they moved the candle further back from the end and carried on working. A mine doctor too considered it common to find a miner in whom the signs of disease were already apparent, struggling on in the hope of just one more lucky strike. One miner stayed working in an unhealthy mine because his children also worked there and he feared for their jobs if he left.[43] Religion too offered explanation and consolation in the face of the ups and downs of tributing. When a Methodist miner had a good run in 1853, he knew who to thank: 'the Lord has greatly prospered me at the mine lately', while for another it was 'Providence' which had blessed his labours. When things went badly, an essay stereotyping the Cornish miner in 1846 suggested that even after months of dismal wages and extreme privation:

> Their hope was in his truth; and often at night, after a long season of labour underground, when the miner returned to his family, and was sitting at his supper of salt fish and potatoes, would he comfort his wife in her trouble, by assuring her that God had said, 'I will never leave thee; I will never forsake thee'.[44]

John Harris wrote of his hatred of work in the mine: 'Yet I never complained, . . . God had placed me there, and I knew it was right.' This article began with a verse from this miner-poet . . . It can end with one from another of his poems:

A miner in his smoky cave,
Amid his course employ
In clouds of darkness visible
Thus sweetly sang for joy
His toil wet face and brow were pale
And very ill he seemed
When carolling those thrilling words
Mankind are all redeemed.[45]

NOTES AND REFERENCES

1. J. Harris, *Wayside Pictures, Hymns and Poems*, 1874, pp. 158–9. This article is mainly concerned with the industry in its most expansive era. After the 1860s decline was rapid but in 1841 the Cornish copper and tin mines employed together around 30,000 people, of whom at least two-thirds worked in the former.
2. J. Harris, *My Autobiography*, 1882, p. 60.
3. *West Briton*, 15 May 1840; S. Shaw, *A Tour to the West of England in 1788*, 1789, p. 383.
4. *Morning Chronicle*, 24 November 1849. For a full discussion of the tribute system see: J.G. Rule, 'The Perfect Wage System? Tributing in the Cornish Mines', in J.G. Rule and R. Wells, *Crime, Protest and Popular Politics in Southern England 1740–1850*, 1997, pp. 53–66.
5. W. Pryce, *Mineralogia Cornubiensis*, 1778, p. 175.
6. On the grain crises see the monumental study by Roger Wells, *Wretched Faces. Famine in Wartime England 1793–1803*, Gloucester, 1988. On the potato crisis see B. Deacon, 'Proto-industrialization and Potatoes: A Revised Narrative for Nineteenth-century Cornwall', in Philip Payton (ed.), *Cornish Studies: Five*, Exeter, 1997, pp. 73–5 and P. Payton, '"Reforming Thirties" and Hungry Forties"—the Genesis of Cornwall's Emigration Trade', in Philip Payton (ed.), *Cornish Studies: Four*, Exeter, 1996, pp. 110–15.
7. For a discussion of the 'mixed economy of welfare' see: A. Kidd, *State, Society and the Poor in Nineteenth-century England*, 1999, chapter 1.
8. BPP 1864, XXIV, *Report of the Royal Commissioners Appointed to Inquire into the Condition of All Mines in Britain etc*, Epitome of Evidence p. 564.
9. *Cornwall Gazette*, 16 March 1838.
10. *Morning Chronicle*, 24 November 1849.
11. C.C. Pascoe, *Walks About St Hilary*, 1879.
12. *Morning Chronicle*, 24 November 1849.
13. Harris, *Autobiography*, 60; BPP 1864, minutes p. 565.
14. Harris, *Autobiography*, p. 5.
15. J. Rowe, *Cornwall in the Age of the Industrial Revolution*, Liverpool, 1953, p. 25; Jenkin MSS, Courtney Library, County Museum, Truro, to J. Britten, 4 April 1802.
16. BPP 1842, XVI, *Report of the Royal Commission on Child Employment*,

pp. 753–4, 830, 837; BPP 1864, p. xxv, BPP 1841, XX, *Report of the Committee of Council on Education*, p. 84. For the use of potato allotments see: B. Deacon, 1997, pp. 60–85.

17. BPP 1842, pp. 754, 848.

18. BPP 1842, p. 840.

19. On the scarcity of employment opportunities for women once through the ages at which surface workers were usually employed see: S.P. Schwartz, 'In Defence of Customary Rights: Labouring Women's Experience of Industrialization in Cornwall *c* 1750–1870', in Philip Payton (ed.), *Cornish Studies: Seven*, Exeter, 1999, pp. 8–31.

20. BPP 1864, p. 45; BPP 1842, pp. 834, 848.

21. BPP 1842, p. 847. The buying strategy for fish, usually pilchard, but sometimes herrings, was to purchase in bulk from the Autumn fisheries and salt a supply in large earthernware vessels known as 'bussas', to last through the winter. If large shoals had not begun coming inshore to the reach of the seine fisheries by the late Autumn, local newspapers began to express concern over the winter food supply for the poor. As purchasers the mining families were eager to take advantage of any unexpectedly large catch in the hope that the glut would make the fish very cheap. When in 1893 a large shoal of herrings was taken unexpectedly at nearby Perranporth late on a winter evening, the town crier of the mining town of Redruth took the news through the town at dawn and the fish were on sale by 8 a.m. (*West Briton*, 13 November 1893). Carts from the mining parishes are reported to have arrived at large landings in their hundreds. The importance of securing a purchase can be seen in the report of a wife and her sister who pushed a wheel barrow from Truro to Perranporth and back, an 18-mile round trip, and brought back 700 pilchards. (7 September 1855).

22. For the sources of these statistics and an analysis of mortality and morbidity see: J.G. Rule, 'A Risky Business: Death, Injury and Religion in Cornish Mining *c*. 1780–1870' in A. Bernard Knapp et al. (ed.) *Social Approaches to an Industrial Past: The Archaeology and Anthropology of Mining*, 1998, pp. 159–62. BPP 1864, pp. 6, 18.

23. On this point see the recent article by R. Burt and S. Kippen, 'Rational Choice and a Lifetime in Metal Mining: Employment Decisions by Nineteenth-Century Cornish Miners', *International Review of Social History*, XLVI, 1, April 2001, pp. 45–76.

24. 'Enquiry into the Health and General Condition of the Mining Population of Cornwall', *Report of the Royal Cornwall Polytechnic Society*, 1841, pp. 133–5.

25. See the discussion in A.K. Hamilton Jenkin, *The Cornish Miner*, 1962 edn, pp. 265–7.

26. M. Gorsky, 'The Growth and Distribution of English Friendly Societies in the Early Nineteenth Century', *Economic History Review*, LI, 1998, pp. 493–5.

27. F.M. Eden, *The State of the Poor* (abridged A.G.L. Rogers), 1928, pp. 146–7.

28. Based on 1801 census and the friendly society returns in BPP 1803/4, xiii. See Gorsky, 1998, p. 459ff. for a valuable discussion of these returns.
29. Kidd, 1991, p. 112.
30. Cited in L.L. Price, *West Barbary or Notes on the System of Work and Wages in the Cornish Mines*, 1891, reprinted in R. Burt (ed.), *Cornish Mining*, Newton Abbot, 1969, p. 162.
31. For the concerns of parish officials for the relief of widows once the new Poor Law of 1834 came into operation see: S. Schwartz and R. Parker, *Lanner. A Cornish Mining Parish*, Tiverton, 1998, p. 29. Further study of the operation of the Poor Law in Cornish Mining parishes seems likely to suggest that officials shared the view usually associated with the industrial north, that the workhouse was not an effective solution to local relief problems.
32. F. Mitchell, *Annals of an Ancient Cornish town—Redruth*, Redruth, 1972, p. 122.
33. R. Blee, 'On the Comparative Longevity of Cornish Miners', *Report of the Royal Cornwall Polytechnic Society*, 1847, p. 18.
34. The expending figures for the unions and districts are conveniently tabulated in the appendix to C. Redding, *An Illustrated Itinerary of Cornwall*, 1842, pp. 247–53. The unions had been established in 1837 following the Poor Law Amendment Act of 1834.
35. The ratios are tabulated in L.H. Lees, *The Solidarities of Strangers. The English Poor Laws and the People, 1700–1948*, p. 199.
36. 'Accident at East Wheal Rose Mine', *Cornish Banner*, August 1846, p. 56.
37. Hawkins Mss. Cornwall RO. DDJ 1227, Letterbook of Henry Tretheway, 7 and 12 June 1847.
38. Courtney Library, Royal Institution of Cornwall, Jenkin Mss. W. Jenkin to A.M. Hunt, 27 February 1799.
39. *Cornwall Gazette*, 9 July 1841.
40. Jenkin to George Hunt, 28 May 1798; Hawkins Mss. Trethewey to J. Hawkins, 2 March 1842.
41. See J.G. Rule, 'Explaining Revivalism: The Case of Cornish Methodism', *Southern History*, 20/1, 1998/9, pp. 168–88 and 'A Risky Business', pp. 162–72. See also the introduction by Philip Payton to C. Noall, *Cornish Mine Disasters*, Redruth, 1989, esp. pp. 7–8.
42. Cited in R. Burt (ed.), *Cornwall's Mines and Miners*, Truro, 1972, pp. 12–14. The verses are from broadsheets in the collections of the Royal Cornwall Museum, Truro, and in the Cornwall County Record Office.
43. BPP 1864, p. 35; BPP 1842, p. 840.
44. Rule, 'Risky Business', p. 159, *Cornish Banner*, July 1846, p. 24.
45. J. Gill, *John Harris the Cornish Poet*, n.d. p. 10; Harris, 1882, p. 36.

CORNWALL'S NEWSPAPER WAR:
THE POLITICAL RIVALRY BETWEEN THE
ROYAL CORNWALL GAZETTE AND THE
WEST BRITON, 1810–1831

Brian Elvins

INTRODUCTION

Today's readers will be familiar with the newspaper 'wars' which regularly flare up, wars that are usually a battle for circulation but which may also have a political dimension. Almost 200 years ago, Cornwall witnessed its own remarkable display of rivalry between the two weekly papers, the *Royal Cornwall Gazette* and the *West Briton*. This 'war' had its origin in a major political battle within Cornwall between Tories and Reformers. The struggle was unrelenting in the years after 1810, certainly continuing for most of the nineteenth century and in a sense it did not cease until 1951 when the two papers were amalgamated.

What is remarkable is that, apart from Claude Berry's account, so little has been written about the rivalry in spite of its significance for the political life of Cornwall.[1] This may be a reflection of the difficulties involved in doing so, and certainly several were encountered in writing this article, for confusion surrounds even some basic facts such as the names and dates of editors and proprietors. There is singularly little material in the surviving private manuscript sources, while no documents of the key figures involved in the foundation of the *West Briton* appear to have survived. Nevertheless, sufficient was found, especially in the two papers themselves, to make an attempt possible and so cast light on a vital area of Cornish life and to rescue from oblivion important individuals such as Edward Budd, the first editor of the *West Briton*.

While scores of students of nineteenth Cornish history have made detailed use of the files of the two papers for their own different research purposes, probably few have appreciated the fact that the papers themselves and their rivalry were part of that history. Any assessment of the importance has to address a number of questions. How far did the advent of the *West Briton*, in 1810, alter the content of the *Gazette*, which had had a monopoly since 1803? What effect did the 'war' have on the readers among the Cornish public and what was the effect on the politics of Cornwall? One needs to consider how the newcomer—the *West Briton*—came to acquire and maintain such a substantial circulation lead over the *Gazette*; a lead which was evident by 1831. Finally, what was the contribution of Budd to making Liberalism the dominant political force in Cornwall in the ninteenth century?

CORNWALL AND 'THE PRINT CULTURE'

Eighteenth-century Britain had seen the expansion of what has been called 'a Print Culture': 'a culture of writers and readers, of authors and editors, of bookshops and printers, of newspapers and periodicals.'[2] The spread of newspaper readership in both London and the provinces was a particularly important part of this culture and has rightly attracted a lot of attention. Both C.A. Cranfield and R.M. Wiles, for instance, published major studies in the 1960s of the early eighteenth century provincial press, highlighting the West Country towns of Bristol, Exeter, Plymouth, Yeovil, Taunton and Sherborne where newspapers existed at some point.[3] More recently, too, Charles Clark has written a unique study of newspapers on both sides of the Atlantic, in the thirteen colonies of North America and in Britain, emphasizing the point that 'by broadening access to current information . . . ordinary readers were invited into . . . a privileged circle, sharing in the ritual of communal identity.'[4]

However, as to the impact of the provincial press on the public politically, Professor Aspinall, a pioneer in this field, contended that it was small as 'at the end of the eighteenth century scarcely one third of the provincial papers had an editor capable of writing a leading article; editors were usually printers'. They were, therefore, non-political. This was to change within a generation but on the whole provincial papers were not important as organs of public opinion, especially since their circulation was 'extremely small'. More recently, too, Jeremy Black has argued the lack of a political edge to newspapers in the eighteenth century and their failure to influence change.[5]

Cornwall was slow to participate fully in this 'print culture', largely because no newspaper was published there. The educated and well-to-do gentry had to be content with two out-of-county papers; the *Sherborne Mercury* and the *Exeter Flying Post*. The former was the more popular, not least because of its efficient distribution system. As early as the 1760s, William Borlase, the famous Cornish anti-quarian, who was Rector of the parish of Ludgvan, three miles outside Penzance, regularly received the paper. Indeed the term 'Sherborne Rider' was used throughout the West Country to designate the men who transferred the papers to branch riders at points along the road between Plymouth and Penzance. Even as late as 1818, the paper boasted that 'Thirty men, and more than twenty horses are employed weekly in its circulation, in every direction, over four counties, extend-ing . . . to Penzance, the land's end in Cornwall . . . Served by men sent for that purpose'.[6]

By that time the dominance of the Sherborne paper had been undermined by the emergence of weekly papers within Cornwall itself, the first being the *Cornwall Gazette and Falmouth Packet*, which began its short existence on 7 March 1801. This paper, priced at 6d, was printed and published in Falmouth. It was owned, along with three other partners, by Thomas Flindell, who acted as its editor. Flindell, a Cornishman, born at Helford in 1767, had varied experience in news-papers. Having served an apprenticeship in Edinburgh, he edited the *Doncaster Gazette* in the 1790s when he was in his twenties. At the end of the decade he returned to live at Helston where he set up the Stannary Press. The last issue of the *Cornwall Gazette*, number 85, came out on Saturday 16 October 1802, for the partners had failed, and Flindell, incapable of sustaining the financial burden alone, was, for a while, imprisoned for debt.[7]

However, according to one source, 'as he was justly reckoned by the gentlemen of Cornwall as a highly suited person to conduct a paper, a subscription was entered into when he was in Bodmin Prison'. With this financial help and the patronage of the Prince of Wales in his role as the Duke of Cornwall, Flindell established what became the *Royal Cornwall Gazette and Falmouth Packet or General Advertiser for the Western Counties*, in Lemon Street, Truro, the first issue coming out on 2 July 1803, price 6d. Of this 3 1/2d was the newspaper or Stamp Tax, a levy which was increased to 4d in 1815. Each copy of the paper carried the amount of the tax stamped in red ink on the front page. Although this meant that the paper could be sent free by post during the 14 days after publication, it clearly had a restricting effect on the readership, placing it beyond the means of all but the well-to-do to purchase. This was even more so after June 1809 when Flindell was forced to increase the price to 6 1/2d.[8] As he remarked in his first editorial:

Cornwall has always been divided betwixt the two rival
empires of Sherborne and Exeter . . . Discouraged a little by
the ill success which attended her efforts last year, she now
feels herself inspirited by the patronage held out to her in
the generosity of the Nobles and Gentry of Cornwall, in the
assistance promised her by the kindness and learning of
the Clergy and in the support assured her by all other ranks
in the County.[9]

Twenty-six prominent Cornish figures, mainly from West and Mid
Cornwall, including both County MPs—Sir William Lemon and Francis
Gregor, two Peers, Viscount Falmouth and Lord De Dunstanville, who
later described Flindell as 'a clever fellow', had contributed to the fund
to finance his paper. It adopted the well-known Welsh motto, 'Gwir en
erbyn y byd' (Truth against all the World), an attempt perhaps to echo
the old Cornish language and even to claim common cultural cause
between Wales and 'West Wales'. Be that as it may, the *Gazette*
flourished and quickly gained sufficient circulation to secure its future
against the competition from the *Sherborne Mercury* and the *Exeter
Flying Post*. By 1806 it claimed it was publishing upwards of 1,500
copies weekly and with 'four score' being sent to London each week. It
flourished not least because it was admirably placed for obtaining news
of the war against Napoleon before anyone else. What was happening
in Spain, for example, in the Peninsular War, both on land and sea, was
known at Falmouth from ships calling in, well before the news reached
London. In 1805 the *Gazette* landed a major scoop, being the first
paper in the country to receive the news of the victory at the battle of
Trafalgar.[10]

Quite consciously, and following the line of many other provincial
papers of the period, Flindell proclaimed the political neutrality of the
paper, stating 'In the treatment of political topics and of public characters, *The Gazette* will shew no partiality but that which veneration for
our Sovereign and a love for the Constitution and Liberties of England
may naturally inspire'. This was clearly evident in its coverage of the
County Elections in 1806 and 1807, despite the clear differences in
political attitudes of the two members involved. Likewise its reporting
of two major County Meetings—June 1805 and May 1809—concerning
scandals which involved government and royal figures was detailed,
and factual, as well as unbiased in its account of the speeches made by
both sides.[11]

THE ORIGINS OF THE *WEST BRITON*

The monopoly enjoyed by the *Gazette* lasted only until 1810 when it was faced with a major challenge from a rival paper—the *West Briton*. This paper's foundation had a distinctive feature. The motive behind it was avowedly political rather than commercial. The 1809 meeting, mentioned above, had witnessed the emergence in Cornwall of a new political group calling itself the Friends of Parliamentary Reform, and demanding changes in Cornwall's unreformed electoral system. The group, made up of minor gentry and clergy, included John Colman Rashleigh (1772–1847), Edward Stackhouse [he assumed the name Pendarves in 1815] (1775–1853), Edmund Glynn (1764–1840), William Lewis Trelawny (1781–1856) and the Rev. Robert Walker (1754–1834), the Vicar of St Winnow near Lostwithiel.[12]

They had been determined, after 1809, to mount a persistent campaign to publicize the cause of Reform in Cornwall. This inevitably involved the use of the only Cornish newspaper. The *Gazette* was inundated with letters and articles on Reform and borough corruption, often with local illustrations from Cornwall's twenty-one boroughs. Rashleigh, writing under the pseudonym of 'Alfred' became involved in a lengthy academic and constitutional debate with Francis Gregor, the Tory MP, writing as 'Freeholder of Cornwall'. The debate in the columns of the paper lasted several months, before both men resorted to publishing pamphlets on their respective positions.[13]

From the outset, the Reform group had been worried about the attitude of the paper and, in fact, in the summer of 1809, had enquired of Flindell 'whether [they] are to consider it as open to them equally with the other party or are they to be excluded?'. Although Flindell had replied that the paper was 'open to both parties', his attitude became less definite as the correspondence controversy between 'Alfred' and 'Freeholder' developed. The Reformers suspected that he was too sympathetic to Gregor to be impartial; a suspicion confirmed in their minds by two events in the spring of 1810. The first was a *Gazette* editorial, approving of the imprisonment of the Radical MP, Sir Francis Burdett for an alleged breach of the privileges of the House of Commons; second, Flindell's refusal to publish a letter, criticizing Gregor, from a Liskeard schoolmaster, Edward Budd.[14]

From the details published in the *Gazette* on 5 May 1810 and subsequent weeks, Walker was the key figure in the abortive meetings with Flindell, arguing 'We must not have things inserted in your paper, which make against the cause we espouse and have the answers refused'. The result was the decision of the group to back their political beliefs with money, by financing the establishment of their own news-paper. This was, indeed, a brave, even risky move, given the state of the war and the economy at the time. Taxation was high, the financial situation was bad, banks were failing and bankruptcies were multiplying. As the paper itself put it 150 years later, 'Few newspapers can have been launched in times more unpropitious than was the *West Briton*'.[15]

The practical problems involved were undertaken by a Cornishman, who, although only 25, had already gained a reputation as a writer and journalist in London. This was Cyrus Redding, born at Penryn, the son of a Baptist Minister, and at that time (1808–13) editor of the *Plymouth Chronicle*. As he wrote in his Recollections published many years later:

> I was requested to meet some gentlemen in Cornwall who wanted another paper in the county, there being but one, which having been secured by the opposite party and having been neutral in position, they thus became deprived of any support from a Tory Press . . . They told me they had an editor ready and a printer as well but that none of them knew how to organise the whole . . . I consented, ordered from London what was necessary, organised the undertaking and returned to my duties . . . Such was the origin of the *West Briton* . . . The promoters . . . [were] including Glynn, some of the Rashleighs, the Stackhouses [Pendarves] and other gentlemen.[16]

The choice of printer and publisher was a Devonshire man, John Heard, then in his 29th year and in partnership with Penaluna of Helston in a printing business. He had previously worked in London both as a printer and bookbinder. On his death in 1823, his wife, Elizabeth (née Goodridge), succeeded him as publisher of the *West Briton* and head of the printing business at Boscawen St, Truro, for the next 44 years until her death in 1867 at the age of 79. Her name first appeared as publisher on Friday 13 June 1823, no. 674.

As editor, the Reformers chose to appoint the Liskeard schoolmaster, mentioned earlier, Edward Budd. Born at Waterford in Ireland, on 26 August 1774, he had taken part in the rebellion of 1798 on the side of the Loyalists, but after failing in some sort of cotton manufacture, he had moved to Cornwall and initially set up a boarding school at Liskeard. The impression he made as a teacher, later in Truro, was recorded by a former pupil, John Gill who subsequently wrote:

Mr Budd . . . kept a boarding and day school of a superior kind. At this school my brother and myself were admitted as one pupil by taking alternate weeks. Mr Budd had a melodious silvery voice; it was a treat to hear him read and I learnt to read poetry from him.

Budd was also a Wesleyan local preacher and first came to the attention of the Reformers as the author of an ostensibly anonymous political pamphlet, strongly attacking De Dunstanville's speech at the 1809 County Meeting. It is likely, too, that Budd's friendship with a Liskeard solicitor, Joseph Childs (1776–1829), who was a member of the Reform group, had much to do with his appointment as editor. Liskeard had apparently been considered as the site for the new paper before it was realized that Truro, as the social centre of Cornwall, was a better choice. Budd, who was 36 when selected, disposed of the school in Liskeard and set about founding another in Truro.[17]

One final detail which had to be decided was the title. There was seemingly no difficulty in fixing on the name *West Briton*, perhaps derived from the *North Briton*, John Wilkes's famous eighteenth century paper, but also reflecting the claims of the Cornish to be 'West Britons', the descendants of 'Ancient Britons' rather than Anglo-Saxons. However, the intention to subtitle it the *Miners Journal* ran into problems. This had to be dropped in the face of opposition from De Dunstanville, Gregor and other Tory notables with mining interests. They organized an Official Protest from 120 Lords, Adventurers, agents and managers of the mines, against the suggestion 'which we think likely to implicate us in . . . discussion of public measures and judgement on the conduct of public men'.[18]

The first issue of the renamed *West Briton and Cornwall Advertiser* with its Latin motto *Prisca Fides*,[19] duly appeared on 20 July 1810, containing four pages with five columns each, measuring approximately 21 inches by 17;—the size of a modern tabloid paper. The paper was closely printed in small type which had been set by hand and without any of the headlines now regarded as normal. All the copies had been struck off on a hand press so it was not unusual for some pages to be smudged. The price was 6 1/2d, the same as The *Gazette*. Of the twenty columns of the first issue, just over four were occupied by advertisements, and four by Cornish news, while the remainder were devoted to a leading article, parliamentary and foreign news, especially news of the war, and a long letter from Budd, justifying the decision to start the paper and setting out its political position. It was, he said:

to give the calumniated advocates of a temperate and
constitutional reform an opportunity of explaining their real
sentiments . . . Reform of some kind is not only expedient but
absolutely necessary for the safety of the state . . . To secure a
free channel for this important enquiry is the first object of
this paper.[20]

THE *GAZETTE* CHALLENGED

The paper's arrival presented an immediate commercial challenge to
the *Gazette* commercially. Leaving aside circulation considerations,
which will be dealt with later, the *West Briton*'s advertisement charges
—fixed on a scale of 6/- for 12 lines, up to 10/- for 36 lines—posed a
threat to the revenue of the *Gazette* for these were considered vital to
the viability of any paper.[21] To every advert, of course, had to be added
a government surcharge of 3/6d whether it was long or short, so that
any household maid wanting a place would have had to pay the same
duty as a large landowner wishing to sell an estate worth £100,000.
There may have been the occasional attempt to avoid using the
advertisement columns of the paper on political grounds,[22] but
that apart it was inevitable that many persons—farmers, mine agents,
seine owners, merchants and solicitors—would avail themselves of a
second outlet for advertising, even if they disliked the politics of the
new paper. It would have been bad business to confine them to
one paper. The *West Briton*, therefore, soon came to be treated on an
equal footing in this respect. When William Rashleigh of Menabilly
was High Sheriff in 1820, he was extremely concerned that publication
of a requisition for a County Meeting should appear in the paper
as well as The *Gazette*, 'particularly as the censure of partiality might
be made for circulating in the paper of one party and not in the
other'.[23]

The *West Briton* had, too, a more general impact on the *Gazette*.
Flindell had to abandon the political neutrality which he had followed
ever since the paper's inception. Sitting on the fence was no longer an
option and so he chose the Anti-Reform or Tory position. This meant
that the paper's content not only became more political but also more
party political. This did not cause him any regrets for later when he was
in charge of the *Western Luminary* in Exeter, a government minister
described it as 'a newspaper which has always taken the side of
Government' and in line for lucrative official adverts from government
departments.[24] Initially, the *Gazette* was put on the defensive by the
West Briton but it reacted with a vigorous counter-attack on several
different fronts. The result, in Claude Berry's words was that 'for three
years, the two Truro editors assailed each other . . . in verbal duels

which matched, if they did not exceed in vituperation that described by Dickens in his "Pickwick Papers" '.

First, Flindell poured scorn on the idea that the new paper could damage the *Gazette*'s circulation, boasting even before the *West Briton* had begun publication that 'the number of weekly subscribers who have dropt [sic] The *Gazette* does not amount to 30 and these have been compensated by the accession of an equal number of new friends, chiefly among the upper classes'. After six months of competition, it declared 'Budd has forgotten to tell his readers that our paper circulates three times the number weekly that his does. Is not the number of the *West Briton* published this week just 531?' This was a reassertion of his earlier claim of a circulation of 1,500 weekly; a figure that must be considered much too high, when it is remembered that a weekly paper such as the *Manchester Gazette* considered 'a weekly sale of six or seven hundred . . . quite satisfactory'.[25]

A major attempt, too, was made in several ways to discredit Budd personally, and, therefore to suggest he was unfit to be an editor. It was alleged that he had been sympathetic to the Irish rebels in 1798, and had betrayed his previous friendship with Flindell. It was also made a matter of adverse criticism that 'Budd had grown up in the habits of the Methodists, sympathised with their feelings and acquired his literary skills in composing Methodist sermons'. Flindell reserved his most spiteful attack till just before his departure in December 1812; 'As the Editor of the *West Briton* has been at pains to inform his readers of the names and godparents of a neighbour's children, lately christened, perhaps he will next week tell them the name of the real father of a child since christened nearer home.'[26] Prominent Tory supporters of the *Gazette* were equally condemnatory of Budd in their private correspondence. Charles Rashleigh of Duporth described him as 'a scoundrel [who] does great mischief . . . and must not be permitted to spread his poison without check'. Dr Richard Taunton went one stage further, describing Budd as 'an arch-fiend' and 'public seducer'.[27]

Similar treatment was meted out to the proprietors of the *West Briton*. The *Gazette* stated they were: the Rev. R. Walker, Rashleigh, Stackhouse (Pendarves), Glynn, along with the senior partner of the Truro Bank, Reuben Magor (1760–1834) and Truro solicitors, John Edwards and Co. Walker, especially, was the subject of much sarcasm ('the reverend and worshipful possessor of 60 or 70,000 pounds') and accused of 'a settled and systematic determination to ruin me as a tradesman'.[28]

Finally and most seriously, the political position of the *West Briton* was attacked. The editor was accused of being 'a Satellite' of Cobbett, the famous Radical owner of the *Weekly Political Register*, and who, when commenting on the war in Portugal, 'labours to divert the hostile feelings of our army from the common enemy and to direct their rage against their own legitimate government'. The following year the *Gazette* alleged that 'the object of all their hopes is the final subjugation of England to the power of France' while the struggle for Parliamentary Reform 'would produce a commotion that shall terminate in a turbulent republic or a military despotism'. Accusations were made, too, that Budd wanted an extreme version of Reform, involving universal suffrage, annual Parliaments, and the eventual establishment of 'a democracy'.[29]

'DIFFERING . . . ON ALMOST EVERY SUBJECT'

The rivalry continued even after Flindell sold what he described as 'his absolute personal property' at the end of 1812, before moving to Exeter to found a new paper, The *Western Luminary*, on the same political principles as he had advocated in the *Gazette*. Boase and Courtney took the view, in *Bibliotheca Cornubiensis*, that Flindell 'seems to have tired of the political warfare in which he was engaged with a rival editor'. However, it would be more credible to suggest that he sold up because he had failed to check the rise of the *West Briton*.[30]

The new owner of the *Gazette* was Peter Nettleton Jnr, only 25 when he took over, most probably with the financial backing of his father, Edward Nettleton, a newspaper proprietor in Plymouth. Francis Gregor, MP and strong supporter of the *Gazette*, plainly approved of the arrangement, commenting to his brother-in-law, 'I have a most excellent letter from Nettleton, precisely what I could have dictated. I shall see him tomorrow about his prospectus. He will certainly do well.'[31] Nettleton ensured the rivalry between the papers continued, albeit without the personal hostility, with his first editorial, stating:

> We have no political connections, no political dependence . . . on one great question, that of Reform, we very fully adopt that decided line of political opinion which has marked the character of the *Cornwall Gazette* since 1809 . . . We cannot believe the country . . . stands in need of the sort of radical reform which has been recommended.[32]

The personal relations between the two editors were evidently cordial. In his obituary notice of Nettleton's death (August 1817), Budd emphasized that:

> differing as we have done on almost every subject of foreign and domestic policy . . . it is gratifying to reflect that there was

one point, at least, upon which we cordially agreed; approbation of the principles of the British and Foreign Bible Society, and in a sincere desire to assist in extending its benign influence, there existed between us a union of sentiment.

That apart, however, the *Gazette* editorials followed on the same lines as before. Nettleton claimed, after a year's operation, 'the circulation of this paper has increased to an extent, far exceeding our most sanguine expectations. It is now one of the largest provincial papers in the Kingdom.' The following summer, it held that 'Budd's own political disposition, as well as that of his turbulent employers, seeks . . . uselessly to agitate the minds of the people of Cornwall', while Rashleigh's motives for Reform derived 'from the spleen of foiled ambition or the love of low popularity'.[33]

While the two agreed on issues such as the Corn Laws of 1815, the Repeal of the Property (Income) Tax in 1816, the need for economy and retrenchment, and in attacking sinecures, the *Gazette* denied that post-war distress would be cured by Parliamentary Reform. It attacked the *West Briton*'s campaign as 'only calculated to excite that levelling spirit, which has too often disgraced, by its public exhibitions, the character of Englishmen'. It disagreed strongly and at length, with its rival for sympathizing with the claims of Roman Catholics and for claiming that County Meetings should be open to all inhabitants rather than confined to freeholders only. In contrast to the *West Briton*, it supported the suspension of Habeas Corpus in 1817, as not being 'productive of serious inconvenience to innocent persons'. By the spring of 1817, it was proclaiming success: 'the indefatigable exertions . . . made for the purpose of convincing the Inhabitants of the County . . . of the necessity of their meeting to procure extreme reform has been completely unsuccessful. Faithful Cornwall disowns the doctrines of the Reformers.'[34]

Nettleton's death, age 29, on 1 August 1817, led to a temporary cessation of hostilities, with Budd paying his former rival a glowing tribute in the columns of the *West Briton*, adding 'We feel a melancholy satisfaction in being able to pay this humble tribute to the character of a political opponent whose good qualities commanded our esteem and whose removal in the prime of life . . is to us a subject of sincere regret'. Dissatisfaction among some Tories at Nettleton's editorship led, at this time, to thoughts of establishing another paper in Cornwall, Charles Rashleigh writing to Pole Carew in September, 'I am decidedly against a third paper . . . (but) most clearly Budd must not be left in full command of the County'. In the event Mrs Nettleton took on editing the paper until the appointment of a new editor, in which according to her, 'the most scrupulous care has been taken in ascertaining that his political opinions were consistent with that line of politics which were pursued by the late Mr Nettleton'.[35]

Frederick Shoberl, whose name first appears in the *Gazette* on 27 June 1818 (no. 783), had no previous connection with Cornwall. He was at the time 43 years of age, of German extraction and had been educated at the School of the United Brethren, a Moravian religious sect, at Fulneck near Leeds. The *Gentleman's Magazine*, describing him as 'mild and unassuming in his manner, amiable and with excellent qualities' claimed in its obituary notice that 'his name is intimately identified with the literature of the 19th century, a succession of valuable and instructive works . . . having emanated from his pen'. He was the founder, co-proprietor and editor of the *New Monthly Magazine* in 1814, and had edited Akerman's Repository of the Arts from 1809 onwards. While 'his literary attainments won for him the friendship and acquaintance of the most enlightened characters at home and abroad', his period at the *Gazette* was not a congenial one, terminating 17 months later on 4 December 1819. He even published his first farewell letter as early as 10 July![36]

Shoberl's tactics were a return to those of Flindell, employing the weapons of sarcasm and invective. Comments on the *West Briton*'s circulation were dismissive: 'Adverts sent to his [Budd's] paper by persons unacquainted with its real circulation fall under limited, very limited observation'; while the *Gazette* 'from its general circulation may justly assume the characteristic distinction of the County Paper'. Budd was subjected to strong attack, being described as a graduate of the 'Jacobin School', one 'who would like to spread sedition to Cornwall' and a man unwilling to accept that 'revolution, not reform, is the aim of those miscreants whose cause, he has long been the avowed advocate'. By contrast, the *Gazette* was presented as a truly patriotic paper, loyal to Crown and Church. One extract from Shoberl's editorial in June encapsulates all these sentiments: 'the very few copies of the most contemptible of all contemptible publications, misnamed the *West Briton*, in the polluted columns of which, not a single sentiment, truly British is anywhere to be found'.[37]

The new owners of the *Gazette*, following its sale by Mrs Nettleton, were the Gillett family, setting up at 33 Boscawen St, a few doors from where the *West Briton* was printed!. They gave it much-needed stability after the frequent changes of the previous years, by remaining in control for, at least, the next sixteen years. Thomas Richard Gillett Jnr, born in London in 1796, became the printer, publisher and proprietor at the age of 23, while his father, also Thomas, who had been born in 1763 in Edinburgh, was installed as editor. In 1832 Gillett Jnr married Louisa Elizabeth, the daughter of John Carthew, a printer in Truro. She, following in the footsteps of her female predecessors, Elizabeth Heard, Matilda Nettleton, and also Mrs Flindell, later carried on both her father's business and briefly edited *The Gazette*, after her husband's sudden death in 1835.[38]

Gillett's first editorial, promising that 'the sound political principles upon which it has always been conducted will be inviolably maintained' ensured that the political rivalry continued throughout the next decade. There were certainly sufficient political issues, on which they disagreed to guarantee this: ranging from the Queen Caroline case in 1821, through agricultural distress, a fierce County Election in 1826, to Catholic emancipation in 1829. The *West Briton* was dismissed as that 'perpetual blister upon the loyalty of the County which has now lost much of its irritating power', while the *Gazette* boasted in 1827 that it was 'the Chief Medium' in the county, because of 'its circulation and the wealth and respectability of its subscribers'.

Pendarves, one of the original proprietors of the *West Briton*, was subjected to a fierce personal attack for having the temerity to stand as a candidate for a County seat in 1826: 'It is a matter of grief that a man should be so blinded by vanity and ambition to grasp at a distinction to which he is not entitled', while the Reform group were 'that dunghill of a party which had almost completed the process of its decay'. Actually this was one of the few occasions encountered, when either paper realized it had gone too far. The Gazette felt obliged to issue a semi-apology the following week; the editor saying it was intended not against Pendarves personally but 'as a mere Philippic' against those backing him.[39]

'A THOROUGH IRISHMAN'

All the different attacks, far from harming Budd or the *West Briton*, probably assisted its consolidation and growth. If nothing else, they raised its profile and that of the Reform cause, the very purpose for which it had been founded, while Budd could and did reply in kind to the attacks. According to Colman Rashleigh, the Reform group 'knew but little' about Budd, when they appointed him editor, 'with a certain salary as compensation for his risk and trouble'. However, whether by luck or judgement, the appointment in 1810 was a successful one, with Budd remaining editor for the next twenty-five years. Rashleigh subsequently made the following lengthy tribute:

I do not believe that an honester man than he was, breathes. He had fair but by no means extraordinary abilities. In disposition, temper, imagination, he was a thorough Irishman; lively, excitable, generous, easily attached and very grateful for kindness, and perhaps a little sensitive . . . more eloquent than judicious, rash and violent when irritated and liable to the two extremes as an Editor . . . of vituperation approaching scurrility and flattery and adulation (blarney). But throughout his long editorship . . . he steadily maintained to the cause to which he had originally professed allegiance, his fealty; . . . Never did he give way to his opponents or abate heart and hope in the conduct of the liberal press what had been so absolutely and so long under his sole management and control.[40]

Budd was so successful in the early verbal battles with Flindell that within two years of the paper's foundation, the original proprietors were able to withdraw, so he became the sole proprietor. As expected loyal supporters of the *Gazette* consistently refused to subscribe to the new paper; Earl Mt Edgcumbe, for instance, remarking to Pole Carew, neighbour and political ally 'I do not see the paper of the Reformers any more than you'. Nevertheless Budd proclaimed within three weeks of starting 'the favour of a generous and discerning public has put all apprehension on the score of its stability at rest. The orders received . . . exceed the most sanguine hopes of its friends. Should not a single additional order be received, the *West Briton* is established.' Further boasts followed on 18 September and 21 December 1810; the latter claiming 'The *West Briton* has the superiority in this county'. While there are no available figures to check the veracity of such claims, there can be little doubt that the paper did become a permanent part of Cornwall's political scene.[41]

Budd was perfectly capable of writing, as he said himself, 'his own vindication' to the attacks. One example of his style was a leader headed 'The Infamous Falsehoods of the *"Royal Cornwall Gazette"* Exposed' and containing the following: 'Checked by no sense of shame and influenced by no principle of honour, the scurrilous advocate of Ministerial imbecility vociferates falsehood after falsehood in order to drown the voice of truth.' He alleged, too, that Flindell had received a place with the government worth £600 a year, while Nettleton was accused of being dependent on the patronage of Lord Falmouth and the Corporation of Truro.[42]

Budd's main tasks, however, were positive ones; to publicize the cause of Reform, whenever possible, and to stress the very moderate nature of the demands of the Reform group. He consistently followed a moderate line, thus making nonsense of the claims that he was a

Jacobin, whose aim was revolution rather than reform. To him 'the main object of the Reformers is the restoration of the Constitution as it existed in the true spirit of the Revolution of 1688 . . . and we shall proceed by slow and cautious steps'. Neither Budd nor the Reform group ever drew up a detailed scheme. However, their ideas clearly included a slight extension in the County franchise (but certainly not universal suffrage), reducing the life of Parliament to three years (though not annual elections), the retention of open voting rather the ballot, and most of all the destruction of the 'corrupt' borough system by an extension of the vote to substantial house-holders.

Budd found in Cornwall's numerous boroughs ('those sinks of infamy') a fruitful field for exploitation and whenever revelations of malpractices became public as in 1818 and 1820, the paper was scathing in its denunciation. His tactics put *The Gazette* on the wrong foot, making it almost inevitable that it would defend the existing electoral system. In fact, when *The Gazette* opposed the disfranchisement of the borough of Grampound in 1821 with 'the Bill is clearly an infringement of the constitutional rights of a considerable number of individuals who have done nothing to forfeit their rights', it seemed to be defending the indefensible.[43]

Budd was just as effective in exploiting a whole range of issues after 1810, to bolster the arguments of Rashleigh and his colleagues on the necessity for Reform. Whether it was in support of the claims of Roman Catholics in 1813, the County's Address to the Prince Regent on the return of peace in 1814, the problem of distress after 1815, the need for retrenchment by the government, protesting at the suspension of Habeas Corpus in 1817, calling for an enquiry into the 'Peterloo Massacre', criticizing the treatment of Queen Caroline in 1821, or sympathizing with Cornish farmers over their problems in 1822, Budd disagreed with the view taken by the *Gazette* and argued the case for Reform. The line taken by Budd that these problems were intimately connected with the unreformed electoral system was clearly a simplistic one but there seems little doubt that it had an increasing effect. He gave enormous coverage to the activities of the Reform group, who mounted a persistent campaign via County Meetings—a total of nine between 1811 and 1822—to popularize the cause. Detailed reports on these meetings, their size, speeches made, and resolutions passed, appeared in the paper, provoking the *Gazette* into argument and debate.

General Election years, 1812, 1818, 1820, 1826, provided oppor-tunity for the *West Briton* to focus on the illegal activities of 'the Borough Mongers', especially well-known local ones such as Sir

Christopher Hawkins and Lord Falmouth. It made the particularly telling point in 1820 that

> while Cornwall sends 42 burgesses to Parliament, it is rather strange that 'the worthy and independent' electors of our numerous Boroughs cannot find above five or six local gentlemen whom they judge worthy of representing them so that two thirds of the Representation of Cornwall are persons whom Cornwall knows only by name.

In 1818, a quiet year politically, much publicity was given to a dinner at Bodmin in honour of Rashleigh as testament to his work for the Reform cause. The *West Briton* later published its report of Rashleigh's 2 1/2 hour speech of thanks in the form of a special supplement, since in Budd's high-flown description it was 'one of the most brilliant displays of eloquence . . . ever heard in the County'! Supplements were issued by the paper on other Reform meetings.[44]

Budd found it difficult to sustain this high level of publicity in the early 1820s when the economy improved.[45] However, the excitement engendered by the 1826 County Election, the downturn in economic conditions in the late 1820s, the sudden emergence of Catholic emancipation in 1829, all helped him revive support for Reform and continue the paper's rivalry with the *Gazette*. The rivalry showed itself, not only in editorials, but also in the correspondence sections of the papers. From the first issue of the *West Briton*, there were regular letter 'wars' between opposing correspondents. While Flindell was supported by Gregor, Budd had the backing of Rashleigh or Walker; the result being letters occupying column after column and extending week after week. After one particular bout of this, Gregor commented to his brother-in-law,'Flindell is clearly defeating Budd by his weekly cannonade . . . a sly hint in the nature of a query on his sales may do good'. A short time later he confided 'I have made the use of the *Cornwall Gazette* that I told you I would'.[46]

Usually the correspondence was conducted under the shield of pseudonyms; such as Alfred, Cornishman, A Friend of the People, and Anti-Pope, though more often Argus, Scrutator, Cornubiensis, Veritas, Algernon, Dion, Britannicus, Mercurius, or Clericus; classical names which perhaps give us some idea of their social background. This correspondence was equally protracted in terms of time and number of columns; sometimes being learned discussions on the arguments for or against Reform; others merely scoring of points. The use which politicians were prepared to make of letter writing of this kind is well illustrated by two examples from the 1826 election campaign, mentioned in a letter by Pendarves, one of the candidates.

> Vyvyan (his opponent) is doing all he can to raise the cry of 'No Popery' but this will effect Tremayne (the moderate Tory candidate) as much as it does me. We thought Cornubiensis was Pole Carew (Vyvyan's main supporter), so probably is Anti-Pope . . . Colman (Rashleigh) is much improved in health and begins to advocate my cause. He was the author of that squib about the Helston canvass in the *West Briton* last month.

While much of this correspondence, in retrospect, seems tedious and repetitive, it did not appear to be so to contemporaries. It is only rarely that one comes across a letter like that in 1811 from 'Constant Reader', requesting Budd to drop the controversy with Flindell, since he is wearied by it! The correspondence 'wars' certainly performed the important function of keeping the volume of political debate high and of maintaining the rivalry between the two papers; both of these suited Budd's aim.[47]

Budd gave prominence, too, to Reform meetings in other parts of the country as well as to votes in the Commons on motions for Reform, such as those of the Radical MP Burdett, in 1817 and 1819 and the Whig, Lord John Russell in 1821 and 1822, and especially the consistent support of Sir William Lemon, the veteran County member, for these motions. Equally the paper highlighted the popular welcome given to Burdett on a visit to the county, in 1822, to see members of the Reform group, while the following year it copied an extract from the *Sherborne Mercury* of 1783 to remind readers of one of the first meetings in Cornwall in favour of Parliamentary Reform.[48]

Although the *West Briton* had been founded for a specific purpose, Budd as editor, did not permit the paper to be devoted just to that one objective, but supported other causes as well. He was, for instance, strongly in favour of freedom of the press against proposed government restrictions in 1817, as well as the right of the people to free assembly. He warned, after the events at St Peter's Fields in 1819, that 'the case of the people of Manchester may be the case of the people of Cornwall . . . whenever their meeting may be disagreeable to Ministers'. He was equally forceful in supporting Rashleigh's argument that non-freeholders had as much right to attend County Meetings as freeholders. He showed obvious concern about the post-war distress; attacking the level of government expenditure, high taxation, and the heavy burden which tithes and local rates placed on the farmers. He

supported their case on the Corn Laws, since 'the foreign grower ought
to pay a duty on importing his corn equal to the amount of taxes
imposed on our farmers . . .that the importer and the farmer may meet
on equal terms in the British market'.[49]

Most of all, Budd sided with Cornish farmers when a major tithe
dispute arose at the end of 1821. This involved the imprisonment of a
farmer, Anthony Geake of Trecarrel, by an ecclesiastical court at
the request of his rector, Rev. Johnes, despite having won an action
against the rector in a civil court. The *West Briton* roundly condemned
Johnes's action. The *Gazette*, after ignoring the case for several weeks,
was put on the defensive, merely expressing its 'regrets' at Geake's
imprisonment and saying that 'the parties should have compromised
this unpleasant affair'.[50] Equally, when the farmers themselves
organized a County Meeting in the spring of 1822 to petition about
agricultural distress, the paper voiced its unqualified approval; 'We
regard the approaching meeting as the most important event that was
ever held in Cornwall. It is the first time that the Yeomanry as a body
have come forward to act for themselves.' It gave detailed coverage,
especially to the speeches of those Reformers who attended the
meeting, which concluded by including a demand for Parliamentary
Reform in the petition drawn up concerning rents, tithes and taxes.
Budd could be well pleased that his efforts had helped towards a
crucial alliance between the farmers and the Reformers. Likewise,
he did much in the paper during the election campaign of 1826, to
propagate the view that the independence of the yeomanry was being
threatened by Tory attempts to win both County seats.[51]

RAISING POLITICAL CONSCIOUSNESS
In appearance, size, price (both were increased to 7d in 1815 because
of the Stamp Duty), and much of their contents, there was little
difference between the two papers. The format, by which the front
page was devoted to advertisements and public notices, was common
to both. Equally, in the other pages, they both provided coverage
of trade and commercial matters important to Cornwall: of tin and
copper prices in the mining industry; of the state of farming and of
corn prices, and of the fortunes of the fishing industry. Sporting events
of particular local interest such as Cornish wrestling contests or the
Porthleven Regatta figured in the papers as did major catastrophes
like the loss of 213 lives from a ship wrecked off Falmouth in 1814.
Items of a curious or sensational nature were, also, well to the fore
in their local news reporting. The death of a 'Cornish Giant'—a
Mr Chillcott—at Tintagel was reported in 1815. Bull-baiting on
Penzance Green was highlighted in 1814 and even worse, 'shameless

transactions' of 'Wife-selling' at Redruth and St Austell were exposed in 1819.

However, on the desirability of Parliamentary Reform and, indeed, most of the major political issues of the time, there was a fundamental divide. What effect did this have on the readers in Cornwall?

They clearly became more knowledgeable, being provided with information on a wide range of issues, including those such as the Corn Laws or the repeal of the Property Tax, where there was little disagreement between the two papers. They were also provided with the arguments, on both sides of the political fence, on those issues like Parliamentary Reform and Catholic emancipation, where there was a major disagreement. The public, for perhaps the first time, were given the opportunity, through reading both papers, to weigh the arguments and make up their minds. In reality though, most probably saw only one of the papers. The incessant outpouring from the *West Briton*, on the need for Reform, meant that the question was constantly before the readers, and in a way that no number of public meetings by the Friends of Parliamentary Reform could ever have done. In so doing it forced the *Gazette* to respond, thus creating fresh controversy.

The political consciousness of the reading public in Cornwall was thus raised to an extent which would have been undreamt of before the establishment of a second paper. The contrast between the meagre amount of political news relating to Cornwall before 1810, and the vast amount of space devoted, after that date, to Reform, Catholic claims, agricultural problems or tithes is truly dramatic. Moreover, the evidence suggests that the readers were not alienated (as perhaps happens now), but stimulated into public discussion and into a demand for more of the same. On rare occasions, as in 1826, it could lead to a crude primitive response. The *Gazette*'s editor was threatened by an irate reader of the *West Briton* with horsewhipping, for calling the crowd at the election 'a Mob': 'You! who have been in this county but a few months and a German too! call the freeholders a mob!' Nothing further seems to have happened on this occasion though the same cannot be said of a later editor of the *West Briton* who was actually assaulted, in 1850, by an irate High Sheriff, wielding a horsewhip![52]

One important question is how widespread was this politicization of the public? It might be argued it remained comparatively narrow, confined to the literate and well-to-do who could afford the high price of either paper. The comments in both, about circulation, were invariably and perhaps deliberately vague, and even when actual figures are given, their reliability has to be doubted. Official figures on the number of stamps issued to the papers are not available for the years before 1831, when the combined annual total for the two amounted to 77,900, or only 1,500 a week.[53] Yet it will be recalled that the *Gazette* claimed as far back as 1806 that its own circulation was 1,500 a week!

However, it is accepted that newspaper readership was far wider than the circulation. Frank O'Gorman has stressed that 'precise circulation figures for newspapers are not of critical significance owing to the multiple use made of each copy and the widespread practice of reading aloud . . . It is reasonable to assume that that members of a family might either read or hear all or part of the contents.' In addition, papers were passed from hand to hand, and people clubbed together to buy them or they were available in coffee shops, taverns and libraries. This was the case in Cornwall, the *Gazette* making great play, on one occasion, of a report that the Reading Room of Penzance Library had resolved to give up the *West Briton*.[54]

It has been estimated that, in London, readership of a single copy was as high as 30. Morever, as Charles Clark has pointed out in his study of eighteenth century papers 'the ritual of reading was not a closed communion. Anyone who could read could participate . . . The bounds of literacy were considerably broader than the publishers' intended audience . . . The newspapers' message almost certainly reached well beyond the audience most publishers had in mind.' The effect of this on politics was clear: 'long before the end of the unreformed period, newspapers had penetrated deep into the voting classes.'[55]

In Cornwall, at the start of the ninteenth century the Cornish electorate had been approximately 2,700, while by 1831 it had risen to around 4,000.[56] Thanks, however, to the combined efforts of the *West Briton* and the Reformers, political consciousness had reached well beyond these freeholders. That many more than this group were both politically aware and active is evident in several ways. The number attending County Meetings clearly increased and equally the number signing petitions in favour of Reform or against Catholic emancipation.

Most of all, the 1826 election showed public excitement and involvement as never before. This was partly because it was the first to be contested since 1790, but there was also something extra. It was a contest between two opposing political views, represented by Pendarves, the Reformer, and Vyvyan, the Ultra-Tory candidate. Alfred Jenkin, the Quaker steward of the Lanhydrock estate and a dispassionate observer of the election, confided privately to the owner, Mrs Agar 'the public feeling in favour of E.W.W. Pendarves has been intense.' The *West Briton*, too, wrote of the final election scenes:

Thus terminated a meeting which will long be remembered in Cornwall . . . The assemblage was unprecedented. Those who remember the last contested election say that, on no day during its continuance were anything like the numbers that crowded the streets of Lostwithiel on Tuesday last, to be seen then. Upwards of 2000 horsemen entered the town with Mr Pendarves, comprising the great bulk of the Yeomanry of the County.[57]

There was similar public excitement in 1829, over Catholic emancipation, and in the Reform years of 1830–1. The opponents of concessions to the Catholics organized a whole series of protest meetings in different localities in Cornwall, with the total signatories to petitions to the Commons amounting to over 9,000. Similarly the greater excitement aroused by the prospect of Reform led to three County Meetings in a single year—January, March, October 1831— all attended by large numbers and with well over 10,000 names to one of the subsequent petitions. All this was clear evidence of public involvement in the political process, which the rivalry between the papers had helped to stimulate.[58]

The emancipation issue seems to have been the only time when Budd was put on the back foot. Faced with strong opposition from some Methodists to concession, it was the *West Briton*, rather than the *Gazette*, which deprecated the public excitement, advocated that the question 'should be left to the deliberations of Parliament', and fell back on the argument that 'the intelligence and property of the County were in favour of those claims', whatever the public felt. [59] However, Budd's adoption of an unpopular line on this issue did not have any adverse effect on, what was clearly by then, the superiority of his paper's circulation over the *Gazette*. The first tangible and fairly reliable evidence, the number of Stamps issued to the respective papers, revealed that, in 1831, the *West Briton*'s circulation was almost twice that of *The Gazette*. While 50,900 stamps were issued to the former, only 27,000 went to its Tory rival.[60]

'THE INDEPENDENCE OF CORNWALL'
One important allied consideration is whether Budd, being a Methodist local preacher, deliberately tailored the views of the paper on certain issues to appeal to Cornwall's many non-conformists. Clearly from the outset, he gave consistent support to the demand for repeal of the Test and Corporation Acts and in 1811 criticized proposals of Lord Sidmouth to stop itinerant preachers. When the Catholic issue arose in 1813, the paper warned the dissenters that if they helped in opposing

concessions, they would be the next to be persecuted. However, in Budd's mind the key consideration was less concern for a religious group but more for Parliamentary Reform. 'Religious and Civil Liberty are inseparable and we are well assured that the only means by which both can be secured . . . is a Reform of the House of Commons.' In 1829, he was not deterred from maintaining his support for emancipation by the evident hostility of many Methodists in Cornwall to concession. Indeed, he took a prominent part at a public meeting in Truro with a two-hour speech in support of Catholic claims.[61]

There is no evidence that the *West Briton*, or indeed the *Gazette*, attempted to make any appeal to any incipient Cornish national feeling. The first long editorial by Budd in July 1810 made no mention of it, despite the newspaper's evocative name, and indeed both papers considered themselves to be in the mainstream of British politics. Yet at times, both thought it advantageous to invoke appeals to Cornwall or 'Cornishness'; the *Gazette*, for example, proclaiming in 1829 'Be the fate of the Catholic question what it may, Cornwall has nobly performed its duty'.

More intriguing are the several references by the *West Briton* or the Reformers to the 'Independence of Cornwall'. It was first used in 1813 in support of the Reformers' efforts to establish the right of inhabitants to attend County Meetings. The next year, after a second such meeting had taken place, involving inhabitants as well as freeholders the paper stated that '16 August will long be remembered as an anniversary of the triumph of the Independence of the County'. Again, in 1817, when it was rumoured that Sir W. Lemon, the pro-Reform County MP might resign and be replaced by a Tory, the *West Briton* warned against 'the complete prostration of the Independence of Cornwall'. It was used, too, by supporters of Pendarves's candidature in 1826, and in his victory speech on the hustings, he told the crowd 'You have secured the Independence of Cornwall'. Most certainly all these references were not to independence literally, but to independence from aristocratic control, or what O'Gorman has defined as 'a repudiation of the politics of oligarchy'. It seems, nevertheless, to have been a term which had a strong appeal to something deep in Cornish culture and identity.[62]

CONCLUSION

In 1810, on the foundation of the *West Briton*, De Dunstanville privately declared that 'I cannot conceive that any House will receive it which is not inclined to go all lengths with the pretended Reformers'. He was still alive some 21 years later to witness the triumph of the Reform cause in Cornwall and the clear superiority of the *West Briton* over its rival. The link between the two was obvious and, as Budd modestly expressed it in an editorial (12 October 1832), 'To us who have had a part in this great contest, to share in the exultation it will excite from the Lands End to the Tamar is ample recompense'.[63]

The reasons for the paper's superiority are evident from the above discussion. In some ways it had been fortunate. A number of issues had arisen that helped its expansion in the years after 1810. Economic problems—post-war distress, taxation, tithes, the plight of Cornish farmers—could all be linked to the question of Parliamentary Reform and likewise the right of non-freeholders to attend County Meetings. These and others had been exploited by the Reform group to preach the necessity of Reform. It had been Budd, however, who had publicized their arguments and speeches to the Cornish public, reaching an audience that no number of meetings could do. In his long editorship, he had adhered without deviation to a consistent line—the case for moderate reform—and so was able to refute accusations of extremism. He had shown great skill in focusing the public's attention upon it in numerous ways. Not only had he given the Reform meetings great publicity, but also references to Parliamentary debates on Reform motions, reports of Reform meetings in other counties and exposure of malpractices in Cornish boroughs, had all reinforced the message. Even the frequent correspondence 'battles' in the two papers had served to assist the cause.

The *Gazette* initially had the advantages of the firm backing of many of Cornwall's wealthier landowners and of being the first in the field. However, it suffered from the frequent changes of editor—four in less than 10 years— and the changing editorial line adopted to meet the challenge posed by the *West Briton*. The *Gazette* was correct in arguing that the granting of Parliamentary Reform would not be a panacea, and that it would not solve many of the problems utilized by the Reformers and the *West Briton* in their campaign. Nevertheless it was difficult to deny the case for some reform, with the many examples of corruption in Cornish boroughs to hand. It was also forced on the defensive on those issues, such as tithes and the right of all inhabitants to attend County Meetings, which mattered to many Cornish. As a result the *West Briton* appeared to be more in tune with the Cornish public than was the *Gazette*.

The tasks before Budd in the post-Reform period were to maintain the lead established by his paper, and to consolidate further the hold which the party of Reform had gained in Cornwall. Consideration of these must, however, be deferred for another occasion. As it turned out, Budd had only four years of his life left to accomplish them, but already his achievements were considerable. Indeed, the Friends of

Parliamentary Reform were much aware of his contribution to their success. As the Rev. Robert Walker emphasized in a letter to the paper, 'it was chiefly through the *West Briton* that Cornwall's sons elevated her among the Counties of England in the great cause of Reform'.[64]

NOTES AND REFERENCES

1. Claude Berry, *The West Briton in Nine Reigns*, 1955, repeated in the 150th anniversary supplement of the paper, 21 July 1960. Berry was, of course, an editor himself of the paper from 1947. Nigel Tangye's article, 'The Newspaper in Cornwall, a Protracted Birth' in *Cornish Studies* 7 (1979) almost amounts to a breach of the Trades Description Act, given the brief references it contains to the foundation of the *Cornwall Gazette*. His *Gazetteer and Finding List of Cornish Newspapers*, published by the Trevithick Society and Institute of Cornish Studies, 1980, is much more useful, despite some factual errors.
2. Frank O'Gorman, *The Long 18th Century, British Political and Social History 1688–1832*, London, 1972, p. 127.
3. G.A. Cranfield, *The Development of the Provincial Newspaper 1700–1760*, 1962, and *Handlist of English Provincial Newspapers 1700–1760*, London, 1952. R.M. Wiles, *Freshest Advices: Early Provincial Newspapers in England*, London, 1965.
4. Charles E. Clark, *The Public Prints: The Newspaper in Anglo-American Culture 1665–1740*, London, 1994.
5. A. Aspinall, *Politics and the Press 1780–1850*, London, 1948, Chap. 15. J. Black, *The English Press in the 18th century*, London, 1987. The verdict is Clark's, 1994, p. 252.
6. A.K. Hamilton Jenkin, *Cornwall and its People*, 1945, p. 147. Wiles, 1965, pp. 129–30. F. O'Gorman, *Voters, Patrons and Parties: The Unreformed Electoral System of Hanoverian England 1734–1832*, London, 1989, p. 287.
7. For all biographical details, see those two indispensable sources on Cornwall, G.C. Boase and W.P. Courtney, *Bibliotheca Cornubiensis*, 1874–82, and G.C. Boase, *Collectanea Cornubiensia*, 1890, as well as, in a few cases, F. Boase, *Modern English Biography*, 1892–1921, and *The Gentleman's Magazine*.
8. Boase and Courtney, 1874–82, p. 151. *Royal Cornwall Gazette* No. 1, 2 July 1803; 3 June 1809.
9. *Royal Cornwall Gazette*, 2 July 1803; 22 November 1806; 9 January 1809. East Cornwall gentry, at first, favoured Plymouth papers which were closer. Earl Mt Edgcumbe referred to a Plymouth paper he took in a letter to R. Pole Carew, 29 November 1819, [C]ornwall [R]ecord [O]ffice, from Antony House, Carew Mss CC/M/52.
10. Berry, 1955; *West Briton* 21 July 1960.
11. *Cornwall Gazette* 7 March 1801; *Royal Cornwall Gazette* 10 June 1805; 25 October 1805; 16 May 1807; 20 May 1809.
12. See W.B. Elvins, 'The Reform Movement and County Politics in Cornwall,

1809–1852', unpublished M.A. thesis, University of Birmingham, and W.B. Elvins, 'Cornwall's Unsung Political Hero: John Colman Rashleigh' in Philip Payton (ed.), *Cornish Studies: Six*, Exeter, 1998. See also Edwin Jaggard's article, 'The Parliamentary Reform Movement in Cornwall, 1805–1826' in *Parliamentary History*, Vol. 2, 1983.

13. *Royal Cornwall Gazette*, 3 June and successive issues till 14 October 1809. Gregor's pamphlet (September 1809) was incurred under the Civil List. *Pensions and Public Offices with observations on the Expenses conduct of Modern Reformers*, price 1/6d. Rashleigh's (October 1809) *Reasons for Reform or a brief consideration of our Representative System*. Both were printed by Flindell at the *Gazette* Office.

14. *Royal Cornwall Gazette*, 7 April 1810, 5 May 1810, 12 May 1810 and subsequent issues.

15. *West Briton*, 21 July 1810.

16. Cyrus Redding, *50 Years Recollections, Literary and Political*, 1863, pp. 146–7.

17. For Gill's remarks, see J.C. Trewin, *Down to the Lion* (1952) p. 175. Budd's pamphlet *Remarks on a pamphlet . . . in a Letter to a Noble Lord*, published 11 October 1809, was, at first, wrongly attributed to Rashleigh. Joseph Childs had clashed with Flindell in 1806 over The *Gazette*'s reporting of the Liskeard election (*Royal Cornwall Gazette*, 22 November 1806, 6 December 1806). The choice of Truro was Redding's, according to Ashley Rowe (*West Briton*, 21 July 1960).

18. *Royal Cornwall Gazette*, 30 June 1810. Budd's defence (*West Briton*, 20 July) was that the title had been selected 'merely as a provincial distinction . . . and a mark of respect for this staple branch of commerce in Cornwall'.

19. Literally translated this means 'old faith'. However, according to Glyn Moore—former colleague and Classicist—both Latin words have layers of meaning which make the phrase difficult to translate. His judgement is that it means 'old (fashioned) loyalties or values'.

20. *West Briton*, 20 July 1810.

21. *West Briton*, 18 Sept 1810.

22. For example, Carew Mss CC/M/52, Dr Richard Taunton, Senior Physician at the Royal Cornwall Infirmary, to Carew 19 November 1819: 'I find that the Advertisement of our Declaration (about Peterloo) with the signatures will be very expensive—about £2-2s, wherefore I have informed Mr Heard printer of the *West Briton* that I was not instructed to have it inserted in his paper . . . As their party has deprived the editor of the *Cornwall Gazette* of their Requisition, it would appear not to be right that they should be furnished with ours.'

23. C.R.O. Rashleigh Mss, W. Rashleigh to T. Robins (Liskeard), Saturday 11 March 1820. The letter adds 'your clerk would have killed his little pony had he proceeded to Truro. He therefore had one of my horses and reached Truro in good time' (for publication).

24. Aspinall, p. 131.

25. *Royal Cornwall Gazette*, 2 June 8 December 1810; Donald Read, *Press and the People 1790–1850*, London, 1961, p. 64. The reference to 'subscribers'

supports Clark's finding, ibid. p.259, that most weekly papers were delivered on a subscription basis to households rather than sold on the streets. Mt Edgcumbe writing to Carew, 29 November 1819 remarked 'As your *Cornwall Gazette* did not arrive as it should have done yesterday, I take the liberty of sending you mine'. Carew Mss CC/M/52.

26. *Royal Cornwall Gazette*, 5 May 1810, 5 December 1812. Personal outbursts from Flindell of this type led him into trouble, being found guilty, on 19 March 1821, of a libel on Queen Caroline in the *Western Luminary* and being sentenced to eight months in prison. He had said 'She was as notoriously devoted to Venus as to Bacchus and that she was such a woman as would . . . be committed to Brideswell and whipped'. Aspinall ibid. p. 131. Seven days later, on 26 March, William Rashleigh wrote telling Flindell to stop sending the paper until further orders (Rashleigh Mss).

27. Carew Mss CC/M/50, Charles Rashleigh to Carew 21 September 1817, and CC/M/52, R. Taunton to Carew 16 November 1819.

28. *Royal Cornwall Gazette*, 22 December 1810; 2 November 1811; 10 April 1812; 26 December 1812.

29. *Royal Cornwall Gazette*, 7 April 1809, 15 September 1810, 27 October 1810, 12 October 1811.

30. Boase and Courtney, p. 151.

31. C.R.O. Gregor Mss, F. Gregor to F. Glanville 11 December 1812. Aspinall, p. 132.

32. *Royal Cornwall Gazette*, 2 January 1813.

33. *West Briton*, 8 August 1817. *Royal Cornwall Gazette*, 31 December 1813, 30 July 1814, 30 November 1816.

34. *Royal Cornwall Gazette*, 2 January 1813, 30 July 1814, 4 February 1815, 9 February 1816, 18 October 1816, 25 October 1816, 1 November 1816, 9 November 1816, 1 March 1817, 15 March 1817, 12 April 1817.

35. *West Briton*, 8 August 1817, *Royal Cornwall Gazette*, 31 December 1817. Carew Mss CC/M/50 Chas Rashleigh to Carew 21, 28 September 1817.

36. *Gentleman's Magazine*, Vol. 39 (1853) pp. 446–7, DNB XVIII p. 147, R.C.G. 10 July 1819. Coincidentally, James Montgomery (1771–1854), editor of the *Sheffield Iris* paper, was also educated at Fulneck. (Reed ibid. p. 72).

37. *Royal Cornwall Gazette*, 2 January 1819, 26 June 1819, 10 July 1819, 21 August 1819, 4 September 1819, 25 September 1819, 4 December 1819. The last editorial expressed strong support for the proposed measures in the aftermath of Peterloo: 'There is not a man in the country, unwarped by party prejudices who can say they are unnecessary.'

38. Flindell died July 1824. His wife was certainly running the *Western Luminary* in 1826. She continued her husband's hostility to the Reformers, and used it to attack Pendarves during the County Election, leading to the threat of legal action. Vyvyan commented to Carew (28 June) 'She has attacked him beyond all measure in this week's paper and I fear . . . I shall hardly succeed in pacifying her'. Carew Mss CC/N/59.

39. *Royal Cornwall Gazette*, 4 December 1819, 6 December 1823, 2 January

1827, 18 December 1824, 25 December 1824. Vyvyan, the Tory candidate, issued 'an unqualified disapprobation' to Pendarves, which probably had much to do with the *Gazette*'s apology, though on 1 January 1825, it attempted to justify the attack.

40. C.R.O. *Memoirs of Sir J.C. Rashleigh*, FS3/1127/2, Pt 2 pp. 37–40. The original four vellum bound notebooks in which it was completed, 1846–7, appear to have disappeared but his great grandson, Edward Colman Rashleigh, completed a typewritten copy in 1931.

41. *Royal Cornwall Gazette*, 25 July 1812; *West Briton*, 3 August 1810, 28 September 1810, 21 December 1810. The reference to 'Orders' suggests that the *West Briton* followed the *Gazette* in delivering to subscribers. There may have been some free copies distributed, for it contended (21 December) 'We circulate none gratis but the usual papers to agents and none in the Mining Districts. It is *The Gazette* which circulates gratis'. Carew Mss CC/M/52, Mt Edgcumbe to Carew 29 November 1819.

42. Berry, 1955. *West Briton* 15 November 1811; 10 November 1815; 24 November 1815. Behind the scenes, Falmouth may have had a financial interest in the paper.

43. *West Briton*, 27 July 1810, 3 August 1810; 5 March 1810, 9 July 1810, 27 August 1819, 7 January 1820; 11 February 1820. *Royal Cornwall Gazette*, 19 May 1821, 26 May 1821. Budd's political outlook was very similar to that of Edward Baines, the famous editor of the *Leeds Mercury* after 1801.

44. *West Briton*, 18 August 1818, 10 February 1820.

45. The *Gazette* claimed, 15 February 1823, that 'the Radical mania in the County is nearly extinct'.

46. Gregor Mss, Gregor to Glanville, 14 August, 22 October 1812.

47. Rashleigh Mss, E.W.W. Pendarves to W. Rashleigh 25 December 1825. *West Briton*, 29 November 1811.

48. A typical example from the *West Briton*, 3 May 1822, on the Russell motion: 'It is unnecessary to say that amongst this Band of Patriots is to be found the venerable Sir W. Lemon, whose unvarying consistency throughout his long public life does honour to the County.' *West Briton*, 30 August 1822; 13 September 1822; 19 September 1823.

49. *West Briton*, 1 March 1813; 3 June 1814; 24 February 1815; 23 May 1817; 10 September 1819.

50. *West Briton*, 9 November 1821; 23 November 1821; 7 December 1821; 14 December 1821. *Royal Cornwall Gazette*, 8 December 1821. John Rowe, *Cornwall in the Age of the Industrial Revolution*, Liverpool, 1953, pp. 243–44.

51. *West Briton*, 22 March 1822; 5 April 1822, and 28 January 1826, especially the speeches of farmers, Snell, Hambly and J.P. Peters. The latter proclaimed 'The Yeomanry know their rights and their strengths. They will never allow two members to be thrust on them by the Aristocracy.'

52. *West Briton*, 14 July 1826. This letter contains some serious mistakes. Although addressed by name to Gillett, the editor, the references to him being German and only in the county a few months are both incorrect.

The only German editor, Shoberl, had resigned in December 1819, so Gillett had been in charge for over six years! In 1850 Sir Samuel Spry was found guilty of an assault on the *West Briton* editor, John Taylor Brown. *West Briton*, 2 August 1850.

53. Figures from the Inland Revenue, Somerset House now located at the Public Record Office, IR 69 1A.
54. *Royal Cornwall Gazette*, 5 December 1812.
55. R.K. Webb, *Modern England*, 1969, p. 159.
56. The 2,700 figure comes from *The House of Commons, 1790–1820*, ed. Roland Thorne, 1986, Vol. 2 p. 40. In 1831 the *West Briton* (3 June) gave a figure of 4,200, while A. Jenkin's letter (19 May) to P. Grenfell had quoted 3,800. [R]oyal [I]nstitution of [C]ornwall, Jenkin Letter Books.
57. *West Briton*, 23 June 1826. RIC Jenkin Letter Book, A. Jenkin to Mrs A.M. Agar, 22 June 1826.
58. *Royal Cornwall Gazette*, 28 February 1829; *West Briton*, 6 March 1829, 21 January 1831, 4 February 1831, 25 March 1831, 28 October 1831.
59. *West Briton*, 2 January 1829; 2 March 1829.
60. See note 53.
61. *West Briton*, 26 April 1811; 8 January 1813, 16 January 1829. *Royal Cornwall Gazette*, 17 January 1829. Philip Ziegler, *Addington*, 1965, p. 298. It is worth emphasizing, too, that while Budd was a Methodist, the founders of the *West Briton* and the Reform group were Anglican gentry or clergymen.
62. *Royal Cornwall Gazette*, 24 January 1829; *West Briton*, 19 February 1813; 19 August 1814; 13 June 1817, 23 June 1826.
63. C.R.O. Tremayne Mss, Bundle 117 De Dunstanville to Rev. H.H. Tremayne 7 June 1810. The former died 5 February 1835, aged 71. *West Briton*, 12 October 1832.
64. *West Briton*, 18 January 1833.

'VOTE LABOR, AND RID SOUTH AUSTRALIA OF A DANGER TO THE PURITY OF OUR RACE': THE CORNISH RADICAL TRADITION IN SOUTH AUSTRALIA, 1900–1939

Philip Payton

INTRODUCTION

In recent years the distinctive characteristics of Cornish politics have received considerable attention, with historians and political scientists pointing to both a discernible 'Cornish political culture' and a particular 'Cornish Radical Tradition', the Liberal-Nonconformist nexus that emerged in the nineteenth century (and which has survived perhaps into the twenty-first) being adjudged their most enduring feature.[1] The place of the 'Great Emigration' in Cornish politics has also received some attention, with observers noting the influence of the emigrant Cornish upon the conduct of politics at home in Cornwall but also, perhaps more importantly, tracing the transplantation of Cornish political culture overseas.[2] The latter study has been attempted most successfully with regard to South Australia, where the role of the Cornish in that State's political development is now an accepted component of Australian historiography.[3] In particular, it has become commonplace to compare and contrast Radical politics in Cornwall and South Australia in the late nineteenth/early twentieth centuries.[4] Such comparisons show how the abrupt demise of Cornish copper (and the subsequent decline of Cornish tin) after 1866 cut short the development of trade unionism and a wider Labour movement in Cornwall, while, by contrast, the mass emigration of Cornwall's 'natural leaders' (including budding trade unionists) and the continuing success of the South Australian copper industry allowed the development in that State of a particular kind of 'Cornish socialism'. On the mines of northern Yorke Peninsula, in the district of Moonta, Wallaroo and Kadina, known colloquially as 'Australia's Little Cornwall', a vibrant trade union movement emerged, its flavour being overwhelmingly 'Cornish' and 'Nonconformist', while the area's Cornish communities made a strong contribution to the growth in South Australia of the United Labor Party.

"Capital! What IS Capital?"
"If you was to ask we to come 'n' 'ave a drink, lad, that would
be capital."

Figure 1: Oswald Pryor's commentary on the Cornish miners' supposed suspicion of advanced socialism on the Yorke Peninsula mines. This and other Pryor cartoons reproduced courtesy of the National Trust of South Australia.

This United Labor Party (ULP) was a peculiarly South Australian phenomenon, essentially Nonconformist in its make-up and outlook and profoundly influenced by the Cornish trade unionists, in many respects distinct from the Irish-Catholic influence in the Labor movement in neighbouring Victoria and New South Wales. Its reputation was for moderation and pragmatism ('eminently practical rather than eloquently visionary', as the Irish Land League agitator Michael Davitt put it when he visited South Australia[5]), with an explicit link between religion and politics. Within the United Labor Party there were certainly echoes of the Liberal-Nonconformist nexus in Cornwall but the ULP claimed a 'socialist' identity and had its power base amongst a strong miners' union. These latter features served to distinguish it from the Liberal-Nonconformist tradition at home but, rather than a repudiation of or deviation from the experience in Cornwall, the development of the United Labor Party in South Australia represented the maturing of Cornish Radicalism in an overseas environment where (unlike Cornwall) mining had survived and trade unionism had flourished.

And yet, if the South Australian experience seemed somehow more 'progressive' in comparison with Cornwall, where the Labour movement was apparently retarded and the Liberals had become 'fossilized' as the Radical opponents of Toryism at a time when politics in much of Britain was becoming a Labour-Conservative contest, it was not long before it too appeared anachronistic. To begin with, the fate that had overcome the Cornish copper industry in 1866 befell the mighty mines of Moonta and Wallaroo after the Great War, both falling silent in 1923, while the characteristics that had marked the ULP became less distinctive and less important as it amalgamated with the continent-wide Australian Labor Party and was thus subsumed in a wider political entity. Moreover, as these bases for the Cornish Radical Tradition were thus eroded, so the agendas that shaped politics in the State became ever more distinctly Australian, from the new political allegiances that emerged after 1900 and the conscription issue of 1916, to the institutionalizing of the 'White Australia' policy and the controversy surrounding the 'Premiers' Plan' of 1933.

A curious paradox thus emerged. On the one hand, public opinion in South Australia continued to equate Labor politics, at least in part, with the Cornish and with Nonconformity, while the make-up of the Labor hierarchy continued to reflect the Cornish, Nonconformist and mining background. Indeed, as Hopgood has noted, even during the 1920s and 1930s the cartoonist's stock stereotype of the South Australian Labor politician was a corpulent Cousin Jack complete with Moonta billy-goat beard and with a red flag hidden behind his back.[6] In the public mind, Labor politics still drew on the Cornish tradition, one which professed moderation but (as the red flag implied) disguised a commitment to at least some kind of socialism. On the other hand, however, as noted above, the cultural and socio-economic basis of the tradition thus stereotyped was under threat, both from structural changes within the State and the emergence of new political agendas. As Lonie concluded in his study of South Australian politics in the inter-war period:

> By 1930, the A.L.P. [Australian Labor Party] itself did not mirror, in its hierarchy, the changes that had taken place in the composition of the work force since the time of the party's inception, and especially since the end of World War I. Rather, its composition and ideology reflected the social situation of the 1890s. Of note was the still very strong Methodist flavour which derived in the first place from the mine workers of Burra and Wallaroo who were of Cornish stock.[7]

'HONEST JOHN' VERRAN

But twenty years before, this mismatch seemed hardly the case, when in the April 1910 State Election the United Labor Party was swept into office for the first time, its leader (and South Australia's new Premier) one John Verran, a Cornish miner and Methodist local preacher. As C.C. James noted in his *History of Gwennap*, Verran was born at Cusgarne in that parish on 9 July 1856.[8] As a youngster he emigrated with his parents to South Australia, where he found work at the Kapunda copper mine as a pickey-boy (ore-sorter). Later, he moved on to Moonta Mines, where he worked underground as a tributer until his election to the Adelaide Parliament in 1901. John McConnell Black, the South Australian essayist and diarist, thought Verran 'the typical Cornish miner, with his burly frame, his goatee and general exuberance',[9] and there is little doubt that Verran's working-class, Cornish background accounted for his popularity amongst the Yorke Peninsula miners as he became involved in local trade unionism and politics. As the Adelaide *Advertiser* was to put it in 1910, 'Mr Verran is the more popular at the Peninsula towns because only nine years ago he was working with his three sons at the 360 fathom level at Taylor's Shaft at Moonta'.[10]

Verran's Methodist allegiance was also important. Brought up a Primitive Methodist, he mixed religious teaching with political debate. An article in the *Plain Dealer* newspaper in 1911, for example, noted how in a sermon delivered in Wallaroo Mines Methodist Church,

Verran used the parable of the 'Barren Fig Tree' to attack 'modern commercialism',[11] while on another occasion he insisted 'that his M.P. (membership of Parliament) was due to his P.M. (Primitive Methodism)'.[12] Another observer thought that 'Had not Methodism first made him a preacher, politics could not know him now as Premier',[13] while to those who argued that religion had no place in politics, Verran replied:

> Religion is citizenship, and the relationship between religion and politics is very close . . . When we come to justice and righteousness and truth these are great elementary principles of religion which affect the basis of our manhood. Religion is not a question of going to heaven. It is a question of living and making the world better for having been in it.[14]

Verran had his first opportunity to put this concept of active citizenship into effect when, as President of the Moonta, Kadina and Wallaroo Branch of the Amalgamated Miners' Association (AMA), he led the miners out on strike in 1891–2 in demand for more favourable employment contracts. Ominously, the strike was not a success. Despite generous donations from miners elsewhere in Australia and from trade unionists in Adelaide, the AMA found it increasingly difficult to maintain strike payments to its members, and as the conflict dragged into its eighteenth week the strike was broken finally by desperate and hungry men going to the mine office to plead for work. The AMA conceded defeat, and in return the mine company promised 'substantial modifications'. to the system of employment.[15] The unfortunate men who had caused the strike to collapse were ostracized by the local community and branded '92ers' (the strike ended in January 1892), a tag that continued to haunt them even if they ventured as far afield as the mines of Broken Hill or the Western Australian goldfields. The local AMA branch itself survived the trauma of 1892, establishing itself further as an integral part of community life and continuing to put pressure on the mine company, negotiating further changes to the contract system and welcoming the company's new workers' welfare policies. It also developed an increasingly political agenda, fostering links with the United Labor Party and putting forward John Verran as a parliamentary candidate.

Verran was first elected to the State Parliament in a by-election in June 1901, having promised in his campaign to pursue 'liberal measures'.[16] He also pledged himself to reform of the Legislative Council, South Australia's always conservative upper house, a commitment to which he adhered—even though it was to precipitate the

"Only one-and-six tribute, Cap'n? Why that edden nuthin'."
"Better take un, boays, nuthin's better than nuthin' 't all."

*Figure 2: Contract negotiation and industrial relations on Yorke Peninsula, as
viewed by Oswald Pryor.*

collapse of his Ministry in 1912. In the State Election of 1902 he was
returned with a handsome majority, and in the Elections of 1905 and
1906 he again topped the poll, the principal issue of the day being
reform of the Legislative Council. A Labor–Radical Liberal coalition
had been returned with increased strength in 1906 but, despite this
popular mandate, the Legislative Council was successful in frustrating
most of its plans. In 1909 the Premier, Tom Price, died. His death put
pressure on the coalition, elements of the Labor Party arguing that, as
they were the dominant coalition partner, the next Premier should also
be chosen from amongst their ranks. In fact, in a sort of 'buggin's turn'
power brokering, A.H. Peake, the Radical Liberal leader, was chosen.
Several Labor members refused to serve under him, and so Peake, with
his coalition collapsing, was forced into a new alliance with country and
conservative members, a prelude to the new political allegiances that
were soon to form.

Verran, in the meantime, had replaced Price as leader of the United Labor Party, and in the Election of April 1910 Labor found itself in office in its own right for the very first time.[17] Verran received a hero's welcome as he returned from Adelaide to Yorke Peninsula as Premier. The conservative *Kadina and Wallaroo Times* claimed that the demonstrations that greeted Verran were 'the most miserable specimens of his irresponsibility . . . Torches and bands and wild words, and gesticulations'.[18] A more sympathetic account observed that:

> There could be no doubt as to the warmth of the welcome which the Cornish miners sought to give to their President on his being raised to place and power, and the gathering will mark an epoch in the history of Moonta. Bunting was flying all over the town, and all Moonta and his wife were out to take part in the gathering. At Kadina and at Wallaroo hundreds of workers joined the train, and the scene on arrival at Moonta was an animated one. The Wallaroo town band and the combined Moonta Commonwealth and Model brass bands discoursed music as the train drew up in the platform.[19]

There followed speeches, and cheering, and even the shedding of tears. But the triumph was premature, for the Labor victory had the effect of galvanizing the hitherto disparate non-Labor factions into a new and strong Opposition force. Ironically, several of the prime movers in this progress towards Opposition were Cornishmen, two of them former Labor supporters to boot. One was John George Bice, born in Callington, Cornwall, in 1853, a Methodist, trade unionist and former blacksmith at Moonta Mines. Following his marriage to Elizabeth Jane Trewenack, a Cornish woman, in 1875 he established a merchant's business in Port Augusta, becoming Mayor of that town in 1888–9 and first entering the Adelaide Parliament in 1894. He opposed 'repressive legislation', he said, and as for women:

> I am in favour of Adult Suffrage and because [I] believe that women are equally as intelligent, equally as capable of studying political questions, and of recording their vote as we are, I think they should have the same privileges as men in this respect. Further, without representation there is no right of taxation and under our present laws women are entrusted with the rights of property and are subjected to taxation —consequently they are entitled to rights of representation.[20]

Such views marked out Bice as a Radical Liberal, and during the
1890s he supported the ULP (although he never formally joined its
ranks), identifying with its moderate and pragmatic form of democratic
socialism and its Cornish-Methodist ethos. However, in 1906, with both
'socialists' and 'conservatives' apparently becoming more organized, he
was instrumental in the formation of the Liberal and Democratic
Union, led by Peake. This, in turn, was fused with the Farmers' and
Producers' Political Union and the Australian National League to form
the centre-right United Liberal Union in June 1910, a little over a
month since Labor's famous victory. The organizing secretary of the
Farmers' and Producers' Political Union was then David Morley Charleston, another of those Cornishmen who were to play an important
role in the emergence of the new Opposition.

Born in St Erth in 1848, Charleston had learned the engineering
trade at Harvey & Co. of Hayle before emigrating to San Francisco in
1874 and arriving in Australia in 1884, in 1887 finding work in the
English and Australian Copper Company's smelting works at Port
Adelaide. In 1889–90 he was President of the Trades and Labor
Council in Adelaide, and in 1891 he was sponsored as a ULP parlia-
mentary candidate. Said to be imbued 'with characteristic Cornish
fervour and enthusiasm',[21] he won the support of the local *Christian
Weekly and Methodist Journal* (which argued that 'the ideals of labour
were consistent with Christianity'[22]) and he argued for a 'broad liberal
Unionism', one which might fuse the ideas of John Stuart Mill and Karl
Marx. Thus, in his opinion, 'To attain happiness is the end and purpose
of life in high and low degree', while 'The State . . . should, if
Democracy means anything, completely control Production and
Distribution, thereby carrying to its logical conclusion the co-operative
system'.[23] This was to be achieved, however, not through revolution or
upheaval but through a slow, evolutionary process in which trade
unions would play a central role. On the strength of such views he
was elected to the Adelaide Parliament as a Labor member in 1891.
However, despite his firm left-of-centre commitment, Charleston
quarrelled with the parliamentary ULP, frustrated that the party's
caucus meetings in parliament were largely irrelevant and unproduc-
tive, with a great part of the talk spent in frivolous talk and barracking.
In the Election that followed, Charleston stood as an 'Independent
Liberal', and was returned with a substantial majority over his ULP
rival. Thereafter, he drifted gradually to the right of the political
spectrum, and entered the new Federal Parliament as a centre-
right Liberal Senator in 1901–3, subsequently lending his energies to
the Farmers' and Producers' Political Union and then, eventually, to
the United Liberal Union.

FROM TRIUMPH TO DISASTER

If the move towards a more coherent party system, and the political polarization that this implied, had served to undermine the Cornish-Methodist coalescence that had previously bound together men such as Verran, Bice and Charleston, then the fortunes of the Verran government in the face of the consolidating Opposition made matters even more difficult. As T.H. Smeaton observed in 1914, 'The path trodden by the Verran Government was not at any time a smooth one; beset as it was by snares skilfully laid by its enemies, as well as by obstacles heedlessly cast there by its friends'.[24] Indeed, the government's first year in office, 1910, was characterized by industrial strife, with more than half-a-dozen major incidents in Adelaide, each one an embarrassment for Verran whose sympathies were with the trade unionists and yet who was under great pressure (not least from the Opposition) to resist what were portrayed as challenges to law and order. In December 1910 the Adelaide cart-drivers' strike erupted, an episode that proved particularly damaging for Verran. Critics suggested he was in league with the strikers, John McConnell Black writing that:

Jack [*sic*] Verran took a jovial interest in the strike and Gunn, the secretary of the union, used to stroll across Victoria Square [in the centre of Adelaide] from the Trades Hall and consult with the Premier, who sat smoking his short pipe with his legs up on the fence of his boarding house in Landrowna Terrace.[25]

Events began to turn ugly when strike-breakers (some of whom were armed) engaged by the local Tramways Trust clashed with the striking drivers, provoking a riot. The State Governor, His Majesty's representative in South Australia, summoned Verran to Government House for a dressing-down, and it was rumoured that a Naval gunboat was about to be deployed to Port Adelaide. In the end, the strike was settled peaceably enough, with the cart-drivers securing better pay and conditions, but the damage to Verran and his government had already been done.

The Opposition had been careful to exploit the situation to the full, and was given additional ammunition in the form of the State mining controversy that unfolded during 1910 and 1911. Verran had decided to acquire the near-defunct Wandilta, Yelta and Paramatta copper mines, all on northern Yorke Peninsula and located within his constituency, with a view to running them as State enterprises, for 'God had put the wealth in the earth for everyone and not just a few people'.[26] To the Opposition this 'nationalization' was seen as evidence of Verran's commitment to 'advanced socialism', though Verran retorted that it was sound business sense. It was a great pity, he said, that promising properties 'should be languishing for want of capital', adding that at one of the mines all that was needed was 'a good Cornish lift pump to get the water out'.[27] Somewhat recklessly, Verran purchased the Yelta and Paramatta mines without reference to parliament and, indeed, without reference to all the relevant officials within his own Department of Mines. He explained angrily, 'I am not going to officers who don't know as much about mining as I do'.[28] Although the Yelta and Paramatta mines had lost £200,000 in the eight years before July 1911, Verran insisted that the Yelta had made a profit of £1,000 a month during the early 1900s and that recent reverses were merely the result of bad management. He envisaged, he said, a return of about 4 per cent on the capital invested, noting that the two properties had been purchased for only £6,000 while the smelting plant at the Yelta was alone worth £20,000.

In the public controversy that ensued, the Labor-sponsored *Daily Herald* supported the purchases but the Adelaide *Register* considered that Verran was 'wasting public money in a vain attempt to resurrect an abandoned property in his district'.[29] On Yorke Peninsula itself, the *Kadina and Wallaroo Times* added its voice to the condemnation of State ownership, while local experts such as Captain Richard Cowling (originally from Gunnislake) advised that Verran's estimation of the mines' worth was unduly optimistic.[30] W.H. Trewenack (ironically, J.G. Bice's brother-in-law) was engaged to run the mines but in the event the experiment in State ownership did not last long, the incoming government in 1913 soon taking measures to close the properties.

In addition to the cart-drivers' strike and the State mining controversy, the Opposition was able to exploit the Verran government's practice of 'tacking', the attaching of provisions for new, hitherto undiscussed, public works to the Appropriation (Budget) Bill. The Opposition argued that 'tacking' was a device employed by Verran to push through legislation of a 'socialist' nature without proper parliamentary scrutiny. In the Appropriation Bill presented to the Adelaide parliament in December 1911 there was a 'tacked' provision for the establishment of a State brickworks. This was used as a pretext by the conservative Legislative Council, the upper house, to defer the Bill, an action tantamount to refusal of the government's supply. This brought to a head a series of confrontations between Verran and the Legislative Council. In the September of 1911 the Council had rejected—for the second time—the Council Veto Bill, a measure to limit the powers of the Legislative Council, while it had also rejected, laid aside or permitted to lapse more than a dozen other Bills, all of them reformist. This was a time when there were parallel moves to restrict the powers of the House of Lords, the United Kingdom's upper house, and Verran secretly approached Asquith, asking for British intervention for 'the Constitution [of South Australia] to be so amended by an Imperial Act as to enable the matured will of the people of South Australia on these and all other questions to become law'.[31] Asquith replied that it would not be proper for him to intervene, and so, with his supply refused, Verran decided to request the dissolution of parliament and seek an election.

The election campaign that followed was described at the time as 'the most important and fiercest political battle ever fought in South Australia'.[32] Verran bitterly attacked Peake, calling him 'a political rogue' and condemning him and his 'so-called Liberals . . . [for] turning from Democrat to Conservative',[33] a recognition of the threat posed to Labor by the newly coherent forces of the centre-right. Indeed, in the election Labor fared badly, losing control of the House of Assembly (the lower house) and thus the government. The only constituency not to follow the anti-Labor trend was Wallaroo, Verran's own seat, showing that Verran had not yet lost his personal following in the mining communities of Yorke Peninsula. However, Verran was discredited by the defeat of February 1912, and he resigned from the Labor leadership in the following year, citing as his reason his wife's continuing ill-health.

Significantly, despite his continued popularity at Moonta, Wallaroo and Kadina, Verran had lost the unequivocal support of the Methodist establishment in South Australia. In February 1912 the *Australian Christian Commonwealth*, a Methodist magazine published in Adelaide, had warned that Verran and his cabinet colleagues had been too 'prepared to take their orders from the more violent and revolutionary forces in their party'[34] and, detecting a sinister Irish hand in this, felt that 'efforts are being made to dominate the Labour Party by the Church of Rome'.[35] This estrangement of Methodism from the Labor Party was soon perpetuated and deepened by the conscription issue which emerged during the Great War, a distancing which did much to dent the Cornish-Methodist tradition within Labor in South Australia.[36]

'A BRITISHER AND A CORNISHMAN'

The debate over whether conscription to the armed forces should be introduced raged throughout Australia. Although essentially a matter of principle and conscience, the anti-conscriptionist lobby was seen by its detractors as a Fenian, Popish and even pro-German plot.[37] In the eastern States of Victoria and New South Wales the Irish-Catholic element was strong within the Labor movement, and when the Labor Party adopted its anti-conscription policy, the worst fears of its critics seemed to be confirmed. Although different in make-up from its eastern States counterparts, the Labor Party in South Australia followed suit and duly adopted the anti-conscription line, immediately aggravating the tension between Methodism and the Labor movement. The Methodist Church, with its increasingly anti-Catholic rhetoric, declared in favour of conscription. The effect was traumatic, especially amongst the Cornish communities on Yorke Peninsula. Those who were Labor men first and Methodists second moved firmly behind their party, while for those for whom religion was politics resignation from the Labor Party was inevitable. A Moonta Anti-Conscription League sprang up but even as it was mobilizing its supporters so John Verran was announcing his resignation from the ULP and the foundation of the Moonta branch of the pro-conscription *National Labor Party*.[38]

Verran managed to hold on to local support but others found a new champion in Robert Stanley (R.S.) Richards, a young trade union activist. Born at Moonta Mines in 1885, he was the son of Richard Richards of Camborne and Mary Jeffery of Tuckingmill. He was a Methodist local preacher but he was noticeably to the left of Verran and the earlier generation of Cornish miners. He was, therefore, an anti-conscriptionist and he had a ready appeal for like-minded younger, second-generation Cousin Jacks. Stanley Whitford, for example, was born at Moonta in 1878. A man especially proud of his Cornish roots, Whitford, like many others from Yorke Peninsula, had been on the Western Australian goldfields in the mid 1890s where 'I was camped with a nest of Cousin Jacks from Moonta'.[39] There he had enjoyed the camaraderie of the miners, Cornish and non-Cornish, and had picked up his ideas about the relationship between bosses and workers and had acquired his Labor credentials. Come the Great War, he was 'opposed to conscription because it violated my ideals as a follower of the International Socialist movement', and he was especially critical of Verran: 'I placed him among my list of damned old humbugs, and he never reinstated himself in my estimation.' Verran was, Whitford said, 'robust, good looking, good voiced, but ignorant . . . [one] in whom I had no trust'.[40] Richards was able to exploit such sentiment in the election of 1918 when, standing as the official Labor Party candidate for Wallaroo, he ousted John Verran, who had stood on the National Labor ticket.

Out of parliament for the first time since 1901, and with his local power base seriously eroded, Verran attempted to win new sources of political support. Indeed, recognizing that his support on the Peninsula was no longer solid, he had cultivated a strong anti-German stance early in the war. He argued that it was necessary for the British Empire to crush Germany so that Europe could be cleaned up, 'just as the Cornish people like their general cleaning up at Christmas'.[41] In parliament in 1916 and 1917 he introduced Bills designed to disenfranchise South Australia's sizeable German community (both Bills narrowly failed to make their way onto the statute book), and in August 1916 he had declared in the House of Assembly:

> It is deplorable to allow those with German blood in their veins to vote in this country. No matter what they cry out, they must have a bias for Germany. I am a Britisher and a Cornishman, and no one can take away my feelings of loyalty to my country.[42]

To some extent Verran was successful in retrieving support through his anti-German stance, one contributor to the Moonta *People's Weekly* asking: 'Who but a Hun would not say that Mr Verran is one of the most popular legislators of the State?'[43] With the end of the war, however, the German question lost its immediacy, and once again Verran found himself politically isolated. The National Labor Party tried to retain the Methodist vote by embracing the 'prohibitionist' cause but Verran failed (albeit narrowly) to regain his Wallaroo seat in 1921, and his alienation from mainstream Labor was now complete. Like Bice and Charleston before him, he was pushed further to the right of the political spectrum, and in 1924 he was contesting Wallaroo as a Liberal. In a campaign speech at Moonta he declared that:

> He could not see how any country could accept socialistic proposals of socialising all means of industry. He considered the Labor Party ideals took away a man's fundamental rights which were the basis of our civilisation. Home life went when communism came on, and he would never favour any policy which took away his right to build his home.[44]

Verran also blamed the collapse of the Wallaroo and Moonta Mines in 1923 on the activities of trade union militants, although, as R.S. Richards pointed out, all this sounded very strange coming from the man who, more than anyone, had been responsible for developing the Labor movement on the Peninsula. Not surprisingly, Verran was defeated in 1924 and, with the exception of a brief spell in the Federal

"*I bain't Coornish, Missus, but feyther an' mawther was.*"

Figure 3: The paradox of Cornish identity on Yorke Peninsula,
caught by Oswald Pryor.

Senate from 1927–8 when he was appointed to fill a casual vacancy, his political career was finished. He died in 1932.

The conscription issue and its aftermath had been a personal trauma for John Verran but it had also been traumatic for the Cornish communities of northern Yorke Peninsula, presenting them with deep and bitter divisions, a marked contrast to the solidarity and cohesion they had displayed before the Great War. The estrangement of Methodism from Labor was especially painful, eroding as it did the nexus that underpinned the Cornish Radical Tradition in South Australia. There was certainly a generational aspect to the divisions that had emerged, the older Cornish-born population striving to preserve the Methodist-Labor link and the younger activists adopting a more militant position over conscription and other issues. There were also issues of identity here. Although all Moonta folk were deemed 'Cousin Jacks ' and 'Cousin Jennies', the older generation had brought their ideological baggage from Cornwall and retained their commitment to Britain and Empire, while the younger people, more susceptible to a nascent Australian nationalism, were likely to be more critical of the Imperial connection and more sensitive to Australian perspectives and Australian agendas.

Of course, the conscription crisis had ramifications for the Cornish (and others) far beyond the bounds of Yorke Peninsula. Jack Scadden, for example, born at Moonta in 1876, went like many other Peninsularites to the Western Australian goldfields in the 1890s, settling there and entering the Legislative Assembly in Perth in 1904 as a Labor member and rapidly rising to become Premier. However, like Verran, the conscription issue forced him from the Labor Party and into the National Labor camp. So too with George Pearce, born 'of Cornish stock' at Mount Barker in South Australia. He also travelled to Western Australia in the 1890s, and by 1910 was representing that State in the Federal Senate as a Labor member. However, like Scadden and Verran, he clashed with his Labor colleagues over conscription and found refuge in the National Labor ranks. Peter Heydon, his biographer and one-time personal secretary and confidante, wrote that for Pearce the conscription issue was 'the dominating, shattering political experience . . . Pearce was not a bigot. A Protestant and of Cornish extraction, he tried to keep the whole conscription issue free of sectarian and Irish political issues'.[45]

THE 'BOGIES', THE 'SPLIT', THE 'BETTERMENT PRINCIPLE'

Meanwhile, back in South Australia, the split in the Labor Party caused by the conscription issue was mirrored in a corresponding split in the miners' union on northern Yorke Peninsula. During 1917 the Amalgamated Miners' Association held a ballot to determine whether it should merge with the Australian Workers' Union (AWU). The younger miners, such as R.S. Richards and his supporters, were in favour of the merger, for 'unity is strength' but the older Cornishmen —including John Verran—opposed the move and feared that 'We will lose control of industrial matters locally'.[46] The merger went ahead, with R.S. Richards becoming President of the Moonta branch of the AWU, but Verran reacted by forming a new organization—officially the Yorke's Peninsula's Miners' and Smelters' Association but known to many local inhabitants as the 'Bogus' Union. The Wallaroo and Moonta company was accused of victimizing the militants who had engineered the AWU merger, while the 'Bogies' (members of Verran's 'Bogus' Union) were in turn victimized by the AWU men and ostracized by sections of the local community. Verran, allegedly in cahoots with the bosses, was bitterly criticized for causing 'much distress in many homes in this district',[47] while he retorted (or so it was claimed) that the AWU was 'led by Pommies who came out from England to escape conscription'.[48] R.S. Richards' electoral victory in 1918 consolidated the position of the AWU but this did not prevent 'Old Cornishman' from writing to the local press to complain about the AWU's supposedly militant tactics.[49]

In the earlier twentieth century, in the years before 'the split' (as it was known), the AMA had enjoyed widepread support on the Peninsula, establishing a coherence and solidarity which created a certain stability within the community and lent the Union stature in dealing with external organizations, not least the bosses. Its behaviour was restrained but it was organized, competent and usually successful in its negotiations with the mine company. As the *Register* had remarked in August 1914, 'Although politically a "red hot Labour centre", the Yorke's Peninsula mines have been remarkably free from labour troubles'.[50] After the strike of 1891–2, the AMA had used its influence to good effect in dealing with the mine management, co-operating with the latter's plan for rapid modernization at the mines in return for the development of an advanced welfare policy, two boom periods (1905–7 and 1911–18) creating the right conditions for this symbiotic relationship to grow. By 1905 an entirely new shaft had been sunk at Wallaroo Mines (J. Moyle, the chief pitman, had been sent to the Great Boulder Mine, Western Australia, to observe the latest shaft-sinking techniques), complete with electrically driven underground pumps, a modern steel headframe and new winding house.[51] By 1906 there were no fewer than 2,700 men employed directly in the mines and at the smelters, with many more in the district whose livelihoods depended upon them.

Integral to this process, as noted above, was the enhancement of the company's welfare provisions. Originally a transplantation of the Cornish-style Club & Doctor Fund and bal-surgeon arrangements established in the mid nineteenth century at the Burra Burra and other major South Australian copper mines, the 'Betterment Principle' as it developed on northern Yorke Peninsula was a part of the modernization and rationalization of company practices and plant undertaken by H. Lipson Hancock, the general manager and son of the famed Captain Henry Richard Hancock. Lipson Hancock felt that welfare policies were useful 'from a political point of view',[52] because they won the loyalty and appreciation of the employees and wider community. Thus when William Lathlean, a young surface worker, was badly mangled by the crusher at Moonta Mines, Lipson Hancock recommended the payment of £90 so that the unfortunate youth might be placed in the Home for Incurables. On another occasion he organized the donation of company land to the Wallaroo Benevolent Society for their proposed old-folks' home.[53]

Hancock explained his Betterment Principle in a booklet describing the mines (first published in 1914) and in an article 'Welfare Work in the Mining Industry' which appeared in 1918.[54] The best exposition of Hancock's welfare work, however, was the report by L.C.E. Gee, Chief Registrar of Mines, in the *South Australian Department of Mines Mining Review* for the half-year ended June 1919. Gee noted that 65.5 per cent of the workforce at Wallaroo and Moonta had been with the company for a decade or more, a measure of its success in retaining its labour. Everywhere, he said, there was a general impression of 'tidiness, space and light',[55] and there were baths and changing houses for employees. At Wallaroo plots of company land were sold freehold to employees on easy terms. In October 1912, for example, James Henry Chynoweth secured allotment No. 222 at East Wallaroo on which to build a house, while in the November Clarence William Opie acquired plot No. 212.[56] At Moonta Mines there was a vigorous tree-planting programme to improve the appearance of the place, and in addition the company supported or supplied the Moonta Mines Institute, the reference and circulating libraries, a billiards room, a recreation hall, the rotunda, tennis courts, and children's playgrounds. At Wallaroo Mines similar amenities were provided, including a pavilion, croquet lawns, a hockey-pitch, and a bowling green with 'a good club house'.[57] Additionally, the company maintained its compulsory Club & Medical Fund. A married man, for example, contributed one shilling a week to the Medical Fund and a further sixpence to the Club, while an adult employee unable to attend work through illness could claim twenty shillings per week from the Fund for six months, and then ten shillings per week for a further six months. Moreover, Gee concluded, the sliding scale of wage determination, introduced by H. Lipson Hancock in the early 1900s as an improvement to the contract system, should also be considered an integral part of the Betterment Principle because it represented a form of profit-sharing which was preferable to other types of employment.

As Hancock had intimated, there were strong pragmatic reasons why the mine company found it useful to develop such welfare policies but there was in the Betterment Principle (as even its nomenclature suggested) more than a hint of the Cornish-Methodist mutual improvement ethos, and it was no coincidence that Hancock was himself an enthusiastic Methodist. This provided a degree of cultural common ground with his workforce, a certain mutual sympathy and understanding, and in furthering the cause of Methodism on Yorke Peninsula he adopted the Rainbow System of Sunday School instruction (already applied with success at the Marion Lawrence School, Toledo, Ohio), precipitating a reorganization which in its manner echoed both his modernization of the mines themselves and the implementation of the Betterment Principle. Methodist Union in South Australia in 1901 had rendered redundant the Primitive Methodist chapel at Moonta Mines, and after 1905 this building became the focus for the new regime. As Hancock wrote:

> This meant a complete reconstruction, necessitating careful thought and much wisdom, and involving considerable expense. The whole teaching arrangements had to be reorganized and suitable rooms provided, together with the needed apparatus for teaching. Led by the present Superintendent of the School [Hancock], the teachers undertook the reconstruction.[58]

However, behind this positive picture of benign busy-ness was the reality of increasing tension on the Peninsula, the crises of John Verran's Premiership compounded by the conscription issue and its aftermath. The estrangement of Methodism from the Labor movement, made worse locally by the split over the AMA-AWU merger, together with the growth of a new mood of Labor militancy across Australia as the war dragged on, undermined the cohesion and consensus that seemed to have marked the first decade of the new century on Yorke Peninsula. Indeed, the split of 1917, with its polarization of conservatives and militants, ushered in a new era of confrontation on the mines, the likes of which had not been seen since 1891–2. This culminated in a brief but bitter strike in 1922, when the AWU's venom was directed equally at the company and the Bogies, an antipathy reflected in the fiery words of one of R.S. Richard's pamphlets:

> Starvation may drive us back into the Mines; Man's inhumanity to Man may make countless thousands continue to mourn; but, whatever the result, we will never forget those men who aided the oppressor, we will never forget those men who played us false, and when the Time comes to show our contempt for them, we will do so in no uncertain manner. In the meantime:
>
>> We will speak out, we will be heard, though all earth's
>>   system crack;

We will not bate one single word or take a letter back,
For the cause that lacks assistance, 'gainst the wrongs that
   need resistance,
For the future in the distance, and the good that we can do.

> R.S. Richards, M.P.
> North Moonta.[59]

When the Moonta and Wallaroo Mines closed in 1923 there were some who blamed the collapse on the AWU, while there were indeed some militants who were happy to see the company go at last into liquidation. Certainly, the Cornish Labor-Methodist nexus that had appeared so intact at the time of John Verran's famous victory in 1910 now seemed hardly relevant, the events immediately before, during and after the Great War having radically altered the industrial and political landscape in South Australia and on Yorke Peninsula in particular. Sensing that the demise of the Cornish Radical Tradition was at hand, one contributor to the Moonta *People's Weekly* wrote sadly in 1927:

> I am not, nor have I ever been, a member of the A.W.U. that caused so much trouble and sorrow at the mining towns. I was a member of the first A.M.A., formed at Moonta Mines, and the leaders were all Cornishmen, right up to the time of the forming of the A.W.U.[60]

'SCATTERIN' THE BAL'

Needless to say, of all the structural changes that had altered the industrial and political landscape, none was more profound nor more final than the closure of the Moonta and Wallaroo Mines in November 1923. The enormity of that moment was still felt keenly some forty years on by Oswald Pryor, son of Captain James Pryor from Wendron:

> Some hot-headed trade union leaders were pleased at the news. The company, they said, had kept up ornate offices in Adelaide, yet the miners had not received an adequate share of the huge profits in the early days of the field—and if an industry couldn't, or wouldn't, pay a decent wage, let it shut up shop! To the Cornish community that had lived in Wallaroo and Moonta for three generations, however, the closing of the mines was a calamity. For a while some thought that the company was only bluffing—that the announcement was just a stunt, designed to scare the miners into accepting a

starvation wage. But they were faced with the fact that, for the first time in the history of the mines, the pumps were idle, water was rising steadily in the workings, and all underground gear worth salvaging was being brought to the surface.[61]

Pryor's distinction between 'hot-headed trade union leaders' and 'the Cornish community' is telling, further insight into the belief that the Labor movement on the Peninsula was now somehow less 'Cornish' than it had been hitherto, a consequence of the Great War and the turbulent post-war years, and that the Cornish inheritance was being marginalized by the new militancy. Be that as it may, the hard fact was that the mines' closure was a result of the slump in demand for copper (and thus in its price) after the cessation of hostilities in 1918. The mines were shut down temporarily from March to September 1919, and there were further periods of inactivity from January to March 1920, January to August 1921, and February to November 1922, before the mines were abandoned finally on 23 October 1923. The company went formally into liquidation in the November, precipitating what the locals called 'scatterin' the bal', the wholesale dismantling and disposal of the mines' plant and infrastructure.[62] Like the Cornish copper industry itself in the 1860s, the South Australian mines had in the 1920s succumbed to the classic combination of low copper prices, soaring costs, and increasing impoverishment of the lodes. Anticipating this crash, many had already left the district, bands of unemployed miners gathering in Adelaide where they formed themselves into a miners' choir and created a flurry of interest, singing their Methodist hymns and Cornish carols. Thereafter, there were various forlorn attempts in the 1920s and even into the 1930s to re-establish mining but none was successful. For example, in 1936 there was a brief attempt by a Kadina Mining Company to restart the long-abandoned New Cornwall mine, while W.J.L. Polmear, born at Landrake in 1877 and a former AMA activist, worked the Poona lease on his own account without success. Slightly more fortunate was the Moonta Prospecting Syndicate, a small outfit with a capital of £3,000 which worked steadily until 1927 when, with a rise in copper prices and the help of R.S. Richards (then Minister of Mines), a form of 'subsist' (a Cornish term) was paid by the State as an advance on earnings. Richards even managed to attract Federal assistance for a time, but these modest attempts at renewal were doomed to failure and had petered out before the Second World War.[63]

In such a climate, the miners' trade union effectively disappeared, as did many of the local population. Some went to the copper mines of Bougainville,[64] an appendage of New Guinea, and in the decade after

SCATTERIN' THE BAL

Figure 4: Oswald Pryor's humorous yet poignant 'Scatterin' the Bal'.

1923 more than 3,000 people left northern Yorke Peninsula for pastures new, some 85 per cent of these migrants originating from the mineral lease settlements at Moonta Mines and Wallaroo Mines. At Wallaroo a 'strong defeatist attitude' was prevalent during the 1920s and 1930s but on the mineral leases at Moonta Mines and Wallaroo Mines, despite the continued leaching of the skilled and the restless, there was a certain stubbornness: 'When the source of employment was removed, the population proved highly resistant to migration. While many left, hundreds clung on, eking out a bare living by casual labour on farms, docks and grain depots until entitled to age or incapacity pensions.'[65] Thus it was principally the younger people who departed, leaving behind 'a high proportion of aged and infirm'.[66]

Unpromising as the post-closure depression of Wallaroo and Moonta seemed for the further development of the Labor movement in South Australia, R.S. Richards and others continued to behave as though little had happened, insinuating themselves into the Labor Party's leadership hierarchy at a time when the basis of their claims to power (the mines) had already vanished. This was the nub of the paradox illuminated by Lonie and Hopgood, the continued prominence of individuals of a Cornish-Methodist-mining background in the Labor Party at a time when this no longer reflected the composition of the State's workforce but when popular opinion was still prepared to recognize a continuing Cornish influence in the State's political culture. But equally, the demise of mining and the loss of much of the erstwhile mining community was itself a diminution of the fabric of the Cornish Radical Tradition in South Australia, the Wallaroo constituency a shadow of its former self and no longer a vibrant focus of the Labor-Methodist nexus.

'A DANGER TO THE PURITY OF OUR RACE'

However, as Lonie intimated, a cursory glance at the composition of the Labor Party in the Adelaide parliament in the 1920s and early1930s revealed a block of some ten members of Cornish birth or descent, mostly Methodists, from his perspective a remarkable legacy from earlier times.[67] And yet, despite their Cornish, Methodist and mining backgrounds, these Labor members for the most part reflected the contemporary preoccupations of Australian politics, a function of the structural changes that had overtaken or sidelined the Cornish impact in South Australia. To some extent this represented a metamorphosis (rather than merely decline) of the Cornish Radical Tradition in the State: the survival of a caucus of active Labor politicians from a traditionally 'Cornish' background but with their embrace of a range of 'new' policies that apparently had little or nothing to do with Cornish sensibilities and everything to do with current Australian concerns.

For example, although the Cornish had shared the traditional hostility to non-white immigrants (especially Chinese mine workers), the White Australia policy that emerged after Federation in 1901 was quintessentially the business of an Australian Labor movement anxious to prevent the flooding of Australia with Asiatic and other cheap labour. In the South Australian State election of 1927, therefore, the White Australia policy emerged as a major issue. Labor's campaign that year was masterminded by Leslie Claude Hunkin, one of the 'Cornish' block identified above, the son of a Cornish mine captain.

Born in Tasmania in 1884, Hunkin came to South Australia while still young, later becoming involved in the Storeman and Packer's Union and the Public Service Union. In managing Labor's campaign, he emphasized traditional 'socialist' issues such as deep drainage, road improvement, social services, housing and monopolies. But the White Australia policy was now also prominent as a Labor issue, one of Hunkin's handbills exhorting voters to: 'VOTE LABOR, AND RID SOUTH AUSTRALIA OF A DANGER TO THE PURITY OF OUR RACE.'[68] To the Cornish electorate on Yorke Peninsula but a decade before, the encouragement to 'VOTE LABOR' would have been familiar enough but the prominence now given to 'racial purity' might have struck them as novel, especially when compared to the more pressing local issues that had always demanded the attention of politics and politicians at Moonta and Wallaroo.

Indeed, South Australia had been hitherto relatively tolerant of 'minorities', the colony allowing Aborigines to vote in its elections long before the new Commonwealth constitution of 1901 prevented it at Federal level. Paradoxically, at precisely the moment that the White Australia policy was taking centre stage in the State's Labor programme, so concern for the future of South Australia's Aboriginal population was beginning to emerge in Labor circles. This concern was reflected in the writings of Henry 'Harry' Kneebone, another of the Cornish 'block', born at Kadina in 1876, the son of Henry Kneebone of Penponds (near Camborne) and Elizabeth Ann Tonkin (born in Cornwall in 1851). A journalist by training, Harry Kneebone was asked to contribute to *The Wonder Book of Empire for Boys and Girls*, published shortly after the Great War in London, Melbourne and Toronto, writing a series of essays on 'Sunny Australia: The All-British Continent'. Although Kneebone shared the prejudices of his contemporaries, asserting that 'The aborigines who have yielded their country to the white settlers . . . are generally poor specimens of humanity', and that in poorly resourced parts of the continent 'the struggle for existence has been fairly keen and tribes have become at times almost cannibals', he demonstrated a genuine concern and affection for Aboriginal peoples which would have been unusual at that time. He identified qualities of selflessness and courage in the Aborigines, and observed that 'They make excellent stockmen' and that, as first-class trackers, 'they have saved the lives of many wanderers in the wilder parts'. Indeed, 'All over Australia aboriginals are attached to the country police stations so that their services may be available for tracking criminals or suspected or lost persons'. Their culture, too, was fascinating, with expert spear-throwing, boomerangs and corroborees: 'Many interesting stories could be told of these folk, and for many reasons it is to be hoped that the efforts which are being made to keep them from dying out will be successful'.[69]

This essential humanity was typical of Kneebone and, like others from Yorke Peninsula, his political views seem to have matured and crystallized during a spell as a miner on the Western Australian gold-fields in the 1890s. His daughter and biographer, Joan Tiver, in her book *Harry Kneebone: A Son of 'Little Cornwall'*, recalled that:

> He was a Socialist in the sense that he considered Jesus Christ a Socialist . . . [he] was entirely democratic in outlook and did not believe that anyone can be born with 'bluer' blood than another. Although he would not have described himself as a Republican, he was not an ardent Royalist. He believed, however, that complete independence must come to Australia some day, as a child sheds its mother's apron strings. He also believed that superiority, if it need be recognised, should spring from achievement by the use and development of one's God-given talents and mental powers, never from the accident of one's birth or the inheritance of wealth.[70]

The concern for Australian independence, like concern for the future of the Aborigines, reflected the prominence of Australian preoccupations in Kneebone's political thought. And yet, the Cornish-Methodist influence was also plain, not least in the assumed link between religion and politics and in the Methodist commitment to self-help. Indeed, Kneebone was careful to cultivate his Cornishness, seeking out family members during a visit to Cornwall and becoming an enthusiastic devotee of the Cornish Association of South Australia.

While still in Western Australia, he had decided to put his journalistic skills to work in the Labor cause by joining the pro-Labor *Coolgardie Miner*, of which newspaper he eventually became editor. In 1910 he returned to South Australia, joining the Labor-sponsored *Daily Herald* in Adelaide and becoming its editor in 1911. This was a position he held, with the exception of a brief period in London, until the paper's collapse in 1924. Significantly, perhaps, his opposite number in the Adelaide *Advertiser* was owner-editor Sir John Langdon Bonython, another enthusiastic Methodist and member of the Cornish Association, who had sat in the Federal parliament as a Radical Liberal from 1901–6 and supported Labor on most issues. Following the demise of the *Herald*, Kneebone entered the Adelaide parliament in 1925 as Labor member for the constituency of East Torrens, moving on to the Federal Senate in 1931.

Of the other members of the Labor 'block', Stanley R. Whitford was, as noted above, a close ally of R.S. Richards. His enormously long and candid autobiography (still unpublished) affords numerous insights into his career and personality, not least those experiences that helped form his Labor principles. He was, he said, profoundly influenced by Eugene Debs (the American leader of the 'Wobblies', the International Workers of the World), and he described the deep impact the visit of Tom Mann to Moonta in 1910 had upon him. But despite the attraction of Marxist thought, he remained a firm Methodist, and was critical of both the Anglican and Roman Catholic churches. He first entered the Adelaide parliament in 1921, as Member of the House of Assembly for the constituency of North Adelaide. He lost his seat in 1927 but was back in parliament in 1929, where he remained until 1941. In 1930 he became Chief Secretary in 'Lightning Lionel' Hill's Labor government, although only a few years later, in 1934, he was dramatically expelled from the Australian Labor Party. This was because he was an advocate of the controversial and divisive 'Premiers' Plan', an economic strategy to try to beat the Depression put together by the several State Premiers in consultation with the Federal government, a belt-tightening exercise that was bitterly opposed by much of the Labor movement.

In an echo of the damaging conscription issue years, the Premiers' Plan controversy split the Labor movement in South Australia, its parliamentary Party dividing into three mutually antagonistic camps: the Australian Labor Party, the (so-called) Parliamentary Labor Party, and Lang Labor (those who supported the anti-Federal position of J.T. 'Jack' Lang, the flamboyant New South Wales Premier who had opened the Sydney Harbour Bridge, was opposed to the Premiers' Plan, and was soon after sacked by the State Governor). Whitford himself continued in parliament as an Independent Labor member, and he recalled that 'This debacle in the ranks of the Labor movement in this State was the worst of my experience'.[71] R.S. Richards, the veteran of the conscription issue and the 'split', came at last to power in South Australia as Labor Premier at the height of this crisis in February 1933, following Hill's resignation. He was Premier for only 64 days, however, for in the State election of 1933 the Liberal Country League was swept into office, the Labor forces being in entire disarray. Only in the Wallaroo constituency did the non-Liberal forces do well, with R.S. Richards returned yet again as the darling of 'Little Cornwall'. In his campaign he had relied skilfully on the support of local power-brokers, such as Bill 'Sponger' Tonkin, chairman of the local Unemployed Association, and his all-important policy speech at Wallaroo Town Hall was given such an easy reception that (his opponents insisted), 'the Cousin Jacks must have thought it an evening church service'.[72]

Significantly, Richards continued to represent Wallaroo until as late as 1949.

Another of Richards' close allies was John Nicholas Pedler, again of Cornish stock, who sat in the Adelaide parliament from 1918 until 1938, along with Richards one of the two members for the constituency of Wallaroo. Then there was Thomas Gluyas, born at Moonta Mines in 1864, who became President of the Adelaide Branch of the Amalgamated Society of Engineers, and who was a member of the Legislative Council in South Australia from 1918 until 1931. John Stanley ('Stan') Verran, born at Moonta in 1883, the son of 'Honest John', held the safe Labor seat of Port Adelaide from 1918 to 1927. Thomas Hawke, born near the Burra of Cornish descent, was the member for Burra Burra from 1921, when he was succeeded by Albert Redvers George Hawke (no relation, apparently), born in the old mining town of Kapunda in 1900, who later went on to become Labor Premier of Western Australia. Thomas Tonkin Edwards, born in Cornwall in 1870, represented Barossa in the State's House of Assembly from 1929 until 1933.

CONCLUSION
Together with Hunkin, Kneebone, Whitford and Richards, these parliamentarians represented that enduring Cornish-Methodist influence in South Australia's Labor Party in the 1920s and 1930s identified by Lonie. The extent to which they consciously self-identified as a Cornish 'block' is unknown, though most thought their Cornish-Methodist backgrounds important to their personal identities and some were active in the State's Cornish Association. Certainly, as Hopgood argued, the South Australian public continued to equate Labor politics with the Cousin Jack influence. Lonie considered that Labor ideology was consequently locked in the 1890s, a sort of 'fossilized' Cornish Radical Tradition rooted in the hey-day of the State's erstwhile mining industry, but the reality was more complex. While aspects of that Tradition did seem increasingly anachronistic, not least as they were overtaken by important structural changes (the most significant of which was the closure of the Yorke Peninsula mines), there was also a degree of metamorphosis as the Labor movement reacted to the changes. Moreover, as Australia-wide issues became of ever greater importance, shifting the gaze of State politicians away from the purely local, so the Cornish-Methodist Labor hierarchy identified by Lonie was drawn increasingly to Australian perspectives and Australian agendas. Thus, for example, the maintenance of White Australia acquired a new prominence in Labor ideology, articulated by Hunkin amongst others, while it was the Premiers' Plan rather than any

"Beats me 'ow they all knawed I coomed from Moonta."

Figure 5: Oswald Pryor's commentary on the South Australian public's sophisticated appreciation of Cornish identity.

purely local issue that caused disarray in the State's Labor ranks in the 1930s.

For Cornish Studies practitioners, the comparative aspects of this experience are especially interesting, pushing forward the comparisons between Cornwall and South Australia to suggest that, if we move our attention from the earlier period (roughly 1848-1912) to the later one examined in this article, then what had appeared to be divergence becomes convergence. In other words, despite the differences in experience between Cornwall and South Australia (not least the relative fortunes of the Labour/Labor movements therein), in the longer term the experience of the latter came to resemble that of the former. Not only did Moonta and Wallaroo go the way of Fowey Consols and United Mines but the residual (albeit metamorphosing) Cornish-Methodist influence in the Labor Party hierarchy in South Australia was at the very least an echo of the situation in Cornwall where, in 'the politics of paralysis' in which Cornwall failed to engage with the new Labour-Conservative alignment happening elsewhere, the Liberal-Nonconformist nexus survived intact well into the twentieth century.

For Australian Studies, this is a yet further reminder that assumptions regarding the ostensibly 'homogeneous' character of pre-1945 Australian society are at best an oversimplification and, at worst, deeply flawed. As well as noting some important differences between the cultural make-up of the several States, and the potential for tension between local and Federal perspectives after the creation of the Commonwealth of Australia in 1901, this article also suggests that community and ethnic identity (in this case, the Cornish) could be more important than is sometimes admitted in shaping differentiated micro-political cultures in different parts of the continent. Certainly, as argued above, the suggestion that 'Cornishness' continued to influence the make-up of the South Australian Labor hierarchy in the 1920s and 1930s, together with its beliefs and behaviour, is persuasive. Indeed, the complex and often paradoxical picture elaborated above may have wider theoretical significance for the study of cultural transfer, adaption, and assimilation (or otherwise) of immigrant ethnic groups and their descendents in new lands.

NOTES AND REFERENCES

1. For example, see the Review Article by Garry Tregidga in this edition of *Cornish Studies*.
2. See Philip Payton, *The Cornish Overseas*, Fowey, 1999.
3. For example, see Migration Museum, *From Many Places: The History and Cultural Traditions of South Australian People*, Adelaide, 1995, pp. 97 and 99.
4. For example, see Philip Payton, *The Making of Modern Cornwall: Historical Experience and the Persistence of 'Difference'*, Redruth, 1992, Chapter 7 'The Politics of Paralysis'.
5. Michael Davitt, *Life and Progress in Australiasia*, London, 1898, p. 53.
6. Donald J. Hopgood, 'A Psephological Examination of the South Australian Labor Party from World War One to the Depression', unpublished Ph.D. thesis, Flinders University of South Australia, 1973, p. 335.
7. John Lonie, 'Conservatism and Class in South Australia during the Depression Years, 1924–1934', unpublished M.A. thesis, University of Adelaide, 1973, p. 173.

8. C.C. James, *A History of the Parish of Gwennap in Cornwall*, Penzance, n.d., p. 90.
9. John McConnell Black, *Memoirs*, Adelaide, 1971, p. 66.
10. *South Australian Advertiser*, 21 June 1910.
11. *Plain Dealer*, 11 March 1911.
12. *People's Weekly*, 7 May 1910.
13. *People's Weekly*, 7 May 1910.
14. *People's Weekly*, 18 May 1917.
15. *People's Weekly*, 30 January 1892.
16. *People's Weekly*, 15 June 1901; 29 June 1901.
17. For an analysis of the fortunes of the Verran government, see R.J. Miller, 'The Fall of the Verran Government 1911–12: The Most Determined Attempt to Abolish the Legislative Council of South Australia, and its Failure', unpublished B.A. (Hons) thesis, University of Adelaide, 1965.
18. Undated cutting from *Kadina and Wallaroo Times* (*c.*June 1910), in Mortlock Library (State Library of South Australia), PRG96, *Oswald Pryor Papers*, Scrapbook: 'Electorate of Wallaroo, John Verran etc'.
19. *People's Weekly*, 25 June 1910.
20. Mortlock Library [ML] 522, *Draft of First Hustings Speech*, by John George Bice, March 1894.
21. According to an unidentified issue of the *Cornishman* newspaper of 1919, reprinted in pamphlet form by the Cornish Association of South Australia, Adelaide, *c.*1910.
22. *Christian Weekly and Methodist Union*, 5 September 1890.
23. D.M. Charleston, *New Unionism*, Adelaide, 1890, pp.1 and 5.
24. T.M. Smeaton, *The People in Politics: A Short History of the Labor Movement in South Australia 1891–1914*, Adelaide, 1914, p. 17.
25. McConnell Black, 1971, p. 66.
26. *South Australian Advertiser*, 2 March 1910; see also Bernard O'Neil, *In Search of Mineral Wealth: The South Australian Geological Survey and Department of Mines to 1914*, Adelaide, 1982, p. 162.
27. *People's Weekly*, 3 August 1910.
28. *Kadina and Wallaroo Times* 1 November 1911.
29. *Daily Herald*, 26 April 1911; 18 May 1912; *South Australian Register*, 6 May 1911.
30. *Kadina and Wallaroo Times*, 13 May 1911.
31. G.D. Combe, *Responsible Government in South Australia*, Adelaide, 1957, p. 145.
32. Combe, 1957, p. 146.
33. *People's Weekly*, 20 January 1912.
34. *Australian Christian Commonwealth*, 16 February 1912.
35. *Australian Christian Commonwealth*, 1 November 1911.
36. See Arnold Hunt, *Methodism Militant: Attitudes to the Great War*, Adelaide, 1976.
37. See Patricia Gibson, 'The Conscription Issue in South Australia, 1916–17' unpublished B.A (Hons) thesis, University of Adelaide, 1959.
38. *People's Weekly*, 21 October 1916; 21 April 1917.

39. ML D3627(L), Stanley Whitford, *An Autobiography*, p. 252.
40. ML D3627(L), pp. 478, 401 and 399.
41. *People's Weekly*, 29 August 1914.
42. *South Australian Parliamentary Debates*, 30 August 1916, p. 1095.
43. *People's Weekly*, 18 August 1917.
44. *People's Weekly*, 15 March 1924.
45. Peter Heydon, *Quiet Decision: A Study of George Foster Pearce*, Melbourne, 1965, pp. 14 and 79.
46. *People's Weekly*, 15 September 1917.
47. *People's Weekly*, 5 April 1918.
48. *People's Weekly*, 18 June 1921.
49. *People's Weekly*, 6 August 1921.
50. *South Australian Register*, 4 August 1914.
51. ML BRG40/1034, *Wallaroo and Moonta Mining and Smelting Company*, Minute Books, 1895–1923, 23 February 1904; 1 March 1904; 3 May 1904.
52. ML BRG40/1034, 10 October 1899.
53. ML BRG40/1034, 4 November 1902; 10 June 1908.
54. H. Lipson Hancock, *The Wallaroo and Moonta Mines*, Adelaide, 1914; H. Lipson Hancock, 'Welfare Work in the Mining Industry', *Australian Chemical Engineering and Mining Review*, October 1918.
55. *South Australian Department of Mines Mining Review*, Half Year Ended June 1919, p. 53.
56. ML BRG40/1034, 29 October 1912; 19 November 1912.
57. *South Australian Department of Mines Mining Review*, Half Year Ended June 1919, p. 54.
58. H. Lipson Hancock and William Shaw, *A Sunday School of Today*, Adelaide, 1912, pp. 21–2; for further details of the 'Rainbow System' see H. Lipson Hancock, *Modern Methods in Sunday School Work*, Adelaide, 1916; H. Lipson Hancock and William R. Penhall, *The Missionary Spirit in Sunday School Work*, Adelaide?, 1918; H. Lipson Hancock, *The Rainbow Course of Bible Study*, Adelaide?, 1919.
59. ML D5341(T), Peter Thomas, *Scrapbook Relating to Kapunda, Burra, Wallaroo, and Moonta Mines*, Pamphlet issued by R.S. Richards, p. 124.
60. *People's Weekly*, 2 July 1927.
61. Oswald Pryor, *Australia's Little Cornwall*, Adelaide, 1962, pp. 187–8.
62. Pryor, 1962, p. 186.
63. *South Australian Department of Mines Mining Review*, Half Year Ended June 1929; Half Year Ended December 1931.
64. *People's Weekly*, 25 May 1935.
65. K.W. Thomson, 'The Changes in Function of Former Mining Settlements: The Wallaroo Copper Belt', *Proceedings of the Royal Geological Society of Australia, South Australian Branch*, 56, 47–58, 1955, p. 57.
66. Thomson, 1957, p. 57.
67. For biographical details of the parliamentarians thus identified, see Howard Coxon, John Playford and Robert Reid, *Biographical Register of the South Australian Parliament 1857–1957*, Adelaide, 1985.

68. ML PRG30/21, *Leslie Claude Hunkin Papers*, Material relating to the Australian Labor Party.
69. H. Kneebone, 'The "Blacks" of Australia and Papua', in Harry Golding (ed.), *The Wonder Book of Empire for Boys and Girls*, London (and Melbourne and Toronto), n.d., pp. 137–42.
70. Joan Tiver, *Harry Kneebone: A Son of 'Little Cornwall'*, Adelaide, n.d., p. 73.
71. ML D3627(L), p. 857.
72. Pryor, 1962, p. 136.

CORNWALL: A VERY DIFFICULT WOMAN? A FEMINIST APPROACH TO ISSUES OF CORNISH IDENTITY

Cheryl Hayden

INTRODUCTION

To apply feminist theory to a population comprising both men and women assumes that the researcher perceives that the subject group is in some way oppressed by a dominant 'other'—that is, by a group that has power over it, sees it as different and 'lesser', and thus treats it accordingly. It also implies that the nature of this relationship and its resultant discrimination is analogous to that experienced by women in a patriarchal society. For Smith such differentiation 'immediately implies processes of categorization and identification based on group characteristics. This means that the concept of difference is inherently political and politicized.'[1] And feminism is inherently political as its purpose is unashamedly to achieve a shift in the balance of power between men and women. To take feminism outside of gender relations into a broader realm is to draw an analogy between men and the dominant 'core' of society, which houses and controls its institutions, and between women and this core's peripheries, which are dependent upon it.

Theoretically, it should be possible to apply feminist theory to any aspect (or representation) of social activity, for example, economics, history, politics or culture. However, to demonstrate how it might be applied across all of these elements as they pertain to a given population is too large a brief for the purposes of this essay. Therefore, this article will focus on the application of feminist theory to Cornish identity as it relates to ethnicity and territory. That is not to say that other aspects of the Cornish experience are in any way separable from identity—indeed, as this paper will show, identity is integral to the categorization process that makes the application of feminist theory both appropriate and useful.

But before looking at a feminist approach to Cornish identity, let us briefly look at how Cornwall fits into feminist theory.

CORNWALL AS A FEMINIZED 'OTHER'

Using the relationship model described above, the application of feminist theory to Cornwall assumes that it is a region occupying a subordinate place in relation to England, the powerful 'core' society that dominates it. So, while English institutions set and maintain traditions, and also occupy the 'neutral' ground of what is considered 'normal', the Cornish are cast into secondary, dependent, even 'backward other', status. And so, we have a situation in which we can argue that Cornwall is to England as woman is to man.

But does Cornwall really fit this model? Perry[2] and Williams[3] are among numerous writers on Cornish matters to demonstrate that Cornwall suffers high unemployment, lower than average wages, poor access to quality housing and lack of access to higher education— similar forms of disadvantage to those experienced by many women. Overriding all of these, however, is the lack of political potence needed to effect change. Of five MPs representing Cornwall in the House of Commons, four are Liberal Democrats, arguably a marginal party with little or no influence over a Labour Government that enjoys a huge majority. The only Labour MP is not Cornish and has often been unable to use her influence to address peculiarly Cornish matters, notably South Crofty mine.[4] In short, it would appear that the Cornish suffer similar material disadvantages to the female populations of many societies because they are a minority group with little political influence.

CORNWALL AND FEMINIST METHODOLOGY

Feminist methodology as characterized by Lengermann[5] and by Brunskell[6] is by, of and for women and, as a 'totalizing' theory, can adopt any number of quantitative and qualitative research techniques and encompass all aspects of social, political and cultural activity.[7] By taking this feminist model and putting the Cornish in the place of women, we can construct a Cornish methodology in which:

the Cornish perspective is the starting point for all investigation;

the Cornish are the centre subjects in the investigative
  process;
theory is critical and activist on behalf of the Cornish.

Such methodology allows us to cross the borders of more rigid
sociological and historical methodologies and theories and thus identify
and explain the impact of behaviouristic and definitional process of
individuals and institutions,[8] all the while keeping in mind that no one
methodology or theory can hope to be '*the* category that will finally
explain all inequality, all oppression, all history'.[9]

A FEMINIST EPISTEMOLOGY: HOW DO WE KNOW ABOUT THE CORNISH?

A feminist approach to epistemology tells us that our knowledge
of Cornwall and the Cornish comes largely from England, whose
historians, sociologists and other educators and communicators
privilege English tradition and perpetuate their own dominance. As
Harding has pointed out, it has not been women's experience to
have the world theorized, tested or explained according to their
experience.[10] Likewise, marginalized populations such as the Cornish
are unused to the world being presented from their own perspective,
just as the 'core' population would find it odd to have their world
explained from a Cornish viewpoint.

However, there are variations to this general theme. A materialist
approach, such as MacKinnon's, explains that 'the world, in its objec-
tivity, is the world of the male gaze in which women are objectified,
reduced to their sexuality, and then subordinated as just that, sexual
beings for them'.[11] In other words, the objectification of the Cornish by
the dominant centre results in the application of certain stereotypes to
which they are then reduced, and henceforth subordinated as 'inferior
others'. MacKinnon's theory contains more than a suggestion of
malicious intent, yet such a process is just as likely to occur as the result
of an unchallenged and uneducated mainstream consciousness that
is self-perpetuating because the mainstream mindset dominates the
messages society receives about itself and others. Its validity in the case
of Cornwall, however, cannot be denied because it seeks to explain
the relationship between a 'backward other' identity (for example,
romantic and timeless backwater that is full of superstitious and rustic
'folk') and the material reality described above.

A post-structuralist feminist epistemology would have us contest
and destabilize concepts and social constructs. In other words, such an
epistemology tells us that what we 'know' about Cornwall is seriously

flawed because it is made up of the concepts and constructs created by the dominant 'core' and can therefore be challenged.

FEMINISM AND CORNISH IDENTITY

The very notion of Cornishness assumes the existence of a distinct identity and, as Ivey and Payton have pointed out, there is widespread acceptance that such an identity does exist and that it is based on territory, language, a significant belief in a Celtic heritage (albeit one that has been hotly debated) and an awareness of a shared history in which England has featured as an often oppressive foreign power.[12] This difference is expressed, mostly within Cornwall, through a variety of customs and behaviours that are both assertive and celebratory.

The 'Celtic' issue is just one aspect of ethnicity and has been the subject of considerable debate. Attempts to prove the existence of a 'Celtic' gene-pool have largely failed, leaving the 'social construct' theory to dominate current discourse.[13] As Hale has pointed out, the ever-changing nature of society means that social constructs, or expressions in meaning and style, are equally valid measuring sticks, leading her to ponder why the Cornish have put so much effort into justifying their claims to Celtic heritage.[14] Today, these expressions, and the icons that signify them—wrestling, hurling, the language, male voice choirs, rugby, tartan and the St Piran's flag—indicate a clear identification with the Celtic world. Conversely, they also highlight the difference or 'otherness' in terms of Cornwall's relationship with England, the central relationship in this debate.

But how can feminist theory be applied to research into the Celtic aspect of Cornishness, and what purpose would it serve? Hale gives us a clue with her statement that 'the project is not to justify or judge . . . but potentially to give voice to those for whom Celtic identities are meaningful'.[15] The question for those who would apply feminist theory is what does this voice want, and how can it be achieved?

First, cultural feminism would accept the existence of 'the Celt' and 'define [them] by their activities and attributes'.[16] Furthermore, it would use reason to argue in favour of a re-evaluation of the differences ascribed to the Celt, so that a claim of Celtic ethnicity is seen as both valid and free of 'negative' stigma. In practical terms, this might take the form of policy decisions at local levels to emphasize the 'positive' elements of Cornish Celtic culture—art, music and literature—over what are perceived by the mainstream as 'negative' qualities such as superstition, rusticity and ornery individualism. Such an approach, of course, still privileges the value system imposed by the dominant centre (in that it accepts that superstition, for example, is undesirable), which might in itself be considered a dilemma, but it nevertheless represents a pragmatic, non-confrontational approach towards effecting change.

Second, Marxist materialist feminism would argue that the centre has either created or redefined the concept of the Celt and ascribed to it a series of negative qualities (such as superstition) in order to further objectify Celtic peoples as 'backward others'. It has then used this 'backwardness' to create and justify a division of labour that results in real-life, material consequences. While this approach is clearly more divisive, it is also more useful in demonstrating the need for political change in that it offers a model upon which to collect and build empirical data on aspects of life such as employment, wages, education, housing and health. Clearly, the social science being practised by and through the Institute of Cornish Studies on Cornwall's behalf, while not necessarily being either Marxist or feminist, uses empirical data to this end and in doing so is extremely 'political'.

Third, a post-structuralist form of feminism would 'attack the category and the concept [of the Celt] through problematizing subjectivity',[17] thus forcing 'vigilant repetition, reassertion, and implementation by those who have endorsed one or another definition.'[18] Post-structuralism and postmodernism have been used by many feminist theorists and for obvious reasons: with their deconstructive elements, they can undermine or discredit widely held assumptions that maintain a *status quo* of oppression and disadvantage. In terms of the Celtic issue, the application of this brand of feminism is a double-edged sword. While it can be used to deconstruct and possibly discredit theories and assumptions of backwardness and inferiority[19] it can also be used to discredit the very difference Cornwall has relied on to gain ethno-regional status and other political and economic accommodations.

IDENTITY AND TERRITORY

Feminist theory is also interested in territory and space and the way the core/periphery relationship allows them to be used. For the Cornish, as mentioned above, territory is a 'core value'[20] and a basis for building solidarity. But what is the nature of that territory and how does feminist theory help to explain it?

Society has traditionally placed a higher value on public space[21] —spaces of government, finance and culture that are traditionally dominated by men—than on private or domestic space to which women have traditionally been confined. Spivak draws a parallel between the public/private dichotomy and that of core/periphery, thus overlaying the private or domestic arena inhabited by women with the relative powerlessness inherent in zones of peripherality. Conversely, the public domain of men is characterized by the power and influence integral to the 'core'.

This analogy goes to the heart of the division of labour and material reality already discussed. Within this model, the 'feminized' Cornish occupy the 'private' space as opposed to the masculine 'public' space of England, and as such are seen as fulfilling 'domestic' tasks. So that while the English are running the country, the Cornish occupy a domestic territory, providing holiday accommodation, golf courses and boat harbours—the economic version of slippers, supper and sex—for their weekend leisure. Fiske's examination of the liminal nature of London music halls provides a microcosmic illustration of this analogy: a mixing of classes on the social edge of 'civilized' society in which the lower class (the women) are employed to entertain the respectable middle class (the male patrons).[22]

Cornwall, however, is arguably more than just 'liminal'. Its 'remote' geography renders it peripheral in terms of distance, while its well-defined border peripheralizes its population and their cultural activities. From a feminist perspective, the activities that are carried out in peripheral societies are deemed to have a 'carnival' atmosphere.[23] That is, they are not only carried out in 'private' or 'domestic' space, but because they are inclusive of everyday 'folk', they are considered amusing and superficial, and deemed to lack seriousness and depth. By contrast, the sombre ritual of the 'establishment' is the privilege of the 'core' and is carried out as an exclusive spectacle in important public space, all the more to reinforce its importance and the privileged status of those it includes.

However, 'carnival' is not always just harmless fun but is frequently to do with confrontation.[24] Fiske supports this argument, citing Rabelais and Bukhtin for whom the carnivalesque is concerned with overt and excessive displays of physical pleasure which are a direct response to social and moral controls imposed from outside.[25] Furthermore, he claims that the carnivalesque is the result of a collision between the 'high, validated language of classical learning enshrined in political and religious power, and the low, vernacular language of the folk'.[26] This theory challenges us to examine Cornish 'folk' spectacles in terms of Cornwall's relationship with the 'dominant core' and to question to what extent they are harmless expressions of identity or subtle but overt and recalcitrant statements to an historically oppressive England.

Regardless of whether Cornwall's relationship with England is described as peripheral, liminal, playground, carnival, private, domestic or home to a race of 'backward others', the constant is its powerlessness. As such, its territory and its identity are subjects ripe for an application of feminist theory.

HOW CAN FEMINIST THEORY BE USED?

The application of feminist theory to research into Cornwall is potentially useful on several levels. First, its interdisciplinary nature allows us to examine many aspects of the Cornish situation and thereby gain a coherent picture of interactions between different spheres of activity and the way they impact on the community. Second, the fact that it comes in a range of styles—cultural, materialist, post-structuralist and postmodernist, to name a few—means that those who might choose to apply its theoretical perspectives can be selective in the way they go about it. Indeed, Ivey and Payton's five stages of cultural identity could prove useful as a guide to the type of feminist theory that might be appropriate to various groups.[27] For example, educationalists wanting to place more emphasis on Cornish culture at primary school level, where children may be at a naïve stage in terms of cultural awareness, might use a cultural feminist methodology to develop a curriculum that would recognize and celebrate the positives of difference without attaching values to either the Cornish or English.

Policy makers more concerned with the local economy might elect to use a materialist model to analyse the impact of stereotyping on real, quality-of-life issues such as jobs, wages and housing and thereby create a solid argument for change. Clearly, such arguments have already been made, as a great deal of research has been done on these issues. A feminist materialist methodology is simply one means of constructing the case.

While post-structuralist and postmodernist approaches to feminism might appear to be less helpful at a 'grass roots' level, used carefully they have the potential to not only eat away at negative constructs but to create new ones. Image makers, such as advertising agencies and the public relations departments of organizations repre-senting Cornwall, should be actively concerned with this task, as should politicians and journalists whose rhetoric finds its way into the public domain at both UK national and local levels.

SOME DIFFICULTIES

While its potential is considerable, the application of feminist theory to the issues affecting a specific cross-gender population is not without its problems. For example, researchers using feminist theory risk doing precisely what they accuse men (or in the Cornish model, England) of doing: categorizing on the basis of difference, constructing stereotypes, and adopting certain behaviours and attitudes accordingly. Applied to

Cornwall, this not only means that certain stereotypes are placed on the English, it also means that there is the risk of putting the entire subject population (the Cornish) in one basket and ignoring those who are on the margins within Cornwall itself. In brief, if we use feminism to progress the cause of the Cornish as a whole, are we assuming that Cornish men and women are equally oppressed? Is there such a thing as the 'Cornish as a whole'? What about Cornish women? What are the ethics of using feminist theory in the name of an ethnic group only to have it ignore that culture's women? Such an outcome would be surely the most sublime irony feminism is likely to face.

Another irony regarding the application of feminist theory to Cornwall is the 'macho' nature of so many Cornish identity icons. Is it simply coincidence that a culture so suited to feminist theory is so overtly masculine? Or perhaps the expression of masculine prowess is a reaction to an underlying awareness of having been feminized in terms of power, or on the other hand, perhaps it is a challenge. This is not the place to examine this issue, yet it is a vexing and interesting one.

Finally, feminist methodology does not allow me, a fourth-generation Australian, to be active on Cornwall's behalf, a premise Hale refutes on the basis of her own research experiences in Cornwall.[28] Hale's experience as an American working in Cornwall showed that the Cornish are more willing to identify and co-operate with others who share 'outsider' status *vis-à-vis* England, especially those from places that have been colonized by the English or where large numbers of Cornish have migrated. This attitude among the Cornish starkly underscores the feminized position Cornwall occupies in its relationship with England, its dominant core.

CONCLUSION

The theoretical perspectives of feminism offer numerous avenues for research into topics relating to any marginalized or disadvantaged group. For Cornwall, its application can provide insight into its relationship with both England, its dominant 'other', models for the advancement of change and an understanding of the Cornish people's own behaviours and attitudes, both at home and abroad. That said, it is not without its risks. As mentioned above, feminist theory can be a dangerous weapon if used to take advantage of the differences that in other contexts it resists or rejects. But here again, feminism provides astute campaigners with a range of methodologies that can be used alone or together to weaken and change values and assumptions, argue facts, and ultimately achieve the desired shift of power and focus.

NOTES AND REFERENCES

1. Susan J. Smith, 'The Cultural Politics of Difference', in D. Massey, J. Allen and P. Sarre (eds), *Human Geography Today*, Cambridge, 1999, p. 129.
2. Ronald Perry, 'Economic Change and Opposition Economics' in Philip Payton (ed.), *Cornwall Since the War*, Redruth, 1993.
3. Malcolm Williams, 'Housing the Cornish', in Payton (ed.), 1993.
4. Philip Payton—information provided by email in response to my query on this issue, 10 June 2000.
5. Patricia M. Lengermann and Jill Niebrugge-Brantley, 'Contemporary Feminist Theory' in G. Ritzer (ed.), *Sociological Theory (2nd edn)*, New York, 1998, p. 400.
6. Heather Brunskell, 'Feminist Methodology' in Clive Seale (ed.), *Researching Society and Culture*, London, 1998, p. 38.
7. Sandra Harding, 'The Instability of the Analytical Categories of Feminist Theory', in M. Malson, J. O'Barr, S. Westphal-Wihl and M. Wyer (eds), *Feminist Theory in Practice and Process*, Chicago, 1989.
8. Lengermann and Niebrugge-Brantley, 1998, p. 401.
9. Joan W. Scott, *Gender and the Politics of History*, New York, 1988, p. 10.
10. Harding, 1989.
11. Catharine MacKinnon, quoted in Drucilla Cornell, *Beyond Accomodation*, New York, 1991, p. 120.
12. A. Ivey and P. Payton, 'Towards a Cornish Identity Theory', in Philip Payton (ed.), *Cornish Studies: Two*, Exeter, 1994, p. 151.
13. Dick Cole, 'The Cornish: Identity and Genetics—An Alternative View' in Philip Payton (ed.), *Cornish Studies: Five*, Exeter, 1997.
14. Amy Hale, 'Rethinking Celtic Cornwall: An Ethnographic Approach' in Payton (ed.), 1997.
15. Hale, 1997, p. 86.
16. Linda Alcoff, 'Cultural Feminism versus Post-structuralism: The Identity Crisis in Feminist Theory' in M. Malson et al. (eds), 1989, p. 297.
17. Alcoff, 1989, p. 297.
18. Scott, 1988, p. 5.
19. Such as those put forward by Borlase, quoted in Hale, 1997, p. 89.
20. Bernard Deacon, quoted in Philip Payton, 'Territory and Identity' in Philip Payton (ed.), 1993, p. 224.
21. Gayatri Spivak, *In Other Worlds: Essays in Cultural Politics*, New York, 1998, p. 103.
22. John Fiske, *Understanding Popular Culture*, London, 1995, p. 77.
23. Smith, 1999.
24. Smith, 1999, p. 134.
25. Fiske, 1995, p. 81.
26. Fiske, 1995, p. 82.
27. Ivey and Payton, 1994, p. 155.
28. Amy Hale—subject raised during a telephone seminar, 1 July 2000.

A QUESTION OF ETHNIC IDENTITY

Philipa Aldous and Malcolm Williams

INTRODUCTION

Whilst there has been much debate in the last decade or so about Cornish identity[1] there have been few attempts to measure or describe Cornish ethnicity as a key variable.[2] In this article we report on such an attempt.

The principal focus of the research was that of attitudes toward migration amongst two cohorts of young people aged 15 to 18 in October 1997, in Cornwall and Devon. Although ethnicity was not the central topic of investigation, it was, however, initially hypothesized that Cornish identity might be an important factor in any differences in attitudes toward migration between young people in Cornwall and Devon.[3] To this end a key variable in the research was that of ethnicity. Here we will not report in any detail the findings in respect of migration intention, but will focus instead on the methodological and sociological issues raised in the measurement of Cornish ethnicity.

The research consisted of four stages:

- Stage One was a sample of school and college students from Year 11 (aged 15–16) and Year 13 (aged 17–18) in Cornwall and Devon and weighted according to the relative difference in resident population in the two locations. The survey was self-completion and administered in the schools/colleges with the help of staff in the Spring of 1997.[4]
- Stage Two consisted of structured interviews with a sub-sample of respondents from Stage One selected on the basis of migration preference, gender education and career intention. These interviews were designed to develop further some of the issues covered by the

initial questionnaire. This sub-sample formed the basis of a longitudinal panel followed over the next two years.

- Stage Three consisted of a further self-administered questionnaire sent to the same sub-sample during the summer of 1998. This questionnaire recorded changes in attitude, circumstance and intention in the intervening period, which for the Year 11 pupils marked a transition to sixth form, college or work and for Year 13 students a transition to work or university (in the latter case mostly involving migration).

At each of these stages ethnic identification was recorded, allowing back-checking for consistency between Stages 1 and 2 and the measurement of change in identification between Stages 2 and 3. The final stage of the research was conducted in the summer of 2000 and consisted of detailed case studies of a group of young people from various parts of Cornwall. The case studies were based on a series of in-depth interviews and, therefore, did not contain a consistent measure of ethnic identity, but instead drew out the personal implications of identity and provided a useful contextualization of the earlier standardized measures.

MEASURING ETHNICITY

The question of the measurement of ethnicity has been a politically and methodologically vexed one for a long time. There have been those who have objected to such measures at all because of a history of their abuse in the punitive treatment of minorities.[5] However, in the last two decades or so these objections have been mostly politically eclipsed by an awareness that non-white groups (in particular) had been and continued to be systematically disadvantaged in respect of employment, housing, education and social services. Consequently, some measure of ethnic monitoring or measurement is used nowadays by most public and voluntary sector organizations. Indeed, many sociologists see one's ethnicity, alongside class and gender, as a key predictor of life chances.[6]

Nevertheless, ethnicity (often wrongly referred to as 'race'[7]) is a slippery concept and cannot be associated unproblematically with any fixed, or relatively fixed, physical or cultural characteristics. The 2001 UK Census, for example, asked respondents to choose between the following categories:

White (*British; Irish; Any other White background*[8])

Mixed (*White and Black Caribbean; White and Black African; White and Asian; Any other Mixed background*)

Asian or Asian British (*Indian; Pakistani; Bangladeshi; Any Other Asian background*)

Black or Black British (*Caribbean; African; Any other Black background*)

Chinese or other ethnic group (*Chinese; Any other*)

These categories are a melange of characteristics of colour, culture and geography and bear little resemblance to unprompted definitions of ethnicity people will themselves usually give.[9] The numeric predominance of the 'White' category produces both statistical problems when making certain comparisons with other groups and obscures an enormous amount of cultural and geographic variation. It is likely that an Indian brought up in the UK will be less culturally distinct from a 'white' person than a Bulgarian Romany will be from a Welsh person. Indeed, the wars of the Yugoslav secession have been fought wholly between 'white' people, but on the (varying) contested basis of religion, language and shared cultural norms.

There have been attempts to improve on the Census and various different ethnic categories have supplemented or replaced Census definitions in other research or monitoring. These have variously included: Greek, Irish, Arabic, European mixed, Black British, and so on.[10] On the insistence of a voluntary sector client, one of the present authors took this inclusiveness to its logical conclusion with an ethnic monitoring question containing 86 categories!

Different ethnic identities will privilege a range of characteristics that can be geographic origin, language, place of birth, religion and cultural affinity, which in itself can be broken down into a number of categories (e.g. caste, diet, kinship).[11] Some or all may be present and where this is 'some' rather than 'all', it does not follow that such an ethnic identity is experienced as being 'weaker'. Furthermore, a number of these characteristics can be acquired (particularly by those 'born' into one ethnic group and subsequently socialized from an early age into another), or one may have a dual ethnicity, with a parent from each of two groups. Although attempts have been made to produce formal definitions of an ethnic group (in particular that of Anthony Smith[12]), for the most part these do not map particularly well onto an individual's self-perception of ethnic identification (or indeed its absence). Yet for all this there remains a need for objective measurement of subjective categories in order to determine the relative opportunities or disadvantages experienced by one group over another, but also to measure the importance of such identification for social solidarity.

A methodological solution to the problem of the inclusivity of different kinds of ethnic groups lies in a 'question testing' approach. History, migration and so on can allow us to hypothesize that certain survey locations will have over-representations of particular ethnic groups. Consequently, a standard ethnic grouping format can be used with the addition of those groups it is believed have a significant representation in the survey population. For example, one might include Irish in Liverpool or Manchester, or Maltese in Cardiff or Plymouth. These additions can be checked through piloting, though of course a pilot study may fail to reveal very many members of a relatively small minority. Finally, the category 'Other' provides an opportunity for self-identification which can be subsequently coded. This methodological strategy not only measures the relative numeric proportion of a group, but also tests for identification with that group. For example, whilst there is no question that a significant number of people in the UK would identify with the ethnic category of Bengali, few in Cornwall would, not because the ethnic identity is weak, but because there are few Bengalis in Cornwall. Conversely, one could invent a category 'Avonish', but one would anticipate there would be very few takers, even in Bristol! A broad conclusion to this is that whilst defining measures of ethnicity is politically and sociologically difficult, even in this way, it is not sociologically blind and can be sensitive to historic-cultural and demographic characteristics.

One final technical problem exists as to where in any list a category should be placed. The Census places 'white' first, presumably on the basis that this will be the largest group. Other surveys have placed 'White British' first and then provided sub-categories, but when this is compared with findings from studies which place the subcategories first, the results in the same population are different, with a favouring of the first category by respondents, whether or not this is a broad or sub-category. It follows then, that measures of Cornish ethnicity may differ according to where in any list the category is placed. In order to produce a stringent test of whether respondents would self-identify as Cornish the present study did not place Cornish first in the list, but third after English and Black British.[13] The ethnic question and categorization was then as follows:

Which of the following groups do you see yourself as belonging to?
(Tick one box only)

English	☐	Scottish		Chinese	☐
Black British	☐	Black African		Other (Please specify)	☐
Cornish	☐	Black Caribbean			
Irish	☐	Indian			
Welsh	☐	Pakistani			

IDENTIFYING AS CORNISH

Overall 29.2 per cent of the sample self-defined as 'Cornish'. This should not be taken as a measure of the number of Cornish in Cornwall, but may be seen as a reasonable estimate of the percentage of the 15–18-year-old population prepared to self-define as Cornish. There is a further caveat which should be entered: although each administrative district was represented by a school/college, not all major towns were represented. For example Truro,[14] Camborne, St Ives, Bodmin, St Austell, Launceston and Saltash were not represented. From the geographic results presented below it seems likely that the inclusion of further schools from West or Mid Cornwall might have produced a higher level of 'Cornish' identification and the inclusion of further schools from East Cornwall may possibly have lowered this. Indeed, as Table 1 shows there is an east–west distance decay in self-identification as Cornish. Two exceptions to this gradient are Camelford and Penwith College. The former serves a relatively sparsely populated area of North Cornwall and the latter is a sixth-form college with no Year 11 pupils. This makes a difference to self-identification as we will show below.

Table 1: Ethnic category and school

% Row Chi^2 res School/College	*Self-defined ethnic category* English		Cornish		Other	
Cape Cornwall School	44.6	(-9.0)	46.4	(9.6)	8.9	(-0.6)
Penwith College	69.6	(2.0)	17.4	(-2.7)	13.0	(-0.7)
Redruth CC	57.0	(-3.7)	34.0	(4.8)	9.0	(-1.1)
Falmouth CC	52.1	(-6.3)	31.5	(1.7)	16.4	(4.6)
Liskeard CC	75.0	(12.6)	18.2	(-9.7)	6.8	(-2.9)
SJS (Camelford)	68.4	(4.4)	22.8	(-3.7)	8.8	(-0.7)
P=.00			n=397			

Identification and birth
Identification as Cornish cannot be viewed simply in terms of birth or length of residence in Cornwall. Whilst, as one would expect, 94 per cent who defined themselves as Cornish had lived all of their lives in Cornwall, only 42 per cent of those who had lived their entire lives in Cornwall defined themselves as Cornish, and this was proportionally higher the greater the distance from the Devon border. This may be a function of a weaker sense of identity in East Cornwall, but is complicated by the fact that maternity facilities serving South-East Cornwall are located in Plymouth. Evidence from the case studies suggests that not being born in Cornwall is seen by some as a disqualification.

Table 2: Ethnic category and parents' birthplace

% Row Chi^2 res *Parents' birthplace*	*Self-defined ethnic category* *English*		*Cornish*		*Other*	
Neither parent born in Cornwall	75.8	(24.5)	9.3	(-31.8)	14.9	(7.3)
One parent born in Cornwall	55.6	(-5.8)	35.0	(7.0)	9.4	(-1,2)
Both parents born in Cornwall	43.0	(-18.8)	52.3	(24.9)	4.7	(-6.1)
P=.00					n=385, missing obs=12	

Despite this there is firm evidence that birthplace of the respondents' parents is a factor in ethnic identification. Table 2 shows parents' known birthplace in relation to self-identification. Of those with both parents born in Cornwall, 48 per cent self-defined as 'English', or a category other than 'Cornish' and of those with one parent born in Cornwall, 66 per cent self defined as 'English', or a category other than 'Cornish'. Only the group with two parents born in Cornwall had a majority identifying as Cornish.

Ethnicity and cohort
Cohort is also significantly associated with identification as Cornish, as is shown in Table 3 below. Overall, only 18 per cent of the Year 13 sample identified as Cornish, as opposed to 33 per cent in Year 11. This suggests three possible explanations:

1. that those defining as Cornish are less likely to continue into post-compulsory education;
2. that some fundamental change occurs in the process of self-identification between the ages of 16 and 18, which causes

individuals to change their self-identification category from Cornish to English;

3. that the macro scale phenomenon of Cornish self-identification is increasing among young people and will become more apparent in successive cohorts of young people in Cornwall.

Explanation #1 suggests that those in Year 11 who self-define as Cornish would be less likely to continue into Further or Higher education. Analyses show, however, that this is not the case and the proportions of Cornish and non-Cornish entering Higher or Further education are similar.

Explanation #2, that ethnic identity changes between Year 11 and Year 13, is testable through a longitudinal analysis of Stage One and Stage Three data.[15] This change does not seem to be occurring. Only nine individuals changed their self-identification and six of those were in fact from English to Cornish.

This leaves the tentative conclusion that a macro scale process of change may be under way and that identification with Cornish ethnicity may be increasing over time, with progressive cohorts increasingly identifying as Cornish.

Table 3: Ethnic category and cohort

% Row Chi^2 res Cohort	*Self-defined ethnic category* English		Cornish		Other	
Year 11	57.1	(-10.9)	32.7	(10.5)	14.9	(0.5)
Year 13	72.3	(10.9)	18.1	(-10.5)	9.4	(-0.5)

WHAT IT MEANS TO BE CORNISH

It has been noted above that ethnicity is not a clearly defined concept. In the case of identification with Cornish ethnicity, this was certainly the case for the respondents in the present study. Self-inclusion or exclusion was based on a variety of factors such as place of birth, parents' place of birth or identification and subjective feelings of 'belonging'. Factors such as birth led to self-exclusion for some, but not others. The subjective basis of identification was explored at Stages 2 (structured interviews) and 4 (depth interviews).

Stage 2 of the research consisted of short structured interviews with a sub-sample of 151 respondents, of which 89 were resident in Cornwall at the time of interview. In the case of the latter respondents a short section designed to access subjective definitions of Cornishness was included in the interview.

Respondents were first asked whether they thought of themselves as Cornish or not. This was asked irrespective of their choice of ethnic category at Stage 1. Of the Stage 2 sample 64 per cent responded positively to this question and 36 per cent negatively. Both groups were then asked to explain, in their own words, the reason for their answers. The open nature of this question allowed potential for a wide variety of responses but, in fact, there was consistency in the answers given. The reasons respondents gave for their answers are not mutually exclusive and in some cases the explanations were multi-faceted and complex.

Among those who did identify as Cornish, the most common reason given was birth in Cornwall (21 cases), parents' birth in Cornwall (22 cases) and life-long residence in Cornwall (29 cases). The last of those reasons was particularly common in Liskeard where several respondents had been born in Plymouth, though had lived in Cornwall since birth. One respondent saw this as a reason for not identifying as Cornish; a further respondent claimed her mother had changed GPs in order that she should be born in Cornwall.

Birthplace of parents was commonly given as a reason for claiming to be Cornish and in a few cases birthplace of grandparents was also cited. Family in Cornwall was also a fairly common reason (16 cases), whilst others mentioned cultural and/or lifestyle differences and 8 said they had been brought up the 'Cornish' way (7 of these were from Redruth). One in this last group referred to specifically 'Cornish' morals and went on to talk about the 'importance of family' and of being able to 'stop and talk to people in the street'. Another referred to the culture of 'doing it directly'.

Amongst those who did not think of themselves as Cornish, the most common reason was the fact that they were not born in Cornwall (15 cases) or had not been resident for long enough (7 cases). Five of the respondents felt they had allegiances to other geographical areas or ethnic groups. Other reasons offered included parents who were born outside of Cornwall and the lack of a Cornish accent. Three respondents reported that being Cornish or not was not something they had ever thought about. Only 2 of the 89 respondents suggested that there was no difference between Cornwall and other areas.

In order to further assess subjective definitions of the boundaries of Cornish ethnicity, a series of statements was provided, offering various criteria for inclusion/exclusion. These questions were presented in the form of a Lickert scale offering a choice of answers ranging from strongly disagree to strongly agree.[16]

Of the 89 members of the sub-sample from Cornwall, only 35.2 per cent agreed that 'You cannot be truly Cornish unless you were born in Cornwall', whilst 52 per cent disagreed and 10 per cent were unsure. Similarly, only 29.5 per cent agreed that 'You can only really call yourself Cornish if you and at least one of your parents were born in Cornwall', whereas 61 per cent disagreed. There was also a largely negative reaction to the suggestion that 'Only those who have lived all their lives in Cornwall have the right to call themselves Cornish', with 72.5 per cent disagreeing and only 22 per cent agreeing.

The fact that these fairly closed definitions of the boundaries of Cornish ethnicity produced a high proportion of negative reactions would suggest the prevalence of an open and inclusive attitude to Cornish identity. However, the suggestion that 'Wherever you were born, once you have lived in Cornwall long enough you become Cornish' produced a negative response in 60 per cent of cases with only 20 per cent agreeing. Yet only 42 per cent disagreed with the statement 'If you feel Cornish, then you are Cornish', as opposed to 35 per cent who agreed and 22 per cent who were unsure.

Fifty-five per cent agreed that 'If you are born in Cornwall, it doesn't matter where you live later in life, you will always feel Cornish'. Twenty-three per cent disagreed and 23 per cent were unsure.

The scores produced by these answers were combined to produce a composite score of attitude to inclusive/exclusive criteria for each individual. A positive score indicated a relatively closed attitude and a negative score a relatively open one. When the results were cross-tabu-lated with the dichotomous variable 'Cornish/non Cornish', 50 per cent of those self-defining as Cornish scored positively, indicating a more closed attitude, whilst 37.5 per cent scored negatively, indicating a relatively open attitude. Conversely, amongst those who did *not* define as Cornish, 53 per cent had scores indicating a relatively open attitude to inclusion, as opposed to 36 per cent with relatively closed attitudes.[17]

The final stage of the research was series of case studies drawn from members of the sample who were resident in Cornwall at Stage 2. This part of the research permitted a more in-depth exploration of the young peoples' attitudes, but crucially attitudes in transition between school/college and work/university and in some cases after migration. One of the young people, 'Anna',[18] who had lived her whole life in West Cornwall was asked about being Cornish. She indicated that whilst she would tick a survey category of Cornish, she would not self-define as Cornish in an 'other' category. If you do this, it was suggested, non-Cornish people do not understand: '*People think you're shit stirring, awkward . . . People think it's silly.*' Yet when asked about her feelings of being Cornish she was quite firm: would she have felt the same if she had been born elsewhere?

No. If I had been born in Devon I wouldn't feel the same . . .
Cornwall is more like Wales and Scotland. Cornwall is *not*
English. It's *like* English, but it's Celtic not English.

A further respondent from West Cornwall (Troon), 'Emily', had
not been born in Cornwall, though her parents were Cornish. She
firmly defined herself as Cornish, justifying this in her perception of a
family blood line. She also emphasized the cultural uniqueness of
Cornwall:

> It's got it's own flag. It's got its own language . . . and I mean
> Celtic connection, as well, and I mean people say they are
> Scottish and Welsh and I know they are separate countries,
> that are more independent and bigger . . . but . . . I mean
> Cornish is, you know, it is like, almost a breed, a race. I don't
> know how to describe it.

Emily also referred to her connections with Brittany and the
Cornish diaspora in Australia and America.[19]
'Steve', who lived in Perranporth at the time of interview[20] had
neither been born in Cornwall nor had Cornish-born parents, yet he
still felt himself to be Cornish. However, because he saw Cornwall as
ethnically distinct he also felt that he would have to say he was English
as well, yet being Cornish for him was a sense of belonging and not
really having much alternative experience to living in a Cornish community. Other respondents who had been born outside of Cornwall,
even if they had Cornish parents, expressed similar ambiguities, though
each stressed similar ideas of what being Cornish consisted of.
One of the case study respondents, 'Rachel', though she had
been born in Devon and lived virtually all her life in Doublebois, in
Caradon, nevertheless did not regard herself as Cornish:

> I came here at, like sixteen months old or something, so I
> suppose I've known no different than ever living in Cornwall
> but, you know . . . I've got family in Devon and Birmingham
> and in other parts of the country and . . . I suppose it's
> down to my parents. They've never sort of pretended to be
> real locals you know, in the community . . . I've never felt
> particularly Cornish.

It is not claimed that the case studies are in any way statistically
representative, but they do throw some light on what people (in this
case young people) think when they tick a box marked 'Cornish' , or

indeed contemplate writing in the category Cornish in an ethnic identity question. For all of the case study respondents, living in Cornwall for all or much of their lives had produced feelings of attachment, yet these feelings were not always the same as feelings of belonging to an ethnic group.

CONCLUSION: A QUESTION OF BEING CORNISH?

The question of the proportion of Cornish in the population of Cornwall is either no longer relevant, or it is at least parasitic upon much more complex questions of what it is to be Cornish. The emergent and changing nature of Cornish identity has perhaps always contained paradoxes. Perhaps its most confident phase was in the nineteenth century when many of its characteristics were the result of industrialization and Methodism.[21] In Wales at least, such changes have been seen as a weakening of traditional identities[22] and in one sense this was true of Cornwall as well. By the end of the nineteenth century not that much remained of the kind of explicit Celtic identity found in North Wales or Brittany and a great deal of what is now celebrated as Celtic can be dated to the Revival of the late nineteenth and early twentieth centuries. Though there is little or no research to demonstrate this, one would anticipate that for many in the generations prior to those who were teenagers in the 1980s and 1990s, the manifestations of the Revival (in the language, music, tartan and so on) would be seen as synthetic. For those generations the 'real' Cornish identity may well have been that of mining and Methodism. Of course, ironically, the growth in sociological research that can tell us about identity and ethnicity is in itself (at least partially) a consequence of that very Revival!

Many of the respondents in the present study cited just those objects of the revival as a basis for their Cornishness. For them the Revival was not synthetic, but part of their lived experience. In itself this does not mean it is the totality of their experience. Young people in most cultures now have complex and multi-layered identities[23] and being Cornish is just one of them and one which many had taken for granted until asked. In expressing one's ethnic identity as Cornish there was both confidence and defensiveness, yet if the greater proportion of the younger cohort preparing to identify themselves as Cornish is the result of macro level change and not an artefact of the study, then something important and unusual is happening. At the same time as high levels of in-migration continue, a greater proportion of young people are prepared to assert their cultural distinctiveness. There is certainly no evidence in the present study that this is the result of a ghettoization of young Cornish people, but more likely, as Deacon and

Payton suggest, that the symbols of Cornishness, both traditional and Revivalist, can be mobilized in a popular culture.[24] However, there may be spatial differences in this process, with an East–West 'distance decay' in identification and a stronger sense of identification in the old industrial areas.[25] The current study did not explore the latter, but evidence from other studies of housing and migration indicates both a firmer Cornish identity in urban areas and lower levels of in-migration[26]

Finally, what of migration and ethnicity? The study provided strong evidence to suggest that there has been a turnaround in attitudes to migration by the Cornish. In both cohorts, those who self-identified as Cornish were much less likely to express an intention or wish to migrate. Conversely, the sons and daughters of in-migrants expressed opposite views. This poses some fascinating questions for Cornish ethnic identity. Is it the case that if one chooses to 'stay' one is more likely to assert a Cornish identity, or is the development of a Cornish identity becoming a factor in deciding to remain in Cornwall? Or, to what extent does the presence or absence of cultural resources to be able to migrate (e.g. access to family networks outside of Cornwall) then determine how one feels about Cornwall?

Perhaps the most fascinating question in the assertion of Cornish ethnicity lies in its voluntary nature. Whilst to an extent all ethnic 'minorities' have some element of choice in their ethnic identification, social factors or those of colour will restrict this. In this study there were some insights as to why such choices are made, but the data are not comprehensive or conclusive. All that we know is that around a third of young people in Cornwall choose to be Cornish and not English.

NOTES AND REFERENCES

1. See for example: P. Payton, 'Territory and Identity', in P. Payton (ed.), *Cornwall Since the War*, Redruth, 1993; B. Deacon and P. Payton 'Re-Inventing Cornwall: Culture Change on the European Periphery', in P. Payton (ed.), *Cornish Studies: One*, Exeter, 1993; D. Cole, 'The Cornish: Identity and Genetics—An Alternative View', in P. Payton (ed.), *Cornish Studies: Five*, Exeter, 1997; B. Deacon, *The Cornish and the Council of Europe Framework Convention for the Protection of National Minorities; The Cornish National Minority Report*, Redruth, 1999.
2. The 2001 Census, for the first time, coded those responses given as 'Cornish' in the Other Ethnic Group category. Unfortunately, because such answers are self-defining and Cornish is not listed as an ethnic category in its own right, this will almost certainly lead to an undercount of

those who would define as Cornish when this category is listed. There is some evidence for this in the current study.

3. The initial hypothesis was that Cornish identity would be a predisposing factor in migration decisions, but as it will be seen this hypothesis was falsified.

4. Total Stage 1 sample size for Cornwall and Devon was 1,853 with a 68 per cent response rate. The achieved sample for Cornwall was 397.

5. W. Ahmad, 'Ethnic Statistics: Better than Nothing or Worse than Nothing?' in D. Dorling and L. Simpson, *Statistics in Society: The Arthimetic of Politics*, London, 1999, p. 128.

6. See T. Modood and R. Berthoud, (eds), *Ethnic Minorities in Britain*, London, 1997.

7. See B. Carter, *Realism and Racism: Concepts of Race in Sociological Research*, London, 2000.

8. As with the Cornish (see note 2 above) 'any other' categories are self-selecting and will not form part of most Census analyses of ethnicity.

9. T. Modood, 'Culture and Identity', in Modood and Berthoud (eds), 1997.

10. D. Coleman and J. Salt, (eds), *Ethnicity in the 1991 Census, Vol. 1: Demographic Characteristics of the Ethnic Minority Population*, London, 1996, p. 12.

11. Ahmad, 1999, p. 129.

12. A. Smith, *National Identity*, Harmondsworth, 1991.

13. The latter was used as a 'test' category to see if placing this category in a privileged position would over-represent this group comparative to the Census—it did not.

14. The independent Truro School was sampled at Stage 1, but the findings were analysed separately.

15. This relates to only 111 cases. A much larger sample would be needed to draw firm conclusions.

16. A. Oppenheim, *Questionnaire Design, Interviewing and Attitude Measurement*, London, 1992.

17. Because numbers were small in the 'non-Cornish' sub-group (in Cornwall) these latter percentages are not statistically significant.

18. Respondent names have been anonymized.

19. See M. Buck, L. Bryant, M. Williams, *Housing and Households in Cornwall*, Plymouth, 1993.

20. Some problems were experienced in tracing/recruiting those no longer in education for Stage 4. 'Steve' was recruited to increase the representatives of this group.

21. See for example P. Payton, *The Making of Modern Cornwall*, Redruth, 1992; Deacon and Payton, 1993.

22. See for example, G. Williams, *When Was Wales? A History of the Welsh*, Harmondsworth, 1985.

23. See for example, S. Miles, *Youth Lifestyles in a Changing World*, Buckingham, 2000.

24. Deacon and Payton, 1993, p. 76.

25. This is not the same as urban areas. For example more respondents identified with the category 'Cornish' in St Just than Liskeard, however in the present study this particular issue is hard to disentangle from the 'distance decay' effect.

26. Buck et al. 1993; C. Williams 'Counterurbanisation, Housing and Households in Cornwall,' unpublished Ph.D. thesis, Plymouth, 1997.

COMMUNITY IDENTITY AND CYBERSPACE: A STUDY OF THE CORNISH COMMUNITY

David Crowther and Chris Carter

INTRODUCTION

The ubiquity of the World Wide Web (WWW) and the Internet provides many opportunities for individuals to combine, to communicate, and to make their respective voices heard. This article considers the potential for Cornish identity to be made explicit via this medium. The article begins by considering the various definitions of 'community' and identifies changes to these definitions arising from transition to the postmodern era. In particular, the use of the WWW as a mechanism for communication and for establishing and maintaining a sense of identity which is separated from geographical location is investigated. This is achieved through an examination of one such community that has established a presence on the Internet, the Cornish community located throughout the world. It is argued that this community has established an identity as a discrete community through its use of the Internet, and that this virtual community is a 'true community' according to its many definitions . Using the Internet as a research tool, the authors entered into a virtual dialogue with members of this community and conducted a series of structured interviews with them. The responses of these community members have been analysed and evaluated in order to demonstrate the uses made of the Internet in creating and reinforcing their sense of Cornish identity. The implications of the use of the Internet in creating and maintaining such cybercommunities are then considered in the context of the current usage of this technology and possible future increased usage.

THE IMPACT OF THE INTERNET AND THE WWW

The increasing availability of access to the Internet has provoked a debate which ranges across the present and likely future impact of this means of communication upon the construction of society and upon the lives of individual members of that society. Much of this discourse is based upon an expectation that the Internet and the WWW will have a significant impact upon the way in which society operates. Thus it is argued that either this technology will be more liberating, participatory and interactive than previous cultural forms,[1] or that it will lead to increasing globalization of politics, culture and social systems.[2] Much of this discourse is concerned with the effects of Internet technology[3] upon society and, by implication, upon individuals within society. The emphasis upon individuals is important because it is at the level of the individual that changes effected by the Internet take place. Indeed, an individual's access to the Internet, and his/her ability to communicate via this technology to other individuals without regard to time and place, can be considered to be a revolutionary redistribution of power.[4] Moreover, the disciplinary practices of society[5] breakdown when the Internet is used because of the lack of spatial contiguity between communicants[6] and because of the effective anonymity of the communication which prevents the normalizing surveillance mechanisms of society[7] from interceding in that communication. Thus the Internet provides a space in which resistance and alternative identities can foment.[8]

The Internet provides the ideal environment for a community of resistance to exist: the Web-structured organization of the Internet means that no separate geographical existence is necessary for a Web-based community, and the nature of the Internet is such that people are only part of an Internet community when they actually choose to participate in the activities of that community. Thus an Internet community is a truly postmodern, 'virtual community'. The information architecture of the Internet means that it is relatively easy for such a community to establish its existence,[9] and so examples of such communities abound. It is relevant to observe that such communities have existed for a considerable period of time in such areas as academic life and social life. However, one essential feature of postmodernity is the changing informational architecture of society, and this both makes virtual communities more prevalent and provides one possible infrastructure for determining community identity. Thus both the territorial and temporal constituents of community disappear, or at least assume diminished significance, in a postmodern environment. At the same time, this argument has been extended to the proposition that any community need have neither any discrete geographical existence nor any continuous temporal existence but may exist as a virtual community having sporadic temporal existence and no territorial existence.[10]

Postmodernist arguments, expounded later in this article, suggest that the technological capability of the Internet will lead to a duality of social structures. This will be manifest in the increasing globalization of social structures and also the increased localization of such structures. In this article, the effect of the technological and communicative capabilities of the Internet are considered from the viewpoint of the localization imperative through a study of the effect of the medium upon one group of people, those who identify themselves as 'Cornish'. But in order to achieve this, it is necessary first of all to consider the meaning of 'community' and the impact of the Internet upon such a consideration.

THE CONCEPT OF COMMUNITY

The concept of 'community' has been used widely to enable an understanding of the structure of society but its meaning is still elusive. Plant[11] points to the essentially evaluative nature of the word, while Hillary[12] listed no fewer than ninety-four definitions of 'community' whose only common denominator was that they all dealt with people. Crow and Allen[13] report Halsey as having argued that community had 'so many meanings as to be meaningless'. Plant draws upon Bryce Gallis' criteria to argue that community is an 'essentially contested' concept, used in both an evaluative and a descriptive way, and incapable of being detached from normative understandings. He states: 'When the term is used in substantive debates about social and public policy it is never used in a neutral fashion. There is always going to be some normative and ideological engagement'.[14] Community thus 'tends to be a God word',[15] and as a concept has often escaped intellectual rigour, being perceived either as a lost ideal past or as a future to be aspired to. Thus 'below the surface of many community studies lurk value judgements of varying degrees of explicitness about what constitutes the good life'.[16]

A key interpretation, however, sees community as a uniform whole within a territorially defined boundary. Plato's Republic and the Aristotelian City State were unified political entities on a small scale which allowed interpersonal contact and involvement. Rousseau's Venetian State was larger but the community remained a unified whole, having a life of its own expressed via the General Will. Hegel's 'Spirit' saw this unity extended to the modern nation-state. But an abiding image of community has also been that of the small, homogeneous entity, rooted in custom and sharing both physical place and commonality of interest; the ideal model here is that of the pre-modern rural village, characterized by a spiritual bond to place, friendship, kin and blood relationships—affective and emotional ties of the kind to be found in Tonnies' ideal type, *Gemeinschaft*.[17] Arguments that community has been lost in modernity stem from such views and a belief that a concentration upon rationality and individual rights, along with the dislocation caused by urbanization and industrialization, have led to the loss of the old emotive ties. Thus the search for community turned to new settings—in the urban centres and the workplace—via sociological investigation. Communities could, for example, now be identified in city neighbourhoods.

However, the logical implication of modernity and its concentration upon individual rights was to emancipate man from the bonds of traditional communities. Liberalism implies natural rights and has the moral primacy of the individual at its centre; there is no one version of the common good. Reason and self-interested calculation are the determinants of action, and the basis of human interaction is contractual. People may thus decide to be members of many communities or of none; any necessary link between community and territory is severed and justification is provided for the 'new' communities which emerge—communities of interest, functional communities, those based upon the division of labour, and professional communities. Attention here is less upon spiritual bonding than upon contractual association: society, containing many sub-groups, is the focus of attention

This is an essentially pluralist vision, characterized by Tonnies' *Gesellschaft*. Broadly, modernity is held to have brought with it political and social freedoms which changed perceptions of community from those emphasizing the 'wholeness' of specific places to ones which emphasized 'communality' or 'social togetherness regardless of physical distance': communities which 'bind man socially whilst allowing him to be physically free', echoing Max Weber's concept of 'community without propinquity'. Attention is thus focused upon sub-units—groups, organizations and associations—prompting Wolin to identify late modernity as an 'Age of Organisation' and to lament the loss of sense of belonging to 'whole' political communities. Durkheim, for example, contrasted what he called 'mechanical' community, which was essentially held together by sameness, with 'organic' community which was a function of industrialization and in which it was the very differences between people which held them together as a whole; it was the interdependence caused by functional differentiation which was important.[18]

One of the presuppositions of any definition of community is that the group of people comprising that community share some commonality of interest, and it is often accepted (uncritically) that this must apply to a group of people sharing a locality as a place of habitation. Harvey and Butler, for example, identify reasons for the existence of local government, and among them is meeting the needs of the 'community'.[19] However, they do not tell us what they mean by community, and in fact the sharing of a locality by individuals need not imply the sharing of all commonalities of interest—people may belong to one community for one purpose and to another for a separate purpose. Community thus construed can be seen to exist in any one of innumerable situations: in the rural village and the urban city, in groups, associations, universities, schools and so on. Here community becomes almost a state of mind, a 'psychological sense of community' which can exist in any size of collectivity provided its members display certain characteristics of togetherness.[20]

However, this very looseness of definition has encouraged yet further divergent approaches to the study of community. For example, attempts to locate community in 'modern' urban settings gave rise to a largely anthropological series of community studies in which geographical place was yet again seen to be a determinant of patterns of life.[21] But new theoretical approaches which sought to link community with wider social processes also emerged.[22] The works of Gans and Pahl, amongst others, questioned whether it was possible to consider the specifically local and asked whether patterns of social behaviour could really be tied to geographic locations.[23] Attention was turned instead to wider economic and social processes and to structural explanations for local variations, so much so that by 1969 Stacey could wonder whether the idea of community was really of value anyway.[24] Later, during the 1980s, 'locality' was once again the focus of attention, with socio-economic variations between localities being viewed as the result of the differential impact of the uneven development of capitalism.[25]

Recently, despite the myriad definitions, approaches and difficulties sketched above, the concept of community has to a degree been rehabilitated in intellectual thought. This has arisen not only out of a concern for the alienation caused by the atomized individualism of modernity but also from a desire to 're-connect' through a return to Civic Republicanism.[26] For example, Bulmer[27] pointed to a renewed interest in the study of local social networks, work which had been pioneered by Barnes[28] and Bott,[29] and which focused attention upon the interaction of primary groups (family, friends). Network analysis could be used to 'map' these interactions; the range and spread of each person's network would vary according to his/her differing structural locations—factors including age, employment, gender, and so on. Community is thus once again an extremely fluid concept, without easily recognizable boundaries; Scherer had in 1972 identified 'modern' social relationships to be 'fluid and vague', involving overlapping and complex associations. Community was not anchored by place or lifestyle and 'still life' studies were no longer appropriate, the emphasis being not upon social balance, cohesion and homogeneity, but upon social exchange. For Scherer this approach allows us to view community as an essentially 'human' construct rather than as an illusory perfect entity. Further, there appeared to remain an area of interaction between people which was not purely personal but which rested between the world of 'primary' relationships and that of the larger organizations of state and society. This called for a refocusing of attention upon the 'intermediary structures' of this area of interaction, in the process casting a new role for the concept of community. Viewed in this way, community 'does address an element or level of social experience which cannot be ignored or done away with,' and as such may be a concept which 'if it did not exist . . . would surely need to be invented'.[30]

POSTMODERNITY AND COMMUNITY IDENTITY

But even if community is a vital concept, it would be unrealistic to assume that a 'community identity' could be derived from an aggregation of the constituents of every individual of which the community comprises. Such a view would ignore the value placed by any individual upon the various *components* of identity. It is here that the concept of postmodernity is useful because it can be used to demonstrate how all the components of identity can be considered and addressed for individuals as separate entities rather than in aggregation.

Postmodernity has been considered as being either epochal, in replacing modernity as the current time frame, or epistemological, in its relativity to other interpretations of social structures, and Newton considers the implications of both uses of the concept for the study of organizations.[31] The concept of postmodernity is, however, considered most fully by Lyotard who questions the continued use of modernist metanarratives which legitimate society as existing for the good of its members, with the consequent presumption that the whole unites the parts as an expression of the common good.[32] Furthermore, this weakening of the macroculture of society detected by Lyotard is accompanied by the rise of an increasingly robust set of subcultures, and these subcultures are operating both at a local level geographically, and at a local level in terms of common interest and identity even when geographically disparate. One conclusion to be drawn from this is that, rather than universal politics, the dominance of local or regional politics becomes paramount. Thus the dominance of community as the agent of local need assumes priority as the expression of societal organization, and local government structures are needed which recognize this. A postmodernist stance also leads to a redefinition of community and divorces it from geographical proximity. Indeed, Harvey argues that one of the significant features of the postmodern era is the compression of space and time, brought about through development in technological and informational architecture of society.[33] This compression of space and time has the effect of removing territorial boundaries from any community and this has the further effect of providing an opportunity for the redefinition of community in terms of organized local societal structures for the provision of local services without any geographical constraint.

This redefinition of community contains within itself one of the inherent contradictions of a postmodernist view of the world, namely the contradiction between the borderlessness of any community organization and the preoccupation with nationalistic inclusion/exclusion criterion. This criterion has the effect of distancing community from the nation-state, while simultaneously widening the concept to embrace inclusion in an expanded state for some purposes and yet at the same time shrinking the idea of community to a local level for other purposes.[34] Indeed, Cooke observes that the nation-state, which has for 150 years held together the tensions between individualism and the 'old' values of community, is now breaking down and becoming obsolete in a global economy, with attention becoming focused upon the global and the local.[35] Thus postmodernity suggests that different spaces are needed for different histories and purposes and that a dominant model of society has no rational meaning. When considering the question of community identity, therefore, and its relationship with societal structure, this suggests that the local structure has dominant importance to the individual and that his/her sense of community is defined circumstantially. Indeed, Lash and Urry observe that people now have an ever-increasing choice of communities to 'throw themselves into'.[36] Thus an individual can consider him/herself to be a member of a community for a particular purpose and a member of a different community for different purposes, with community identity being defined in terms of commonality of interest for specific purposes rather than being an overriding part of a definition of self. The advent of cyberspace, as a cultural form, enhances this ability of individuals to exercise such choice, allowing them to construct their own identity through selection of groups to belong to by opting for community memberships to meet their own personal needs.

This redefinition of the relationship between self and community is in perfect accord with the concept of liberal democratic pluralism which requires a separation of social spheres in order to maximize individual welfare.[37] This definition is also in perfect accordance with the concept of communitarianism which regards the self as atomistic and aiming to maximize value (in the liberal sense of welfare) to the lonely self through acting in a community for any specific purpose.[38]

A postmodernist view of community organizations, as structures, is that they are sustained by the rules governing their existence and by the resource appropriation mechanisms which apply to them, rather than by any real need from the people whom they purport to serve. Thus the legitimation of their very existence is not founded upon this redefinition of community identity and community need. Rather, this redefinition of community suggests that a very different type of community structure is needed in order to cater for the needs of the individuals who aggregate for one common purpose while atomizing (or aggregating with different individuals) for others. Such a structure has been defined by Heckscher as a post-bureaucratic structure, with its rationale for continuing existence not being through self-referential normalizing mechanisms but rather through the maintenance of an interactive dialogue, based upon consensus, with the individual members of the community which the organization exists to serve.[39] This organization structure can be extended to exclude a territorial basis for existence whereby the organization, through the use of informational and communicational technology, need be little more than a virtual organization existing in a virtual environment as the need arises.[40] Thus the continuing existence, either temporally or geographically, of any community organization, as a unit, has no meaning in its own right, as the organization has no purpose other than the provision of the services mandated to it by the community it serves.

Postmodern analysis of society and its organs is fully coincidental with this view. Baudrillard claims that there is a need to break with all forms of enlightened conceptual critiques and that 'truth' in the postmodern era is obsolete,[41] while Fish claims that 'truth' and 'belief' are synonymous for all practical purposes.[42] If this is so, then there is a need to consider community identity and structure from a post-modernist standpoint, independent of the prevailing dominant hegemony. This, in turn, requires a reconsideration of the purpose of community organization within the context of this redefinition of community identity.

REDEFINING COMMUNITY IDENTITY

A redefinition of community to mean an aggregation of individualities with a commonality of interest for a particular purpose and at a particular time suggests that an individual can be a member of a variety of different communities at the same time but for different purposes. It also suggests that any such community to which an individual belongs is not defined in any mutually exclusive geographical terms and that communities for different purposes can overlap geographically without any necessary conflict. At the same time, it is apparent that any community need not have any discrete geographical existence but may exist as a virtual community, having sporadic temporal existence and no territorial existence. The information architecture of the Internet means that examples of such communities abound, but such communities have existed for a considerable period of time in such areas as academic life and social life. One essential feature of postmodernity, however, is the changing informational architecture of society and this both makes virtual communities more prevalent and also provides one possible infrastructure for determining community identity. Thus both the territorial and temporal constituents of community disappear, or at least assume diminished significance, in a postmodern environment.

One such virtual community which has come into existence due to the development of accessibility of the Internet is the Cornish Studies group which is indeed a virtual community having no territorial existence and only a sporadic temporal existence, as its members participate in the activities of the community group as and when they wish without any likelihood of individual members of the group meeting collectively in a physical context. Such a group can be defined as a community in the Benthamite sense of allowing the individuals within the group to pursue their own ends and also in the Hegelian sense of the individuals having a commonality of interest—in this case an interest in Cornish matters and the maintenance of at least part of their identity as 'Cornish'. In order to consider the existence and operation of such a virtual community, it is first necessary to consider what it is about Cornwall, a small part of a small nation-state (the United Kingdom), which generates such a strong feeling of identity among a disparate collection of individuals.

THE CORNISH CONTEXT OF IDENTITY

Cornwall is commonly represented as just another English county and as a location associated with picturesque fishing villages, pasties, cream teas and stunning coastal views. Cornwall's image as a sleepy, rural idyll at the south-westerly tip of England is reinforced today by the lack of both heavy industry and large urban conurbations;

unsurprisingly the prime industry is tourism. In broader economic terms, Cornwall is viewed as being an integral part of the south-west of England region which stretches from Cornwall to Gloucester, with the capital being in Bristol.

A cursory glance, then, might suggest to the uninitiated that Cornwall's identity and its relationship with England is straightforward. However, such a view is widely contested and is seen by many Cornish people as a very 'English' representation of Cornwall. Thus an alternative view rejects the notion of Cornwall as being part of England and instead articulates a separate Cornish identity. Typically, the construction of this alternative view of Cornwall broadly revolves around the following assertions:

1. Cornwall's relationship with England is not as simple as that of being merely a county. In a Royal Charter of 1337 it was established that the first-born son of an English monarch was to be the quasi-ruler of the Duchy of Cornwall. In this sense Cornwall's relationship with England is similar to that of Wales. Cornwall also appeared as a separate Country in the Mappa Mundi (an eleventh-century map of the world), and in medieval state documents references were made to '*Anglia et Cornubia*' as separate entities.

2. Cornwall was ruled throughout the middle ages and into the modern age through a legal system separate from that of England, the Stannaries, bound up with the Cornish mining industry. The Cornish were also involved in various uprisings against the English, the most celebrated being in 1497 when the Cornish army reached London.

3. The Cornish are Celts with their own separate language, 'Kernewek'. The Cornish language is a Celtic language that shares close links with Welsh and Breton. The use of the language declined in the sixteenth and seventeenth centuries before dying out in the nineteenth century. The Cornish language has been revived in the twentieth century, and there is at present a small number of fluent speakers.

The Cornish case against being part of England is, therefore, based on a set of historical differences, with the insistence of being a distinct Celtic nation. As many of these differences precede the notion of the nation-state it is perhaps surprising that this sense of identity persists. However, there are many contemporary manifestations of a sense of Cornishness, such as:

- Organized resistance in the 1970s that led to the abandonment of a proposal to hive off the south-eastern part of Cornwall into a new county 'Tamarside' centred on Plymouth. At the same time a scheme to create an overspill new town in West Cornwall to be populated by Londoners was successfully resisted.
- The emergence of a nationalist party, Mebyon Kernow, which, although it has not achieved any notable electoral success, has forced the main political parties to take Cornish issues into account when campaigning in Cornwall.

   In understanding Cornwall and Cornishness, and the perpetuation of the Cornish identity to the present, Payton argues that 'The experience of Cornwall, indeed, can only be understood against the wider background of diversity and centre–periphery relationships within the UK as a whole'.[43] This view is supported by Hechter who sees Cornwall as being part of the Celtic fringe along with Wales, Scotland, the Isle of Man and Ireland.[44] An added dimension to understanding Cornishness is that it is not restricted to the spatial boundaries of Cornwall but is very much an international identity. This is grounded in the Great Emigration from Cornwall in the nineteenth century when thousands of miners and others left to seek new opportunities overseas;[45] this encompassed Australia (particularly South Australia), the United States, Canada, Mexico, South America, South Africa, New Zealand, and elsewhere. One consequence of large numbers of miners leaving together and then creating 'Little Cornwalls' in their new locations, such as the Yorke Peninsula in South Australia, was that they transplanted and then sustained their sense of Cornishness.

   However, as nations such as Australia forged their own identities, and communities dissolved, so the old ties with Cornwall began to recede. And yet, in recent times there has been a resurgence in the idea of Cornishness in the New World; for example, the largest ethnic festival in Australia is said to be South Australia's 'Kernewek Lowender' on Yorke Peninsula, celebrating the State's Cornish heritage.

STUDYING A VIRTUAL COMMUNITY
This resurgence is manifested in the existence of organizations such as the Cornish Society of Greater Milwaukee, the Cornish Association of South Australia, and the New Zealand Cornish Association, and the advent of the Internet has enabled 'Cornish people' from these diverse geographical localities to interact and develop their common interest in Cornwall and its culture. The only way to study such a virtual community, given that it only exists sporadically via the Internet, is to

communicate with the members of the community via the Internet itself.

In order to conduct this research, therefore, a survey was undertaken of members of the Cornish Studies community active on the Internet. This was by means of a questionnaire posted to the discussion group, explaining the purpose of the survey and asking for assistance.[46] Discussion groups via the Internet provide a surrogate for conversation between members of the group. With this in mind, the questionnaire was deliberately designed to mimic a structured interview rather than to operate as a conventional questionnaire type of survey. One problem with this type of survey is that, unlike true structured interviews, no supplementary questions can be asked to elicit further explanations, and so the questionnaire was deliberately designed to be open ended and to explore three main issues:

• the Cornish connection of members of the community;
• the use of the Internet in developing this sense of identity;
• the use of the Internet to develop other aspects of community identity.

Accordingly just five questions were posed in the questionnaire; these were as follows:

1. What is your link with Cornwall?
2. Do you feel Cornish above other identities?
3. Has the WWW played a role in your sense of identity?
4. Do you have any other involvement in Cornish issues/activities?
5. What other community identity uses do you make of the WWW?

In contrast to most other types of postal survey, the responses to this questionnaire were both speedy and enthusiastic, illustrating the way in which Internet communication simulates real conversation. It is estimated that approximately one third of the members of this community responded within four days of the questionnaire being posted to the discussion group, while the total response rate exceeded 75 per cent. The enthusiasm of the respondents was manifest both in the extent of detail and openness in the responses to the questions asked and also by additional comments such as 'I think this is a fantastic area of study', 'thanks for your interest' and 'glad to help' as well as suggestions for other contacts to pursue in extending this research. In general, the survey produced much interesting data to enable us to consider the use of the Internet in establishing and maintaining a virtual community.

THE VIRTUAL CORNISH COMMUNITY

Of the respondents to the survey only one person was currently living in Cornwall, although 40 per cent had been born there. The rest of the respondents all had Cornish ancestry from between two and five generations previously. Not surprisingly, respondents were currently located in all the main areas of the Cornish diaspora with significant numbers being located in Australia, New Zealand and the USA, as well as other parts of the UK.

Approximately 50 per cent of the respondents defined themselves as Cornish first and as another identity second, while the remainder identified primarily with the country or area in which they were currently living, with Cornishness being a subsidiary part of their identity. Examples of this dualism in identity are as follows:

> *Anglo-Australian is stronger but after that Cornish takes first place.*

> *I am first of all a US citizen and then a Cornish American.*

> *I am an American first and foremost with a deep Cornish background.*

Two respondents defined themselves as Cornish exclusively and refused to recognize any other national identity. They responded thus:

> *I define myself as Cornish only, and perhaps Celtic, never British or UK. There is no need for any further reference.*

> *It comes before all other possible loyalties and I proudly announce that I am Cornish whenever possible.*

Notwithstanding the views of the last two respondents, this dualism of identity is prevalent throughout the discourse and can be taken to indicate identity with the current geographical location but also a need to validate a sense of personal identity through reference to the respondents' origins. Thus it is argued that a person's identity is constructed both through reference to the present and reference to the past. This reference to the past, as demonstrated through this sense of Cornish identity, can be seen in part as a reference to an idealized past: commonly a pastiche of the rural idyll as described in the concept of *Gemeinschaft* and the romantic view of the 'mystic Celt'. This dualism is more apparent in members residing in the 'New World', where individuals have possibly a greater need to validate their sense of identity through their ancestry. This was encapsulated by one respondent who stated a feeling of Cornishness 'slightly above my other cultural identities'. Conversely, a Cornish-born respondent living in another part of the UK stated that his feeling of Cornishness transcended other senses of identity 'only because I feel different from the new community I live in'. In general, the sense of identity of Cornish-born respondents seemed to be more straightforward with less need for self-validation through reference to past ancestry.

Not surprisingly, given their active participation on the Internet, most respondents felt that the Internet helped them in defining or maintaining their Cornish identity. In such a virtual community it is a good deal easier to join or leave compared to more geographically bounded community groupings, with no pressure to become more active in the community group, in contrast to the pressure that is frequently brought to bear in groups which meet in person. In such a community the members can be active or inactive, members or non-members as they choose at any particular point in time. Indeed, membership of the community group is only manifest at those points in time when any person participates in the group activity, either actively or passively, through the discussion group. Thus features of geographically bounded groups such as commitment and peer pressure do not exist in a virtual community, and self-interest is the only defining constituent of membership. Such a virtual community can be considered to be both stronger, in term of commitment and sustain-ability, and weaker, in terms of direction, than the more conventional community groups that have a greater temporal and geographical existence, and this contrast is worthy of further exploration.

The uses made of and value gained from membership of the community varies greatly from one person to another, and examples quoted include:

> *exploring Cornish culture*
> *communicating with friends sharing a similar identity*
> *a means of research*
> *contacting other Cornish emigrants*
> *exploring my heritage*

In this respect there were distinctly divergent views between Cornish-born and Cornish-ancestry respondents. The Cornish-born reported that membership of the community had relatively little effect on their sense of Cornish identity, which was already well established through their cultural upbringing. For those Cornish-born living outside Cornwall membership was also seen as a good way of keeping in touch with Cornish issues, of providing a type of newspaper or journal relating to Cornish issues. For example, one respondent replied:

> *It is a great medium for being able to 'feel at home' sometimes. It's also interesting to join in or observe discussions about the politics of Cornish rural life, regional cookery tips and local history.*

On the other hand the Cornish-ancestry respondents were more likely to feel that membership had played a significant role in forging their sense of Cornish identity. For instance:

> *Cornish is the part of my heritage which is most difficult to follow, research, learn about.*

> *WWW has linked me with Cornish around the world and provided me with a means of research and has indeed strengthened my sense of identity.*

One of the advantages of such a community is that the benefits felt by members are entirely personal and need not be held in common with other members. All that is necessary is a shared interest and sense of identity to hold members together, without any need for joint decision making, joint action or even joint communication, as all communication is common to all members of the group without the need for any private conversation between individual group members to the exclusion of others. Indeed, one of the features of a virtual community is that the inclusion/exclusion criteria applied within society in general do not exist, and inclusion or exclusion is self-selected rather than being determined externally to the individual concerned. One of the significant features of the Internet is its anarchic structure, which enables truly open communities to exist without any impact upon others, and perhaps this is one feature of cyberspace which will bring about a significant change in the way in which society's structures operate.

Approximately 60 per cent of respondents were involved in other Cornish activities, and these ranged from participation in geographically local societies to subscription to Cornish journals, and a significant number was actively learning the Cornish language (a facility offered through the user group). This desire to learn Cornish, which is essentially a revived language and has not been the spoken vernacular of Cornwall for two hundred years, might suggest an interpretation of community which transcends the bounds of cyberspace and is more in tune with Tonnies' concept of *Gemeinschaft*, a symbolic link with 'the rural idyll' with which a revivalist/romantic view of Cornish heritage might be said to have much in common. There is, however, a paradox here, a dichotomous view of community in which the virtual community of cyberspace is linked to an apparent search for an older conception of community. It would seem, though, that this dichotomy is not recognized by the members of this Cornish virtual community, or at least is not in need of explanation. It is interesting to observe, therefore, that the modern technology of the Internet is helping a return to links with the romantic idyll of the past, and it would seem that the collapse of time identified in postmodernist theory can be interpreted to be not just the collapse of present time but also a collapse of the distinction between past, present and future into the virtual time suggested by quantum theory.[47]

Approximately 35 per cent of respondents made use of the Internet for establishing an identity that was not just Cornish but was broader and more complex, a complexity that was apparent in their membership of other discussion groups. Without exception, such other groupings were entirely Celtic in nature, encompassing discussion groups such as the Welsh and Breton, and this suggests that while the majority see Cornishness as a distinct sense of community identity, others view it as part of a larger Celtic cultural identity. It can be argued, therefore, that the boundaries of community fostered by the Internet are fluid and imprecise, with participants simultaneously belonging to the same and different communities, each individual with his/her own perspective of which communities he/she is a part. It is also possible to argue that these people each belong to different communities at different times and for different purposes, or even belong to the same community (such as the Cornish cybercommunity) at different times for different purposes. Either way, the concept of community identity in a virtual environment is thus further complicated, and is an area for further exploration in future research.

CONCLUSION

It is apparent from this research that the Internet user group has provided a forum for Cornish-born people and people of Cornish ancestry to communicate with each other, thereby creating and cementing a living, international cybercommunity. This living community has had important implications for people with Cornish ancestry by strengthening/augmenting their sense of Cornishness. Those respondents with Cornish ancestry living in the New World seem often to have identities that are a pastiche, drawing on ancestral origins which are generally subordinate to the nation-state in which they live. For example, Norman Davies, in his book *The Isles: A History*, noted that overseas 'Cornish Associations were among the most energetic on the worldwide Celtic circuit', observing that 'One could even contact Los Hijos de Kernow in Albuquerque, NM'.[48] Exponential growth in Internet access could create a strong, vibrant cross-border sense of Cornishness which could have an impact on the way users identify themselves, and in reflexive terms, on the Cornish identity itself. Thus the Internet is able to both strengthen and to redefine a sense of identity; this is of potentially significant impact upon the maintenance of minority identities and cultures as the population of such cultures is extended beyond a territorial boundary. As Payton has concluded elsewhere:

> Individual Cornish enthusiasts across the globe are in almost constant contact through e.mail communication, creating what is in effect a Cornish 'virtual community' in which the international [Cornish] identity has become 'deterritorialised' (to use Professor Robin Cohen's term), bridging the gap between the global and the local. Here globalisation, not least the power of communication and information technology, may be seen as a positive asset in the further enhancement of a Cornish international identity (or identities).[49]

It is also clear from the responses to the survey that respondents viewed the Internet discussion group as a virtual community of common interest. They also, overwhelmingly but not unanimously, viewed this cybercommunity as part of a larger community of Cornish people, some of whom they were in contact with through the Internet or geographically local activities, with still others 'out there' with whom they were not yet in touch but with whom they might make contact at some point in the future. The cybercommunity, therefore, served as one mechanism amongst several for locating their community identity as 'Cornish'. Thus it is questionable whether cyberspace alone is yet able to provide a comprehensive sense of community identity in its own right. It is certainly possible for cyberspace to create a community of people interested in cyberspace itself but it remains uncertain whether it is able to create communities of other individuals motivated solely by the desire to establish communication and share interests. It may be, indeed, that communities such as the Cornish cybercommunity cannot exist in any self-maintaining manner as communities in their own right, and that cyberspace merely provides a localization mechanism for a community identity which exists in any event and is manifest through a variety of mechanisms—of which cyberspace is but one. The projected growth in use of the Internet as a means of communication is, however, likely to change this considerably, as those with little interest in cyberspace are nonetheless increasingly exposed to the Internet, and this may eventually alter radically our current conceptions of community identity. Payton has hypothesized that 'As Cornwall is confronted continually by threats to its own territorial integrity and identity . . . it may be that it is in the "deterritorialized virtual community" of the newly re-emergent Cornish diaspora that the future of Cornish ethnicity rests'[50] but this seems at present a very long way off.

NOTES AND REFERENCES

1. V. Sobchack, 'Democratic Franchise and the Electronic Frontier', in Z. Sardar and J.R. Ravetz (eds), *Cyberfutures*, London, 1996.
2. B. Axford, *The Global System*, Cambridge, 1995.
3. In using the term Internet this is meant to encompass all related electronic communications media such as email and the world wide web (www). Equally the word technology is used to mean hardware, software and communications mechanisms. It is not the intention of the author to debate these technologies but rather to consider their use by individuals. Consequently terms such as the Internet, the web and cyberspace are used generically in this paper, without any attempt to attach specific and separate meanings to each.
4. B. Russell, *Power*, London, 1975.
5. See M. Foucault, *Discipline and Punish*, trans. A. Sheridan, London, 1977.
6. See C. Carter and M. Grieco, 'New Deals, No Wheels: Social Exclusion, Tele-options and Electronic Ontology', paper presented to Odyssey Workshop, Cornell University, August 1999 regarding the emerging electronic ontologies.
7. S.R. Clegg, *Frameworks of Power*, London, 1989.
8. K. Robins, 'Cyberspace and the World we Live in', in M. Featherstone and R. Burrows (eds), *Cyberspace/Cyberbodies/Cyberpunk*, London, 1995.
9. H. Rheingold, *The Virtual Community*, London, 1994.
10. N.J. Barnett and D.E.A. Crowther, 'Community Identity in the 21st Century: A Postmodernist Evaluation of Local Government Structure', *International Journal of Public Sector Management* 11 (6/7), 1998, pp. 425–39.
11. R. Plant, *Community and Ideology*, London, 1974; R. Plant, 'Community: Concept, Conception and Ideology', *Politics and Society* 8, 1978, pp. 79–107.
12. G.A. Hillary, 'Definitions of Community: Areas of Agreement', *Rural Sociology* 20, 1955, pp. 134–47.
13. G. Crow and G. Allen, *Community Life: An Introduction to Local Social Relations*, Hemel Hempstead, 1994.
14. Plant, 1978, p. 106.

15. C. Bell and H. Newby, *Community Studies: An Introduction to the Sociology of the Local Community*, London, 1971, p. 16.
16. Ibid.
17. F. Tonnies, *Community and Society*, trans. C.P. Loomis, New York, 1957.
18. E. Durkheim, *The Division of Labour in Society*, trans. G. Simpson, London, 1947.
19. J. Harvey and J. Butler, *The British Constitution*, London, 1965.
20. See, for example, D.W. McMillan and D.M. Chavis, 'Sense of Community —A Definition and a Theory', *Journal of Community Psychology* 14, 1986, pp. 6–23.
21. For example, R. Redfield, *Little Community: Comparative Studies of Cultures and Civilisations*, Chicago, 1955.
22. See, for example, R.L. Warren, *The Community in America*, Chicago, 1963.
23. H.J. Gans, 'Urbanisation and Sub-urbanisation as Ways of Life' in A.M. Rose (ed.), *Human Behaviour in Social Processes*, London, 1952; R.E. Pahl (ed.), *Readings in Urban Sociology*, Oxford, 1968.
24. M. Stacey, 'The Myth of Community Studies', *British Journal of Sociology* 20, 1969.
25. See D. Massey, *Spatial Divisions of Labour*, London 1984.
26. This is, broadly, the 'Communitarian' critique of Bellah, Booth Fowler, Taylor and others.
27. M. Bulmer, 'The Re-juvenation of Community Studies: Neighbours, Networks and Policy', *Sociological Review* 33(3), 1985, pp. 430–48.
28. J.M. Barnes, 'Class and Committees in a Norwegian Island Parish', *Human Relations* 7, 1954, pp. 430–48.
29. E. Bott, *Family and Social Network*, London, 1957.
30. Crow and Allen, 1994.
31. T. Newton, 'Postmodernism and Action', *Organization* 3(1), 1996, pp. 7–29.
32. J.F. Lyotard, *The Post Modern Condition*, trans. G. Bennington and B. Massumi, Minneapolis, 1984.
33. D. Harvey, *The Condition of Postmodernity*, Oxford, 1990.
34. R. Radhakrishnan, 'Postmodernism and the Rest of the Work', *Organization* 1(2), 1994, pp. 305–40.
35. P. Cooke, *Back to the Future: Modernity, Postmodernity and Locality*, London, 1990.
36. S. Lash and J. Urry, *Economies of Signs and Space*, London, 1994.
37. P. du Gay, 'Colossal Immodesties and Hopeful Monsters: Pluralism and Organisational Conduct', *Organization* 1(1), 1994, pp. 125–48.
38. C.J. Fox and H.T. Miller, *Postmodern Public Administration: Towards Discourse*, London, 1995.
39. C. Heckscher, 'Defining the Post-bureaucratic Type' in C. Heckscher and A. Donnellon (eds), *The Post-Bureaucratic Organisation*, London, 1994, pp. 14–62.
40. N. Nohria and J.D Berkley, 'The Virtual Organisation', in Heckscher and Donnellon (eds), 1994, pp. 108–28.

41. J. Baudrillard, in M. Poster (ed.), *Jean Baudrillard: Selected Writings*, Cambridge, 1988.
42. S. Fish, 'Is there a Text in this Class?', in W.T.J. Mitchell (ed.), *Against Theory*, Chicago, 1985.
43. P. Payton, *The Making of Modern Cornwall*, Redruth, 1992, p. 20.
44. M. Hechter, *Internal Colonialism: The Celtic Fringe in British National Development*, 1536–1966, London, 1975.
45. P. Payton, *The Cornish Miner in Australia: Cousin Jack Down Under*, Redruth, 1984; and, especially, P. Payton, *The Cornish Overseas*, Fowey, 1999.
46. The standards of 'netiquette' (Z. Sardar and J.R. Ravetz, 'Reaping the Technological Whirlwind' in Sardar and Ravetz (eds), 1996) were observed both in asking for assistance and in posting the results of the research to the discussion group.
47. D. Miller, *Organization, a Quantum View*, London, 1984.
48. N. Davies, *The Isles: A History*, London, 1999, p. 976.
49. P. Payton, 1999, p. 398.
50. Ibid.

REVIEW ARTICLE

'A MODERN AND SCHOLARLY CORNISH-ENGLISH DICTIONARY': KEN GEORGE'S *GERLYVER KERNEWEK KEMMYN* (1993)

N.J.A. Williams

Ken George, *Gerlyver Kernewek Kemmyn*, Cornish Language Board/ Kesva an Taves Kernewek, Saltash, 1993, hardback, 338 pp., ISBN 0 907064 079

INTRODUCTION

In 1993 Ken George published his *Gerlyver Kernewek Kemmyn* [GKK], a book which is described on its back cover as 'A modern and scholarly Cornish–English dictionary.' The Cornish used is Kernewek Kemmyn or Common Cornish, a system of George's own devising. George claims that the orthography of Kernewek Kemmyn and its underlying sound system reflect more accurately than Unified Cornish the phonology of the traditional language. George also claims that his new orthography is phonemic. The term 'phonemic' means that any one sound in the language is always represented by the same letter or group of letters. It is not necessary to scrutinize GKK thoroughly to realize that the claims of the orthography to be phonemic are unwarranted. In the following list of words from GKK, for example, the same 'phoneme' or set of 'phonemes' is spelt differently:

kavoes 'to get' (< OC -*uit*) but *eglos* 'church' (< OC -*uis*)

prena 'to buy' (W. *prynu*), *krena* 'to tremble' (W. *crynu*) but *warlyna* 'last year' (W. *y llynedd*)

bywek 'lively' (W. *bywiog*) but *Kernewek* 'Cornish' (W. *Cernyweg*)

Dewnens 'Devonshire' (W. *Dyfnaint*) but *bywnans* (cf. W. *bywyd*)

defendya 'to defend' but *diformya* 'to deform'

politek 'politic' (< Greek *politikos*) but *krytyk* 'critic' (< Greek *kritikos*)

epystyl 'epistle' (W. *epistol*) but *pistyll* 'spout' (W. *pistyll*)

kyst 'box' (W. *cist*) but *trist* 'sad' (W. *trist*)

arsmetryk 'arithmetic' but *eretik* 'heretic'

gwerthys 'shuttle' (B. *gwerzhid*) but *gonis* 'work' (B. *gounid*)

chalys 'chalice' but *servis* 'service'

palys 'palace' (W. *palas*) but *solas* 'solace' (W. *solas*)

jentyl 'well-born' (< OF *gentil*) but *sivil* 'civil' (< OF *civil*)

favour 'favour' but *sokor* 'succour'

diskarga 'to discharge' (B. *diskargan*) but *dyskybel* 'disciple' (B. *diskibl*)

edifia 'to edify' but *justifya* 'to justify'

frya 'to free' but *fia* 'to flee'

annia 'to vex' but *agrya* 'to agree'

gokki 'foolish', *gokkineth* 'folly' but *gokkyes* 'fools'

trynyta 'trinity', *cheryta* 'charity' but *antikwita* 'antiquity'

konviktya 'to convict' but *vyktori* 'victory'

kemmyska 'to mix' (< *ken* + *mysky*; cf. W. *cymysgu*) but *kemusur* 'symmetry' (< *ken* + *musur*; cf. W. *cymesur*)

demondya 'to demand' (< OF *demander*) but *kommondya* 'to command' (< OF *comander*)

gwannder 'weakness' (B. *gwander*) but *glander* 'cleanness' (B. *glander*)

klyket 'clicket' but *boekket* 'bucket'

fashyon 'fashion' but *passhyon* 'passion'

dessayt 'deceit' (< ME *deceite*) but *resayt* 'recipe' (< ME *receite*)

nesa 'to approach' (W. *nesu, nesau*) but *nessa* 'next' (W. *nesaf*)

klokk 'clock' but *luk* 'luck'

charet 'chariot' but *gargett* 'garter'

fyttya 'to fit' but *akwitya* 'to acquit' (*aquyttya* in the texts)

plattya 'to crouch' but *skwatya* 'to squash'

hwypp 'whip' but *skryp* 'scrip'

botell 'bottle' but *sotel* 'subtle'

referya 'to refer', and *preferya* 'to prefer' but *konkerrya* 'to conquer' and *gwerrya* 'to wage war'

sertan 'certain' but *bargen* 'bargain'

fesont 'pheasant' and *plesont* 'pleasant' but *remenant* 'remnant' and *semlant* 'appearance' (< ME *semlant*)
pemont 'payment' (< ME *paiement*) but *fisment* 'face' (< ME *visement*)
tulyfant 'tulip' but *olifans* 'elephant'

GKK writes *kons* 'pavement' with a long vowel but *kons* 'vagina' and *pons* 'bridge' with a short one. Why do we not find *kons*, **konns* and **ponns*? Similarly GKK has *fondya* 'to found' with a long vowel but *londya* 'to land' with a short one. Why is it not *fondya* and **lonndya*? GKK writes *tont* 'impertinent' with a long stressed vowel but *marchont*, etc., with a short unstressed one. GKK geminates after unstressed vowels in *kribenn*, *eythinenn*, *linenn*, etc. Why, then, does it not write **marchonnt*, **fesonnt*, **plesonnt*, **serponnt*, etc? Perhaps the most bizarre departure from a 'phonemic' spelling in GKK occurs in the derivatives of *naw* 'nine'. We find *naw* 'nine', *nawves* 'ninth' but *nownsek* 'nineteen' and *nownsegves* 'nineteenth.'

Unified Cornish spelling does not claim to be phonemic, but it is firmly rooted in Middle Cornish scribal practice. The spelling of GKK on the other hand is hypothetical and often confused. Phonemic it is not.

THE ACCURACY OF GEORGE'S DATABASE

The question remains how George's revised phonology and orthography came to be so inconsistent. Kernewek Kemmyn is, we are told, based on a computer analysis of the traditional Cornish texts. George's database is not in the public domain and it is impossible, therefore, to submit it to scrutiny. In GKK, however, each headword is accompanied by authentication and frequency codes, themselves based upon George's computer analysis of the Cornish texts. By comparing these codes with the actual attestation of words in traditional Cornish, we can assess the accuracy or otherwise of George's Cornish database.

George's frequency and authentication codes are explained in the introduction to GKK, pp. 8–17. In the body of the dictionary the codes are given within curled brackets. The codes {4: M: 1 (BM. 3220)}, for example, after **greons** 'greyhound', means that the word in question is a loanword assimilated to Cornish phonetic type {4}, is confined to Middle Cornish {M} and occurs once only {1}, the occurrence being cited as line 3220 of *Beunans Meriasek*. The codes {1: D: 0 (38)} after **gwalgh** 'glut' mean that the word is a native one {1}, that it occurs in Cornish English dialect {D}, is unattested in any traditional Cornish text but has been taken from Nance's 1938 dictionary {0 (38)}. The codes after the verb **diskevera** are {4: L: 2}. Here again {4} means the word is a loan that has been assimilated to Cornish phonology, {L} means that the word is exclusively Late Cornish, while {2} suggests that the etymon occurs 2-3 times.

It will be seen that the figure given in third place in George's authentication and frequency codes represents the number of times that any etymon is said to occur. The numbers used are to be interpreted as follows: 0 = unattested; 1 = occurs once only; 2 = occurs 2 or 3 times; 3 = occurs between 4 and 9 times; 4 = occurs between 10 and 31 times; 5 = occurs 32 to 99 times. The highest frequency code given is 9, which means that an item occurs more than 3162 times. In the following pages we will not concern ourselves with any etymon that bears a frequency code higher than 5. We will see below, however, that there are many discrepancies between the frequencies given in GKK and the actual occurrences of the corresponding words in the Cornish texts themselves. Approximately 370 erroneous entries are listed below. This and further notable inaccuracies in the codes would lead the impartial observer to suspect that George's database of Cornish is less than perfect. In that case the statistics in any of George's published works on Cornish should be treated with caution.

Notice that in the following list headwords are given in Kernewek Kemmyn followed by UC(R) in square brackets. Notice further that yogh <ʒ> in PA, BM and CW is represented below as <z>.

abas [abas] 'abbot': GKK says this word is confined to a single instance in OCV. This is incorrect: *Corn.* **Abaz** glossing *An Abbot* AB: 270a.

aghskrif [aghscryf] 'pedigree': GKK says this is a modern neologism taken from Nance's 1955 dictionary. This is incorrect: *ple ma faut a Koth* **ahskref** AB: 224; *dho'n* **Ah-skrefo** *Zouznak* AB: 224.

akordya [acordya] 'to agree': GKK says this verb is confined to a single instance in PA. This is incorrect: *trest am bus boys* **acordys** BM 494.

akusashyon [acusacyon] 'accusation': GKK says this word does not occur in the texts but has been taken from Nance's 1938 dictionary. This is incorrect: *oppressys gans fals* **accusacion** TH 25.

akusya [acusya] 'to accuse': GKK says this word is confined to one instance in PC. This is incorrect: *may hyllyn y* **acusye** PC 1625; *pan fue genough* **acusyys** PC 1859; *kepar del fus* **acusyys** PC 1999; *pan fue* **acussys** PC 2386; *a* **akiuzya** *ha damnya* AB: 224.

alhwedha [alwhedha] 'to lock': GKK says this verb is confined to a single instance in Lhuyd: *Dho* **lyhuetha** glossing *Claudo, To shut; to lock* AB: 48b. This is incorrect: *in ov cofyr sur gorys oma* **alhwethys** *certeyn* BM 3643-4.

alow [alaw] 'water lily': GKK says this word occurs in place-names but is otherwise unattested. This is incorrect. Lhuyd has *Nymphaea, Alau. White water-lily.* AB: 101c. Borlase writes *Alau, White Water Lillies* 376c and Pryce has *alow water lily* opposite G K k.

ama 'me': GKK says this is a Late Cornish pronominal form that arose when 'a phrase like *gene' mevy* "with me" was re-interpreted as *gen ama vy'*. This is incorrect. *-ama* is already a Middle Cornish form: *te a vyth yn keth golow yn paradis* **genama** PA 193d.

amontya [amontya] 'to count': GKK says that this word is confined to two instances in PA (e.g. *ny yl den vyth* **amontye** PA 40b; *den vyth ny yl* **amontye** PA 59c). This is incorrect: *pandra* **amount** *thy'n gonys* OM 1223; *ny* **amont** *travyt* PC 439; *tra uyth ny* **amont** RD 559; *rag thym ny* **ammont** *defry* BM 2055; *ny* **ammont** *ov peiadov* BM 3624; *ny* **amownt** *whelas mercye* CW 527; *ny* **amownt** *gwythell duwhan* CW 1712; *ny* **amownt** *thymma resna* CW 2395.

anella [anella] 'to breathe': GKK says that this verb is confined to two instances in TH. This is incorrect: *fatell rug du* **anella** TH 2; *Ha wosa* **anella** TH 36; *hag a rug* **enella** *warnetha* TH 38a.

angra [angra] 'to anger': GKK claims that this word is confined to a single instance in PA. This is incorrect: *hag a* **angras** *du* TH 7a; *me a* **angras** CW 1683; *Nena Herod . . . yw* **engrez** RC 23: 199. GKK cites **engrez** as a separate headword.

anhedhek, anhudhek [anhedhek]: GKK has two separate headwords. The first, we are told, is an adverb meaning 'incessantly' which occurs once in BM, the second is an adjective meaning 'easeless' and occurs twice in BM. This is incorrect. The two are, of course, the same word. *Anhedhek* is a compound of *hedhy* 'to cease' and means either 'without respite, afflicted' (adj.) or 'without respite, unceasingly' (adv.) See Nance's 1938 dictionary s.v. There are *four* examples in BM: *kynth este claff* **anhethek** BM 1853; *me yv vexijs* **anhethek** BM 2630; *drefen ov boys* **anhethek** BM 3072; *assoff guan hag* **anhethek** BM 4181.

anhweg [anwhek] 'bitter, grim': GKK claims that this word has been taken from Nance's 1938 dictionary, being unattested in the texts. This is incorrect: *cachaf y ben pur* **anwhek** OM 2816; *me a's doro pur* **anwhek** PC 2332; *mar* **anwhek** *dyghtys* PC 3188-9; *lavyr pur* **anwek** BM 451; *peynis* **anwek** BM 2380; **Anwhek**, *unsweet, unsweetly* Pryce.

arader [arader] 'plough': GKK says this word is confined to OCV and a single instance in Lhuyd (i.e. at AB: 43b). This is incorrect: *W. Aradr, Corn.* **Ardar**, *A Plow* 7b; *Dean* **ardar**, †*ardhur* glossing *Arator, A Plow-man* 43b; **Ardar** glossing *Aratrum, A Plow* 43b; *Dorn* **ardar** glossing *Stiva, The plough-tail or handle* AB: 155a; **Ardar** *and* **aradr**, *A plow; Aratrum* AB: 241a; **Ardar** glossing

ARATRUM AB: 290a. The word also occurs in Pryce: *Gora an ohan en* ***arder*** 'put the oxen to the plough' F f 2.

arbennik [arbennek] 'special': GKK's headword on p. 34 is <arbennik> and the compiler has a note: 'The suffix is -IK, not -EK'. Under *speshyal* on p. 295 the compiler has a note: 'Use **arbennek** for the aj.' [with -EK rather than the recommended -IK]. On p. 34 the word <arbennik> is described as a recent coinage, unattested in the texts. This is incorrect: *yu'n* ***arbednek*** *ha'n ydnek* AB: 224; ***Arbednek,*** *used, customary* Borlase 377; ***Arbednec*** *adj Usual, customary* Pryce. *This is a later form of* **arbennec** LCB.

arghel [arghel] 'archangel': according to GKK the plural is not attested until *arthelath* at CW 61. This is incorrect: *neg esa ow desuethas theugh elath nanyle* ***arthelath*** SA 60a.

argument [argument] 'argument': GKK says this word is confined to a single instance at PC 1661. This is incorrect, since the plural ***argumentys*** is attested at SA 61a.

arloedhes [arlodhes] 'lady': GKK says this word is confined to Old Cornish and place-names. This is incorrect. It is attested in both Middle and Late Cornish: *meystres hedyr vywy hag* ***harluzes*** CF; ***arlothes*** *ker my a wra* PC 1965; *ov* ***arlothes*** *sur gyne* PC 2194; *hag* ***arluthes*** *a vyth gurys* RD 1701; *lowena zyvgh* ***arlothes*** BM 237; *neb* ***arlothes*** *worthy* BM 330; *Rag an* ***Arlothas*** *an wolas Kernow* BF: 9; *rag gun* ***Arlothas*** *da* BF: 11; *lever bean rebbam dro tho an* ***Arlothas*** *Curnow* BF: 37; *lever an Have an* ***Arlothas*** *Kernow* BF: 37.

askall [ascal] 'thistles': GKK gives this as the collective plural of *ascallen* 'thistle' but says this form (as distinct from the singular) is not attested. This is incorrect: *Spearn ha* ***askal*** *ra e dry rag theeze* RC 23: 182; *Askallen* [*pl.* ***askal***] glossing *Carduus, A Thistle* AB: 46b.

askus [ascus] 'excuse': GKK says this noun is not attested. It is likely, however, that [əs'ku:s] is the pronunciation of <excus> in the two following examples: *oll* ***excuses*** *a'n par na* TH 14 and *yth ethans y heb* ***excusse*** TH 14.

assaya [assaya] 'to try': GKK says this verb is confined to a single example each in RD and CW. This is incorrect: *tra vyth* ***assaye*** OM 2477; ***asaye*** *ow arluth ker* RD 2051; *dus nes hag* ***assy*** *an poyt* BM 3325; ***assays*** *ha teball pynchis* TH 34; *gwraf* ***assaya*** CW 201; *manaf* ***saya*** CW 472.

assendya [ascendya] 'to ascend': GKK says this word is confined to a single instance in TH. This is incorrect: *agan lef yn* ***ascendys*** RD 174-75; ***assendijs*** *the'n neff in ban* BM 4052; *then neff* ***assendias*** *inweth* BM 4084; *fatell rug Crist* ***assendia*** *thy'n neff* TH 33a; *agyn Arluth ha'n Saviour ew* ***ascendis*** *the'n nef* SA 59; *mas Dew*

ascendias *the'n neff* SA 60. The word **ascensyon** is not listed by GKK but it occurs at TH 36, 37a, 44a and 52.

assentya [assentya] 'to assent': GKK says this verb is confined to two instances in the *Ordinalia*. This is incorrect: *a vynnegh ol* **assentye** PC 2037; **assentye** *ol the henna* RD 583; *ha myns* **assentyas** *genas* CW 247; **assentyes** *yth yns sera* CW 272; *yn* **assentys** *te a glow* CW 654.

avisia [avysya] 'to take note': GKK says this is confined to a single instance in CW. This is incorrect: *an beth me re* **avysyas** RD 399; **avesijs** *off* BM 577; *beth* **avysyys** BM 840; **avesyans** *eff a hena* BM 1031; *byth* **avysshes** CW 1755; **avice** *pub tra* CW 1799; *me a vyn skon* **avycya** CW 1803; *bethowgh* **avysshes** CW 2367.

avisment [avysment] 'advice, counsel': GKK says this word does not occur in the texts but has been taken from Nance (1955). This is incorrect: *rag nyna tus a gymmer* **advisement** *bras* TH 1.

avowa [avowa] 'to avow, admit': GKK says this verb is confined to a single instance in PC. This is incorrect: *myns a wruk me a'n* **avow** PC 1301; *ma na veath y* **avowe** PC 1783; *me a'nn* **avow** *dyougel* RD 2120; *hager lower os me an* **avow** CW 480; *me an* **advow** CW 2353.

awelek [awelek] 'windy': GKK says this is unattested, being taken from Nance's 1955 dictionary. This is incorrect: **Auelek***, windy* Borlase 378.

aweyl [awayl] 'gospel': GKK gives as the plural **aweylyow*, which is not attested. The compiler does not seem to have noticed that there is a plural in the texts: *a scryffas* **aweylys** TH 37a; *a thyscas y* **aweylys** TH 38; *aga* **aweylys** TH 52a.

aweyler [aweyler] 'evangelist': GKK gives the plural *aweylers*, and says it is confined to 2-3 instances in TH. This is incorrect: *ran* **aweilers** TH 33a; *ran* **aweylers** TH 42; *appostres,* **aweilers** TH 42; *Ran an* **aweylors** TH 53; *onyn vith an* **Aweylers** TH 53; *onyn vith an* **aweylers** TH 53a; *dell vsy an* **Awaylers** TH 53a *onyn vith an* **Aweylers** TH 53a; *onyn vyth an* **Aweylers** TH 54.

aysel [aysel] 'vinegar': GKK says this is confined to a single instance in the *Ordinalia* (i.e. at PC 2978). This is incorrect. The word is also attested in PA: **eysyll** *bestyll kemyskis* PA 202b.

banadhlek [banallek] 'place of broom': GKK says this is unattested outside place-names. Note, however, . . . *whence our bannal,* **banathlek, bennathlick,** *a place in Constenton; also the proper name* **Bennalack** Pryce, *opposite L.* The surname is, of course, based on the toponym.

banadhlenn [banallen] 'broom (plant)': GKK says the singular is confined to a single instance at AB: 240c. This is incorrect: *Banhadlen in Welsh, signifies Broom; Corn* **Bynollan***, A Beesom* AB: 3a;

Scopa . . . A beesom. C. **Bynolan** AB: 146b; **Bannolan**, *A broom* AB; 240c. Cf. also **Bynollan**, *a Beesom; Broom* Borlase 380; **Bannolan**, *a broom* Pryce, opposite L. GKK also says that the collective *banal* occurs in dialect, in place-names and once in OCV but not elsewhere. This is also incorrect: *S.W. & Corn. Banal. Arm. Balan, Broom* AB: 7c; *Genista . . . Broom. C. Banal* AB: 63a.

bargenya [bargynya] 'to bargain': GKK suggests that the verb is confined to a single instance in Lhuyd. This is incorrect: *Dho* **bargidnia** glossing *Consentio, To consent* AB: 50c; **Bargidnias** glossing *Pactus* AB: 111a; *chei a* **varginiaz** *rag trei penz* BF: 15; *Nenna chei a* **varginiaz** *rag vlethan moy* BF: 15; *Enna chei a* **varginiaz** *rag blethan moy* BF: 16; **Bargidnia**, *dho* **bargidnia,** *to bargain, to contract* Pryce, L; **Bargidnia** *gen dean da mose da whele sten* Pryce.

barr [bar] 'branch, top': GKK says the plural **barrow** is unattested. This is incorrect: *an wethan han* **barrow** TH 4a; *an buddes, an* **barrow** TH 8a; *oll thyn* **barrow** TH 39a.

basket [basket] 'basket': GKK says this word is confined to a single instance in Lhuyd. This is incorrect: **Basket** glossing *Calathus, A Basket, a hampier or pannier* AB: 45b; **Basket** *dorn, a hand-basket* s.v. *Corbis* AB: 51c.

bejeth [bejeth] 'face': GKK suggests that the word is confined to a single instance in Late Cornish, i.e. in Keigwin. This is incorrect. In the first place the author is Chirgwin, not Keigwin. In the second place there is more than one source. In the third place there are at least six examples: *ha spiriz Deu reeg guaya var* **budgeth** *an dour* BF: 51; *Gen agaz* **bedgeth** *gwin, ha agaz blew mellyn* Edward Chirgwin x 5 (quoted in LAM: 228-30).

benfis [benfys] 'benefice': GKK says this is confined to a single occurrence at OM 2612. This is incorrect: *pan lafuryens rag* **benefys** BM 2827.

besydh [besyth] 'baptism': GKK says that the word is unattested in the texts, being derived from Nance (1938). This is incorrect: *Solem ro in aga* **begeth** *the cresy* TH 20; *ow cows a'n* **beseth** *a'n flehis* TH 37.

bleydh [bleydh] 'wolf': GKK says the plural <bleydhi> occurs in BM. This is incorrect. *Blythy* in BM is the plural of *bledhen* 'year': *kuntullugh an flehysygyov a vo pur certen achy the try* **blythy** 'gather the children, that may be right certainly within three years of age' BM: 1535-7. The only plural of the word for 'wolf' attested in the texts is Tregear's *blythes*. GKK mentions this form and says it occurs once. This is incorrect. It occurs twice: *yth yns y in golan ramping* **blythes**, *settys rag devorya. yma agan Savyour worth aga gylwall y* **blythes** TH 19a.

blydhen [bledhen] 'year': GKK spells this word <blydhen> (why is it not **blydhenn* in *Kernewek Kemmyn?*) and tells us that the plural is *blydhynyow*. The compiler adds a note: 'for <y> in plural cf. *fentynyow*'. He is apparently unaware that a plural without <y> is well attested: *nep dew cans a* **vlethynnow** OM 657; *Ober* **bledhynno** *yu* AB: 223.

borlewenn [berlewen] 'morning star': GKK says this is confined to a single instance in Lhuyd. This is incorrect: *may teffa an Jeth hag egery, ha'n* **vurluan** *agery in agys colonow* TH 18. Cf. **Byr-luan**, *the Morning Star* Borlase 380.

bowji [bowjy] 'cow-shed': GKK says that apart from toponyms this word is confined to two instances in Lhuyd. This is incorrect: *W. Boydy & Beydy, A Cow-house; Corn.* **Boudzhi** AB: 10b; **Boudzhi**, *a Fold* glossing *Caula* AB: 47a; **Boudzhe** *devaz* glossing *Ovile, A sheep-coat, a fold, a sheep-house* AB: 110c.

bragya [bragya] 'to threaten': GKK says this word is confined to a single instance in BM. This is incorrect on both counts: *na* **vrakgy** *e rak ef a sur* RD 2018; *Ty horsen [n]agen* **brag** *ny* BM 1228; *na* **vragyogh** *brays lafarov* BM 1597; *[n]am* **brag** *vy* BM 3491; *neb ur* **braggye** BM 3507; *ef a's* **braggyas** *y'n vaner ma* TH 40.

Breton [Breton] 'Breton' [inhabitant]: GKK says that this word is unattested in the texts and has been taken from Nance's 1938 dictionary. This is incorrect. Nicholas Boson writes *an* **Bretten** *ha an Kembreeanz ha an Curnowean* BF: 29; *rag an* **Bretten** *ha an Curnowean* ibid.

brin [bryn] 'brine': GKK says this word is unattested being taken from Nance's 1955 dictionary. This is incorrect. Lhuyd gives Cornish **Bryn** glossing *Muria, Brine* AB: 96a.

broennenn [bronnen] 'rush *(Scirpus)*': according to GKK the singular is attested three times, once each in OCV, RD and Lhuyd (AB: 146b). This is incorrect, since Lhuyd cites it twice: *W. Bruynen, A Rush; Corn.* **Brydnan** AB: 10b; †**Brunnen, brudnan** glossing *Scirpus, A rush without a knot* AB: 146b.

brottel [brottel] 'frail, brittle': GKK says this word is from Middle English 'with change of vowel' —which the dictionary does not attempt to explain. The compiler does not seem to have noticed that the word occurs in Cornish with an unrounded stressed vowel: *the'n dore* **brytyll** *prye* TH 9; **Brettal**, *Brittle* (in a list of Cornish words agreeing with English) AB: 33c.

brys [brys] 'womb': GKK says the word is confined to a single instance in BM. This is incorrect: *creator a* **brys** *benen* RD 191; *deuones a* **brys** *benen* RD 1350; *in* **breys** *benen* BM 846; *a thuth in* **breys** *Maria* BM 856; *a ve benegas in* **breis** *y vam* TH 8.

Brythonek [Brethonek] 'British': GKK says that the word is taken from Nance's 1938 dictionary, being unattested in the texts. This is incorrect: *an Tavaz* **Brethonek** AB: 222; **Brethonek** *Kembrîan* AB: 222; *Dialeksho* **Brethonek** AB: 222; *Skot-***Vrethonek** AB: 222; *lavarnanz priez an Tavas* **Brethonek** AB: 222; *Gal-***Vrethonek** AB: 222; *an gerlevran bian* **Brethonek**-*ma* AB: 222; **Brethonek** *Pou Lezou* AB: 222; *gerrio* **Brethonek** AB: 223; **Brethonek** *Kernou* AB: 223; *an Mytern* **Brethonek** AB: 224; *gen Tiz* **Brethonek** AB: 224; *uar anuo* **Brethonek** AB: 224; Cf. also **Brethonek** *British* Pryce and **Brethonec**, *adj. British, the British or Welsh language* LCB s.v.

bryvya [bryvya] 'to bleat': according to GKK this verb is confined to a single instance in Lhuyd. This is incorrect: *Dho* **privia** glossing *Balo, To Bleat* AB: 44b; *Ma'n dhavaz a* **privia**, *The sheep bleats* AB: 230c; *A* **privia**, *Bleating* AB: 248a.

byrla [byrla] 'to embrace': GKK says this is attested once. I have noted two examples: *Amplector, To Embrace; C.* **Byrla** AB: 42c; *Kensa blethan,* **byrla** *a' baye* William Allen (quoted in LAM: 236).

chast [chast] 'chaste': GKK says this word is confined to a single example in TH. This is incorrect: *an* **chast** *spowse a crist* TH 33; *in* **chast** *gwren ny kesvewa* CW 1314.

chastia [chastya] 'to chastise': GKK says that the verb is confined to a single instance in BM. This is incorrect: *me an* **chasty** PA 127c; *mar ny vethe* **chastijs** BM 810; *rag* **chastya** *an crustunyon* BM 1180.

chasya [chassya] 'to chase': the frequency code {2} for this word in GKK implies that the word occurs three times at the most. This is incorrect: *rag y* **chasye** PA 163d; *pan vef* **chacys** OM 706; *me a's* **chas** *yn mes* PC 317; **chasshes** *on a baradice* CW 1764; *alena aga* **chassya** CW 1823; **Chacyes**, *pursued* AB: 226c.

chayn [chayn] 'chain': GKK says the singular is not attested. This is incorrect: *gans* **chayne** *tane adro thymo* CW 331.

chaynya [chaynya] 'to chain': GKK says that the word is unattested in traditional Cornish and has been derived from Nance's 1938 dictionary. This is incorrect: *pur fast yth os* **chenys** BM 3809; **cheynys** *in keth vaner ma* BM 3825; *Awoys ov bones* **cheynys** BM 3826.

chyften [chyften] 'chieftain': GKK says this word is confined to a single instance at OM 1445. This is incorrect: *war an gwlascur* **cheften** BM 3.

daffar [dafar] 'apparatus, receptacle': GKK's frequency code {2} means that this word is attested at most three times. This is incorrect: **daver** *vyth wy ny zecsyugh* PA 50b; *cafas* **daffar** *pur parys* PA 105d; **dafyr** *lathva* [= ammunition] Keigwin (King Charles's

Letter); **Daffar**, *Conveniences, Furniture* Borlase 383; **Daver**, *a script, a pouch, a budget* Pryce, opposite N.

damma-wyn [dama wyn] 'grandmother': (why the hyphen?) GKK says the word is confined to a single instance in Lhuyd. This is incorrect: *Corn Taz gwydn [& Sira wydn] a Grand-father, and* **Dama wydn**, *a Grand-mother* AB: 3b; **Dama widn**, *i.e. W. Mam wen* glossing *Avia, A Grand-mother* AB: 44a.

darn [darn] 'piece': GKK says the plural *darnow* is unattested in the texts. This is incorrect: *dywolow yfarn a squerdyas corf iudas ol ze* **zarnow** PA 106c.

dasserghyans [dasserghyans] 'resurrection': GKK says there are at most three examples of this word in Middle and Late Cornish together. This is incorrect: *na vyth moy a'th* **daserghyans** RD 2545; *a* **thasserghyens** *cryst* RD 2632; *wosa y* **thethyrryans** TH 49; **Thasurrans** *an Corf* BF: 56; **thethoryanz** *a'n corf* Pryce; **dedhoryans** *an corf* LCB: 396.

deboner [deboner] 'debonair': GKK implies that the two instances of this word are from PA. This is incorrect. There is one instance at PA 129c: *a gewsys* **dyboner**. The other example is from the Charter Fragment: *curtes yw ha* **deboner** (quoted in LAM: 30).

dehweles [dewheles] 'to return': GKK says this verb is confined to one instance in the *Ordinalia*. This is incorrect: *kyns* **dewheles** *my a'd pys* OM 728; *an varghvran na* **thywhele** OM 1105; *sav byner re* **thewhylly** OM 2196; *may* **tewhyllyf** *arte thu'm gulas* RD 879; *rag bener re* **thewellen** BM 3439; *na byth moy na* **zewylly** BM 4146.

dekkweyth [degweyth] 'ten times': GKK says the word is unattested. This is incorrect: **Deguyth**, *Ten times* AB: 248c. KK's <-kkw-> for -*gw*- in this word is pure invention.

delyow [delyow] 'leaves': GKK says that the word is found as *delkiow* in Late Cornish. This is only partially true. *Delkiow* is certainly well attested in Late Cornish, e.g. **Delkiou**, *Leaves* AB: 243b; **delkyow** RC 23: 177; **delkiow** *sevi* x 6 Chirgwin (LAM: 228-30) but *delyow* also occurs in the later language: **delyow** AB: 243b and **dellyow** CW 93.

dena [dena] 'to suck': GKK says the word is confined to a single instance in Lhuyd. This is incorrect: *hag ef gensy ow* **tene** PA 161c; *na ve zeze* **denys** *bron* PA 169d; *pan* **denys** *bron* OM 1755; *an bronnow na* **thenes** *flehesyggow* PC 2649; *ha specyly re ov* **tena** BM 1509; *Dho* **tena** glossing *Sugo, To suck* AB: 158.

densek [densek] 'toothy': GKK correctly points out that this word occurs in OCV (**denshoc** *dour luceus* [pike]). The dictionary fails to mention, however, that Borlase gives **denjack** 'hake' and that **tinsack** 'hake' survived in dialect at St Ives (GCSW: 72). GKK adds a note that there is no need for *i*-affection in *densek*. This is incorrect, since there is already *i*-affection in OCV; *denshoc* is a compound of *dens* 'teeth' + *oc* rather than *dans* 'tooth' + *-oc*.

derwenn [derowen, derwen] 'oak tree': GKK says the word, the singular of *derow* 'oaks' is unattested. This is incorrect: *Derven, an oak* Borlase 383.

despitia [despytya] 'to insult': GKK says the word is unattested in the texts being derived from Nance's 1938 dictionary. This is incorrect: *gureugh y **thyspytye** PC 1397.

destryppya [dystryppya] 'to strip': GKK says this verb is confined to one example in PA (i.e. *Whare y an **dystryppyas** PA 13a). This is incorrect: *me a **thystryp** ow dyllas* PC 250. In view of <diruska> it is difficult to see why GKK does not spell this word <distryppya>.

desygha [deseha] 'to dry': GKK says the word is confined to a single example in the *Ordinalia*. This is incorrect: *pan vs gveyth ov **tesehe*** OM 1128; *dor **dyseghys** OM 1144; *may fens y **dysehys** OM 1833; *pan vons **dysehys** gulan* OM 1838.

devorya [devorya] 'to devour': GKK says the word is confined to 2-3 instances in TH. This is incorrect. It does indeed occur once at TH 4 and twice at TH 19a. GKK is apparently unaware, however, that the verb also occurs in BM: *lues oma **deworijs** BM 4178.

dewdhegves [dewdhegves] 'twelfth': GKK says that this word is confined to a single instance in TH. I am unable to find it. The only example of 'twelfth' known to me is Pryce's ***Dow degvas**, the twelfth*.

Dewnens [Dewnans] 'Devonshire': GKK says the form is confined to a single instance in Lhuyd. This is incorrect: *Kernou ha **Deunanz** AB: 224; *auoz an dzhyi rygkuitha **Deunanz** AB: 224; *ha lîaz en **Deunanz** AB: 224

diank [dyank] 'to escape': GKK says this verb is confined to one occurrence (i.e. PC 1180). This is incorrect: *y ze **zeank** yndella* PA 251b; *mars yv **dyenkys** RD 520; *maras ywe **dyenkys** BM: 3732.

dibenna [dybenna] 'to behead': GKK says the word is confined to a single instance in Lhuyd. This is incorrect: *ran cregys ran **debynnys** BM 1351.

diber [dyber] 'saddle': GKK tells us this word is attested in Old, Middle and Late Cornish and in toponyms. The frequency code given is {5}, which suggests that the word occurs between 32 and 99 times. This is incorrect. According to Padel it is attested in the single place-name *Carrack an **deeber** (1613) in Zennor. Apart from that I have collected the following instances: ***diber** glossing *sella* 'saddle' OCV 955; ***deeber** Richard Symonds *ca* 1644; ***Dibre** [a saddle]* glossing *Dorsuale* AB: 55c; ***Debr** dour [i.e. sella pluvialis]* s.v.

Galerus, A hat AB: 62b; ***Diber*** glossing *sella equina* AB: 148a. The frequency code should be emended from {5} to {3}.

diek [dyek] 'lazy': GKK says this word is confined to a single occurrence each in OCV and BM. This is incorrect: *nyng o **dyag** the wull* TH 2a.

difyga [dyfygya] 'to fail, to tire': GKK says this word is unattested. This is incorrect: *an ioy na **thyfyk** nefra* OM 517; *byth na **thyfyc*** RD 76; *ioy na **thyfyk*** RD 1310; *byth na **thyfyk*** RD 1434. GKK implicitly criticizes Nance for having written the verbal noun <dyfygya>. Nance was, it seems, more right than GKK: ***Tefigia**, To tire, W. Dyffygio* AB: 245a. Cf. ***Tefighia**, to tire; **Tevigia**, id.* Borlase 408; ***Tefigia** v.n. To tire, to be tired. Llwyd, 245. W. difygio* LCB.

digesson [dygesson] 'discordant': GKK says this word is unattested in the texts and has been taken from Nance's 1938 dictionary. This is incorrect: *an laveryanz anydha yu muy kalliz ha **dygesson*** AB: 223.

dinas [dynas] 'city': GKK says this word is unattested except in toponyms and has been taken from Nance's 1938 dictionary. This is incorrect: ***Dinaz**, †brenniat* glossing *Propugnaculum, A fortress, a bulwark, a rampart* AB: 130; *Urbs . . . A city, a wall[']d town. C. **Dinaz*** AB: 177c; *C[ornish]* ***Dinas*** glossing *URBS* AB: 298b. Cf. ***Dinaz, Dinas**, a bulwark, a fortress; also, a city, a walled town* Pryce.

dinerenn [deneren] '(single) penny': GKK says the word is confined to a single instance in BM. This is incorrect: *A Penny, C[ornish] **Dinar** & **Dinaryn*** AB: 283a.

dineythi [denethy] 'to give birth': GKK says the word occurs at most three times in Middle and Late Cornish together. This is incorrect: *mar quren flogh vyth **denythy*** OM 390; *na caym pan yu **dynythys*** OM 618; *ef a wra **dynythy*** OM 638; *ny a **thynyth** vn flogh da* OM 664; *gans y gorf a'm **dynythys*** OM 863; *a dor ov mam **dynythys*** OM 1754; *a vaghteth gulan **dynythys*** PC 1727; *ty a vyth mabe **denethys*** CW 1323; *flehys am bef **denethys*** CW 1979; ***Denethes** Dar an Speris zance* BF: 41; ***Denethes** der Spiriz Sanz* BF: 56; *than fleghys tha **denethy*** Keigwin (King Charles's Letter).

diruska [dyrusca] 'to peel, scrape off skin': GKK says the verb is unattested. This is incorrect: *ha hy warbarth **dyruskys*** OM 787; *trogh ha **dyruskys*** PC 2687.

disesya [dysesya] 'to discomfort': GKK says that this verb is unattested in traditional Cornish and has been derived from Nance's 1938 dictionary. This is incorrect: *ragh ovn the vos **desesys*** PC 97; ***desesijs** bras off deffry* BM 1771.

diskrysi [dyscrejy] 'to disbelieve': GKK says the verb is confined to a single instance in Middle Cornish. This is incorrect: *na*

thyscryssough *dev a nef* OM 1657; *kafus ken the* ***thyscrysy*** OM 1826; *yn sur re re* ***thyscryssys*** RD 1040; ***Dezkrissa****, To distrust* AB: 249c.

diskudha [dyscudha] 'to uncover': GKK says the verb is confined to one instance in Middle Cornish. This is incorrect: *an gorhel gvren* ***dyscuthe*** OM 1146; *me a vyn y* ***thyscuthe*** PC 1393; *lemmyn* ***dyskuth*** *ha lauar* PC 2852; *awos* ***descotha*** CW 1369; *As Dizkuedha and* ***Dyzkydha****, To discover* AB: 249c.

displesya [dysplesya] 'to displease': GKK says this verb is confined to a single instance in TH. This is incorrect: *na vewy* ***dysplesys*** BM 119; *na vewy* ***dysplesijs*** BM 322; *genes yth off* ***dysplesijs*** BM 400; ***dysplesijs*** *purguir genas* BM 490; *Kynth ogh geneff* ***dysplesijs*** BM 492.

disprevi [dysprevy] 'to disprove': GKK says that this is a modern neologism unattested in the texts. This is incorrect: *inweth the prevy ha the* ***dhisprevy*** *pup tra scriffis* TH 36.

diveth [dyveth] 'shameless': GKK says this word is not attested and has been taken from Nance's 1938 dictionary. This is incorrect: *bost a wrens tyn ha* ***deveth*** PA 242d

diwoesa [dewosa] 'to bleed': GKK says that the word is confined to BM where it occurs 2-3 times. This is incorrect. There are *four* examples: *may hallons boys* ***dewogys*** BM 1556; *parys thage* ***dewosa*** BM1575; *gruegh scon age* ***dewose*** BM 1584; *hag a'n* ***dewoys*** *knak oma* BM 1652.

diworth [deworth] 'from': GKK gives this word a frequency code of {5}, i.e. between 32 and 99 times. As Ray Edwards has pointed out (*Notennow Kernowek* 3 (1999)) *dyworth* occurs 7 times in the texts. *A-dhyworth* is less common, occurring 6 times. The most frequent form is *dhyworth* (*dheworth*) which occurs 167 times. Under *dhiworth* GKK says: 'commoner than *diworth*', but gives no figure for its frequency. The two entries in GKK, therefore, are misleading and the frequency code given is not accurate.

dons [dons] 'dance': GKK says the word is unattested outside toponyms. This is incorrect: *high stones (called* ***Daunce*** *mine)* BF: 10; . . . *the name they go by most commonly that that of* ***Dawns-*** *men, that is, the Stone-Dance* Borlase 183; ***Dawnse*** *in Cornish, signifies a Dance* Borlase 183; ***Dawns****, a Dance* Borlase 383.

dotya [dotya] 'to dote, to rave': GKK says this verb is confined to a single instance in BM. I have noted two examples: *mar mynnyth* ***dotya*** BM 346; ***dotyys*** *oys vyl* BM 462.

downder [downder] 'depth, deep': GKK says this occurs 2-3 times in Late Cornish. This is incorrect: *W. Dyvnder, Depth; C.* ***Dounder*** AB: 19b; ***Dounder*** *glossing Profundum, A gulf, a bottomless pit,* *the deep, the sea* AB: 129c; **Dounder**, *Dep[t]h* AB: 240b; *rag mer a* **dounder** BF: 51; **downder**, *a gulf, depth* Pryce; *ha tewolgow ese war enep an* **downder** LCB: 395.

dreysenn [dreysen] 'brambles': GKK says that this word is confined to a single instance in Lhuyd. This is incorrect: *C[ornish]* **Dreizan** glossing *Rubus, A bramble, a bush* AB: 141c; *C[ornish]* **Dreizan** glossing *A Bramble* AB: 272b.

drivya [dryvya] 'to drive': GKK says this verb is confined to a single instance in TH. This is incorrect: *aga* **dryvya** *in mes* TH 13; *Eff a ve* **dryvys** *war theller*TH 49a.

drokpollat [drogpollat] 'scoundrel': GKK tells us (p. 84) that it is from *drog + pollat*, with a geminate <ll>. The simplex *pollat*, however, is given as a separate headword on p. 257, where it is spelt with a single <l> as <polat>.

dywolow [dewolow] 'devils': GKK says that this form occurs twice, once in TH and once in CW. This is incorrect: **dywolow** *yfarn a squerdyas* PA 106c; *ena golmas* **dewolow** PA 212b; *ha* **dewolow** *hep nyuer* OM 569; *ha fethys an* **dywolow** PC 77; *an* **thewolow** PC 3057; *pryncys a'n* **dewolow** RD 97; *er bos* **dywolow** RD 301; *re'n kergho an* **dewolow** RD 2277; *rak deuones* **dewolow** RD 2302; *ow* **dewolow** *duegh gynef* RD 2307; *skrymba bras a'n* **dewolow** RD 2344; *orth temtacyon* **dewolow** BM 145; *sur* **dewolov** *ens y* BM 916; *warbyn an* **dywolow** TH 28; *oll an* **thewollow** CW 481; *an* **thevllow** *pub onyn* CW 2010; *yma an* **thewollow** CW 2021; *comerez gen an* **Jowlov** RC 23: 193 (and see emendation in RC 24: 100).

dughanhe [duhanhe] 'to grieve, afflict': GKK says that this verb is confined to a single instance in the *Ordinalia*. This is incorrect: *yth oma pur* **dewhanhees** CW 1225.

dyerbynna [dyerbyn, dyerbyna] 'to meet': GKK is apparently unaware of *dyerbyn* as a verbal noun. It says that the verb is attested once only in Middle Cornish. This is incorrect: *arte zy* **dyerbyne** PA 167c; *Vn den as* **dyerbynnas** PA 174a; *why a* **thyerbyn** *wharre* PC 628; *a's* **dyerbyn** *dyougel* PC 897; *ny alsen y* **thyerbyn** PC 2276; *eff a* **deerbyn** *trestyns* BM 2255. As is clear from the above examples the verb is always transitive. GKK's distinction between *dyerbynna gans* 'meet' (going the same direction) and *dyerbynna orth* 'meet' (going in opposite directions) is both ungrammatical and entirely without foundation.

dynnerghi [dynerhy] 'to greet': GKK says the verb is confined to a single occurrence in Lhuyd. This is incorrect: *herodes reth tenyrghys* PA 115b; *a'th* **dynyrghys** *hag a'th pys* PC 565; *genef ythos* **dynerghys** RD 1628; †**Dynerxy** *[or* ‡**Dynerhy**] *To Greet or Salute* AB: 249c.

dyssembla 'to dissemble': there are two occurrences of this verb: *Na rewgh* **dyssymbla** TH 40a; *Dho* **dissembla** glossing *Simulo, To feign, to counterfeit* AB: 150c. Curiously, the word appears to be wanting from GKK.

dyssipel, -plys [dyscypyl, -plys] 'disciple': GKK says the word is unattested outside TH. This is incorrect: *ha'y* **zyscyplys** *a'n sewyas* PA 52b; *z'y* **zyscyplys** *y trylyas* PA 55c.

dyw [dew] 'god': GKK says the plural *dewow* is unattested outside toponyms. This is incorrect: *y fyeugh yn surredy yn ur na avel* **dewow** OM 177-78; *a worth* **dewow** *tebel* OM 1818; *fals* **duwow** OM 1882; **dewov** *nowyth* OM 2732; *thum* **dewov** *tek* BM 914; *theth* **dewov** *try mylwyth fy* BM 915; *ov* **dewov** *flour* BM 922; *nyns o an re na* **dewov** BM 1801; *naha* **dewov** *nag yv vas* BM 2519; *why a vith kepar ha* **duow** TH 3a; *saw a pony* **dewyow** *gwryes* CW 812; *For we read* **Deuon** *and* **Deuou**, *Gods* AB: 243b; **Deauon**, *Gods;* **Deuiou** *id.* Borlase 383; *Ty nyn vyth thy* **Dewyow** *eraill mez me* Pryce.

Ebrow [Ebrow] 'Hebrew': GKK says this word is confined to a single instance in the *Ordinalia* (i.e. *fleghes* **ebbrow** PC 239). This is incorrect. The word is also attested in Late Cornish: *En Tavaz Greka, Lathen ha'n* **Hebra** BF: 59. Notice further: *in second chapter thyn* **hebrues** TH 13; *tha Greckian,* **Hebran** BF: 27.

edifia [edyfya] 'to edify, to build up': GKK says this word is confined to a single instance in TH. This is incorrect: *rag* **edifia** *corfe crist* TH 31; *rag* **edyfya** *an corfe a crist* TH 42; *Rag* **edyfya** *spiritually* TH 42.

eksperyans [experyans] 'experience': GKK says the word is confined to a single instance: BM 4318 [*recte* 4391]. This is incorrect: *Ith esa dhe'n profet Job* **experience** TH 7; *na ve an catholyk egglos the ry thym* **experiens** TH 37a; *an pith a ren ny the aswone dre* **experiens** TH 40.

ekwal [equal] 'equal; equivalent': GKK says this word is confined to two instances in CW (i.e. at 604 and 2198). This is incorrect: **equall** *recompens* TH 24; *war y wull* **equall** *ha kepar* TH 28a.

enep [enep] 'face': GKK says that this word is attested 2-3 times in OCV and Lhuyd. This is incorrect: **eneb** glossing *pagina* OCV 754; **enap** glossing *Facies, A face, a visage* AB: 58a; *Tyrnehuan lîven,* †**Enep** glossing *Pagina, The side of a leaf or page* AB: 111b; *C[ornish]* †**Enap** glossing *A Face* AB: 276; *agas* **enep** 'your face' quoted from Borlase MS by Nance (1938) s.v.

entent [entent] 'intent': GKK says this word is confined to a single instance at CW 496. This is incorrect: *heb colynwall gans* **intentys** *ha ordynans anethe* TH 40a; *rag an* **entent** *neb a ve an pen ha'n dalleth* TH 47-47a; *nyng ew thyn* **entent** TH 55a.

er [er] 'heir': GKK says this word is confined to a single instance at BM

372. This is incorrect: *neg ew ef ow kill **heare** nep ne theffa regardya an keth gyrryow ma* SA 59.

erba, -bys [erba, -bys] 'herb': GKK says that neither the singular nor the plural is attested. This is incorrect: *palm ha bayys, byxyn **erbys*** PC 261; *hag **erbys** an goverou* BM 1971; *ha'n **earbes** a'n keth dor na* CW 948

eretons [eretons] 'inheritance': GKK says the word is confined to two instances in BM (i.e. at 1953 and 3469). This is incorrect: *in ov **hertons** deth na nos* BM 2452; *ha ry then ny an **herytans** in gwlas neff* TH 41.

ermit [ermyt] 'hermit': GKK says this word is confined to Old Cornish, occurring once in OCV (as *hermit*). This is incorrect. The word also occurs in Middle Cornish: *ena **ermet** purguir boys* BM 1133; *avel **hermyt** pur thevry* BM 1948; *avel **hermyt** y'n guelfos* BM 1964.

ervira [ervyra] 'to decide': GKK says the word is confined to two instances in PA. This is incorrect: *my a **yrvyr*** OM 1229; ***yrverys** eu ru'm levte* OM 2611; *del of **yrvyrys*** PC 493; *war veyns ol of **yruyrys*** PC 854; *rak satnas yv **yrvyrys*** PC 880; *an porpos yv **erverys*** BM 988.

eskerens [eskerens] 'enemies': GKK's authentication code {I} for *eskerens*, the plural of *escar* 'enemy', suggests that the form is unattested and has been inferred from 'derivatives and the rules of grammar'. This is incorrect: *nan kemerre y **yskerans*** PA 241b; *tho'm **yskerens*** PC 737; *tha **eskerans*** BM 1176; ***eskerans** ov du soly* BM 1197; *gwregh cara agys **yskerens*** TH 22; *ow exortya y **yskerens*** TH 22; *mas inweth y **yskerens*** TH 22a; *pan en ny y **yskerans*** TH 24; *the cara agan **yskerans*** TH 24; *So the cara agan **yskerens*** TH 24; *dre y **yskerans*** TH 24; *the gara y **yskerens*** TH 24; *theworth aga **yskerens*** TH 25; *cothmans hag **yskerenns*** TH 26; *warbyn agan gostly **eskerens*** TH 28; *warbyn y **yskerens** ha **yskerens** a onyn vith* TH 50a.

eskisyow [eskyjyow] 'shoes': GKK says the plural of *eskys* 'shoe', is confined to OCV and Lhuyd. This is incorrect: *dysk the **skyggyow** quyk the ves* OM 1406; *unworthy rag bocla y **skyggyow*** TH 8.

Est [Est] 'August': the compiler asserts on p. 92 that *Est* 'August' is confined to a single instance in Gwavas. This is presumably a reference to *Durt Newlin in Bleau Pawle 22 **East**, 1711* (LAM: 238). The compiler's observation is incorrect. *Est* 'August' is attested elsewhere: *W. Aust, August; Corn. **East*** AB: 14c. He further claims on p. 222 that *mis-Est* (why the hyphen?) is a recent invention. This is also incorrect: *in **meys est** an viijves deth an secund feer sur a veth sensys in pov benytha* BM 2197-9; *on 22ves*

mys Est, *1711* Gwavas (LAM: 238); *Ni-trehes e bigel en miz-east* Gwavas (LAM: 242); *Miz-East (August)* Pryce.

Est [Yst] 'East': GKK says that this word is confined to BM 664 and CW 1742. This is incorrect: *Wor duath Gwra gwenz Noor East whetha pell* BF: 44; *a reeg doaze teeze veer thor an Est* RC 23 (Rowe): 194; *Rag ma gwellez genani e steran en Est* ibid.; *ha pel da East ev a Travaliaz* BF: 15.

estren [estren] 'stranger': GKK says the word is unattested. This is incorrect: *geffya e foto dho Estren pel-pou* AB: 222.

ewines [ewynas] '(finger)nails': GKK says that the plural of *ewin* 'fingernail' is confined to a single instance in Lhuyd. This is incorrect: *W. Ewinedh, Nails; C. Winaz* AB: 28a; *Unguis . . . A nail, a claw, a talon.C. Euin & iuin, plur. iuinaz* AB: 176b.

eyrin [eyryn] collective 'sloes': GKK says this word is unattested. This is incorrect: *W[elsh] Eirin, Plums; Corn Aeran* AB: 15c; and cf. *Aeran, Plumbs* Borlase 376; *Aeran, a plumb, a prune* Pryce, opposite K 2.

eythinenn [eythynen] 'gorse bush': GKK says the singular is confined to a single instance in OCV. This is incorrect: *glastanen, eithinen, brox* AB: 223; *Eithinan, A furze-bush* AB: 240c. GKK also claims that apart from toponyms the collective *eythin* [eythyn] is attested twice only. This is also incorrect: *Bagaz eithin, a Bush of furze* AB: 33c; *bagaz eithin, a bush of furze* glossing *Dumus* 56a; *Eithin* glossing *Genista spinosa* AB: 63a; *Tskekke'r eithin* glossing *Parus, A titmouse, a muskin* AB: 113c; *Whelas poble tha trehe ithen* Pryce, F f 2. According to Nance Gwavas gives *cromman eythyn* 'furze-hook' (1938, p. 30; *crobman ithen* according to Gendall) and Pryce's MS gives in a note *begh eythyn* 'a burn [load] of furze (Nance 1938: 10).

favera [favera] 'to favour': GKK says this verb is confined to one instance in TH (i.e. TH 51). This is incorrect: *a ser arluth faverugh ny* BM 3349.

figura [fygura] 'to figure': GKK says the word is unattested and has been taken from Nance's 1955 dictionary. This is incorrect: *kepar del ve va fuguris in la goyth* TH 38a; *ha'n dra a ve figurys i'n pascall oyen in la coith* TH 52a.

fisyshyen [fysycyen] 'physician': GKK says this word is confined to a single instance in BM. This is incorrect: *ov boys fecycyen connek* BM 1421: *fecessyon ny thereff nefra* BM: 1482; *in bys ma rag fecycyen* BM 1484; *Eff ew an phisicion ha'n metheg a rug sawya oll agan deseyses* TH 11.

flourenn [flowren] 'flower': GKK cites this *hapax legomenon* from TH and glosses it 'fine specimen'. This is incorrect. The word means 'flower' in the botanical sense: *eff a deffe in ban kepar ha flowren, eff a clomder* 'he grows up like a flower, he withers' TH 7.

foly 'folly': this word is well attested: *mvr a foly ew thotho* OM 191; *rag gul foly* OM 708; *me ny wruk foly* PC 1295; *yth apyas thy'm gul foly* PC 1438; *myns a geusys foly* PC 1782; *na temptyogh vy the foly* BM 501; *ow foly z[y]mmo gava* CW 429; *henna yth o tha folly gye* CW 1013; *ow folly yth ew mar vras* CW 1522. The word does not appear to be in GKK.

fondya [fundya] 'to found': GKK says that this verb is confined to a single instance at BM 1150. This is incorrect: *omma lemmen fondya plays* BM 720: *Omma me re fundyas plas* BM 990; *ov chy fundia* BM 1150; *Eff a fowndyas y egglos* TH 45a; *fatel ve hy foundyes dre an auncient appostles* TH 47a

form, -ys [form, -ys] 'bench': GKK says this word occurs in Cornish English but is not attested in the texts. This is incorrect: *me a's ordyn though wharre, cheyrys ha formys plente; ysethough syre iustis* 'I'll order them for you immediately, chairs and plenty of benches; be seated, sir justice' PC 2228-2230.

forsakya [forsakya] 'to forsake': GKK says this word is confined to two instances in TH. This is incorrect: *forsakyans byen ha muer* BM 384; *ny forsakyn y hanow* BM 1212: *forsakis y das hay vam* BM 1941; *the forsakya pub tra* TH 21a; *deneya ha forsakya* TH 33a; *an ledran a forsakiaz an Vertshants* BF: 17.

fowt [fowt] 'error': GKK suggests that the plural *fowtow* is a recent coinage, given by Nance (1938) but otherwise unattested. The compiler adds a note: 'MidC *fawtys* is the attested plural occurring twice in TH, but Nance gave *fowtow* and this is in common use.' Both main entry and note are incorrect. The plural form *fowtys* occurs *three* times in TH: *ow rebukya aga fautes* TH 22a; *an offences ha fawtys* TH 25; *ha kemeras sham a'ga fawtys* TH 29a. Moreover *fowtow* is attested: *geffya y foto dho Estren pel-pou* AB: 222; *try fotou idzhanz* AB: 223; *an fotou erel* AB: 223.

Frynk 'France; French': GKK's treatment of this word is very misleading. The basic form is **Frank* 'a Frank, a Frenchman' < Lat. *Francus*. Because the Frank was a freeman, unlike the subject Gauls, the word also came to be an adjective meaning 'free'. This is seen in Cornish in the Godolphin motto *Frank ha leal etto ge* 'Free and loyal art thou' Pryce, opposite p. F f. The Lat. plural *Franci* became *Ffrainc* 'Franks, French people, France' in Welsh and *Frynk/Frenk* in Cornish. With the use of the plural of the population name to mean the country cf. *Cymry* 'Welshmen' and *Cymru* 'Wales', both from **Kombrogi* 'fellow-countrymen, Welshmen', the difference between *Cymry* and *Cymru* being one of spelling only. The Cornish form was **Kembry* 'Wales', but this had reduced to *Kembra, Kimbra* by the Late Cornish period. The original <y> is seen in the recharacterized plural *Kembrian* 'Welshmen' (AB: 222, 223, 242c) < **Kembry + on*. GKK says the <y> in *Frynk* 'is unexpected but is found twice in Late Cornish'. This is incorrect on both counts. I have counted six examples: *ha ugge hedda mose tho* **Frenk** N. Boson, BF: 29; *Pou Lezou en* **Vrink** AB: 222; *Kynyphan frenk* 'nut of France, walnut' AB: 74a; *Pokkys* **Frenk** 'pox of France' AB: 82a; *Nenna e eath car rag* **Frink** Tonkin (LAM: 226); *Materen* **Frink** Tonkin (LAM: 226). The hesitation between *y* and *e* is regular in Cornish; cf. **santi > sens/syns* 'saints' and **danti > dens/dyns*. George says the vowel *y* is unexpected presumably because he would have expected *a* in the singular **Frank*. As we have seen *Frynk/Frenk* is a plural and always means 'France' or the 'French' (pl.). A plural *Frankaz* 'Frenchmen' based on the singular **Frank* 'Frank, Frenchman' is used by Gwavas (cited by Gendall). GKK's main mistake here is to attempt to treat *Frynk* 'France' and **Frank* 'Frenchman' under the same heading. Notice incidentally that Pryce cites the word *frank* 'free at liberty' and in his lament on the death of William III Lhuyd uses *Frank* to mean 'France': *Dhort henna war* **Frank** *ha war Span* LAM: 234. Moreover Nicholas Boson writes **Francan**-*belgan* 'Franco-Belgian' BF: 31.

Frynkek [Frynkek] 'French language': GKK says this is 'actually found as *Frencock* in Late Cornish.' This is incorrect. N. Boson writes *an* **Frenkock** (not **Frencock*) *feen* BF: 29 and J. Boson writes *En* **Frenkock** *ha Carnoack* BF: 59. One also finds **Vrinkak** glossing *Gallica lingua, The French Tongue* AB: 62b; *Arvorek ha* **Frenkek** AB: 222; *avez a* **Frenkek** AB: 223. Welsh *Ffrangeg* 'French language' is from **Frank* singular + *eg*. Cornish *Frynkek* is from *Frynk* plural + *ek*, hence the difference in vocalism.

gast [gast] 'bitch': GKK says the word is confined to a single instance in Lhuyd. This is incorrect: *W.* **Gast**, *A Bitch; Corn.* **Gest** AB: 14c; **gest** AB: 46a (s.v. *Canis*); **gest**, *A bitch* AB: 241b; *CANIS . . . Kei, †ki,* **gest** AB: 291a.

gavar mor [gavar mor] 'crayfish; spider crab': GKK cites this s.v. *gavar* <gaver> and arbitrarily lenites the initial consonant of *mor* to give **gaver vor*. The dictionary also asserts that apart from Cornish dialect the word is confined to a single occurrence in Lhuyd. This is incorrect: *. . . called otherwise by the Cornish* **Gavar mor** s.v. *Legast, a Lobster* AB: 5a; *Corn.* **Gavar mor** *[i.e. Sea-goat] A sort of Lobster, so call'd from its long horns* AB: 34b; **Gavar mor**

glossing *Locusta, A lobster* AB: 81a; **Gavar mor**, *A segar or long oister* AB: 241bc.

gaver [gavar] 'goat': GKK cites *gever* on p. 108 as the plural of *gavar* 'goat' and says that the form is confined to place-names. This is incorrect: *eue a reeg pederre war* **Gever**, *ha meskeeges dro tho Anko, eue levarraz droua* **Gever** *ul* BF: 25; *Devas, ean,* **gever** *ha menas* Bilbao MS; *Gavar, A goat,* **Gever** AB: 243a. GKK does not mention the earliest instance of the plural of *gavar*, i.e. *gyfras: na the offra in ban the Thu ley, oghan, devas ha* **gyffras** TH 27a.

gedya [gedya] 'to guide': GKK says that this verb is confined to one instance in BM. This is incorrect: *the teller da rum* **gedya** BM 629; *grua ov* **gedya** *vy* BM 637; *me agis* **gyd** BM 981; *rum* **gedya** *in forth wella* BM 1099; **gedyogh** *dymo* BM 2089; *ov bevnans oma* **gedya** BM 2541; *reth* **gedya** *del vo plesijs* BM 3015.

gedyer [gedyer] 'guide': GKK says that this word is derived from Nance (1955), being unattested in the texts. This is incorrect: *ow tristya fatell ota* **gydyar** *the'n re ew dall* TH 14a.

genesigeth [genesygeth] 'birth': GKK says this occurs 2-3 times in BM and TH. This is incorrect: *ay* **genesygeth** BM 4387; *mortall* **genesegeth** TH 6a; *then* **genesegath** TH 8; *dre* **genesegeth** TH 26; *ha 'enegegath* SA 61a.

genn [gen] 'wedge, chisel'; GKK says this word is confined to a single instance in Lhuyd. This is incorrect: *A Wedge; Corn[ish]* **Gedn** AB: 14c; **gedn** glossing *Cuneus, A Wedge* AB: 53a; **Gedn** *is Cornish for a wedge* Pryce (LAM: 308).

gerlyver [gerlyver] 'dictionary': GKK says this word is confined to a single instance in Pryce. This is incorrect: *neb 'ramtekek ha* **gerlevar** AB: 222; *mar peue* **gerlevar** AB: 222; *hay* **gerlevro** *e honan* AB: 222; *e* **'erlevar** *Kembrian* AB: 223; *en an* **ger-levar** *Ladin ha Keltek* AB: 223.

gerlyvrynn [gerlyvryn] 'glossary, short dictionary': GKK says this word is confined to a single instance in Lhuyd. This is incorrect: **ger-levran** *Kernuak* AB: 222; *na huath* **gerlevran** *veth* AB: 222; *ha'n* **gerlevran** *Arvorek* AB: 222; *neb* **'Erlevran** *Brethonek* AB: 222; *e* **gerlevran** *Kembrian* AB: 222; *mez* **gerlevran** *Kernuak* AB: 222; **gerlevran** *bian Brethonek* AB: 222; *an* **gerlevran**-na AB: 223; *an* **gerlevran**-ma AB: 223; *vez a'n hoth* **Erlevran**-ma AB: 223; **gerlevran** *Kernuak Levarva Cotton* AB: 223; *en an* **gerlevran** *Kernuak-ma* AB: 223; *en an* **gerlevran-ma** AB: 223.

gil [gyl] 'deceit, guile': GKK says that this word is confined to a single instance in the *Ordinalia*. This is incorrect: *rag ovn genes bones* **gyl** OM 196; *seruont hep* **gyl** OM 2402; *hep toll na* **gyl** OM 2559; *deceypt vith na* **gyll** TH 11.

glanhe [glanhe] 'to clean': GKK says that this verb is confined to two occurrences in TH. This is incorrect: *yth ough **glanhys** PC 865; genen yv **glanheys** BM 4523; an nenaf a veth **glanhis** SA 60a.*

glena [glena] 'to stick': GKK says that this verb is confined to two instances in TH. This is incorrect: *orto fast navng o **glenys** PA 176c; th'y thyller arte **glenes** PC 1154; worto an kyc a **glene** RD 2594; y **glynes** hardlych RD 2597; a russa **glena** TH 19a; **glena** agys honyn TH 58; Dho **glenys** [sic]* glossing *Haereo, To stick, to cleave,* etc. AB: 65a.

glew [glew] 'sharp, penetrating': GKK says that this word is confined to three instances in the *Ordinalia* (i.e. OM 2062, PC 2088 and RD 2582). This is incorrect: *peynys **glu** BM 765.*

glyb [glyb, gleb] 'wet': GKK says that apart from dialect survivals, this word is confined to two examples in Lhuyd. This is incorrect: ***Gleab*** glossing *Fluidus* AB: 60b; ***Gleb*** glossing *Humidus* AB: 66b; ***Gleb*** glossing *Madidus* AB: 83c; *Dedh **gleb**, A wet day* AB: 243c; *Keuar '**leb**, Wet weather* ibid.

glybya [glybya] 'to wet, to moisten': GKK says that this verb is confined to a single instance in BM (line 3276). This is incorrect: *yma daggrow ow **klybye** the dreys* PC 482-3.

godra [godra] 'to milk': GKK says this word is confined to a single occurrence in Lhuyd. This is incorrect: *W. **Godro**, To Milk; Cor. **Gudra** AB: 17b; Buket **gudra** glossing Mulctra, A milk-pail* AB: 95a; *dhort **gudra** an devaz han gour* AB: 240b; ***Gudra**, to milk or milch* Borlase 390.

godrevedh [godreva] 'third day hence': GKK says the word is taken from Nance's 1955 dictionary, being otherwise unattested. This is incorrect: ***gydreva**, The third day hence* AB: 249a; ***gydreva**, the third day hence* Pryce; ***Gudreva**, the third Day hence* Borlase 390; ***gydreva**, adv. The third day hence* LCB. GKK also implicitly criticizes Nance for spelling the word <godreva>. It is GKK's unhistorical <godrevedh> that is unjustified.

goel [gol] 'sail': GKK says that this word is confined to three instances (i.e. OCV, RD 2331 and BM 1085). This is incorrect: *tenneugh a thysempys y **goyl** yn ban* RD 2291-92; *tennogh dyson an **goyl** thym in ban lemen* BM 597-98; *Guelan **gol**, the sail-yard* AB: 3a; *C. **Gol**, Velum* AB: 33a; ***Gol**, **guyl*** glossing *Velum, A veil, a curtain or sail* AB: 170c.

goellys [gullys] 'gulls': GKK says that this word, the plural of *goella* [gulla] 'gull' is confined to a single instance in Lhuyd. This is incorrect: ***gulles**, Guls* AB: 243a; *an **gullez** ha'n idhen mor aral* AB: 245a.

Goelowann [Golowan] 'St John's Eve, Midsummer': GKK says this is confined to one instance in Late Cornish. This is incorrect: *Guave en Have terebah* **Goluan** Ustick MSS; . . . *Midsummer is thence, in the Cornish tongue, call'd* **Goluan** Borlase 130.

goen [gon] 'sheath': GKK says this is confined to Old and Middle Cornish. This is incorrect: *Gun,* †*guain* glossing *Vagina, A sheath or scabbard* AB: 169a.

goesogenn [gojogen] 'black pudding': GKK says this word comes from Nance (1955), being unattested in the texts. This is incorrect: *Gudzhygan, A black Pudding, from the old word guaedogen, of the same signification* AB: 4c; *W.* †*gwaedogen, A Pudding; C. Gudzhygan* AB: 10b; *Gudzhygan (a black pudding)* s.v. *Fartum, A pudding, a farce* AB: 58c. The word is also in Nance (1938) s.vv. *gojogen* and *gosogen* and Nance (1952) s.v. 'pudding'.

gokkyes [gockyes] 'fools': GKK cites this as a separate headword distinct from *gocky* <gokki> and says that the word is unattested. This is doubly incorrect. *Gockyes* is merely the plural of *gocky* 'foolish, foolish person' and means 'fools'. It is attested: *gorteugh lymmyn* **gockyes** 'stay now, you fools' PC 1149; *nyns ough lemmyn* **gokyes** 'you are nothing but fools' RD 1136.

golowi [golowy] 'to lighten': according to GKK this is confined to one instance each in BM, CW and Lhuyd. This is incorrect: *re* **woloways** *ov skyans* BM 213; *han presan ov* **colowhy** BM 3714; *an kigg ew touchis gans dowla rag malla an nenaf bos* **golowis** *gans an Spiris Sans* SA 60a; *ow* **collowye** CW 125; *Dho* **gylyua** glossing *Fulgeo, to shine, glister or glitter; to lighten* AB: 61c-62a; *Dho* **Gouloua** glossing *Lumino, To light, to enlighten* AB: 82b; **Kylyui**, *To lighten* AB: 245b; *Patl yzhi a* **kylyui** *ha trenna* AB: 248.

golvan [golvan] 'sparrow': GKK says this word is confined to one instance each in OCV and Lhuyd. This is incorrect: **goluan** glossing *passer* OCV 515; *Arm. & Corn.* **Golvan** *[a Sparrow]* AB: 38a; **Gylvan** *ge* glossing *Curruca, A hedge-sparrow* AB: 53b; *Passer . . . A sparrow . . . C.* **gylvan**, †*golvan* AB: 114a; **Golvan**, *A sparrow* AB: 241b; *A Sparrow, C & Ar.* **Golvan** AB: 286b.

gorheri [gorhery] 'to cover': GKK says this verb is confined to a single instance in the *Ordinalia*. This is incorrect: *tha'gas* **gorhery** *hep gow* PC: 2655; *goole powze crohan ha ez* **goreraz** RC 23: 183; *Ha* **gwarrow** *goz pennow genz lidziw glaz* Lhuyd (LAM: 232).

gorlewin [gorlewen] 'west': GKK says that this word is confined to a single instance in Lhuyd. This is incorrect: *an boble en* **Gorleuen** *Kernou* AB: 222; *en* **uorleuen** *an G'laskor-ma* AB: 224; *kenza* **gorleuen** *an 'Ulaskor-ma* AB: 224.

gossen [gossen] 'rust, ferruginous earth': GKK says that apart from

English dialect the word is unattested. This is incorrect. Pryce writes, **Gozan, Gossan,** *rust, iron ochre, ferruginous* [sic].

gour-gath [gourgath] 'tomcat': GKK says this word, which is otherwise unattested, has been derived from Nance's 1952 dictionary. This is incorrect: **Gurkath,** *A he-cat* AB: 241b. Moreover, the word is already in Nance's 1938 dictionary, s.v. *cath* 'cat' on p. 21.

governya [governya] 'to govern': GKK says that this verb is confined to 2-3 examples in the *Ordinalia* and CW and adds a note that the variant *governa* occurs in TH. In fact *governya* is confined to the *Ordinalia*: *rag* **governye** *ow bewnans* OM 89; *rak* **governye** *oll an beys* PC 930. CW has *governa*, i.e. the same form as in TH: *omma thagan* **governa** CW 181. GKK fails to mention that the word is also cited by Lhuyd: **Govarna,** *Govern* AB: 248a.

gramasek [gramasek] 'grammar': GKK asserts that this word is unattested in the texts, being derived from Nance's 1952 dictionary. George adds a note: 'Nance's Cornicisation of E. *grammatic(al)*'. None of this is really correct. Lhuyd uses the term *gramatek* (e.g. **Gramatek** *ha ger-levran Kernuak* AB: 222) of which *gramasek* is Nance's more fully Cornicized form. *Gramatek/gramasek* is based on Welsh *gramadeg* 'grammar', itself the regular development of Latin *grammatica* (cf. Irish *gramadach*). English *grammatical* is irrelevent.

Grekys [Grekys] 'Greeks': GKK's code {I} means that the plural is deduced from the singular *Greca* 'Greek' and that *Grekys* itself does not actually occur. This is incorrect. The plural occurs twice: *Oecumenius, den auncient in egglos an* **Grekys** TH 26a; *athea'n egglos a'n* **Grickys** TH 56.

grevons [grevons] 'grievance': GKK says that this word is confined to a single instance in BM. This is incorrect: **Grefons** *ha cleves seson* BM 1000; *y* **grefons** *sewagya* BM 1004; *nyns yv* **grefons** *me an geyl* BM 1438.

grondya [grondya] 'to found': GKK says the word occurs 2-3 times in Middle Cornish. This is incorrect: *war fals yz ens* **growndys** PA 118b; *Nans yw* **groundyys** *genef vy* OM 2321; *sur ha* **grondya** BM 1151; **groundya** *aga honyn* TH 32a; *a res bos* **groundys** TH 51a.

grugyerik [grugyeryk] '(young) partridge': GKK says that the word is confined to a single instance in Lhuyd. This is incorrect: **Gyrgirik,** *A Partridge* AB: 5a; **gyrgirik** glossing *Perdix, A partridge* AB: 117b; **Gyrgirik,** *A Partridge* AB: 241b.

gwaneth [gwaneth] 'wheat': GKK says this word is confined to two instances in Late Cornish. This is incorrect: *kerth, barlys ha* **gwaneth** CW 1066; *Barles* **gwanath** *ha keer* Bilbao MS; *W. Guenith, Wheat; Corn.* **Guanath** AB: 15b; **Guanath** glossing

Triticum, Wheat AB: 167a; *C[ornish]* **Guanath** glossing *TRITICUM* AB: 297b; **Guanath**, *wheat; bara* **guanath**, *wheaten bread* Pryce, Q.

gwannder [gwander] 'weakness': GKK says the word is unattested. This is incorrect: *rag* **gwander** *y a gozas* PA 68c; *Rag* **gwander** *war ben dowlyn* PA 171c; *doun an grows rag* **gwander** PA 173d; *rag* **guander** *ef re cothas* PC 2618; **Guander**, *Weakness* AB: 240b.

gwary-myr 'play, pageant': this word is cited as **guirremears** by Scawen (LAM: 282); **Guirimir** by Borlase 196 and cf. **guarry-meers**, *interludes played in the rounds; amphitheatres* Pryce, opposite Q 2. The word is in Nance (1938, 1951 and 1955). It appears to be wanting from GKK.

gwaynya [gwaynya] 'to gain': GKK says the word is confined to one instance in Lhuyd. This is incorrect: *hag eff a* **gvayn** *roov cans* BM 388; *hag a* **guayn** *pur sempellos* BM 2256; *Dho* **guaynia** glossing *Lucror, To gain, to win* AB: 81c; *To Win or Gain, C[ornish]* **Guaynia** AB: 289b.

gwaytya [gwaytya, gwetyas] 'to expect': GKK says the verbal noun is not attested. This is incorrect: *pan a dra a ren ny* **gwettyas** TH 15a; *fatell yllans* **gwetias** 55a; *uz na ellen skant* **quatiez** BG: 25; *Mattern James rig* **quachas** *e stoppia* LAM: 224; *Eva rig* **quachas** *moaze* LAM: 224.

gwenenenn [gwenenen] 'bee', *gwenen* [gwenyn] collective 'bees': GKK follows Nance in making *gwenenen* the singular and *gwenen* the plural. **Guenenen** 'apis' [i.e. 'bee' singular] occurs in OCV. Lhuyd, however, makes *guanan* his singular: *W. Guenynen, A Bee; Corn.* **Guanan** AB: 13c; *W. Guenynen, A Bee; Corn* **Guanan** AB: 15b; *Apes vel apis, Guenynen, A Bee; C.* **Guanan**, *[pl.* **guenyn**] AB: [4]3a; **Guanan**, *A bee* AB: 240c. The plural *gwenyn* occurs in *Kaual* **guanan** glossing *Alveare, A Bee-Hive* AB: 42b; *Ha ma leiaz bennen Pokare an* **guenen** Pryce and *Corgwenyn Bees-wax* Borlase 382b. It would seem, then, that in Late Cornish *gwenen/gwenyn* was both singular and plural. According to GKK *gwenen* occurs twice. We have noted above *eight* examples.

gwenton [gwaynten] 'spring': GKK says the word is confined to OCV and Lhuyd. This is incorrect: *Houl sooth, Tor lean, paravy an* **gwaynten** Scawen MSS.

gwiader [gwyader] 'weaver': GKK says that this word is confined to Lhuyd. This is incorrect, since Gwavas writes: *Why ladar* **gweder**, *Lavarro guz pader* LAM: 242.

gwibenn [gwyben] 'fly': GKK says this word is confined to a single instance in Lhuyd. This is incorrect: *A Flie; Corn[ish]* **Guiban** AB:

13c; **Guiban** glossing *Insectum, A Fly, an Insect* AB: 71b; **Guiban** glossing *Musca, a fly* AB: 96a.

gwikoryon [gwycoryon] 'merchants': GKK says that this plural is confined to two instances in PC. This is incorrect: *crist a gafas* **gwycoryan** PA 30c.

gwius [gwyus] 'winding': GKK says that this is unattested in the texts and has been taken from Nance's 1955 dictionary. This is incorrect: *the belha ha the* **weusa** *a vova ow mois in rag* TH 17a.

gwlesik [gwlesyk] 'leader': GKK says this word is confined to place-names. This is incorrect: *en termen Maksen* **Ulezek** AB: 224.

gwragh 'old woman': GKK says that this word is confined to Old Cornish and place-names. This is incorrect: *Anus . . . An Old Woman . . . C. Bennen goath;* **gurah** AB: 33a; *Vetula . . . An old woman or wife. C. Benyn goth,* †**gurah** AB: 173a. It also occurs in dialect as *wrah, wraugh, wraff* with the sense 'wrasse' (a fish with hag-like features) GCSW: 174.

gwrannenn [gwrannen] 'wren': GKK says this word is attested 2-3 times in Lhuyd who, we are told, spells it <gwradnan>. This is incorrect on both counts: *English. A Wren, Corn* **Guradn** AB: 9c; **Guradnan,** *A Wren* AB: 33c; **Guradnan** glossing *Troglodytes, A wren* AB: 167a; **Guradnan,** *A wren* AB: 241b. Nowhere does Lhuyd spell the word with initial <gw>.

gwreydhenn [gwredhen] 'root': GKK says that the singular in *-enn* [-en] is confined to OCV and Lhuyd. This is incorrect: *dell ons y aga dew an* **wrethyan** *dretha mayth o res the lynyath mab den dos, han* **wreythan** *unwith o corruptys ha nyns o vas, fatel ylly an wethan ha'n barrow ow tos mes a'n* **wreythan** *na bos vas?* TH 4a; *theworth an* **wreythan** TH 8a. GKK also suggests that TH contains two instances of a word *****gwreydhyans** 'foundation'. I am unable to locate either of them.

gwreydhya [gwredhya] 'to take root': GKK says the word is unattested. This is incorrect: **gurythyoug** *ha tyvoug arte* OM 1894; *yn dor ymons ol* **gurythyys** OM 2084.

gwrys [gwrys] 'crystal'. GKK says that no cognates have been identified. This is incorrect. In his glossary to *Beunans Meriasek* (*Archiv für Celtische Lexicographie* 1 (1900): 121) Stokes suggested that *grueys* at BM 1288 was from *****gwysr* < *uitrum*. I would suggest further that *gwrys* represents the regular Cornish development of *****uritu-*, an early British metathesis of Latin *uitrum* 'glass'. The unmetathesized variant *uitru-* developed regularly in Cornish as *gweder*.

Gwydhelek [Godhalek] 'Irish, Gaelic': GKK says that the word has been taken from Nance's 1938 dictionary, since it is unattested in the texts. This is incorrect: *ha gerlevar rag oz Tavaz huei ha rag an* **Godhalek** AB: 222; *mar peue gerlevar &c Kernuak ha* **Godhalek** AB: 222. Cf. **Godhalec** *adj. Irish Pryce* in LCB.

gwyr [gwer] 'green': GKK says this word is confined to two instances in Lhuyd. This is incorrect: *W. Guyrdh, Green; Corn* **Guer.** AB: 12b; *W. Guyrdh, Green; Corn* **Guer** AB: 18c; *C. Delkio* **guer** glossing *Frons* AB: 61c; *C.* **Guer,** *guirdh [guirt]* AB: 174c; *Ky* **guer** *vel an guelz, As green as grass* AB: 248c.

gwyrgh [gwergh] 'virginal, pure, innocent': GKK says the word is unattested in the texts. This is incorrect: *dre'n pyte a gemeras orth flehys* **gruegh** *ha byen* 'through the mercy he showed to children innocent and small' BM 1691-2; *drefen kemeres pyta a'n flehys* **gruergh** *del rusta* 'because of taking pity upon the innocent children as you did' BM 1704-5; *tremmyl flogh* **gruergh** *the latha* 'to kill three thousand innocent children' BM 1776.

hager-awel [hager-awel] 'storm': GKK cites this under *hager* and suggests that it is confined to a single instance in Pryce. This is incorrect: *Kensa, vrt an* **hagar auall** *iggeva gweell do derevoll* BF: 9; *Kensa, urt a* **hagar-awal** *iggeva gweel do derevoll* BF: 12; *Keuar,* **hagar-auel** glossing *Tempestas, A tempest or storm* AB: 161c.

hanasenn [hanajen] 'sigh': GKK says the word is confined to a single instance in Lhuyd. This is incorrect: *A Sigh. Arm. Huanal. Corn.* **Hanadzhan** AB: 8c; *Suspirium . . . A sigh; A short breathing . . . C.* **Hanadzhan** AB: 159c; **Hannadzian** *down ha garm krev* LAM: 232. It is probable also that **Hynadzhas** glossing *Gemitus, a groan or sigh* at AB: 62c is a misprint for **Hynadzhan.*

handla [handla] 'to handle, to touch': GKK says this verb is confined to a single instance in BM. This is incorrect: *drok* **handle** *del om kyry* PC 991; *ny alla* **handle** *toul vyth* PC 2678; *gesough vy th'y* **handle** PC 3165; *galles* **handle** PC 3194; *erna* **hyndlyf** *y golon* RD 1531; *thy* **handla** *sur eff am gays* BM 1113; *le mayth eua drok***hendelys** BM 3760.

hangya [hangya] 'to hang': GKK says that this verb is confined to a single instance at BM 1245. This is incorrect: *oll an la ha'n prophetys ow* **hangya** TH 20a.

hansel [hansel] 'breakfast': GKK says this word is confined to two instances in BM (i.e. at lines 110 and 960). This is incorrect: *Jentaculum . . . A break-fast. C.* **Haunsel** AB: 67b; **Haunsel,** *a Breakfast* Borlase 392; *Gwag o ve, ra ve gawas* **haunsell?** 'I am hungry, shall I have breakfast?' Pryce, opposite F f 2.

hanter-kans [hantercans] 'fifty': GKK says that this word is attested 2-3 times in Middle and Late Cornish. This is incorrect: *ha* **hanter cans** *keuelyn* OM 957; *ha* **hanter cans** *y gyle* PC 506; *ha* **hantercans**

kevellen CW 2262; *C.* **Hanter kanz** glossing *Quinquaginta* AB: 135a.

harber [harber] 'refuge': GKK says this word has been taken from Nance's 1938 dictionary, being unattested in the texts. This is incorrect: *ena purguir an poddren thotho prest re ruk* **harber** BM 2290-91; *malbe yeman in* **harber** BM 3303. *Erberow* OM 32 is probably the plural.

heligenn [helygen] '(single) willow tree': GKK says the singular in *-enn* [-en] is unattested apart from toponyms. This is incorrect: **heligen**: *salix* OCV 707; *Salix . . . A willow or sallow tree, an osier . . . C. Helagan,* †*heligen* AB: 143c.

hembronk [hembronk, humbrank] 'to lead, to conduct': GKK gives this word the codes {M: 2}, by which is meant that the word is confined to Middle Cornish and occurs between two and three times. This is incorrect: *y'n* **hombronkyas** PA 16a; **hombronkis** PA 61c; *e'n* **hombronky** PA 62b; *y a'n* **hombronkyas** PA 76c; *a'n* **hombronkyas** PA 114c; *a ve* **hombronkis** PA 163c; *a's* **hembronk** OM 1874; *may feen* **hembrynkys** OM 1973; *yth* **hembrenkygh** PC 204; **hembrynkys** PC 584; **hembrynkeugh** PC 1195; *a'm* **hembroncas** PC 1205; **humbrak** *mab den in mes* TH 3; **humbrynkes** *the beha* TH 3a; *agan* **humbrag** *ny* TH 11a. Moreover the word is attested in Late Cornish: *a ve Jesus* **humbregez** RC 23: 185.

hernya 'to shoe a horse'. This word is in Pryce: *Moas tha an gove tha* **herniah** *an verh* 'To go to the smith to shoe the horses' F f 2. It appears to be wanting in GKK.

hora [hora] 'whore': GKK suggests that this word is attested in Late Cornish only (i.e. as *hora* by Lhuyd and *whorra* by Carew). This is incorrect: *gas vy the thehesy gans morben bom trewysy the'n vyl* **hora** *war an taal* OM 2703-5.

howlsedhes [howlsedhas] 'sunset': GKK suggests this word is confined to a single instance in Lhuyd, **Houlzedhas** glossing *Occasus,. sun-setting, The west* AB: 104c. This is incorrect: *na oren pana tu, Thuryan,* **houlzethas***, po Gleth po Dihow* Pryce, opposite F f.

hurtya 'to hurt': this verb occurs three times in TH: *the lee* **hurtys** TH 26; *theth* **hurtya** *ge* TH 48 x 2 and is attested by Lhuyd as *dho* **hertia** glossing *Laedo, To hurt* AB: 75b. It does not seem to be in GKK.

hwaff [whaf] 'blow': GKK suggests that this word is confined to three instances in OM (i.e. OM 2711, 2747 and 2755). This is incorrect. The word is also attested in TH with the sense 'gust of wind': *ledys gans pub* **wave** *ha cowas gwyns* TH 31; *ow shackya gans pub* **waffe** TH 42.

hwedner [whednar] 'sixpence': GKK says this is known only from

Borlase. This is incorrect: **Hue dinar** glossing *Semisolidus, Sixpence* AB: 148a; **Hue dinair**, *sixpence* Pryce.

hwetegves [whetegves] 'sixteenth': GKK says that the word occurs once in TH and nowhere else. This is probably an allusion to *in xvi-as chapter* TH 43a, which is not an example. The only occurrence of the word known to me is *Whe **degvas**, the sixteenth* Pryce.

hwiogenn [whyogen] 'dinner cake': GKK says that this word is unattested, being taken from Nance's 1938 dictionary. GKK also gives as a separate headword *hogenn* [hogen] 'pastry', which is, according to GKK, similarly not attested. *Whyogen* and *hogen* are variants of the same word. The item is attested. Lhuyd writes: **Huigan**, *medulla panis* ['dough, pastry'] AB: 87c; cf. *hot **fuggans** (cakes)* Bottrell (LAM: 328).

hwithra [whythra] 'to examine': GKK asserts that this word is confined to a single instance in OM. This is incorrect: **whythyr** *pup tra* OM 748; *a **whythre** warnas* OM 1414; **whythrough** *hetheu* PC 1113.

hwithrans [whythrans] 'research': GKK ascribes this to K[en] J. G[eorge]. This is incorrect: the word was in use in the nineteen-sixties: *rak dysquedhes dhe'n bys deweth **whythrans** byghan* 'to show to the world the end result of a small amount of research' ALK 87 (1964).

hynsa [hynsa] 'peers': GKK says this word is confined to a single instance each in OM and BM. This is incorrect: *ha the oll aga **hynsa*** TH 44; *a ugh aga **hensa*** TH 44a; *ugh oll aga **hensa*** TH 45a; *uth oll aga **hensa*** TH 49a.

igolenn [agolen] 'whetstone': GKK says that the word occurs the place-name *Nancegollan* and is otherwise confined to a single instance in Lhuyd. This is incorrect: *W. Galen [r. Hogalen] A Whet-stone; Corn. **Agolan*** AB: 15a; *W. Hogalen, A Whet-Stone, Cor. **Agolan*** AB: 16c; **Agolan** glossing *Cos, A whetstone* AB: 51c.

igor [ygor] 'open': GKK's code {ML: 3} suggests that this word is well attested in both Middle and Late Cornish. This is incorrect. The word is not attested anywhere in the texts, being replaced by *opyn*. If he had looked at Nance (1938), the compiler would have seen that Nance derived the word from Breton *(d)igor*.

jarn [jarn] 'garden': GKK says this word is confined to one occurrence in Lhuyd. This is incorrect: **Dzharn**, *An Orchard* AB: 33c; *Luar, **Dzharn** glossing Hortus, A garden or orchard* AB: 66a; **Dzharn** glossing *Pomarium, An orchard* 123b. It is also well attested in toponyms, e.g. *Park an **Jarne**, Park **Jearn**, Park an **Jarns*** (Padel: 141).

Jentilys [Jentyls] pl. 'Gentiles': GKK says that the word is confined to a single instance in Late Cornish. This is incorrect: *in myske an Jentyls* TH 14a; *in mysk an Gentyls* TH 45a; *Allale an Gentelles* RC 23: 190.

Kablys [Cablys] 'Maundy Thursday': GKK says that this word is confined to a single instance in Middle Cornish (i.e. PC 654) where it is spelt *duyow hamlos*. This is incorrect: *en gyth o deyow hablys* PA 41c; *nyng egy cowse vith a deow habblys* SA 66.

kachya [cachya] 'to catch, to seize': GKK says that this verb is confined to a single instance in PC. This is incorrect: *ha chechys yntre dewla* PA 48d; *cachaf y ben* OM 2816; *y cachye* PC 55; *a'n chache uskys* PC 615; *me a cache* PC 452; *yn cacher wythovte nay* PC 987; *kychough ef yn vryongen* PC 1007; *hag a cach an cercot bras* PC 2074; *y a yl bones kechys* PC 2293; *kycheugh ef* PC 2523; *war skwych kychys the ves gans dywthorn* RD 2595-6; *Mose tha an mor tha catchah pyzgaz* Pryce; *ketchys, taken* Borlase 395.

kala [cala] 'straw': Although it cites OCV 802 and PC 680, GKK says that the word occurs once only. This is incorrect. The word is common: *marnes in cala garov* BM 4447; *me ny settyaf gwaile gala* CW 1355; *Kala, Straw* (in a list of current Cornish words) AB: 4c; *moran kala [& sivi] a Straw-berry* AB: 44b; *Kala, straw* glossing *Culmus* AB: 53a; *Kala* glossing *Stramen, Straw, litter, stubble* AB: 155b; *Straw, C[ornish] Kala* AB: 287a; *gorah an vose tha shakiah an kala* Pryce, opposite F f 2; *Cala rag Whethlow* motto of Carminow (LAM: 248).

Kalann [Calan] 'first day of month': GKK's discussion of this word is not entirely clear, since the dictionary suggests erroneously s.v. <Halann> that the etymon occurs in CW. Under *Kalann* we are told that the word is confined to 2-3 instances in Late Cornish. This is incorrect. The word is attested twice in Middle Cornish: *ix nobyl a Cala Me* BM 3338; *dew whallon gwa metton in eglos de Lalant* Consistory Court Deposition 1572 (Wakelin: 89). Under *Calendae* Lhuyd writes *Kalan; halan; Deu halan guav, All Saints Day* AB: 45c. Taking all these instances together, we have five examples.

kalgh [cal] 'penis': GKK says this word is confined to one instance each in Lhuyd and John Boson. This is incorrect: *C. & Arm. Kal* glossing *Mentula, a Man's privy member* AB: 89a; *Lost, kal* glossing *Penis, A tail, a man's yard* AB: 116c; *Kal* glossing *Veretrum, A man's privy member* AB: 171c; *goz Kal* BF: 58; *Kal. A Phallus, Membrum Virile* Pryce (LAM: 308).

kammdybyans [camdybyans] 'mistake': GKK says this word has been taken from Nance (1938) and is not attested in the texts. This is incorrect: *Mez an kabmdybianz hedda eu gorryzz ker* AB: 223.

kampoella [campolla] 'to mention': GKK says that this verb is confined to a single instance in the seventeenth century. This is presumably a reference to *Ha me reeg clowaz an poble compla* by James Jenkins (LAM: 230). The assertion in GKK is incorrect, however, since the verb is well attested in BM: *Vn ger na campol a gryst* BM 903; *purguir campollys* BM 2204; *na gampol crist* BM 2439; *pan gampollys* BM 2791.

kankweyth [canqueyth] 'a hundred times': GKK says this is confined to a single instance in the *Ordinalia* (a reference to PC 574, *dek canquyth thy's lowene*). This is incorrect. The variant *kanzuyth* is cited by Lhuyd, AB: 248c.

Karesk [Keresk] 'Exeter': GKK omits to remark that this toponym is stressed on the second syllable. The dictionary says the toponym is confined to 2-3 instances. This is incorrect: *toaz dre mez an fear Ka'rEsk* BF: 16; *dre mes an fer Karesk* BF: 17; *ha tha vethes tha Careesk* LAM: 224; *Kaer Esk, the City of Exeter* [sic] AB: 5a; *Ispak Kar-esk* AB: 222; *gorra emez a'n Kar-esk* AB: 224; *Karesk, Exeter City* Borlase 394.

karg [carg] 'load, burden': GKK says this is a recent coinage taken from Nance (1938) but is otherwise unattested. This is incorrect: *Ha rag hedda an karg a kodhaz uarnav* AB: 222.

karoli [caroly] 'to dance': GKK says the word is unattested. This is incorrect: *C[ornish] Korolli* glossing *To Dance* AB: 274c.

kav [caf] 'cave': GKK says the word is confined to a single instance in BM. This is incorrect: *in caff oma rebon ny* BM 3906; *an dragon vrays us in caff* BM 3965.

kegis [kegys] 'hemlock; umbellifer': GKK says that the word is confined to a single instance in Lhuyd. This is incorrect: *W. Kegid, Hemlock; Corn. Kegaz* AB: 16b; *W. Kegid, Hemlock; C. Kegaz* AB: 28a; *Kegaz* glossing *Cicuta, Hemlock* AB: 47c.

Keltek [Keltek] 'Celtic': GKK says this word is a modern neologism taken from Nance's 1938 dictionary. This is incorrect: *ger-levar Ladin ha Keltek* AB: 223.

kelynenn [kelynen] '(single) holly tree': GKK says the singular is not attested. This is incorrect: *Kelinen, Holly* AB: 241c.

Kembra [Kembra] 'Wales': GKK says this word is confined to a single example in Late Cornish. This is incorrect: *pednzhivikio Kembra* AB: 222; *en Kembra* AB: 222; *Tiz Kimbra* AB: 222; *Tiz Kembra* AB: 223; *adhorton nei Tiz Kembra* AB: 223; *Tiz Guenez Kembra* AB: 223; *en Kembra* AB: 224.

Kembryon [Kembryon] 'Welshmen': GKK suggests that this, the plural of *Kembro*, is confined to 2-3 instances in Late Cornish. This is incorrect: *ha an Kembreeanz ha an Curnowean* BF: 29; *drel an*

Kembreean BF: 31; *Brethonek **Kembrian*** AB: 222; *Tavaz **Kembrian*** AB: 222; *e gerlevran **Kembrian*** AB: 222; *den veth **Kembrian*** AB: 223; *mar peva e **Kembrian*** AB: 223; *e 'erlevar **Kembrian*** AB: 223; *re **Kembrian*** AB: 223; *Dialek **Kembrian*** AB: 223; *liaz pednzhevik **Kembrian*** AB: 224; ***Kembrion**, The Welsh* AB: 242c

kemmynn [kemmyn] 'legacy, testament': GKK says this word is not attested anywhere in the texts but has taken instead from Nance's 1938 dictionary. This is incorrect: *An **gymmyn** ma Luther a leverys* TH 50a, where it appears to be feminine.

kemmynna [kemmynna, kemmyn] 'to bequeath': GKK says this verb is confined to a single instance in CW. This is incorrect: *ov map gruaff the **kemynna** BM 503, me a gemen* BM 1263; *the'n re na neb a wrussens **kymmyn** an egglos* TH 37.

kendon [kendon] 'debt': GKK says this word is confined to a single instance in Lhuyd. This is incorrect: *Dho bos en **kyndan*** glossing *Debeo* AB: 53c; ***Kyndan*** glossing *Debitum* AB: 53c; *bos mer an **gyndan** uarnav* AB: 222; *Ni vedn e nevra dos vez a **gyndan*** AB: 230a-c

Kernewek [Kernowek] 'Cornish': GKK states that this word is not attested in Middle Cornish. This is incorrect. The first attestation of the word is as *Cornowok* from 1572 (Wakelin: 89; LAM: 268). Since George dates Late Cornish from 1575-1800, *Kernewek* [Kernowek] should be considered Middle Cornish.

kesen, pl. **kesow** 'turf': this word is cited as ***kezan [pl. kezau]*** by Lhuyd s.v. *Caespes* AB: 45b. It appears to be wanting in GKK.

kesson [kesson] 'consonant; harmonious': GKK distinguishes the adjective *kesson* 'harmonious' from the noun *kessonenn* 'consonant'. Neither is attested according to GKK. This is incorrect, since Lhuyd uses the first as a noun: *an re Kernuak a kuitha an **Kessonnyo** hedda* AB: 223.

keth [keth] 'servile, base; dependent': GKK claims that this word is confined to two instances in OCV. This is incorrect: *an iovl **keth*** BM 159; *ol the varogyen **keth*** BM 2433. Nance translates *marogyen **keth*** as 'liege knights.'

keus [cues] 'cheese': GKK says that this word is attested only three times in Cornish. This is incorrect: ***caus*** and ***cos*** glossing *caseus* [cheese] OCV; *W. **Kaus**, Cheese; Corn **Kez*** AB: 14c; *Caseus . . . Cheese; C. **Kez*** AB: 46c; ***Kez**, Cheese; Caseus* AB: 241a; *Ez **Kez**? ez, po neg ez; ma sez **kez**, Dro **kez**; po negez **Kez**, dro peth ez* Pryce, F f; *a **kes** glas, out of green cheese* Borlase 376.

kewargh [kewargh] 'hemp': GKK says this word is confined to a single instance in Lhuyd. This is incorrect: *W. **Kyuarx**, Hemp; Corn. **Kuer***

AB: 12a; **Kuer** glossing *Cannabis, Hemp* AB: 46a; **Kuer** glossing *CANNABIS* AB: 291.

klamder [clamder] 'faintness, swoon': GKK says this word is confined to the two instances PC 2593 and TH 7. This is doubly incorrect. In the first place there are two occurrences (not one occurrence) at TH 7: *an flowre a **glomder*** and *eff a **clomder** hag a in kerth*. In the second place, both forms in TH are the third person singular of the present-future of the verb *clamdera* 'to faint'; neither is a noun as stated in GKK.

klerhe [clerhe] 'clear, brighten': GKK says this verb is unattested in the texts and has been taken from Nance (1938). This is incorrect: *hagys lagasow a vith **clerys** ha why a vith kepar ha duow* 'and your eyes will be brightened and you will be like gods' TH 3a.

kloesya [clojya] 'to harrow': GKK says that this word has been taken from Nance (1938), being unattested in the texts. This is incorrect: *Dho **klodzha*** glossing *Occo, To harrow, to break the clods in a plough'd field* AB: 104c.

*klos [clos] 'close, closely': GKK includes the noun **klos** 'enclosure, close, precinct' which is not attested. It omits the adjective/adverb **clos** 'close; closely' which is well attested in the texts: *the'n beth men yv **clos*** RD 389; *degeys an darasov **cloys*** BM 1728; *aban oma **close** entrys* CW 529; *agen prevetta pur **glose*** CW 859.

knowenn [knofen] 'nut': GKK says this word is confined to a single instance in Lhuyd. This is incorrect: *W. Kneyen, A Nut, Corn. **Kynyphan*** AB: 8c; *Guedhan **knyfan*** glossing *Corylus, An hasle-tree* AB: 51c; **Kynyphan** *frenk* glossing *Juglans, A Wall-nut* AB: 74a; **Kynyfan** glossing *Nux, a nut* AB: 101a.

knyv [knew] 'fleece': GKK says this word is confined to a single instance in TH (i.e. TH 23). This is incorrect. Lhuyd gives **Kneu** *glan* glossing *Vellus* 'a fleece of wool' AB: 170c.

knyvyas [knyvyas] 'to shear': GKK says this verb is confined to a single instance in Lhuyd. This is incorrect: *the vos **knevys** y knew the ves* TH 23.

kober [cober] 'copper': GKK says this word occurs is confined to a single instance each in OCV and Lhuyd. This is incorrect. I have noted the following instances in Late Cornish: *Corn. **Kober**, Copper* AB: 21b; *Brest, **Kober*** glossing *Aes, Brass, Copper* AB: 41c; **Kober** glossing *Cuprum, Copper* AB: 53a; *Copper C[ornish]* **Kober** AB: 274b; *Wheal **cober**, a copper work* Pryce, opposite B b 2.

koen [con] 'supper': GKK says this is confined to a single instance in Lhuyd. This is incorrect: *crist worth an **goyn** a warnyas* PA 42c; *bener re gyffy the **con*** BM 1020.

koer [cor] 'wax': GKK says this word is confined to one instance each in OCV and PC 2723. This is incorrect, since Lhuyd cites the word more than once and it is also cited by Borlase: *W. Kuyr, Wax; Corn Kor* AB: 18a; *C. Kor, †koir* glossing *Cera* AB: 47b; *Corgwenyn Bees-wax* Borlase 382.

kofer [cofyr] 'coffer, strong-box': GKK says this word is confined to 2 instances in Lhuyd. This is incorrect: *in ov cofyr sur gorys* BM 3643.

kog [cog] 'cuckoo': GKK says this is confined to two instances (i.e. PC 2890 and Lhuyd 52c). This is incorrect: *Kog, A cuckoo* AB: 241b; *Ma an Gog a'n Luar wartha* from the Ustick MSS.

kommen [comen] 'common': GKK asserts that this adjective occurs only in the phrase *comen voys* BM 2710. This is incorrect: *not commyn the vab den* TH 5; *commine la a nature* TH 14a; *in agyn comyn talke* TH 21a; *an common welth* TH 25, 26; *yn common welth* TH 40a; *yn agan commyn eyth* TH 57a; *eth ew commyn trade* TH 57a; *rag common bara ha dewas* SA 63a.

konfondya [confundya] 'to confound': GKK says the word is confined to a single instance in TH. This is incorrect: *dretho a veth confundijs* BM 2033.

konsekratya [consecratya] 'to consecrate': GKK says this word is confined to a single instance in BM. This is incorrect: *may halla an nenaf bos consecratis* SA 60a; *Rag henna tha orybe gee: nyng o corf Christ kyns ef the vos consecratis, bus osa the vos consecratis me a laver the gee, eth ew lymmen corf agen Arluth Jesu Christ* SA 62; *an bois the vos consecratis* SA 63; *Kyns an bara the vos consecratis ith thew bara* SA 62; *ny pan vo va consecratis* SA 63a.

konsevya [concevya] 'to conceive': GKK asserts that the word is confined to a single instance in TH. This is incorrect: *bones flogh vyth concevijs* BM 846; *concevijs y fue the guir* BM 859; *an map a fue concevijs* BM 887; *conceyvys yn mostethes* TH 7; *me a ve conceviis* TH 8a; *conceviis secretly* TH 28; *concevya anger* TH 28a.

kontentya [contentya] 'to content': GKK says this is confined to a single instance in CW. This is incorrect: *satisfies ha contentys gans mab den* TH 10a.

kornhwilenn [cornwhylen] 'lapwing': GKK says that the plural of this word is unattested outside place-names and alludes to Padel. GKK does not mention the occurrence of the name in 'Jowan Chy an Horth': Lhuyd writes *dho Kuz karn na huìla en Borrian* at JCH¶ 37 (AB: 253a). Nance renders this *dhe Gos Kernwhyly yn Beryan* 'to Cotnewilly Wood [the wood of the desolate place; lit. of the lapwings] in Buryan' CFA: 45.

kortesi [cortesy] 'courtesy': GKK says this word is confined to a single instance in CW (i.e. *in* **curtessye** CW 763). This is incorrect: *mar luen oys a* **corteysy** BM 299.

kosel [cosel] 'quiet, peaceful': GKK claims that this word is confined to two examples, one each in BM and Lhuyd. This is incorrect: *Cosel my re bowesas* OM 2073; *purguir sevel in* **cosel** BM 2426; *Kozal* glossing *Piger, Slow, slothfull, etc.* AB: 120b; *Kuzal* glossing *Serenus, Clear, quiet, etc.* AB: 149a; *cosel, softly, quietly* Pryce; *Cusal ha teg, sirra wheage, Moaz pell* Pryce, F f.

kost [cost] 'coast': GKK says this word is taken from Nance (1938) and is otherwise unattested. This is incorrect: *py* **cost** *yma trygys* OM 1552; *Jhesus a theth then* **costes** *a Cesarye Philippi* TH 43a; *eff a gemeras owne a drega na fella in* **cost** *na* TH 46a.

kostenn [costen] 'shield, target': GKK says that this word is confined to a single instance in Lhuyd. This is incorrect: *Kostan* glossing *Clypeus, A shield, buckler or target* AB: 48a; *Kostan* glossing *Parma, A little round shield, target or buckler* AB: 113b; *Kostan* glossing *Scutum, A buckler, a shield, a target, a scutcheon* AB: 147a; *C[ornish]* **Kostan** glossing *SCUTUM* AB: 297a; *Komero' gostanow, marhow, ha kledhow* LAM: 232.

kowl [cowl] 'soup': GKK says this word is confined to OCV. This is incorrect: *bynytha ny efyth* **coul** OM 2701; *bynytha na effo* **coul** PC 1610; *the guthel* **covle** BM 2392; *As Evos* **kowl**, *Sup up your broth; for Evough agos* **kowl** AB: 231c; *Kaul, Broth from Caulis* AB: 241a.

kowsesyow [cowsesow, cowsejyow] abstract pl. 'heart, conscience': GKK says the word is confined to a single instance in BM. This is incorrect: *na dreyle y* **gousesow** PC 885.

krakkya [crackya] 'to crack': GKK says this word is confined to two instances in PA (i.e. PA 139a and 164b). This is incorrect: *ran a* **crakkyas** BM: 1582.

krambla [crambla] 'to climb': GKK says this verb is confined to one occurrence in Lhuyd. This is incorrect: *Dho* **grambla** glossing *Ascendo, To Climb, to Ascend* AB: 43c; *Dho* **grambla** glossing *Scando, To mount, to climb or get up* AB: 145b.

kreghyn [crehyn] pl. 'skins': GKK says this, the plural of *kroghen* [crohen] 'skin', is confined to a single instance in CW (i.e. line 1477). This is incorrect: *fatell rons y dos in* **crehyn** *devas* TH 19a.

kreupya [cruppya] 'to creep': GKK says that this word is confined to one instance in CW. This is incorrect: *a wra* **cruppya** *ha slynckya* CW 912-13; *me a vyn dallath* **cruppya** *ha slyncya* CW 923-24.

krevhe [crefhe] 'to strengthen': GKK says this verb is confined to a single instance from Nicholas Boson. This is incorrect: *A ra* **creffe**

an collonow TH 52; *sertifyes* (*vel* **crefeis**) TH 56; *the* **creffe** *agen corfow* SA 63a.

kria [crya] 'to cry': GKK says this verb is confined to a single instance in the *Ordinalia*. This is incorrect: *ov* **crye** OM 1418; *ha mercy* **crye** PC 2062; *ow* **crye** PC 2242; *the* **crye** PC 2249; *warbarth ol sur* **crye** PC 2475; **cryeugh** *fast* PC 2477; *pup ol ese ow* **crye** PC 3127; *ymons ow* **crye** RD 2304; *mar* **creya** *war crist* BM 617; **cryaff** *warnogh* BM 1047; *agen* **creya** BM 1531; *war crist y* **creya** BM 1816; *ha* **creya** *pup vr* BM 1825; *na ve* **creya** *warnogh why* BM 2169; *am* **creya** *vy* BM 3620; *ny a* **cry** BM 3961; *mercy* **creyays** BM 4432; **crya** *mercy* TH 9a; *ow* **crya** *out* TH 40a; **creiez** *chei a Horr* BF: 15; *Adam a* **gryaze** RC 23: 185; *e* **griaz** *thonze* RC 23: 192; **kreiez** *en Ladin* AB: 223.

kribenn [cryben] 'comb': GKK says this word is confined to a single instance in Lhuyd. This is incorrect: *W*. **Krib**, *A Comb; Corn*. **Kriban**: **Kriban** *kuliog, a Cock's Comb* AB: 13c; **Kriban** *glossing Crista, A crest* AB: 52b; **Kriban** *mel glossing Favus, A honey-comb* AB: 59a; **Kriban**, *A birds crest* AB: 240c.

kristonya [crystonya] 'to christen': GKK says this verb is not attested in the texts but has been taken from Nance's 1955 dictionary. This is incorrect: *an re na a throlla an flehis the vos besitthis ha* **cristonys** TH 37a.

kriv [cryf] 'raw, unripe': GKK says this word is derived from Cornish English dialect, since it is not attested in the texts. This is incorrect: *Bara ew trylys theworth ann eyl elyment th'e gela rag an vosan ny mar gwan ow kemeras skruth tha thybbry kygg* **kreff** 'bread is converted from one element to another because we are so weak as to shudder at eating raw flesh' SA 66a; **Kriv** *glossing Crudus, Crude [or cold] raw; green or new made; unripe* AB: 52c; **Criv**, *crude, raw* Pryce.

kroenek [cronek] 'toad': GKK says this word occurs between 4-9 times. This is incorrect: **croinoc** *glossing rubeta* [toad] OCV 619; *may zo gweth agis* **cronek** PA 47d; *gans* **cronek** *dv* OM 1778; *the weth vythons the'n* **cronek** PC 2732; *Latin. Rana, Corn*. **Kranag**, *A Frog* AB: 9b; *Corn*. **Kranag**, *A Frog* AB: 11c; *C*. **Cranag**, *Rana* AB: 33a; **Kranag** *diu glossing Bufo, A Toad* AB: 45a; *Kuilken,* **kranag** *melyn; pedn diu.* †*Guilskin,* †**kroniok** *glossing Rana, A frog, a paddock* AB: 136b; **Kranag**, *A frog or toad*; AB: 240c; *C[ornish]* **K-ranag** *glossing A Frog* AB: 277a; **Croinoc**, *a Land Toad* . . . **Cronek**, *id.* Borlase 382.

krommenn [cromman] 'sickle, hook': GKK says this word is confined to a single occurrence in Lhuyd. This is incorrect: *Krymman, A Hook; Corn*. **Krobman** AB: 9b; **krobman** . . . **kromman** AB: 223;

Krobman, *a Hook* Borlase 396. According to Gendall Gwavas gives *crobman ithen*.

kronk, -ys [cronk, -ys] 'blow': according to GKK the word unattested in the texts. This is incorrect: *eff a suffras ragan ny lyas rebuk, keffrys cronkys ha'n moyha cruell myrnans* TH 24.

kropya [cropya] 'to penetrate': GKK claims that this word is confined to a single instance each in PA and CW. This is incorrect: *ha dreyn lym ha scharp ynne a grup bys yn empynyon* PC 2119-20.

krothek [crothak] 'big-bellied': GKK spells says this word is not attested. This is incorrect: *te foole crothacke* 'you big-bellied fool' CW 1105.

kroust [crowst] 'picnic lunch': GKK says this word is confined to the *Ordinalia* and Lhuyd and occurs 2-3 times in all. This is incorrect: *kemeres croust hag eve* OM 1901; *Krust* glossing *Merenda, A beaver or afternoons nuncheon* AB: 89b; *Crwst, Eating between Meals* Borlase 382; *Krust, An Afternoon's Luncheon* Borlase 396; *Croust, an afternoon's nuncheon; a beaver* Pryce; *croust, the afternoon's refreshment* Wiliam Bottrell (quoted in LAM: 328).

krowsvaner [crowsvaner] 'banner with cross': GKK says that this word is not attested in the texts. This is incorrect: *ganso del fethas yn cas worth crousbaner* RD 579-80.

krowsya [crowsya] 'to crucify': GKK says this verb is confined to 2-3 instances in the *Ordinalia*. This is incorrect: *rag an keth re ren crowse* PA 185b; *rag bos Ihesus crist crowsys* PA 189c; *crousyough ef* PC 2166; *the'th crousye* PC 2184; *agas myghtern crousys* PC 2360; *bos crousys* PC 2390; *may fo an ihesu crousys* PC 2478; *ha crous ihesu an fals guas* PC 2486; *may fo crousys* PC 2504; *pren th'y crousye* PC 2535; *kepar hag ef on crousys* PC 2900; *a fue crousys* RD 737; *the vos crowsyys* TH 47.

kryjyans [crejyans] 'faith, belief': GKK criticizes Nance for taking this word to be feminine and cites the line *helma ov cregyans yth yv* BM 838 as proof that the word is masculine. As contrary evidence one might cite *mar tregowhe in gregyans na* CW 176. It is true that most words in *-ans* are masculine, but is quite likely that *crejyans* in some forms of Cornish had attracted to itself the gender of *feth, fyth* 'faith'.

krytyk [crytyk] 'critic': GKK says this word is unattested and has been taken from Nance (1955). This is incorrect: *ha frederyanz an Creteco ha'n Koth-skreferyon* 'and the opinion of the critics and the historians' AB: 224.

kulyek-kenys [culyek-kenys] '*cock-crow': GKK says that this term means 'cock-crow' but is not attested in the texts, being taken from Nance's 1938 dictionary. This is doubly incorrect. The phrase is attested but has been misunderstood. (Nance gives *culyek-kenys* 'cock-crow' without an asterisk, implying that the term is attested). Jesus says to Peter at the last supper: *peder, me a leuer thy's kyns ys bos **kullyek kenys** terguyth y wregh ov naghe* PC 901-3. *Kenys* here is not a noun, but the verbal adjective *kenys* of *cana* used actively. One should translate: 'Peter, I say unto thee: before that the cock shall have crowed, three times thou shalt deny me.' The active use of the verbal adjective is common in Middle Cornish, particularly with *devethys* 'come', *gyllys* 'gone', *cothys* 'fallen', etc.

kuruna [curuna] 'to crown': GKK says this verb is confined to 2-3 occurrences in Middle Cornish. This is incorrect: *te yw mygtern **cvrvnys*** PA 136c; *gans spern **curunys*** PA 165b; *salmon ov map **koroneugh*** OM 2347; *may hallo bos **kerenys*** OM 2374; *ha **kerenys** a ver dermyn* OM 2381; *whare myghtern **kervnys*** OM 2391; *rag why thu'm **kerune*** OM 2398; *guregh y **curene*** PC 2064; *me a vyn y **curune*** PC 2116; *nowyth **curunys*** PC 2124; *emperour **curunys*** BM 2515; *gans curen sperne **curuneys*** BM 3037.

kusulya [cusulya] 'to advise': GKK's attestation code suggests that this verb is attested in Middle Cornish only. This is incorrect. The word occurs in CW: *ny vynsan theth **cossylya*** CW 670; *hag a'the **cossyllyas*** CW 771.

kykesow [kekesow] 'Cornish heath (*Erica vagans*)': this word survived in Cornish dialect as *kekezza*. GKK says must be a late form, since *-k-* is not Cornish. GKK is mistaken. *Kekesow* is almost certainly in origin two words. The second element I take to be *kesow* 'turf'. The first element may be *cuf* 'dear one' or *cugh* 'hood'. Most probably, however, it is *clegh* 'bells' and **clegh kesow* 'bells of the turf' has been simplified (probably in English dialect) to *ke' kesow*. With the name cf. the vernacular term for *Erica cinerea* i.e. 'bell-heather'. **Kekesow** is not a 'late form', but rather a noun phrase.

kystven [kystven] 'stone coffin': GKK correctly says this word is from Borlase. The dictionary suggests incorrectly that it occurs once only. The word in the form **Kist-vaen** is used by Borlase on pp. 151, 182, 197 x 3, 214 x 2, 217 and 218 x 5.

lafyl [lafyl] 'lawful': GKK says that this word is confined to a single occurrence at BM 3401 [*recte* 4301]. This is incorrect: *an pith nag o ragan **leafull*** TH 10; *an pith a rella desyrya theworta **lafull*** TH 39a; *nyns ew **lawfull** folysly the wull resystens* TH 50a.

latimer [latymer] 'translator': GKK says this word is a modern neologism taken from Nance's 1938 dictionary. This is incorrect, since William Hals (1655-1737?) of Ventongimps wrote a Cornish vocabulary variously called *An **Ladymer** ay Kernow, An **Latimer***

ay Kernou or *An* **Lhadymer** *ay Kernou*, which is now in the National Library of Wales (see Ellis: 105-6). Edward Lhuyd refers to **Latimer** *ay Kernow* in one of his letters ('I am very glad the Cornish Latimar goes on' LAM: 302). Cf. Jenner's comments in his discussion of the Bilbao MS, where he suggests that Hals made up the word *Ladymer* from Welsh *Lladmer*.

lemmel [lemmel] 'to leap': GKK says that the word is confined to a single occurrence in Lhuyd. This is incorrect: *Dho* **lebmal** glossing *Salio, To leap, dance, hop, etc.* AB: 143c; *Dho* **lebmal** glossing Salto *To dance, hop or skip* AB: 143c; †*lemal, To leap, now* **Lebmal** AB: 231b; †**Lemmel** †*lebmal, To leap* AB: 245b; *reys yw meeras dueth, ken* **lemmel** *uneth* Scawen MSS. Notice also *driz***lebmal** AB: 222 and cf. *Driz-lebmal* Pryce.

leswedh [lejer] 'frying pan': GKK claims that this word is confined to a single instance in Lhuyd. This is incorrect. There are two instances in Lhuyd, one at AB: 61c where **Letshar** glosses *Frixorium; A frying-pan* and the other at AB: 144 where **Letshar** glosses *Sartago, A frying-pan.* The etymology is uncertain. Perhaps we should spell the word **lecher*.

leveryans [leveryans] 'pronunciation': GKK says that the singular of this word is unattested. This is incorrect: *uar lerh* **Laveryanz** *an Termen nei* AB: 223; *ha aban yu an* **laveryanz** *anydha,* **laverryanz** *kergorryz* AB: 223; *Enradn rag bos an* **laveryanz** *anydha hedh lauer* AB: 223; *uel an* **laveryanz** *ney ha* **laveryanz** *Tiz Lezou* AB: 223.

lieskweyth [lyesgweyth] 'many times': GKK says this word comes from Nance (1952) since it is not attested in the texts. This is incorrect: *lyes guyth me re bysys* PC 884; *mes company* **leasgwyth** *a bub beast* CW 1673. The word is already in Nance (1938), where he cites PC as his source.

Lostwydhyel [Lostwydhyel] 'Lostwithiel': GKK says the toponym is confined to a single reference in BM. This is incorrect. The name occurs not in BM, but in OM: **lostuthyel** *ha lanerchy* OM 2400.

Loundres [Loundres] 'London': according to GKK this place-name is confined to between two and three instances in the texts. This is incorrect: *Pes myllder eus alemma de* **Londres** Borde; *Senezeriou Pou Kernou en* **Loundrez** AB: 222; *Leverva Cotten en* **Loundrez** AB: 222; *reb vor* **Loundres** *Tur* BF: 58; *Mee rese mos tha* **Loundres** *mes a thorow* Bilbao MS; *an Tempel K'res en* **Loundres** Gwavas (in LAM: 238); *an tiz a* **Loundrez** *a credgi boz gwir* Gwavas (quoted in Ellis: 96).

lughesenn [luhesen] 'lightning': GKK says the word is confined to a single occurrence in BM. I am unable to find the example in BM, but have noted one instance at RD 293: *th'y lesky vn* **luhesen**.

luk [luck] 'luck; enough': GKK says this is both a noun meaning 'luck' and an adjective meaning 'enough'. It not an adjective, but an adverb. Curiously GKK, without specifying which sense is involved, says that the word is confined to a single occurrence in Lhuyd. This is incorrect. The adverb is common in Late Cornish: *Satis . . . sufficiently, enough. C.* **Lyk,** *laur* AB: 144c; *The Adverbs* **Lyk** *and Laur or laver [enough] are placed contrary to what we use, after the Noun: . . . They say Pysgoz* **lyk** *and pysgoz laver* AB: 248c; **Lyk** *laur and lauer, Enough* AB: 249a; *Ha skienz* **lyk** *en Tavaz Pou* BF: 46; *Eu an bara pebes* **luck**? Pryce, opposite F f 2; *Ese leath* **luck** *gen veu?* Pryce, F f 2. I can find only one example of the noun: *ma kalliz* **luk** *dha nei* BF: 18.

lymma [lemma] 'to sharpen, to whet': GKK says this word derives from Nance (1938) being unattested in the texts. This is incorrect: *gans ow boell nowyth* **lemmys** CW 2282; *Dho* **lebma** glossing *Acuo, To Whet or Sharpen* AB; 41b.

lytherenn [lytheren] 'letter': GKK says this word is confined to two occurrences, one in OCV and one in Pryce. This is incorrect: *gorra an* **litheren** *b, arag an* **litheren** *m* AB: 223; *gorra an* **letheren** *d, arag an* **letheren** *n* AB: 223; *gorra an* **letheren** *d arag s* AB: 223; *an uynyn* **letheren** *g* AB: 223; *an* **letheren** *t, rag ch* AB: 223; *an* **letheren** *t, rag s* AB: 223. Lhuyd's plural is not **lytherennow** but **lytherow**: *Litera . . . a letter in a book; a bill or scroll; ones hand writing C* †**Litheren** *plur. Litherou* AB: 80b; *ter* **lethero** *kessonyz an deau Davadzheth ma* AB: 223.

mayn [mayn] 'means': GKK says that this word is confined to one example each in PA and BM. This is incorrect: **mayn** *yntreze a ve gurys* PA 8c; **meen** *drethon a veth kefys* BM 1406; *an* **mean** *vs intra du ha den* TH 11; **mean** *a vova gothvethis* TH 50a.

melyn [melen] 'yellow': GKK cites this word as an adjective. It omits to mention that the word is also used as a noun: **Melyn** *oi* glossing *Vitellus, The yolk of an egg* AB: 175a; **Melyn-oi** *yellow of an egg* Borlase 399. Nance (1938: 107) has *melen-oy* 'egg yolk'.

menyster [menyster] 'minister': GKK says that neither the singular nor the plural is attested, both being taken from Nance (1938). This is incorrect: *obedyens res thyn* **minister** TH 42a; *an re na a ve in* **ministers** *in egglos a Crist* TH 41a; *appoyntya the vos pen* **ministers** *war oll y misteris* TH 52a; *the vos* **mynisters** *a'n kythsame sacrament benegas ma* TH 52a.

menystra [menystra] 'to administer': GKK says that this word is confined to a single occurrence at BM 523. This is incorrect: *han* *sacrements vii kefris gol ha guyth* **menystrys** *wose helma* BM 997-9; *the wull an obereth a* **mynystra** *rag edyfya an corfe a Crist* TH 42.

meri [mery] 'merry': GKK says the word is confined to one instance each in OM and BM. This is incorrect: *ny a yl bos fest* **mery** OM 2466; *bethugh* **mery** BM 292; *maga fery avel hok* BM 1901; *bos pur* **very** CW 601; *bos pur* **verry** CW 692.

merk [merk, mark] 'mark': GKK says the plural **merkyow* occurs in TH. This is incorrect and appears to be the result of misreading the second plural imperative of *merkya, markya* 'notice' (see next note).

merkya [merkya, markya] 'to mark': GKK says this verb is confined to TH, where it is attested 2-3 times. This is incorrect on both counts: *Rag the* **verkye** *me a gura* OM 602; *avel wy* **mark** *attahy* 'like an egg, behold her, look!' BM: 3953; *lemmyn* **merkyow** TH 1a; **markyow** *in ta* TH 6; **merkyow** *an exampill ma* TH 6a; **merkyow** *gyrryow crist* TH 27a; **markyow** *pandr' egy* TH 32; **merkya**, *notya, ha done in keth* TH 34a; *mar menogh* **merkya** TH 38a; *the vos* **merkyys** TH 52a; **merkyow** *pan dra* TH 53; *ow mabe* **merke** *an gyrryow ma* CW 1952; *Mi ryg***markia** AB: 223; *gerrio-ma* **markyz** AB: 223.

Meryasek 'Meriasek': GKK says the name is confined to Middle Cornish. This is incorrect: *adro an vledhan 388 dadn Kenan* **Meriazhek** AB: 224. In the forms *Maerrasicks, Merrasickers, Moragicks, Mearagaks, Merry-geeks* and *Mera-jacks* it also survived in Cornish English (Williams 1990: 255). This is not mentioned by GKK.

methek [methek] 'ashamed': GKK says the word is confined to a single instance in TH. This is incorrect: *Myterne Davith o* **methek** *rag y pehosow* TH 8a; *nyns o ef* **methek** *the confessia* TH 8a; *na esow ny the vos* **methek** *the confessia an stat* TH 9a; *Ha na esow ny the vos* **methek** *the confessia nag ony* TH 9a; *na esow ny the vos* **methek** *the confessia agan foly* TH 9a; *bos* **methek** *ha kemeras sham* TH 29a.

Meurth [Merth] 'Tuesday; March; Mars': GKK that this word is confined to a single instance in Lhuyd. This is incorrect: *W. Dydh Maurth, Tuesday; Corn. De* **Merh** AB: 14c; *tuesday . . . C. De* **merh** AB: 54c; *De***mer**, *Tuesday* Borlase 383b; *De* **Merh**, *Tuesday* Pryce, opposite N 2.

milweyth [mylweyth] 'a thousand times': GKK says that this word has been taken from Nance (1938), since it is unattested in the texts. This is incorrect: *me re'n cusullyes* **mylwyth** PC 1811; *wolcom* **myl-wyth** *yn ow hel* PC 937; *Theth dewov try* **mylwyth** *fy* BM 915; *thys* **mylwyth** *ha ze crist fy* BM 1229; *fy* **mylwyth** *then crustunyon* BM 3510; **mylwyth** *in nos* BM 4452; *Ha* **mylwyth** *purguir in geth*

BM 4455; **Miluyth**, *A thousand times* AB: 248c. Cf. **Miluith**, *a thousand times* Pryce.

mingow [myngow] 'with lying mouth': GKK says this word is confined to a single instance in BM. This is incorrect: *an plos* **myngov** BM 2379; *dyso* **myngov** BM 2655.

mis-Ebryl, mis-Est, mis-Genver, mis-Hwevrer [mys Ebrel, mys Est, mys Genver, mys Whevrel] 'April, August, January, February': I have mentioned *mis-Est* above. GKK says all these month names are unattested. This is incorrect. Pryce lists all the months as follows (I omit his English and etymologies) *Mis-GENVER; Mis-HUEVRAL; MIZ-MERH; MIZ-EBRALL; MIZ-ME; MIZ-EPHAN; MIZ-GOREPHAN; MIZ-EAST; MIZ-GUEDN-GALA; MIZ-HEDRA; MIZ-DIU; MIZ-KEVARDHU.* Notice also **Miz ebral** glossing *Aprilis* AB: [4]3b and **Miz Ebral** *Pempas Dydh, sitack canz ha Deg* BF: 46.

mis-Hedra [mys Hedra] 'October': GKK says that this is confined to a single instance in Lhuyd. This is incorrect. It is also in Pryce (see previous note) and in Thomas Boson's hurling-ball inscription: *an Kensa journa a* **messe Heddra** *an Centle* BF: 38.

mis-Metheven [mys Efen] 'June': GKK says the name is confined to a single instance in Lhuyd. This is incorrect: *Ov gol a veth suer in* **mes metheven** BM 4302-3; *C[ornish]* **Efin**, *Junius* AB: 33a; **MIZ-EPHAN** (*June*) Pryce. George adds a note: 'Lhuyd actually wrote *miz ephan*, which may mean the month's name was shortened in LateC, as in colloquial Breton *miz even* for *miz mezheven*.' The compiler is clearly unaware of Lhuyd's *Efin*.

mita, -tys [myta, mytys] 'mite, mites': GKK asserts that this word has been taken from Nance (1938) and is unattested in the texts. This is incorrect: *a ruke offrennia ii* **mittes** SA 64.

miter [myter] 'mitre': GKK says that the singular occurs once in BM and the plural once in OM. This is incorrect. Both instances are singular: *kymmer the* **vytour** *whare* OM 2615; *settyn* **muter** *war y ben* BM 3010.

moen [mun] 'ore': GKK says the word is unattested apart from place-names. This is incorrect. Borlase writes **Mun** (*Mooun, or Moowyn id. W[elsh]*) *any fusible Metal* 400.

mokkya [mockya] 'to mock': GKK says the word is confined to a single instance in TH. This is incorrect: *why ew* **mockys** *gonsa* TH 14a; *seducia ha ga* **mockya** TH 49a;

molas [molas] 'molasses': GKK says this word comes from Nance (1938), being unattested in the texts. This is incorrect. Nance got the word from Borlase; see Nance (1938) s.v. *lollas*.

mollothek [mollothek] 'accursed': GKK says this word is confined to two examples in PA. This is incorrect. The word occurs once only in PA (i.e. at PA 47c). The word does occur twice in BM, however: *ty map molothek* BM 781; *ty yv thymo molothek* BM 2651.

morthol [morthol] 'hammer': GKK says that the singular is confined to a single instance in Lhuyd. This is incorrect: *Morthol* glossing *Malleus, A mallet, a hammer* AB: 84c; *Morthol bian* glossing *Malleolus, A little hammer, a beetle* AB: 84b; *Morthol, a hammer, beetle, or maul* Pryce; *Mortholl, a Hammer* Borlase 400.

morvil [morvyl] 'whale': GKK says recommends the plural **morviles* on the grounds that the plural is unattested in the texts. This is incorrect. The plural is attested: *Morvil, s.m. A whale . . . Pl. morvilow* LCB s.v.; *Ha Dew a wrug an morvilow bras* LCB: 395.

movya [muvya] 'to move': GKK says this word is confined to 2-3 examples in TH. This is incorrect on both counts: *ihesus crist a ve mevijs* PA 4b; *my a vyn kyns es dybarth muvye omma certan tra* BM 259-60; *del ens y moviis* TH 18; *yth yll bos movyes* TH 29a; *ow movya thotha* TH 37a; *thega movya y* TH 44a; *ow movya ve* TH 50.

Moyses [Moyses] 'Moses': GKK says this personal name is confined to a single instance in the *Ordinalia*. This is incorrect: *moyses moyses saf ena* OM 1403; *del lauaraf thy's moyses* OM 1433; *lauer moyses* OM 1443; *py tyller yma moyses* OM 1551; *reys yv thy's gorre moyses* OM 1572; *the geusel sur orth moyses* OM 1583; *moyses me a commond thy's* OM 1585; *gallas moyses ha'y pobel* OM 1627; *moyses thy'so lauara* OM 1645; *dev a erghys thy's moyses* OM 1663; *yma moyses pel gyllys* OM 1682; *dev moyses a wruk hemma* OM 1702; *moyses whek ny a dreha* OM 1715; *moyses del oge den mas* OM 1767; *Ellas moyses ogh tru tru* OM 1777; *moyses mar sos profus lel* OM 1799; *moyses kemer the welen* OM 1841; *moyses sur my re beghas* OM 1863; *a plansas moyses hep mar* OM 1931; *a wruk moyses the planse* OM 1946; *laha moyses thy'm yma* OM 2644; *pur wyr a thalleth moyses* RD 1484; *in tyrmyn moyses* TH 14; *an la a a moyses* TH 14; *a la moyses* TH 26a; *heno an la moyses* TH 27; *in la moyses* TH 27a; *the wetha lais moyses* TH 27a; *folya an la moyses* TH 27a; *in chare moyses* TH 34.

musura [musura] 'to measure': GKK says this verb is confined to a single unnamed occurrence in Middle Cornish. This is incorrect: *musur y trylles* OM 393; *musurough ef yn len* OM 2506; *my a'n musur* OM 2507; *otteve musurys da* OM 2513; *mar len musurys* OM 2550; *may hallo bos musurys* OM 2566; *my re wruk y vusure* OM 2568; *myserough tol th'y thule* PC 2740.

mynn [myn] 'kid': GKK recommends the plural **mynnow*, because the plural is unattested. This is incorrect: *Devas ean gever ha* **menas** *Sheep lambs goats and kids* Bilbao MS.

mysteri [mystery] 'mystery': GKK suggests that this word is confined to a single instance in CW (i.e. CW 2119). This is incorrect: *war oll y* **misteris** TH 52a; *y bos an sacrament ma marvelus worthy* **mystery** TH 52-52a; *i'n* **mystery** *na* TH 52a; *pan veny oll endewis gans an* **mysteris** *benegas ma* SA 60; *eth esan ny o recevia dan an lell* **mystery** *kigg a'y corf benegas* SA 61.

Nadelik [Nadelek] 'Christmas': GKK implies that this word occurs once in Lhuyd and once in Pryce. This is incorrect: *Corn.* **Nedelik** AB: 17a; *C.* **Nadelik**; *Deu* **nadelik** AB: 97a; *Miz-du ken* **Nadelik** Pryce; *Ha Have en Guave terebah* **Nedelack** Ustick MSS. George adds a note: 'Regular development would have given **Nadolyk.*' The original form was **Natālicia*, where the originally unstressed long *ā* would have given *o* in Welsh quite regularly, whence Welsh *Nadolig*. In Cornish and Breton, however, unstressed long *ā* would have given *e* via *æ*?. Lhuyd's *Nadelik* is exactly what one would expect the Cornish form to be. Compare Breton *Nedeleg*. George's note is mistaken.

naswydh [nasweth] 'needle': GKK says this word occurs is confined to 2-3 instances in Middle and Late Cornish together. This is incorrect: *der crov* **nasweth** BM 468; *W. Nodwydh, A Needle; Corn.* **Nadzhedh** AB: 10b; **Nadzhedh** glossing *Acus, A Needle* AB: 41b; *C.* **Nadzhedh** glossing *ACUS* AB: 290a. Lhuyd also writes **nadzha** in his unpublished glossary.

nawves [nawves] 'ninth': GKK says this is confined to Lhuyd where it occurs twice. This is incorrect: **Nauhuas** glossing *Nonus, The ninth* AB: 100a; **Nahuaz**, *The ninth* AB: 243b; **Nawas**, *the ninth* Pryce.

negedhek [negedhek] 'negative': GKK ascribes this modern neologism to J[ulyan] G. H[olmes]. This is incorrect. The word is in both Nance's 1938 dictionary (p. 117) and his 1952 dictionary s.v. *negative* (p. 115).

neythow [neythow] 'nests': GKK says that this plural occurs once in Cornish, i.e. in PA. This is incorrect. The word does not occur in PA, although the verb **nyezy** 'to nest' occurs at PA 206c. The compiler seems indvertently to have repeated the reference to PA in his entry on *neythi* 'to nest' in the discussion of the plural of *neyth*. The plural of *neyth* 'nest' is in fact confined to two instances in Lhuyd: **Neitho**, *Nests* AB: 242c; *Mi 'rig guelaz an Karnou idzha an gullez ha'n idhen mor aral kil y ge* **neitho** AB: 245a.

nivera [nyvera] 'to enumerate': GKK says this verb is confined to one occurrence in PA (i.e. **neuera** *oll y yscren* PA 183c). This is incorrect: *ny yllons bos nyfyrys* OM 1544; *ny yllons bos nyfyrys* RD 558; *Nivera, Reckon or number; Nivyryz, Reckon'd* AB: 248a.

nomber [nomber] 'number': GKK's code {M: 3} means that this word is confined to 4-9 instances in Middle Cornish. This is incorrect on both counts: *cans vyl yn nomber* OM 1614; *numbyr a tremmyl* BM 1516; *heb numbyr* BM 3999; *number a persons* TH 1a; *mar ver in number* TH 8a; *plurel number* TH 8a; *an number an elect* TH 22a; *numbyr bras* TH 31a; *numbyr a lyas* TH 44a; *heb number* CW 1321; *heb number* CW 1990.

offrynna [offrynna] 'to offer, to sacrifice': GKK's code {3} means that this word occurs between 4 and 9 times. This is incorrect: *thotho gvetyeugh offrynne* OM 441; *ny vynnaf offrynne* OM 500; *hag a offryn thy's whare* OM 512; *warnythy my a offryn* OM 1183; *bugh offrynne my a vyn* OM 1185; *my a offryn hep lettye* OM 1194; *goth dek scon my a offryn* OM 1195; *my a offrynn mallart da* OM 1199; *my a offryn scon aral* OM 1205; *y offrynne reys yv thy's* OM 1280; *ow map ysac offrynnys* OM 1287; *rag offrynna* OM 1307; *may fythe gy offrynnys* OM 1327; *offrynnye an keth mols-ma* OM 1384; *offrynnya sur me a vyn* BM 3392; *offrynnyaff pen margh* BM 3400; *me a offren* BM 3407; *me a offren lawen cath* BM 3413; *a ruke offrennia ii mittes* SA 64.

osta [osta] 'thou art': GKK says this form is not attested in Middle Cornish. This is incorrect. It occurs in TH: *benegas osta ge* 'blessed art thou' TH 44.

outray [outray] 'outrage': GKK says this word is unattested. This is incorrect: *Del yw scrifys prest yma adro zynny gans otry* PA 21a, rhyming with *pray* and *joy*. The word should perhaps be spelt <otray>.

oy [oy] 'egg': GKK says the plural of this word is unattested. This is incorrect: *Mathtath drewgh eyo hag amanyn de vi* 'Mayde, brynge me egges and butter' Borde.

palas [palas] 'to dig': GKK says that this verb occurs 2-3 times in Middle and Late Cornish together. This is incorrect: *ty the honyn the balas* OM 345; *the thallath palas* OM 370; *the bales ha the wonys* OM 414; *mos the balas* OM 681; *my a vyn palas* OM 865; *te tha honyn tha ballas* CW 975; *ages tooles tha ballas* CW 982; *me a vyn dallath palas* CW 1033.

panes [panes] 'parsnips': GKK says this form occurs once in Lhuyd. This is incorrect: *S.W. Pannas, Parsnip; Cor. Panez* AB: 14c; *C. & Ar. Panez, S.W. Pannas, Lat. Pastinaca [latifolia]* AB: 33a; *panan [pl. panez]* glossing *Pastinaca, A parsnip, a carrot* AB: 114a. Notice also that GKK arbitrarily changes the attested singular *panen* to **panesenn*. Lhuyd is emphatic that the singular is *panen* (see the citation from AB: 114a above and cf. *panan, A parsnip* AB: 240b.) Nance (1938) gives as singular both **panesen* and *panen*.

paper [paper] 'paper': GKK says that the plural is not attested. This is incorrect: *ny vendzha vesga argrafa an **papyrio** hemma* AB: 222.

parson 'parson': this word occurs in BM: *ser **parson**, bona dyes* BM 1905. It is also attested in place-names: *Lowerth-Lavender-en-**parson*** (Padel: 154). The word is omitted from GKK. Although the dictionary cites *person*, it does not give the specialized sense 'parson' in the entry there. Nance (1952: 124) gives *person* as the Cornish for 'parson'.

paynt [paynt, pent] 'paint': this neologism is credited by GKK to G[raham] S[andercock]. This is incorrect. The word, spelt <pent>, is in Nance (1952: 123).

payntya [payntya, pentya] 'to paint': GKK says that this word has been taken from Nance's 1952 dictionary, since it is not attested in the texts. This is incorrect: *yma S Paul worth agan **payntia** ny in mes in colors in leas tellar in scriptur* TH 7a.

pellder [pellder] 'length of time, distance': GKK says this word is confined to two instances in CW. This is incorrect: *ha pana **peldar** a ruga bewa ena* TH 47a.

Penkast [Pencast] 'Whitsun': GKK says this is confined to a single instance in Lhuyd. This is incorrect on both counts: *war du **fencost** myttyn* TH 44a; *Corn **Pencas**, Whitson-Tide* AB: 20a; *Penkast [Corn.] Pentecoste* AB: 32b-c; *Pentecoste . . . The fiftieth day after Easter, Whitsundtide. C. **Penkast*** AB: 116c; *Penkast, Whitsuntide, Pentecoste* AB: 241a.

pennow-ys [pennow ys] 'ears of corn': GKK says the plural of *penn-ys* [pen ys] 'ear of corn' is unattested. This is incorrect: *we find that we call the Ears of Corn Tyvus, which are term'd by the Armoric Britans Pennou it, by the Cornish **Pednou** is* AB: 267.

perenn [peren] 'pear': GKK says this is confined to a single instance in Lhuyd. This is incorrect: *Per, **peran*** glossing *Pyrum, A pear* AB: 133a; *Guedhan **peran**, †perbren* glossing *Pyrus, A pear tree* ibid.

*perfumya '*to perfume': GKK claims that this word is used by Tregear with the meaning 'to perfume'. This is incorrect. The word in TH is a bad spelling for *performya* 'perform': *kepar dell rug eff nena promysya, in della wosa henna eff a rug y **perfumya*** 'as he then promised, thus thereafter did he perform it' TH 51a.

pervers [pervers] 'setback': GKK says this word is unattested. This is incorrect: *otte vn **purvers** da lemyn wharfethys* OM 882-3.

peswardhegves [peswardhegves] 'fourteenth': GKK says this word is confined to 2-3 occurrences in the Tregear manuscript. This is incorrect. The word does not occur anywhere in the Tregear manuscript. The only examples of the word known to me is *Peswar degvas, the fourteenth* Pryce.

piba [pyba] 'to pipe': GKK says that this verb is confined to Lhuyd. This is incorrect: *menstrels a ras **pebough** whare* OM 2845-6; *now menstrels **pybygh** bysy* RD 2644; *mynstrels growgh theny **peba*** CW 2546.

pilars [pyllars] 'pillars': GKK says the plural of *pyllar* is confined to a single instance in TH. This is incorrect: *principall **pillers*** TH 35a; *an **pillars** ytowns parys* CW 2192.

plagya [plagya] 'to plague, to afflict': GKK's authentication code seems to imply that this verb is confined to a single instance in Late Cornish. This is incorrect: *yma ow leverell fatell rug Du **plagia** cities* TH 53a; *lemyn yth oma **plagys*** CW 1576; *a v[yth] **plagys** creys za ve* CW 1616; ***plages** y fetha ragtha* CW 1642.

plenta [plenta] 'plenty': GKK says this word is attested three times only, i.e. at OM 2247, 2262 and PC 2229. This is incorrect: *yth esa **plentye** a bup kynde* TH 2; ***plenty** a redemcion* TH 10a; *mar **plenty** dysquethys* TH 11; *ha grace ew **plenty** res* TH 28; *ha'n mowyssye lower **plentye*** CW 1455; ***plenty** lower in pur thefry* CW 1497.

pliskenn [plysken] 'shell, husk': GKK says this word is unattested outside Cornish English dialect. This is incorrect. Lhuyd writes: ***Pliskin,** Testa ovi* [eggshell] AB: 163a.

ploumenn [plumen] 'a plum': GKK says this word is confined to a single instance in Lhuyd. This is incorrect: *Mean **plymon** glossing Ossiculum, A little bone; also the stone of a fruit, etc.* AB: 110b; ***Pluman** glossing Prunum, A prune or damson, a plum* AB: 131ab; *Guedhan **pluman,** †plumbren glossing Prunus, A plum-tree* AB: 131b.

pojer [pojer] 'small bowl': GKK says this word is not attested, being known only from dialect. This is incorrect: ***podzhar,** a porringer* Pryce, opposite X; ***Podzher,** a little Dish* Borlase 403.

pokkys [pockys] 'pox': GKK says that this word is confined to a single instance in Lhuyd. This is incorrect: ***Pokkys** Frenk glossing Lues, The pox* AB: 82a; ***Pokkys** miniz glossing Variolae, Measles* AB: 169.

polat [pollat] 'fellow': GKK says that the word is confined to CW. This is incorrect. The word is also attested in 'Jowan Chy an Horth': *an guadn-gyrti genz e **follat** 'the adulterous woman with her paramour'* BF: 18.

porposya [purposya] 'to purpose': GKK says this has been derived from Nance (1955), since it is not attested in the texts. This is incorrect. The word is attested: *a vynna **purposia** na predery the wull* TH 29; *Rag yth off **purposys** dre weras a thu* TH 31; *Ith off ve* *dre weras a thu* **purposys** TH 35. Moreover *porposya* is given s.v. *purpose* in Nance (1952).

porthow [porthow] 'gates': GKK says the plural of *porth* 'gate' is confined to a single instance in PC (i.e. line 3040). This is incorrect: *hag a dorras an* **porzow** PA 212a; *egereugh an* **porthow** RD 98; *rak an* **porthow** *hep dyweth* RD 101; *worto an* **porthow** *ny sef* RD 119; *gallas an* **porthow** *brewyon* RD 126; *kyn fo* **porthov** *neff degeys* BM 1255; *leb es gyi de* **porthow** Pryce.

posseshyon [possessyon] 'possession': GKK says that this word is confined to a single instance in BM. This is incorrect: *nanelle* **possessyon** *an bys* TH 28.

pottya [pottya] 'to put': GKK says that this verb is confined to a single instance at BM 3486. This is incorrect: *eff a* **putt** *then dore* TH 13.

poyntys [poyntys] 'points': GKK says the plural of *poynt* is confined to two instances in CW. This is incorrect: *An kyth sam* **poyntys** TH 34; *in pana* **poyntys** *speciall* TH 36.

poyson [poyson] 'poison': GKK says the word is confined to a single instance in TH. This is incorrect: *an* **poyson** *a serpons* TH 7a; *an* **poyson** *a heresy* TH 42.

prays [prays] 'praise': GKK says that *praysys*, the plural of this noun occurs once in BM. This is incorrect, since **preysys** at BM 2352 is a verbal adjective: *the larchya* **preysys** *fethogh* 'the more you will be praised'.

prederys [prederys] 'worried': GKK says this word was invented by W[ella] B[rown], being unattested in the texts. This is incorrect. Nance (1938: 134) gives *prederüs, prederys* (C. Voc. *priderys*) 'careful, solicitous, anxious'. *Prederys* is in origin the same word as *prederus* (cited by GKK), which carries a similar meaning. Notice also: **Pryderys** glossing *Solicitus, Solicitous, crefull, pensive, troubl'd, busie* AB: 151c; **prederez** *en Kothnanz Tavazo* AB: 222.

prederyans [prederyans] 'opinion': GKK says that the plural is unattested. This is incorrect: *nebez* **brederyanzo** AB: 222.

present 'present' adj.: this word is missing from GKK, even though *presens* and *presentya* are both included (and *presens* is out of alphabetical sequence). *Present* adj. occurs at TH 5, 19a, 26, 34, 37a, 43 and 49. *Present* 'present, gift' occurs at BM 3397, 3402 but does not seem to be included in GKK either.

pris [prys] 'price, value': although the number of occurrences is not given, GKK says that this word is confined to Middle Cornish. This is incorrect. The word is widely attested in Late Cornish: *Price; Corn* **Priz** AB: 30b; *Pretium . . . A price given for a thing that is bought, a reward, a hire, a fee, a bribe. C.* **Priz** AB: 128a; *Pana* **priz** *rag hearne?* **Priz** *dah.* Pryce, opposite F f 2; *nages* **prize** *veeth* *es moase whath ragt'angi* Gwavas (LAM: 238); *rag **prijse** da eu gwell* Gwavas (ibid).

proces 'process': GKK includes the words *procedya* from TH and *processyon* from BM. It does not appear to include *proces* which is attested at TH 43, 46, 49a and 53a x2.

profet [profet] 'prophet': GKK says that this word is confined to instances in TH. This is incorrect, since the word is also attested in Late Cornish: *screffez gen an **prophet** RC 23: 195; *Jerman an **prophet** ibid. 199.

provia [provya] 'to provide': GKK says this verb is confined to 2-3 instances in TH and Lhuyd. This is incorrect: *ware me a **provy** moy* BM 1870; *ef a **provyas** ragan ny* TH 10a; *praga na ruga **provia** rag tra an parna* TH 29; *ha **provya** mariag rag y vab* TH 31; *yma peyke thym **provyes*** CW 2290; ***Pryvia*** glossing *Procuro, To do or solicit another man's business. To Procure* AB: 129b. This is not the same verb as ***pro·vya*** 'offer' at BM 485, 1116, 2880.

provochya 'to provoke': GKK calls this Late C. and correctly cites Lhuyd as the source. It does not mention, however, that the variant *provokya* occurs in TH: *Du a ve **provokys** warbyn an bys* TH 7.

punshya [punsya] 'to punish': GKK says this verb is confined to 4-9 instances in Middle Cornish. This is incorrect on both counts: ***punscie** y tus mar calas* OM 1482; *ef a wra tyn the **punssye*** OM 1527; *genes gy pan os **punsys*** OM 1563; *ty a vyth **punsys*** OM 1600: *correctya ha **punsya** vicys* TH 25; ***punsya** ha correctia* TH 25; *the **punsya** an drog pobill* TH 25; *the **punyssya**, ha correctya* TH 38; *the **punyssya** oll an rena* TH 38; *agan **punyssya*** TH 40a; *gweffa the vos **punyshes*** CW 587.

purkat [purcat] 'pulpit': GKK says this word is confined to a single instance in Lhuyd. This is incorrect: *Rostra . . . A pulpit, a pleading place. C. **Pyrkat** AB; 141c; *Suggestum . . . A chair, a pulpit. C. **Pyrkat** AB: 158a.

pychya 'to stab': GKK asserts that this verb is not attested in the texts and is a modern neologism taken from Nance's 1938 dictionary. This is incorrect: *en gew lym ef a **bechye** pur ewn yn dan an asow* PA 218cd. GKK wrongly puts the form in PA under its own headword. <e> for stressed *y* is common in PA.

pymthegves [pymthegves] 'fifteenth': GKK says the word is not attested. This is incorrect. Pryce writes ***Pemp degvas,** the fifteenth.*

pyseul [pysuel] 'how many': GKK says this word is confined to a single instance in TH. This is incorrect on both counts: ***pesuell** one ny kylmys* TH 11; ***Pysell** defferans* TH 27; ***paseil** moy gallus* SA 62a;

Kynifer, **pezealla** (< *pysuel ha*) glossing *Quot, How many?* AB: 135c.

pystik [pystyk] 'hurt': GKK recommends *pystigow as the plural, no plural being attested in the texts. This is incorrect: *oll sortow clevas ha oll* **pesticks** *mesk an boble* RC 23: 192 (Rowe).

rebuk [rebuk] 'rebuke': GKK suggests that the plural *rebukys* 'rebukes' is confined to a single instance in TH. This is incorrect: *fatell ew kynde an parna an* **rebukys** TH 29a; *ha dre* **rebukys** TH 29a; *han kithsame kende me a* **rebukys** TH 29a.

rebukya 'to rebuke': GKK suggests that this verb is confined to a number of instances in TH. This is incorrect: *Ragon menough* **rebekis** PA 2c; *ena y an* **rebukyas** PA 112a; *ef a ve veyll* **rebukis** PA 156a.

remova [remuvya] 'to remove, to move': GKK says this verb is confined to a single instance in OM. This is incorrect: **remmvys** *the gen tyller* OM 2045; *a fyl aga* **remmvve** OM 2057; *yn certan mar* **remvfe** RD 396.

reperya [reperya] 'to repair': GKK points out that this word is attested in TH and recommends using *ewnhe* instead. This is not very good advice since the word *reperya* in TH is used only in the sense 'repair to, take refuge with': *the thos ha the (the)* **reperya** *thethy* TH 17; *oll an re ew feithfull (po lene a feth) pennagill a vons y, a res assembla po* **reperya** *thethy* TH 48.

repreva [repreva] 'to reprove': GKK says this occurs 2-3 times in Middle Cornish and implies that it is confined to OM and TH. This is incorrect: *pendra wreugh ov* **repryfa** OM 1500; *na* **repreff** *tus vohosek* BM 3120; *why a yll ow* **reprovia** TH 11; *rebukys ha* **reprovys** TH 46a.

resek [resek] 'to run': GKK says *resek* means 'to run for pleasure' whereas *ponya* means 'to run in earnest'. This distinction is difficult to maintain: *whath ny rowns y in ta understondia an scryptur lell mas pub ur* **resak** *pelha ha pelha in error* TH 17a; *nena ny russa den vith* **resak** *in heresy* TH 19a; *Alak, tus vas, ha pell ew mer an bobill* **resys** *hethow in jeth theworth an kithsam rulle ma!* TH 37. Tregear even uses the two words together as synonyms: *lyas onyn a rug* **resak** *ha* **ponya** *in stray* TH 30a.

restorya 'to restore': GKK cites the noun *restoryta* from BM 2178. It fails to mention the verb, however, which is not uncommon: *ha* **restoria** *thymo vy* BM 3594; *thymo* **restoryans** *hy* BM 3778; *drefen nag es* **restorijs** BM 3786; **restorijs** *ov esely* BM 4235; *ov golek thym* **restoryes** BM 4398; *the* **restoria** *mab den* TH 12a.

reyn [rayn] 'reign': GKK says the word is based on Nance's 1955 dictionary since it is unattested in the texts. This is incorrect: *in* *dew[e]tha blethan a* **reign** *an cruell Emperour* TH 47; *an xiii-as a* **reign** *Nero* TH 47.

robbya 'to rob': GKK says this word is attested 2-3 times. This is incorrect: *na vova* **robijs** *in suer* BM 2064; *yth esas ow* **robbya** *sans egglos* TH 14a; *eff a yll* **robbya** *lyas den* TH 25a; *Pan egllossyow a ve* **robbys** TH 40a; *Dho* **robbia** glossing *Depraedor* AB: 54b; **Robbiaz** glossing *Spoliatus, Robb'd* AB: 153c.

rolya [rolya] 'to roll': GKK says this verb, unattested in the texts, has been taken from Nance (1938). The word is spelt <rhullia> by Lhuyd. Both he and Borlase cite the proverb *An men us ow* **rullya** *ny vyn nefra cuntell best* 'A rolling stone gathers no moss' [quoted here from Nance (1938) s.v. **best**].

ronson [raunson] 'ransom': GKK says this word is confined to TH. This is incorrect: *heb* **rawnson** *vetholl na fyne* CW 250. The compiler adds a note: 'The 2nd vowel was nasal in F. and this nasality spread to the 1st vowel in the spelling *raunson* in TH.' I do not understand this. Both vowels were, and indeed are, nasal in French, where the modern spelling is <rançon>. The compiler is perhaps not aware that <raunson> is a common spelling in Middle English.

rosellen 'whirl, whorl': GKK includes the verb **rosella* 'spin, whirl', a neologism taken from Nance's 1938 dictionary. It omits the noun *rosellen* 'whirl', even though the word is cited by Lhuyd: **Rozellen** glossing *Verticula, A whirl for a spindle* AB: 172b.

rudh [rudh] 'red, scarlet': GKK says that apart from place-names this adjective is confined to Old and Middle Cornish where it occurs 4-9 times. I have collected the following examples from Old, Middle and Late Cornish: **rud** glossing *ruber* [red] OCV 486; *the'n mor* **ruyth** OM 1622; *an mor* **ruyth** OM 1635; *queth* **ruth** PC 2127; *mar* **ruth** *the thylles* RD 2512; **ruth** *the thyllas* RD 2529; **ruth** *y couth thy'mmo bones* RD 2535; *dyllas* **ruth** RD 2547; *pur* **ruth** *age myn* BM 3309; **ruth** *gans e gos* SA 60; **Rydh** glossing *Ruber, Red, ruddy* AB: 141c; *Pedn-***rydh**, *Red-hair'd* AB: 142a; *Risk ha reden* **rydh** *[Bark and red Fern]* AB: 229a; **Rydh** glossing *RUBER* AB: 296b; †**Rud**, *Red, now corrupted to* **Rooz**; *pedn* **rooz**, *a red head;* **Rudh, Ruth, Rydh**, *id.* Pryce; **Rydh**, *Red:* **Rydik**, *Reddish* Borlase 405.

rudhek [rudhak] 'robin (*Erithacus rubecula*)': GKK recommends the plural **rudhogyon* devised by K[en] J. G[eorge]. The dictionary is apparently unaware that the plural is already *rudhogas*; see Brian Webb, *Dornlyver Ydhyn* (1984) s.v. Webb's excellent little book is not mentioned in the introduction to GKK and one can only conclude that the compiler was unaware of it. Given that the work was published by Cowethas an Yeth Kernewek, this is a remarkable omission.

rutya [ruttya] 'to rub': GKK says this word is confined to a single instance in Lhuyd. This is incorrect: *Dho **rhittia*** glossing *Frico, to rub, chafe or fret* AB: 61b; *Dho **rhyttia** 'n dha* glossing *Perfrico, To rub all over* AB: 118a.

sabenn [saben]'pine': GKK says this word is confined to 2-3 instances in Lhuyd. This is incorrect: *C. **Zaban**, L. Sapinus* AB: 33a; ***Zaban*** glossing *Abies, A Fir-Tree* AB: 41a; *Aval **zaban*** glossing *Conus, A cone or pine-apple* AB: 51b; *Plankys **zaban**, Deal-boards* AB: 242a; ***Zaban*** glossing *A Fir-tree* AB: 276b; *C[ornish] **Zaban*** glossing *The Pitch tree* AB: 283a; ***Zaban**, a fir tree* Pryce.

Sadorn [sadorn] 'Saturn, Saturday': GKK says this is confined to a single instance in Lhuyd. This is incorrect: *W. **Sadurn**, Saturn; C. **Zadarn*** AB: 30b; *Saturday: De **Zadarn*** AB: 54c; *De **Zadarn*** Pryce; ***Dezadarn*** Borlase 384a.

scavel cronek 'toadstool': GKK omits this neologism although it is in Nance (1938, 1952, 1955) and is used by Caradar: *mos war an bronyon dhe guntell nebes **scavellow-cronek*** (KemK: 39)

selya [selya] 'to seal': GKK says this word is taken from Nance's 1938 dictionary since it is not attested in the texts. This is incorrect: *An kigg ew **selis** may halla an enaf bos defendis* '[caro] signatur ut anima muniatur' SA 60a. GKK believes *selis* to be for **sellys* 'salted' but this is unlikely in view of the Latin *signatur* 'is sealed'.

sens: GKK omits the word *sens* 'sense' which is attested in TH: *an letterall **sens** a la Moyses* TH 26a; *an lell **sens** ha'n understondyng a'n scryptur* TH 36.

sessya [cessya] 'to cease': GKK asserts that this is confined to TH. This is incorrect: *ha homma vyth ny **sestyas*** [read *sescyas* < *cessyas*] *aban duthe yn chy thy's pup ur ol amme thu'm treys* PC 523-5. Sandercock's edition of PC reads *ha homma byth ny **cessyas**, aban dhutha y'n chy dhys, pup ur-oll amma dhe'm treys.*

sesya [sesya] 'to seize': GKK says that this verb is confined to 2-3 instances in Middle Cornish. This is incorrect on both counts: *bethens **sesijs*** BM 972; *praga na ruk y **sesya*** BM 1032; *gene ateve **sesijs*** BM 1886; ***sesyogh** thymmo* BM 3526; *nag onen vyth **sesijs*** BM 3545; *me re ruk sur y **sesia*** BM 3547; *Dho Kymera, dho sindzha, dho **sesia*** glossing *Comprehendo, To take or lay hold on, etc.* AB: 50a.

seytegves [seytegves] 'seventeenth': according to GKK the word is confined to a single instance in TH. This is incorrect. The compiler is probably thinking of *in **xvii-as** sermon* TH 46, which is not an example of *seytegves*. The only real example is **Seith degvas**, *the seventeenth* in Pryce, which GKK does not mention.

seythgweyth [seythgweyth] 'seven times': GKK says this word is unattested. If GKK accepts *vxii-as* as *seytegves* then **vij gwythe** *y wra acquyttya* CW 1537 ought to be accepted as an example of **seythgweyth**.

shakya [shakya] 'to shake': GKK says this verb is confined to 2-3 occurrences. This is incorrect: *aga fen y a* **sackye** PA 195b; *y a* **shaky** *age barvou* BM 2313; **shackys** *ha tossys* TH 30; *kepar ha flehes ow* **shackya** TH 42; *gorah an vose tha* **shakiah** *an kala* Pryce.

sita [cyta] 'city': GKK says that the plural is attested once only, i.e. **cytes** *rych* PC 132. This is incorrect: *fatell rug Du plagia* **cities**, *trevow ha pow* TH 53a. In spite of the Anglicized spelling *cities* in TH is identical with *cytes* in PC.

sitysan [cytysan] 'citizen': GKK says this word was taken from Nance's 1955 dictionary, because the word is unattested in the texts. This is incorrect: *mas yth owhy* **citesens** *gansans an syns* TH 33.

skaldya [scaldya] 'to scald': GKK tells us that this verb is confined to a single instance in the *Ordinalia*. This is incorrect. It does not occur in the *Ordinalia*, but is attested twice in BM: *ny a veth* **skaldys** BM 2107; *ov golyov luen a plos prest ov* **sclaldya** [leg. **scaldya**] BM 3059.

skapya [scappya] 'to escape': GKK says there are only 2-3 occurrences of this verb in Middle and Late Cornish together. This is incorrect: *nyns us* **scapya** OM 1656; *ny wren* **scapye** OM 1706; *na* **scapyo** PC 990; *byth na* **scapye** PC 1888; *mar* **scap** RD 378; *pur wyr ny* **scap** RD 383; *ny* **skap** RD 2019; *byth na* **schapye** RD 2270; *y vos* **scappys** BM 1030; *byth ny* **schappyons** BM 2469; *nyg eas* **scappya** CW 1973.

skavell-droes [scavel dros] 'footstool': GKK says that this expression is confined to a single instance in CW. This is incorrect: *gwregh honora* **scavall** *e dryes* SA 64a; *pandr' ew an* **scavall** *e drys eff* SA 64a; *an grond ew an* **skavall** *ow thrys ve* SA 64a; *rag honora* **scavall** *y drys* SA 64a.

skaw [scaw] 'elder trees': GKK says that this collective plural is unattested. This is incorrect. Polwhele writes: **Scaw** *is still in use for an elder in Cornwall* (quoted in LCB). Cf. **Scao**, *an Elder-tree* Borlase 405.

skentoleth [skentoleth] 'wisdom': GKK says this word, which occurs in the *Ordinalia* and BM, is a short form of '**skiantoleth*'. GKK is apparently unaware that *skyantoleth* is attested: *yma an lyver a* **skyantoleth** *ow remembra thyn* TH 6a.

skiber [skyber] 'barn': GKK says that this word is confined to two instances in PA. This is incorrect: **Skibor** glossing *Horreum, A barn or corn-house* AB: 66a; *Gorah tees en an* **skeber** *tha drushen* Pryce, opposite F f 2.

sklandra [sclandra] 'to offend': GKK says that this verb is confined to a single instance in BM. This is incorrect: *na vo den aral* **sclandrys** PC 743; *pur wyr* **sclandrys** PC 891; *kyn fons y ol* **sclandrys** PC 899; *ov* **sclandra** BM 3747.

skoler [scolar] 'scholar': GKK says this word is confined to a single instance in Lhuyd. This is incorrect: *Helias asas e mantall in ded gans e* **scholar** SA 60. GKK also says that the plural *skoloryon* [scoloryon] is not attested. This is also incorrect: **Skylyrion,** *Scholars* AB: 242c.

skorjya [scurjya] 'to scourge': GKK says this word occurs is confined to a single instance in PA, i.e. line 1303a [*recte* 130a]. This is incorrect: **scorgis** *gans an zethewon* BM 2602; *kylmys gans lovonow,* **scurgys** TH 15a.

skourya [scurya] 'to scour': GKK says this word is not attested in the texts but is taken from Nance's 1938 dictionary. This is incorrect: *crist a rug agery an fentan ma arta ha's purgias ha's* **scurryas** TH 22. GKK cites Tregear's **scurryas** as <skorrya> but gives no meaning for it.

skrifer [screfer] 'scribe, writer': GKK says the singular is not attested. This is incorrect: **Skrepher** *an gerlevran-na* AB: 223.

sogh [sogh] 'ploughshare': GKK says this word is confined to OCV and Lhuyd. This is incorrect: *Gora an* **soch** *ha an troher tha an gove* Pryce, F f 2.

sojet [sojet] 'subject': GKK mentions that the singular of this word at CW 379 is spelt <subject> and says the plural is confined to a single instance in PA. This is incorrect. The plural is also attested in TH: *myterneth gwlasow,* **subiectys,** *tus ientyll* TH 6a.

solempna [solempna] 'solemn': GKK says this adjective is unattested. This is incorrect. It is found as <solem> in TH: *the wull* **solem** *ro in aga begeth* TH 20; *gull* **solem** *promys a vois* TH 51a. The compiler also says he got the word from Nance's 1955 dictionary. The word, however, is cited by Nance in both his earlier dictionaries (1938: 153; 1952: 160).

soveran [soveran] 'sovereign': GKK says this word is confined to one instance each in OM, BM and TH. This is incorrect: *agan arluth* **sefryn** OM 2189; *agan* **soueran** BM 246; **Souereign** *rewler* TH 2; *po y* **soveran** TH 4a; *blonogath y* **soveran** TH 4a.

Sows [Saws] 'Englishman': There are at least four errors in this entry in GKK. First, GKK suggests that the word *Saws* is attested once only. I have noted: **Zouz** glossing *Anglus, An English-man* AB: 42c and *boz* **Zouz**, *Dan po Norman* AB: 224; cf. **Zouz**, *an English Man* Borlase 413. Secondly, GKK suggests that the plural **Sawson** <Sowson> occurs 4-9 times. I have collected the following examples: *car dreeg an* **Sausen** *e thanen* BF: 24; *durt an* **Sausen** BF: 29; *ha whaeh an* **Sousen** BF: 31; **Sousen**-*Curnow* BF: 31; *Pou an* **Zouzn** glossing *Anglia, England* AB: 42c; *ny aldzha an* **Zouzon** AB: 224; *Mytern ol an* **Zouzon** AB: 224; *mesk an* **Zouzon** AB: 224; *neb Koth-***Zouzon** AB: 224; **Zouzon**, *The English* AB: 242c; *Dhan* **Zowzan** *kovaithak* (from Lhuyd's lament for William III) LAM: 234. Third, GKK suggests that Cornish *Saws* derives from Latin *Saxo*. This is incorrect. *Saxo* quite regularly gave **Seys* in Cornish, a form attested in surnames like *Seys, le Seys* and in toponyms like *Carsize, Tresayes, Trezise, Chyseise* (see Padel: 208). *Saws* is a back-formation from *Sawson* < *Saxones*. Fourth, GKK suggests that the Welsh for 'Englishman' is **Saws*. It is not. The Welsh is *Sais*, pl. *Saeson*.

Sowsnek [Sawsnek] 'English': GKK says that this word is confined to 4-9 instances in Late Cornish. This is incorrect: *mouy* **Sousenack** *clappies* BF: 25; *ha clappia* **Sousenack** BF: 25; *an Tavaz* **Sousenack** BF: 25; *tho Ve buz* **Sousenack** BF: 29; *Latten, po an* **Sousenack** BF: 29: *ha an* **Sousenack** *nobla* BF: 29; *gen an* **Sousenack** BF: 31; *meea na vidna cowza* **sawsneck** Carew (Ellis: 73); W. *Saisneg, English;* C. **Zasnak** AB: 30b; **Zouznak** glossing *Lingua Anglicana, the English Tongue* AB: 42c; *'ryg traylia an levrouma dhan* **Zouznak** AB: 222; *gerrio* **Zouznak** AB: 223; *dhort an Koth-***Zouznak** AB: 223; *Kernuak-***Zouznak** AB: 223; *skrefyanz an* **Zouznak** AB: 223; *an gerrio* **Zouznak** AB: 223; *en* **Zouznak** *koth* AB: 224; *Ah-skrefo* **Zouznak** AB: 224; *pordha kouz* **Zouznak** AB: 224; *a kouz* **Zouznak** AB: 224; *Kothskreferyon* **Zouznak** AB: 224; *edn ger* **Sowsnack** Bodinar; **Sawsneck** Pryce.

Spayn [Spayn] 'Spain': GKK says that this name is confined to a single instance in RD. This is incorrect *Dhort henna war Frank ha war* **Span** Lhuyd (LAM: 234).

spena [spena] 'to spend': GKK says this verb is confined to BM. This is incorrect: *y* **speynas** *y gyk hay wos* PA 10c.

spera [spera] 'spear': GKK says that this word is confined to a single instance at CW 1994. This is incorrect: *gwenys dre an assow the'n golon gans* **spera** TH 15a.

spikys [spykys] 'spikes': GKK says that the plural of *spik* 'spike' is confined to a single instance at PC 2140. This is incorrect: **spykys** *bras a horn* TH 15a.

takkya [tackya] 'to nail, to fasten': GKK says this verb is confined to 2-3 instances. This is incorrect: *ha'y yll leff a ve* **tackys** PA 179b;

En lybell a vue **tackis** PA 189a; **tackis** *fast* PA 223c; *ynny hy*
bethens **tackys** PC 2164; *bethens* **tackys** PC 2518; *rag* **takkye** *an fals*
profus PC 2672; *me a* **tak** *y luef gleth* PC 2747; **tackeugh** *e a hugh y*
ben PC 2793; *the* **tackye** PC 2807; *fast* **tackyes** PC 2939; **tackys** *y'n*
grous RD 1116; *Figo . . . to fix, to fasten; . . . C. Dho kelmy, dho*
takkia AB: 59c.

Tamer [Tamar] 'Tamar': GKK says this river name is confined to a
single instance in Middle Cornish. This is incorrect: *an barz ma ze*
pons **tamar** CF 20; *a* **tamer** *the pen an vlays* BM 2208.

tavolenn [tavolen] 'dock plant': GKK asserts that the singular is
unattested. This is incorrect: *W. Tavolen, A Dock; Corn.* **Tavolan**
AB: 15b; †**Tavolen** *glossing Lapathum, Dock* AB: 76b; **Tavolan,** *a*
dock AB: 240c

tavoseth [tavaseth] 'dialect, idiom': GKK says that this word is
confined to a single instance in Lhuyd. This is incorrect: *adro'n*
Tavazeth *Kernuak* AB: 222; *a'n* **Tavazeth** *Kernuak* AB: 222; *en*
Tavazeth *Kernuak* AB: 222; *en* **Tavadzh** *Guenez* AB: 223

tebel-el 'devil': Instead of the word *dyawl* Tregear uses *tebel-el*, e.g. at
3, 3a x 3, 5, 10, 13, 15 x 2, 15a x 2, 16, 23a, 25, 28a, 32a. Noteworthy
is the expression *an bys, an kyge ha'n* **tebel-el** 'the world, the flesh
and the devil' at TH 9a. Cf. *esel yv then* **tebel el** BM 969. *Tebel-el*
'devil' is wholly absent from GKK.

tegys [tegys] 'choked': GKK says the word is unattested. This is
incorrect: *Suffocatus . . . Chok'd or throtl'd. C[ornish].* **Tegez** AB:
157c.

tekhe [tekhe] 'beautify': GKK says this verb is not attested. This is
incorrect: *may fo* **tekkeys** *eredy* 'that he may be beautified indeed'
BM 1601.

tender [tender] 'tender': GKK says this is attested only at BM 115. This
is incorrect: *an* **tendyr** *kerensa a du an tas* TH 1.

tewal [tewal] 'dark gloomy': GKK cites both this and the monosyllabic
form *tewl* as separate headwords. The dictionary also states that
tewal is unattested. This is incorrect: **Teual** *glossing Obscurus,*
Obscure, dark, etc. AB: 103a.

tewel [tewel] 'to be silent': GKK says this verb is confined to 2-3
instances in Middle and Late Cornish. This is incorrect: *a* **taw**
cowyth OM 2749; **taw,** *an el a bregewthy* OM 229; *pan wreta* **tewel**
PC 1320; **tewel** *auel vn bobba* PC 2385; *nep a* **tawo** *yn pow-ma* PC
2387; **taw** *foul a soge gocky* PC 2897; **tau** *sy cowys renothas* RD
405; **tau** *harlot out of my sygth* RD 619; **teweugh** *awos lucyfer* RD
669; *awos ovn my ny* **tauwaf** RD 923; *ty a* **tew** RD 984; *mara colyth*
ty a **tew** RD 1388; **teweugh** *rak meth* RD 1495; *ny ny* **tywyn** *ow*
cane RD 2527; *A* **taw** *na gowse a henna* CW 171: **Taw** *lucyfer*

melegas CW 283; **Taw Taw** *eva* 665; **taw** *theth cregye* CW 1103; **Tau** glossing *Tace* [be silent] AB: 160b; **Teuel**, *To be silent* AB: 245b. The expression *taw tavas* 'shut up!' survives in English. GKK puts it under the headword *taw* 'silence'. This is incorrect. *Taw tavas* is the 2nd person imperative followed by the direct object *tavas*. The phrase means literally 'Silence your tongue!'

ti [ty] 'to thatch, to roof': GKK says that this verb is confined to two occurrences in OM. This is incorrect: *tyy py ny agan beth meth* OM 1078; *hag a's ty gans plynkennow* OM 2475; *tyeugh an temple* OM 2485; *ken agesough why ny's ty* OM 2490. Cf. also **Tey**, *to thatch, or cover with straw* Borlase 408; **Ty**, *to cover a house either with stones or thatch* Pryce, opposite A a 2.

titel [tytel] 'title': GKK glosses this 'legal right' (i.e. legal title) and says it is confined to a single instance in BM. This is incorrect: *oll tytyll ha henow* TH 6; *aga thytyll* TH 6a.

tobacco 'tobacco': Lhuyd gives **Tybakko** glossing *Tabacum, Tobacco* AB: 160b. The word seems to be mising from GKK, though it is in Nance (1938, 1952).

toemma [tomma] 'to heat': GKK says the verb is confined to Lhuyd and Pryce. This is incorrect: **tommans** *onan dour war tan* PC 833; *yma dour* **tommys** PC 839.

toemmder [tomder] 'heat': GKK claims that this word is confined to 2-3 instances in Old and Late Cornish. This incorrect: **tunder** (read **tumder**) glossing *calor* OCV 471; *rag* **tomder** *ef a wese* PA 58c; *hag y ny russans clowas* **tomder** *vith* TH 56a; **tomdar** *ha yender* CW 1668; *in* **tomdar** *tane* CW 1724; *Corn[ish] Tom &* **Tomder** glossing *Warm* and *Warmth* AB: 18a; **Tomder** glossing *Calor, Heat, warmth* AB: 45c; *Mygilder and* **tymder**, *Warmth, heat* AB: 240b.

toes [tos] 'dough': GKK says this word is not attested. This is incorrect: **Toas**, *Paste* Borlase 409.

tollva [tollva] 'tax office': GKK says this word is derived from Nance's dictionary being unattested in the texts. This is incorrect: **Tolva**, *a Custom House* Borlase 409.

tollven [tollven] 'hollow stone': GKK suggests that this word is attested in place-names only. This is not strictly speaking true: *It's common name in Cornwall and Scilly is* **Tolmen**; *that is, the Hole of Stone* Borlase 166; *The two* **Tolmens** *at Scilly* Borlase 167. Cf. **Tolmen** Borlase 238.

torment [torment] 'torment': GKK says the plural is unattested. This is incorrect: *ha paynys intollerabill ha* **turmontys** TH 15a.

torr [tor] 'belly, womb': GKK says that this word is confined to one instance in OCV. This is incorrect: *pan veva genys a* **dor** *y vam zen bys ma* PA 43d; *a* **dor** *ov mam dynythys* OM 1754; *cosk war the* **tor**

ha powes OM 2070; *guregh y cronkye* **tor** *ha keyn* PC 2057; *kyns doys a* **dor** *ov dama* BM 796; *genis a* **dore** *y vam* TH 44a-45; **Tor** *an daorn* glossing *Palma, The palm of the hand* AB: 111c; **Tor;** **tor** *braoz* glossing *Venter, The belly or panch; the stomach,* etc. AB: 171b; *Houl sooth,* **Tor** *lean, paravy an gwaynten* Scawen MSS. GKK says that the plural is unattested. This is also incorrect: *may fyth* **torrow** *benegas bythqueth na allas e zon* PA 169c; *may fenygough an* **torrow** PC 2646.

torrva [torva] 'breach': GKK says that the word is unattested in the texts. This is incorrect: *an violacion ha'n* **torva** *a cherite* TH 28; *an keth same* **torva** *me a cherite* TH 28-28a.

traow [traow] 'things': GKK says the plural of *tra* is unattested. This is incorrect: *ha porskientek en* **traou** *erel* AB: 224. **Traow* is Lhuyd's form and is not otherwise attested, being replaced by *taclow* or *taclennow*.

trelyans [treylyans] 'translation': GKK says that the plural of this word is unattested. This is incorrect: *Lenner Brethonek ra medra uar* **traillianzo** *an gerrio Ladin ma* AB: 222.

treven [treven] 'houses': this plural of *tref* according to GKK is confined to a single instance in Late Cornish. This is incorrect on both counts: *y vab po y virth, chy,* **trevyn** *po tyrryow* TH 21a; *Na dale deiw gwell* **treaven** *war an treath* J. Jenkins (LAM: 230); *oagoaze tha e* **drevon** BF: 39; *Tshyi [plur* **Treven**] glossing *Domus, An house, a lodging* AB: 55c.

treveth [treveth] 'occasion': GKK says the word is confined to a single instance in Nicholas Boson. This is incorrect: *ke weth tresse* **treveth** *th'y* OM 799; *lyes* **trefeth** *y'n clewys* PC 1724; *vii* **trevath** TH 8; *rag an* **drevath** *ma* TH 35; *an tryssa* **trevath** TH 43; **trevath** *arell* TH 53.

trybedh [trebeth] 'trivet, tripod': GKK says this word is confined to OCV. This is incorrect: *W.* **Trybedh,** *A Trivet or Brand-Iron; Cornish* **Trebath** AB: 19a; **Trebath** glossing *Tripes* AB: 166c. Ironically Lhuyd's first citation occurs in a section dealing with the alternation of Welsh <y>with Cornish <e>, a feature of which Kernewek Kemmyn is unaware. Nance correctly spelt the Cornish word <trebeth> and UCR follows him.

tryger [treger] 'inhabitant': GKK says that the plural *tregoryon* is unattested in the texts being derived by analogy. This is incorrect: **Tregoryon** *an Enez-ma* AB: 223; *dhort an* **Tregoryon** *kenza* AB: 223.

trynyta [trynyta] 'trinity': GKK says that this word is confined to a single instance in OM. This is incorrect: *tus ha mab in* **trinitie** CW 344.

turnypenn [turnypen] 'turnip': GKK says the singular is not attested.

This is incorrect: **Turnupan**, *A Turnip* AB: 34a and *Rapum . . . A rape, a turnip or navew C.* **tyrnypan** AB: 136b. Cf. **Turnupan**, *a Turnip* Borlase 410b; **Turnupan**, *a Turnip* Pryce, A a.

tykki-Dyw [tycky Dew] 'butterfly': (why the hyphen?) GKK says that this word is confined to a single instance in Lhuyd. This is incorrect: *W. Gloyn Dyu (i.e. Carbo dei) A Butter-fly; Corn.* **Tikki Deu** AB: 34a; *C.* **Tikki deu** glossing *Papilio* AB: 112b.

tys-ha-tas [tys ha tas] 'tit for tat': GKK says that this phrase is confined to a single instance in PC. This is incorrect: *ha knoukye prest* **tys-ha-tas** PC 2077; *gans ov scorge* **tys-ha-tas** PC 2107; *ha knouk an horn* **tys ha tas** PC 2719; **Tyshatas**, *leisurly, by stroke and stroke* Pryce, opposite A a 2.

ugheldir [uheldyr] 'highlands': GKK says that this word is unattested in the texts. This is incorrect: *en* **Ehual-dir** *an Alban hag en G'laskor Uordhyn* AB: 222.

usa [usa, uja] 'to yell, to hoot': GKK says this word is confined to a single instance in CW 1309. This is incorrrect: *yma agys yskar an tebel-ell kepar ha lyon owh* **uga** TH 3a.

uvelder [uvelder] 'humility': GKK says this occurs 2-3 times in Middle Cornish. This is incorrect: *der the* **vvelder** BM 2941; *in* **vvelder** BM 4328; *virtu ha* **vvelder** TH 6; *pana* **vveldar** TH 6a; *gans* **vvelder** TH 39.

veksya [vexya] 'to vex': GKK says this verb is confined to a single instance at TH 22. This is incorrect: *me yv* **vexijs** *anhethek* BM 2630.

verb [verb] 'verb': GKK ascribes this neologism to *An Gannas* 1984. The word is older than that since it occurs in Nance and Smith's *Termow Gramasek* of the 1940s. It occurs in CS2 (first published 1955), p. 32: *amserow a'n* **verb***-ma*. It is moreover not uncommon in ALK: *rag rosa yu parth an* **verb** *ry* ALK 57 (1957); *Gwerth a yl bos hanow "sale",* **verb** *"he sells", ha gys gorhemmynek ynweth* ALK 70 (1960); *Tynkyal yu* **verb** *dyspar* ALK 70 (1960); *deu form dhe nebes* **verbow** ALK 72 (1960); **Verbow:** *- bugelya, devynnes.* ALK 102 (1968); **Verbow** *ha dhedha -a ha -ya* ALK: 127 (1975).

vogalen 'vowel': GKK spells this word <bogalenn> and ascribes it to K[en] J. G[eorge]. With initial <v> it was already in use in the 1940s. Note these instances from ALK: *An* **vogalennow** *Y hyr ha Y cot yu kemmyskys* ALK 57 (1957); **vogalen***—vowel* ibid.

walkya [walkya] 'to walk': GKK says this verb is confined to a single instance in TH. This is incorrect: **Walkyow** *ha gwandrow* TH 16a; *ef a* **walkias** *i'n kigg na* SA 64a.

yaghhe [yaghhe] 'to heal': GKK says this verb is confined to one instance at RD 1687. This is incorrect: *ow colon yv sur* **yaghys** OM

1381; *ny allaf bos* **yagheys** RD 1591; *bones* **yagheys** RD 1675; *bos*
yaghes *thotho yv reys* RD 1708; *te a vyth* **yagheys** RD 1730; *yth of*
vy **yaghys** RD 1741; **yagheys** *aban os* RD 1749; *ny yllogh bones*
yaghheys BM 1500.

yn [yn] adverbial particle: under this item GKK gives *yn hwir* 'truly'
and says it occurs between 4 and 9 times in Middle and Late
Cornish. This is not true, since the form **yn whyr* is unattested
anywhere in traditional Cornish. 'Truly' in the texts is always *yn*
gwyr. This was first pointed out by Caradar (†1950) in his second
supplement to CS (published 1955). See now CS2: 31. The
expression *an gwyr* 'the truth' is common in the texts. It is likely
therefore that *yn gwyr* 'truly' does not contain the adverbial
particle *yn* but the preposition *yn* + the definite article *an*. It is for
this reason that in the phrase *yn gwyr* the initial *gw* is not mutated.
Indeed we should probably write *y'n gwyr* rather than *yn gwyr*.
GKK's **yn hwir* is wholly spurious. Here are some examples from
the texts of *y'n gwyr*: **en gwyr** *ze zustynee* PA 210d; *tres aral re got*
in guyr OM 2549; *lauar* **en guyr** *thy'm certan* OM 2234; *dew vody*
tha ough **yn guyr** OM 2461; *a gevelyn da* **yn guyr** OM 2541. I can
find no instances in BM, TH or CW. Notice, however, that Lhuyd
writes **En uir** 'truly' with lenition (not mixed mutation) glossing
Certe at AB: 47b and *Quidem* at AB: 134c.

yn nes [yn nes] 'near, by': GKK says that this is confined to a single
instance in BM. This is incorrect: **in neys** *rum caradevder* BM 1309;
saff **in neys** BM 3470; **in nes** *in cres paradis* TH 3a; **in nese** *an ii*
commondment ma TH 20a.

ynkressya [encressya] 'to increase': GKK observes that there is also an
aphetic form *cressya*. The dictionary says that the full form
<ynkressya> is confined to a single instance in CW. This is in-
correct: **encressyens** *ha bewens pel* OM 48; **encresshys** *gans charite*
TH 49; *theth hays a wra* **incressya** CW 1318; *yth ew* **incresshys** CW
1989.

ynocent 'innocent': this adjective is attested in TH: **innocent** *corffe* TH
15a; *ew da ha* **innocent** TH 25. The plural as a substantive is also
attested: *then* **ynocens** *oma* BM 1708; *gans* **Innocentys** TH 24a. The
word does not appear to be in GKK.

Ynys [Enys] 'Shrovetide': GKK says this is a recent coinage taken from
Nance's 1938 dictionary. This is incorrect: *Carnisprivium, ynyd;*
Shrovetide; C[ornish] **Enez** AB: 46b.

ys [ys] 'corn': GKK says that this word is confined to two instances in
Old Cornish. This is incorrect: *gorre hag* **eys** *kemyskys* OM 1058;
an dour ha'n **eys** *yv posnys* OM 1559; *avel* **ys** *y[n] nothlennow* PC
881; *bara gwrys a* **eys** TH 57a; *gwrys a kynde vyth a* **eys** TH 57a; *rag*

rowlya **eys** *ha chattell* CW 1064; *an* **eys** *na'n frutes* CW 1089; *shower a* **yees** CW 1189; *Whelas megourion tha medge an* **isse** 'Look reapers to reap the corn' Pryce, F f 2; *Whelas colmurian tha kelme an* **isse** 'Look binders to bind the corn' ibid; **Ise** *en noare* 'Corn in the ground' Bilbao MS; **Iz** *bara* glossing *frumentum* AB: 61c; **iz, iz** *saval* glossing *Seges, Standing corn* AB: 147c; *Pedn* **iz** glossing *Spica, The ear of Corn* AB: 153a.

yskar [yscar] 'canvas, sackcloth': GKK cites this word but suggests that it is unattested in the texts being taken from Nance's 1955 dictionary. This is incorrect: *a rug usia gwyska* **yscar** *ha canfas garow, an pith a vetha gwrys syehar anotha* TH 6a; *gans* **yskar** *ha canfas ha gans dowst ha lusew* TH 6a.

yssew [yssew] 'issue': GKK says this word is confined to CW. This is incorrect: *oll an* **ussew** *a Adam ha Eva* TH 3.

ystory [ə'stori] 'history': GKK says this word has been taken from Nance (1938), being unattested in the texts. This is incorrect: *in seconde lever a Eusebius, Ecclesiastical* **Historye** TH 46a; *an lever a Eusebius, Ecclesiastical* **History** TH 47a; *yma S Jherom ow recordya in dalleth a'y* **story** *De Ecclesiasticis Scriptoribus* TH 47.

The errors listed above are neither trivial in nature nor few in number. They do, however, represent only a fraction of the mistakes in *Gerlyver Kernewek Kemmyn*. Because of lack of time and space I have not checked the occurrence of words given a frequency code of {4} or higher. Further research would reveal many more errors throughout the work. Certainly, GKK (quite apart from its questionable orthography) compares unfavourably with any of Morton Nance's Cornish dictionaries.

GEORGE, CORNISH AND COMPUTERS

George first described his computational approach to Cornish in a paper 'The Use of a Mainframe Computer to Analyse Cornish Orthography' presented to the Congress of Celtic Studies in Ottawa in 1986 and published in NACCC: 89-115. In the published version of the paper George cites a number of etyma and their various spellings in the texts. In figure 11 (p. 109) of this article George assures us among other things that the word *ayr(e)* 'air' is unattested in the *Ordinalia*. This is incorrect, for the word is attested in PC: *neb a thue th'agan brugy yn* **ayr** *deth brus pup huny* PC 1668-69.

Another etymon discussed by George is the Cornish name for *Timothy* which George says is confined to two instances in TH (figure 12, p. 111). He is mistaken, since the name occurs *seven* times in TH: *in iii chapter the* **Tymothe** TH 17a; *ow scriifa the* **timothe** TH 18a; *O* *thimothye* TH 18a; *in y tressa chapter the* **Thimothe** TH 18a; *Inweth S paule the* **Tymothe** TH 25; *eff a appoyntyas inweth* **Thimothe** TH 33a; *dell rug S paule ordeynya* **Tymothe** TH 33a.

In the same place George asserts that Lhuyd uses the spelling <ithik> for UC *uthek* 'terrible' *on one accasion only*. I have noticed the following nine examples: **Ithik** glossing *Immanis, outrageous, fierce* AB: 68a; **Ithik**, *braz* glossing *Immensus, Unmeasurable, huge* AB: 68a; †*Hail, Leadan,* **ithick**, *braoz* glossing *Largus, Huge, very great; free-hearted, bountiful,* etc. AB: 76c; *Teu, bor, braoz,* **ithik** glossing *Obesus* AB: 102a; **Ithik** *tra* glossing *Plurimum, Most of all,* etc. AB: 122b; *Krev,* **ithik** glossing *Strenuus, Valiant, stout, hardy,* etc. AB: 155c; **ithik** *tra* glossing *Valde* AB: 169a; **ithik** *koth* AB: 223 †4 line 8; **Ithig**, *Hugely* AB: 249a.

EPILOGUE

George read an early draft of these notes and in a personal communication has explained the errors in GKK as follows:

> Rann vrassa anedha yw sevys drefenn: (a) nag esa genev dasskrif kowal a Pryce; (b) ow thowlenn dhe hwilas henwyn-verb hepken; (c) na wrug vri orth ragskrif Lhuyd in A[rchæologia] B[ritannica] awos y vos "idiosyncratic and highly Cymricised".

> [The majority of them have arisen because: (a) I did not have a complete copy of Pryce; (b) my computer program searched for verbal nouns only; (c) I ignored Lhuyd's preface in AB because it was "idiosyncratic and highly Cymricised" (a quotation from the article by me in *Studia Celtica* 32 (1998), 129-54 on pre-occlusion)].

A researcher working on a complete computer database of Cornish ought surely to have acquired a copy or photocopy of Pryce's important book. If the program used in GKK searched for verbal nouns only, it was clearly unsuited to its task. Besides, George's policy with respect to the inclusion of verbal forms in GKK is very inconsistent. GKK includes many idiosyncratic and Cymricized words from Lhuyd. It is not clear why GKK accepts some and repudiates others. The majority of George's omissions from Lhuyd involve the body of *Archæologia Britannica* rather than the few pages (AB: 222-4) of Lhuyd's Cornish preface. In any case it is not apparent why the limitations and qualifications (a), (b) and (c) cited by George were not mentioned in the introduction to GKK.

George's explanation says nothing about the remarkable omissions in GKK from the Middle and Late Cornish texts nor about the other numerous errors of fact. The simplest and most obvious reason for the mistakes in the dictionary is that George's database was inadequate for the task. The database used in compiling GKK, however, had already been used in the construction of Kernewek Kemmyn itself. Given that the database was faulty, it is perhaps no wonder that Kernewek Kemmyn is so mistaken. A recent attempt by Paul Dunbar and George (KK21) to vindicate Kernewek Kemmyn is unconvincing. Indeed, Mills (1999) has drawn attention to the shortcomings of Dunbar and George: 'To demonstrate individually that each of George's analyses is wrong would take a very long time, simply because there are a lot of analyses and there is very little that could be said to be right about any of them.'[1]

And he adds:

> Furthermore, when one compares the data reported by George with the primary sources, they do not match. His results and conclusions are, therefore, spurious. George's work thus makes claims about Cornish phonology which are not really justified. Since George's investigation of Cornish phonology is badly flawed, the switch to Kernewek Kemmyn seems to have been an expensive waste of time and energy.[2]

Mills is critical of all George's work on Cornish phonology and lexicography:

> George's study is, therefore, based on conjecture and so, despite his claims, he has not reconstructed the phonology of Cornish. It must be concluded that George's phonology of Cornish is largely invention . . . Consensus for an orthography for Revived Cornish will only be reached if that orthography can be demonstrated to be academically sound. It is not for an individual to propose an orthography based on his putative reconstruction of Cornish phonology and then shift the burden of proof by requiring that others demonstrate its shortcomings.[3]

Quite independently of my analysis Mills has arrived at a conclusion identical with mine, namely, that Kernewek Kemmyn is a failed experiment in orthographic reform.

NOTES AND REFERENCES

1. John Mills, 'Reconstructive Phonology and Contrastive Lexicography: Problems with the *Gerlyver Kernewek Kemmyn*', in Philip Payton (ed.), *Cornish Studies: Seven*, Exeter, 1999, p. 201.
2. Mills, 1999, p. 214.
3. Mills, 1999, pp. 200–1.

ABBREVIATIONS

AB = Edward Lhuyd, *Archæologia Britannica* (London 1707 [reprinted Shannon, 1971])

ALK = *An Lef Kernewek*

B. = Breton

BF = O.J. Padel, *The Cornish Writings of the Boson Family* (Redruth, 1975)

Bilbao MS = Henry Jenner, 'The Cornish Manuscript in the provincial library at Bilbao, Spain', *Journal of the Royal Institution of Cornwall* 21 (1924–5): 421–37

BM = Whitley Stokes, *Beunans Meriasek: the life of Saint Meriasek* (London 1872)

Borde = Andrew Borde cited from J. Loth, 'Cornique modern', *Archiv für Celtische Lexicographie* 1 (1900): 224–8

Borlase = William Borlase, *Antiquities of the County of Cornwall* (Oxford, 1754)

Carew = F.E. Halliday (ed.), *Richard Carew of Antony: the survey of Cornwall* (London, 1953)

CF = The Charter Fragment

CFA = R. Morton Nance, *Cornish For All: A Guide to Unified Cornish* (revised edition, St Ives, 1949)

CS = A.S.D. Smith, *Cornish Simplified* (Camborne, 1972)

CS2 = A.S.D. Smith, E.G.R. Hooper (eds) *Cornish Simplified* 2 (Redruth 1984) [originally published 1954-63]

CW = Whitley Stokes, 'Gwreans an Bys: the Creation of the World', *Transactions of the Philological Society* (1863, part iv)

Ellis = P. Berresford Ellis, *The Cornish Language and its Literature* (London, 1974)

GCSW = R. Morton Nance, *A Glossary of Cornish Sea-words*, edited by P.A.S. Pool (Marazion, 1963)

Gendall = R.R.M. Gendall, *A Students' Dictionary of Modern Cornish* (fourth edition, Menheniot, 1992)

GKK = Ken George, *Gerlyver Kernewek Kemmyn* (Cornish Language Board, 1993)

KemK = E.G.R. Hooper (ed.), *Kemysk Kernewek: A Cornish Miscellany* (Camborne, 1964)

KK21 = Paul Dunbar and Ken George, *Kernewek Kemmyn: Cornish for the Twenty-First Century* (Saltash, 1997)

LAM = Alan M. Kent and Tim Saunders, *Looking at the Mermaid: A Reader in Cornish Literature 900-1900* (London, 2000)

LCB = R. Williams, *Lexicon Cornu-Britannicum* (Llandovery, 1865)

ME = Middle English

Mills (1999) = Jon Mills, 'Reconstructive Phonology and Contrastive Lexicology: Problems with the *Gerlyver Kernewek Kemmyn*', *Cornish Studies: Seven* (Exeter), 193-218

NACCS = Gordon W. Maclennan, *Proceedings of the First North American Congress of Celtic Studies* (Ottawa, 1988)

Nance (1938) = R. Morton Nance, *New Cornish-English Dictionary* [reprinted as the first part of *Gerlyver Noweth Kernewek-Sawsnek ha Sawsnek-Kernewek* (Redruth, 1990)]

Nance (1952) = R. Morton Nance, *An English-Cornish Dictionary* (Marazion, 1952) [reprinted as the second part of *Gerlyver Noweth Kernewek-Sawsnek ha Sawsnek-Kernewek* (Redruth, 1990)]

Nance (1955) = R. Morton Nance, A Cornish-English Dictionary (Marazion, 1955)

OCV = *The Old Cornish Vocabulary* [quoted from Norris 1859 ii: 311–435]

OF = Old French

OM = 'Origo Mundi' in Norris, *Ancient Cornish Drama* (London, 1859 [reprinted New York, 1968]) i: 1-219

PA = Whitley Stokes, 'Pascon agan Arluth: the Passion of our Lord', *Transactions of the Philological Society* (1860–1, Appendix 1–100)

Padel = O.J. Padel, *Cornish Place-name Elements* (Nottingham, 1985)

PC = 'Passio Domini Nostri Jhesu Christi' in Norris, *Ancient Cornish Drama* i: 221–479

Pryce = William Pryce, *Archæologia Cornu-Britannica* (Sherborne, 1790)

RC = *Revue Celtique*

RD = 'Resurrexio Domini Nostri Jhesu Christi', in Norris, *Ancient Cornish Drama* ii: 1–199

SA = *Sacrament an Alter*, the last sermon in the Tregear manuscript ff 59–66a, pp. 38–45 in Bice's edition

TH = John Tregear, *Homelyes xiii in Cornysche* (British Library Additional MS 46, 397) [quoted from a cyclostyled text published by Christopher Bice (no place [1969])]

UC(R) = Unified Cornish or Unified Cornish Revised

W. = Welsh

Wakelin = M.F. Wakelin, *Language and History in Cornwall* (Leicester, 1975)

Williams (1990) = N.J.A. Williams, 'A Problem in Cornish Phonology', in Martin J. Ball, James Fife, Erich Poppe and Jenny Rowland, *Celtic Linguistics: Ieithyddiaeth Geltaidd* (Amsterdam and Philadelphia), 241–74.

REVIEW ARTICLE

GERLYVER SAWSNEK-KERNOWEK

Neil Kennedy

N.J.A. Williams, *English-Cornish Dictionary: Gerlyver Sawsnek-Kernowek*, Everson Gunn Teoranta and Agan Tavas, Dublin & Redruth, 2000, hardback, 485 pp., ISBN 1-988082-03-4/ISBN 1 901409 04 X.

We have to admire the energy, commitment and focus that Nicholas Williams has brought to Cornish language research in recent years. Within the span of a few years and with little assistance, he has developed a comprehensive project to reform R.M. Nance's Unified Cornish (UC), publishing two books of note: *Cornish Today* (1995)[1] (reviewed in *Cornish Studies: Four*) and *Clappya Kernowek* (1997)[2] as well as supplements and journal articles. Williams's examinations of Revived Cornish, in its various guises, may be regarded by some as unnecessarily abrasive and nit-picking, rather too concerned with discrediting other approaches, but, whilst he is unlikely to win any prizes for diplomacy, his interrogation of the language has encouraged rigour and the exchange of ideas. He has helped to bring debates about the future shape of Cornish into the open where the issues can be subjected to the full scrutiny of academics and grass-roots revivalists alike.

Williams's revision of UC touches all aspects of the language: pronunciation, orthography, vocabulary, grammar and idiom. He attempts to shift the emphasis from the plays of the *Ordinalia* to the later writings of John Tregear (*c.*1570) and William Jordan (1611), calling his revised version 'Unified Cornish Revised' (UCR). This, arguably, positions UCR between Middle and Late Cornish. *Clappya Kernowek* introduced the grammar of UCR in a concise and not too controversial form. This dictionary, by contrast, provides an extensive vocabulary for twenty-first-century use and in doing so enters into major areas of controversy surrounding language planning, some of which I would like to refer to here.

In trying to revive Cornish, how do we reconcile our wishes to be true to the historical language with the practical requirements of the twenty-first century? How should we deal with lexical gaps, for example, and how should we express recent concepts and notions that the language has never had to cope with?

Whilst learners might well imagine that the language of their course books is a straightforward reproduction of historical Cornish, the reality is that conscious choice has been exercised in presenting every aspect of it. To achieve a practical standard, revivalists have had to cut-and-paste, reconciling diverse sources from different periods. In other words, Cornish has been shaped by the exercise of personal taste and preference. Selections have been made in compiling standard lexicons, in fixing grammatical forms and in standardizing ortho-graphies. At the same time Revived Cornish has come under the intense, often hostile, scrutiny of professional linguists and amateur detractors, forcing revivalists to enter into academic and media debates.[3] In this environment no one can speak Cornish innocently and matters of historical accuracy and verbal hygiene become a cause of anxiety and a source of strife.

Recent debates have tended to echo the supposed opposition between *descriptive* and *prescriptive approaches* to language. The move away from judgmental notions of correct language towards relativist positions, from which all forms of language are seen as valid, means that linguists are concerned with describing language as found rather than prescribing 'correct' forms. As Deborah Cameron observes in *Verbal Hygiene* (1995): 'the term "prescriptivism" has a particular value attached to it, a negative connotation that is almost impossible to avoid.'[4]

Cameron, however, points out that normative processes are always at work in language communities, serving to define and police the boundaries of acceptable speech and writing. She considers whether prescriptions by public commentators or linguists are fundamentally different from these apparently 'natural', seemingly common-sense, processes, questioning the belief that it is possible to 'leave your language alone' and recognizing that 'making value judgements on language is an integral part of using it'. If common-sense, taken-for-granted prescriptivism is always at work, do the prescriptions of revivalists, whether conservative or reformist, differ fundamentally from these everyday practices? It is an important question to ask in considering a publication of this scope and ambition. With its 24,000 headwords, Williams's dictionary is twice the size of Nance's *An English-Cornish Dictionary*[5] and offers Cornish equivalents for many objects and concepts never recorded or expressed in the historical texts: air-terminal, airlock, alliteration, biochemist, bourgeois, calculator, cartoon, communist, dynamo and so on. In other words, Williams has attempted to provide a twenty-first-century vocabulary, sifting through the considerable literature of Revived Cornish for useful neologisms and devising hundreds of his own. Inevitably, what we are presented with is a personal exercise in language planning, even allowing for Williams's careful consultation of UC users; but is there an alternative? Even if a committee could produce such a dictionary, the end result would still be the product of conscious verbal hygiene.

The notion of certain selections being natural and neutral is especially unrealistic in the case of a revived language where all of the adult speakers have made a choice to learn it. Cornish is obviously a special case, as Wella Brown points out: 'Speakers of Modern Cornish are not yet numerous enough to have created a natural criterion [of what is correct]. There is no one to whom we can go and ask whether a particular utterance is acceptable as to its structure, its vocabulary or its pronunciation.'[6]

The prescription versus description debate has been centre stage in recent arguments. Should revivalists attempt to present the language as found, confining themselves strictly to historically attested forms, or should they attempt to 'improve' and tidy it up? The readiness of critics to denounce Revived Cornish as a 'made-up language' and the extreme liberties taken by some revivalists both serve to produce a conservative, descriptivist response. Similarly, the desire to use Cornish as an everyday language and the imperatives of learning and teaching tend to produce innovation and prescriptivist standardizations. This may be seen simplistically as a choice between a hands-off approach, driven by notions of historical accuracy or an interventionist, hands-on project that attempts to produce consistency and unity. Despite having formerly accepted this opposition myself, I now see it as an unhelpful and overly simplistic way of understanding the issues. The accurate description of historical Cornish need not exclude standardization of its orthography or the coining of new words.

Williams's approach is particularly interesting. He is descriptive in his acceptance of historical vocabulary from all sources and his evident rejection of the extreme 'Celtic' purisms that have characterized Revived Cornish. Thus he includes many of the numerous English borrowings that are a feature of historical Cornish: *byldya, excludya, stoppya, understonya*, and so on. (though I note that he is somewhat selective with Tregear's vocabulary, omitting for example: *prodigall, holy, beautiful*). This in marked contrast to the established practice in both UC and Kernewek Kemmyn (KK) where there has been a gradual weeding out or deselection of English vocabulary to produce forms that differ from the historical texts in composition and character. Williams's own writing is notable for having a general feel or flavour that is reminiscent of Cornish from the Tudor period and he seems to have been guided by this objective in compiling his dictionary. He frequently provides neologisms, based on English, that closely resemble borrowings already found in Middle Cornish. Ken George's *An Gerlyver Meur* (1993),[7] by contrast, includes some of the historically attested, English vocabulary but directs the reader to purist alternatives with such entries as:

byldya, VN build . . . N.B. Use drehevel.

dampnashyon: MN damnation, N.B. The modern replacement dampnyans is preferred.

I am not offering a critique of either approach in terms of right and wrong, though my own taste and practice is closer to that of Williams. I am worried, though, by the apparent closeness of language purism to essentialist notions of identity. Williams's avoidance of purism is therefore welcome and brings UCR close to the recent practice of Richard Gendall (2000).[8] Until recently the elimination of English vocabulary has been assumed to be desirable. Removing the traces of English is still seen by some as part of the process of language recovery. Cornish, it seems, must be unambiguously separate, ethnically cleansed of impurities and 'corruption'. This reveals an understanding of Cornish identity as separate or rather a desire to construct it as absolutely distinct from Englishness in ways that remove any fuzzy boundaries. More than this though, it shows an understanding of language as ideally pure. There is an evident unwillingness to live with the impurities and indeterminacies of historical Cornish because it offends the desired oppositions of Cornish/English, Celt/Saxon, Colonized/Colonizer and forces us to live with a blurring of categories. Williams's approach, like that of Gendall, is remarkable for its relative freedom from such anxieties.

I am less comfortable with Williams's readiness to form new words from Cornish elements, not because I am against the practice, but because I wonder if more restraint should be exercised. In an environment where Cornish revivalists are accused of inventing their language it would perhaps be wise to be more cautious. Obviously, there is not an easy answer. Cornish speakers want to use the language in all domains and to do so they need a full vocabulary but it is often possible to explain concepts simply and at length rather than devising neat neologisms that translate English equivalents. Do we, for example, need *ysaswonvosek*: subconscious, *ysambos*: subcontract or *yskevarweth*: subdirectory? I do not think so. These particular examples raise another difficulty; how far should we go in making use of prefixes and suffixes that had become dormant by the Middle Cornish period? The prefix used here is ys: lower, sub-, mainly known from place-names that pre-date the emergence of Cornish as a distinct language. Again, I'm not sure that there is any easy alternative but it seems that by Tudor times Cornish formed relatively few new words from suffixes and prefixes. Should that discourage us now?

Advocates of linguistic diversity are fond of telling us that individual languages represent particular worlds of thought, distinctive cultural perspectives and outlooks. If that is the case, do we not compromise the particularity of Cornish by devising a neologism to translate every word in English? The bilingual dictionary has a bearing on this, its dual-columns serving as a sort of DNA template for the lexical reconstruction of Cornish in the image of English. Where the English entry has no corresponding Cornish equivalent we are tempted to devise one. Thus Williams has: creativity: *creaster*, invisibility: *anweladewder*, linear: *lynek*, libertarian: *lybertarek*, internationalize: *keskenedhlegy*. Such one-word solutions to perceived lexical gaps subtly change the character of Cornish. It certainly alters the thought-world of Cornish to one in which such concepts as creativity suddenly exist. Of course, we need answers but perhaps these should include partial solutions, not the tidy insistence on neat semantic equivalents. This requires recognition that Cornish brings the benefit of different perspectives and subjectivities and that this has implications for vocabulary. Williams is far too sophisticated a linguist to be unaware of the issues but the cumulative effect of his neologisms is, nevertheless, a radical reshaping of Cornish. I do not know if that is bad but it does feel as though some of the particularity of the language is lost with every act of modernization and expansion.

The processes of verbal hygiene in language planning are plain examples of people acting with an apparently high degree of agency in shaping the language that they use. Williams's UCR project is the latest instance of individuals or small groups attempting to produce holistic, codified systems of pronunciation, orthography, standard grammar and approved lexicon. The peculiar circumstances of Cornish make these triumphant prescriptions somewhat inevitable but we should still be cautious. Revived Cornish has a history of infallible patriarchs, an apostolic tradition that has resulted in forms that disproportionately reflect their personal tastes as individuals. We have naturalized the idea of monumental figures producing standards that are rubber-stamped by committees of disciples. Academic commentators reinforce this paradigm, assuming the established norm of independent male leaders and decision-makers with rank and file followers. Thus, UC becomes '*Mordonek*' or '*Nancian*' whilst KK and Revived Late Cornish are referred to as Ken George's and Dick Gendall's Cornish respectively. Grass-roots loyalty to gurus works against the productive exchange of research and knowledge between groups, making it difficult for rank-and-file learners to co-operate on practical projects. It is also hard to explore hybrid, compromise forms through consensus and experimentation. Instead, change may only take place through the emergence of assertive challengers who present fully crafted alternatives and gather supporters.

All of these standards seek to impose upon the language a monoglossic form that eliminates the rich variety of historical Cornishes. If UCR, or any other standard, is to contribute fully then perhaps it needs be permissive enough for individuals to draw upon this diversity and allow traces of past Cornishes to show through. If the presence of alternative Revived Cornishes has given us anything positive it is the ability to draw upon internal variety and express our selves differently. Of course, we need a greater degree of mutual intelligibility than we have now. It will be disastrous, for example, if the various factions continue to develop neologisms independently in the manner of this dictionary. Nevertheless, it would be a great pity to lose some of the heterogolossic richness provided by the current situation.[9] Williams's UCR seems well placed to contribute to the idea of a united but plural Cornish, a situation that might allow the various standards to inform each other and overlap. In vocabulary, grammar and even pronunciation UCR comes much closer to Late Cornish than either UC or KK and seems to occupy a position between all of these alternatives. Williams has been cautious and pragmatic in revising Nance's orthography so is unlikely to lose the support of conservative UC learners. Although I will not endear myself to fellow speakers of Late Cornish by saying so, the plain fact is that the appearance of UCR makes all forms of the language more viable by aiding mutual intelligibility.

NOTES ON PRESENTATION
The technical standard of this publication, in terms of layout and printing, is high. There will be some disappointment that sources are not indicated for individual words, though such an undertaking would be easier in a Cornish-English dictionary. Curiously, only feminine gender is marked, masculine gender being assumed to be the norm.

NOTES AND REFERENCES

1. N.J.A. Williams, *Cornish Today: An Examination of the Revived Language*, Sutton Coldfield, 1995. See also N.J.A. Williams, *A Supplement to Cornish Today: Some Further Problems in Kernewek Kemmyn*, Dublin, n.d.; N.J.A. Williams, ' "Linguistically Sound Principles": The Case against Kernewek Kemmyn', in Philip Payton (ed.), *Cornish Studies: Four*, Exeter, 1996, pp.64–87.
2. N.J.A. Williams, *Clappya Kernowek: An Introduction to Unified Cornish Revised*, Redruth, 1997.
3. Payton discusses the issue of academic detractions in Philip Payton, 'The Ideology of Language Revival in Modern Cornwall', in R. Black, W. Gillies and R. O'Maolalaigh (eds), *Celtic Connections: Proceedings of the Tenth International Congress of Celtic Studies, Volume 1, Language, Literature, History, Culture*, Edinburgh, 1999, pp. 395–424.
4. D. Cameron, *Verbal Hygiene*, London, 1995, p. 3.
5. R.M. Nance, *An English-Cornish Dictionary*, Marazion, 1952.
6. W. Brown, *A Grammar of Modern Cornish*, Saltash, 1984, p. v.
7. K.J. George, *Gerlyver Kernewek Kemmyn: An Gerlyver Meur*, Saltash, 1993.
8. See for example, R.M.M. Gendall, *Tavas a Ragadazow*, Menheniot, 2000. Gendall is the main advocate of Late Cornish.
9. Mikhail Bakhtin valued 'heteroglossia' as the dynamic contestation of plural dialects and voices within a language. He views languages as inevitably an amalgam. See for example, M.M. Bakhtin, *The Dialogic Imagination*, Austin (Texas), 1998 and P. Morris, *The Bakhtin Reader*, London, 1994.

REVIEW ARTICLE

CORNISH POLITICS:
CONTINUITY AND CHANGE

Garry Tregidga

Edwin Jaggard, *Cornwall Politics in the Age of Reform*, The Royal Historical Society in conjunction with the Boydell Press, London & Cambridge, 1999, 238 pp., ISBN 0 86193 243 9,

Edwin Jaggard, *Liberalism in West Cornwall: The 1868 Election Papers of A. Pendarves Vivian, MP*, Devon and Cornwall Record Society, Exeter, New Series, Volume 42, 2000, 154 pp., ISBN 0 901853 42 9,

Over the past decade there has been a renewed interest in the subject of Cornish politics. Perspectives on the twentieth century range from Payton's seminal work in the early 1990s on the relationship between political culture and regional identity to Crago's recent consideration of gender as a factor in electoral realignment.[1] A steady stream of articles by historians like Jaggard and Elvins indicates that the political dynamics of the previous century are also being exposed to academic scrutiny and this process has recently been extended by the publication of two books on the subject. Consequently, apart from outlining the principal features of Jaggard's publications, my review article will also consider how his work has implications for future research in this wider field.

Cornwall Politics in the Age of Reform is a compelling and absorbing book that traces the story of Cornish electioneering from the unreformed system existing at the end of the eighteenth century to the rise of mass politics in the 1880s. Using Cornwall as a case study the author challenges the conventional view that the 1832 Reform Act was the critical factor in moving from patronage politics, with ideological debate believed to be non-existent, to a new order based on issues and principles. Jaggard argues convincingly that the region, despite the corruption and aristocratic interference associated with its notorious parliamentary representation of forty-four MPs, witnessed growing tensions as issues like parliamentary reform and Catholic emancipation were debated at public meetings and in the local press. Paradoxically, the politics of patronage was to linger on after 1832 in certain boroughs like St Ives and Launceston. This view of change and continuity is set against the background of the area's unique socio-economic characteristics. A separate chapter considers factors like landscape, society and the economy, with Cornwall being described as 'very much part of the "Celtic fringe", those distant and peripheral regions including Scotland, Wales and Ireland, where cultural distinctions have long been and remain evident' (p. 7). Bearing this point in mind, however, it might have been expected that the author would have subsequently made some political comparisons with the Celtic nations, especially nonconformist Wales, rather than just English counties like Essex and Buckinghamshire (pp. 100 and 135). Jaggard's clear attention to detail, however, ensures that the book certainly extends our general understanding of this period.

His latest publication continues this process by focusing on the campaign of a Liberal candidate in Cornwall at the 1868 general election. As the author points out, Arthur Pendarves Vivian, MP for West Cornwall from 1868–85, enjoyed 'an unexceptional career, only his defeat by the radical Charles Conybeare attracting national attention' (p. xiii). Nonetheless, this edited collection of papers from the year when Vivian first entered the House of Commons provides a fascinating insight into the personalities that dominated the political and social life of nineteenth-century Cornwall. Interestingly, this included Elizabeth Williams, the wife of Vivian's principal supporter and niece of Richard Davey, the retiring Liberal MP. Fifty years before women were first given the right to vote she was playing a leading role in the election campaign, keeping Vivian informed of developments in the division and identifying potential supporters (p. 54). Her background role was indicative of the wider nature of electioneering in West Cornwall. In a seat which had not been contested since its creation in 1832 the desire was to ensure a smooth transition in representation, with party notables manipulating the 'complex commercial, industrial and political networks of the division' and a careful registration of newly qualified voters in case of a possible challenge by the Conservatives (p. xiv). A useful forty-two-page introduction places the issues raised by these letters in context. The final result is an informative and skilful presentation of original documents.

We also need to consider the core themes of Jaggard's work. A welcome aspect of his approach is the way in which he gives equal consideration to the mining, fishing and agricultural parts of the region. Ignoring the tendency to focus on the cultural and economic predominance of Cornish mining, he points out that agriculture 'employed more families than any other industry' at the beginning of the nineteenth century (1999: 11). The political implications were significant. By 1815 a farmer-reformer alliance was providing the vanguard of the local parliamentary reform campaign, linking agricultural issues with the need for greater democracy and forcing out a sitting Tory MP in favour of a reformer at the 1826 general election. After 1832 the politics of the rural division of East Cornwall in particular revolved around agricultural issues, with local farmers challenging the gentry and aristocracy for political supremacy. As Jaggard indicates, the farmers soon acquired a reputation as an independent but pivotal force, defecting to the Conservatives in the late 1830s over the issue of protection before running their own candidate in the 1852 general election. On this occasion Nicholas Kendall, over thirty years before Conybeare's anti-establishment challenge in industrial Cornwall, defeated William Pole Carew, the sitting Conservative MP. This result, according to Jaggard, marked the demise of the socio-political dominance of Cornwall's landed interest: 'Never again would they be allowed to play their formerly self-appointed role in county politics, for it was the yeomen and tenant farmers who now controlled the division' (1999: 146).

It is worth noting that the author's emphasis on the pivotal role of the farming vote, combined with his recognition of intra-Cornwall differences between West and East, can also be applied to subsequent periods of the region's history. Even a cursory glance at developments after the First World War suggests a basic continuity with the past. For example, the strange survival of Cornish Liberalism was not a Cornwall-wide phenomenon. Only in the eastern divisions of Bodmin and North Cornwall, where rural politics was still based on the 'independent activism' of the farming community, did the Liberals continue as the main alternative to the Conservatives after 1945.[2] Detailed research along these lines would provide new research opportunities for both historians and political scientists looking at the Cornish experience.

Running parallel to this sense of change and continuity in the countryside was the emergence of a new political power in the towns and industrial areas of the region. Successive extensions of the franchise provided the framework for this process, with the middle class, albeit gradually in some boroughs, exercising their influence after 1832, which was followed by the greater involvement of working men as a result of the Third Reform Act of 1885. Even by the late 1870s this had resulted in greater tension between the Whig and Radical wings of the Liberal party, with demands for the introduction of public meetings with the Cornish MPs and divisions over policy issues. Vivian was the obvious victim of the emerging era of mass politics. Formerly he had been able to rely on an informal network of upper middle-class organizers in the West Cornwall division. Boundary changes in 1885 meant that Vivian found himself contesting the new seat of Camborne, described by his former colleague John St Aubyn as the stronghold of 'the extreme, and I am afraid violent, party about Redruth and Camborne' (1999: 203). His subsequent defeat by Conybeare represented the triumph of public politics. As the author concludes, 'middle- and working-class people, especially the latter in a division like Camborne, were now the political centre of gravity' (1999: 219).

However, one could argue that research on this subject should be extended beyond 1885. The Liberal split in the following year over Irish Home Rule led senior Whigs like St Aubyn and Williams, along with Leonard Courtney, the middle-class MP for Bodmin, to go over to the Unionist cause. It was now the turn of the Liberals, like their Conservative opponents earlier in the century, to experience difficulties in attracting prominent candidates from the local community. Virtually all of their nominees thereafter came from outside the region, with Thomas Agar Robartes (Bodmin, 1906 and St Austell, 1908–15) the only Liberal MP from 1887 to 1915 to be born and bred in Cornwall.[3] It was also significant that Robartes represented the old landed interest. This was in stark contrast to Wales where the strength of nonconformity, combined with the influence of the local press, created an alternative political culture. By 1892 over two-thirds of MPs representing the Principality 'were Welsh-born, many of humble origins'.[4] Why was this experience not repeated in Cornwall? Was the absence of local 'middle- and working-class' candidates a legacy of the enervating cultural environment that apparently followed the collapse of the mining industry? Can it therefore be explained on the grounds of Payton's theory of the 'Politics of Paralysis'? Was it influenced by other factors? Whatever the explanation, these issues need to be addressed so that we can establish a broader picture of Cornish politics in the last quarter of the nineteenth century.

My final comments relate to religious nonconformity. The classic Liberal-Methodist nexus, which was still influencing the nature of

Cornish politics in the mid-twentieth century, had its origins during the years covered by Jaggard. Not surprisingly, therefore, this is a theme that the author develops in both publications. He argues that even in the 1820s the Methodists, along with the 'other Dissenters were often among the leaders of the agitation' for reform (1999: 65). A variety of grievances, from the prohibition on marriage in nonconformist chapels to the obligation to pay tithes and rates to the Anglican Church, led an increasing number of Cornish Methodists into the Liberal fold. By the mid nineteenth century the numerical supremacy of the Methodists ensured that the Conservatives 'regarded their position as near hopeless' (2000: xxiii). This was certainly the case at West Cornwall in 1868 where Vivian and St Aubyn were the obvious beneficiaries of religious nonconformity:

> We have the great advantage in the 'South Country' that most of the farmers are Wesleyans and from the time that Mr W. Bickford Smith spoke at the great Camborne meeting . . . in the name of his father and the 20,000 male Wesleyans in the division, followed as he was by Dr Lyth (the superintendent Minister) coming forward at the Redruth meeting and proposing the vote of Confidence in you, the Wesleyans have been with us to a man. I need not point out to you the vast importance of this fact (2000: 46–7).

Yet Jaggard's work also reveals the need for a major study of the relationship between religion and politics in a Cornish context. The author admits that local Wesleyans were not always loyal to the Liberal cause, particularly in earlier years when there was an 'obvious tendency for a greater percentage of Methodists to vote Conservative than their Baptist and other Dissenting counterparts' (1999: 131). In 1827 opposition to Catholic emancipation undermined the progress of the Cornish reform movement, with some Methodist ministers co-operating with Cornwall's high Tories in defence of the Protestant constitution. Was this simply a product of Wesleyan loyalty to the Established Church? Did it reflect an inherent anti-Catholic dimension to Cornish politics that was to be repeated in the rise of Liberal Unionism in the 1880s and the 'Prayer Book' election of 1929? Ongoing research by Milden raises further issues. Her view is that the supremacy of the conservative Wesleyan denomination, combined with the unique 'conversion' experience of Cornish Revivalism, discouraged the early rise of working-class politics. This was particularly evident in the local reluctance to embrace the Chartists, a group that Jaggard does not really focus on.[5] Given the centrality of religion to Cornish politics in the nineteenth and twentieth centuries a project that focuses on this subject is long overdue.

CONCLUSION

Publication reviews offer an appropriate opportunity to assess broader developments taking place in particular fields of research. With Jaggard's recent work on the nineteenth century it is evident that the study of electoral politics is currently one of the core areas of inquiry in Cornish Studies. This new insight into the changing political culture of the early period can now go alongside studies of the later period, such as established research into the rise of anti-metropolitanism after 1945 and the current work by the Cornish Audio Visual Archive on qualitative micro-politics.[6] These publications also offer pointers to other areas of inquiry like rural politics, questions of class, and the complex links with religion. In that sense the wider significance of Jaggard's work is that it provides the foundations for further research on Cornish politics within the interdisciplinary framework of New Cornish Studies.

NOTES AND REFERENCES

1. P. Payton, *The Making of Modern Cornwall: Historical Experience and the Persistence of 'Difference'*, Redruth, 1992; P. Payton, 'Labour Failure and Liberal Tenacity: Radical Politics and Cornish Political Culture', in Philip Payton (ed.), *Cornish Studies: One*, Exeter, 1994; T. Crago, 'Play the Game as Men Play It: Women in Politics during the Era of the "Cornish-Proto-Alignment" 1918–1922', in Philip Payton (ed.), *Cornish Studies: Eight*, Exeter, 2000.
2. G. Tregidga, 'Socialism and the Old Left: The Labour Party in Cornwall during the Inter-War Period', in Philip Payton (ed.), *Cornish Studies: Seven*, Exeter, 1999, p. 90.
3. *The Times*, 2 February 1892; *Royal Cornwall Gazette*, 30 June 1892; J. Vincent and M. Stenton (eds), *McCalmont's Parliamentary Poll Book: British Election Results, 1832–1918*, Brighton, 1971, pp. 49–51 and 196.
4. K.O. Morgan, *Wales in British Politics, 1868–1922*, Cardiff, 1970, pp. 112–19.
5. K. Milden, 'Cornish Methodism: A Culture of Conversion', in the *Cornish History Network Newsletter*, December 2000, Issue 9, pp. 10–12; K. Milden, 'Culture of Conversion: Religion and Politics in the Cornish Mining Communities', paper presented at the third annual conference of the Cornish History Network, 27 January 2001.
6. T. Crago, 'Cornish Audio Visual Archive: Voices of a Nation', paper presented at the annual conference of the Oral History Society, London Guildhall University, 22–3 June 2001.

NOTES ON CONTRIBUTORS

Manuel Alberro is a retired research scientist and university Professor. He holds first degrees from the Universities of Oviedo (Spain) and Uppsala (Sweden), together with a doctorate from the University of Guelph (Canada). He is resident in Uppsala, Sweden, where he is currently pursuing his interest in Celtic Studies. He is the author of several books and numerous articles, and recent publications include 'El NW de la Peninsula Ibérica como parte de la Zona Atlántica de la Edad del Bronce', *Historia Antiqua*, XXV, 2001; 'Significancia de las referencias a España en las sagas célticas de la época pagana recogidas en los manuscritos medievales de Irlanda, Gales y Escocia', *Veleia*, 2001; and 'La colonización de Irlanda y Escocia por grupos celtas procedentes de la peninsula Ibérica según los manuscritos medievales escocéses', in S. Crespo Ortiz de Zarate and A. Alonso Avila (eds), *Scripta Antiqua in Honorem A. Montegro Duque et J.M. Blázequez Martínez*, University of Valladolid, 2001.

Philipa Aldous joined the University of Plymouth in 1996. She has recently completed her Ph.D. thesis on attitudes to migration amongst young people in Cornwall and Devon.

Chris Carter is Research Fellow in Knowledge Management at the University of Leicester. He is a native of Cornwall and is interested in its history and culture. He shares David Crowther's interest in the opportunities presented by the World Wide Web.

Paul Cockerham practises full-time as a veterinary surgeon in Cornwall, but is also a postgraduate student at the Institute of Cornish Studies, University of Exeter, researching the funeral monument industry of early modern Cornwall. He is a Fellow of the Society of Antiquaries, a consultant to the Diocesan Advisory Committee in Truro, and has published several articles on the cultural signifance of church monuments in Cornwall, Brittany, France and Ireland. Recent publications include 'Seventeenth-century Tile-tombs in Normandy— An Interim Appraisal' (with John Coales), in *Journal of the British Archaeological Association*, 153, 2000.

David Crowther is Reader in Marketing and Director of Research at the University of North London Business School and has a strong research interest in the World Wide Web as a mechanism for communication and developing community spirit. He lives in Derbyshire, which he insists is the last remaining Celtic stronghold in Britain. Consequently, he has a lifelong interest in Celtic history and tradition.

Brian Elvins, a native of Mevagissey, was formerly head of the sixth form at the Kings of Wessex Upper School in Cheddar, Somerset. He was an authority on the politics of nineteenth-century Cornwall, articles on which he contributed to both *Cornish Studies* and the *Journal of the Royal Institution of Cornwall*. Sadly, he died while this edition of *Cornish Studies* was in press, and his article is published as a posthumous memorial to his outstanding contribution to the political history of modern Cornwall.

Andrew Hawke is the Assistant Editor/Systems Manager of *Geiriadur Prifysgol Cymru* (the University of Wales Dictionary of the Welsh Language) at Aberystwyth. He was an Honorary Research Fellow of the Institute of Cornish Studies, University of Exeter, in 1981–3, when he was working on a new historical dictionary of Cornish, a project he still hopes to complete. He is particularly interested in surviving manuscripts in Cornish and contributed several articles on them to the First Series of *Cornish Studies*.

Cheryl Hayden teaches journalism at the University of Queensland, Australia and the Queensland University of Technology, and is an M.A. student on the University of Exeter's Institute of Cornish Studies/Department of Lifelong Learning on-line, distance-learning programme in Cornish Studies.

Neil Kennedy is Lecturer in Cultural Studies at Falmouth College of Arts. Since 1985 he has worked with Richard Gendall to develop and promote a standard form of Revived Late/Modern Cornish. He is an active teacher of Cornish and has produced several books and recordings for beginners. He is interested in developing new ways of learning, and recently published *Imagination in the Teaching of Cornish* (2000).

Philip Payton is Professor of Cornish Studies at the University of Exeter and Director of the Institute of Cornish Studies in Truro. He holds doctorates from the Universities of Adelaide (1979) and Plymouth (1990), and is the author of numerous articles and books, including *The Making of Modern Cornwall* (1992), *Cornwall* (1996) and *The Cornish Overseas* (1999).

John Rule is Professor of History at the University of Southampton. Born in Redruth, his doctoral thesis in 1971 was on the social history of Cornish mining communities in the eighteenth and nineteenth centuries. As well as a number of essays on Cornish history, he has written numerous books and articles on British social and labour history. His major two-volumed study of the economy and society of Hanoverian England—*The Vital Century: England's Developing Economy 1714–1815* and *Albion's People: English Society 1714–1815*, was published in 1992.

Sharron P. Schwartz is a postgraduate student and Honorary University Fellow at the Institute of Cornish Studies, University of Exeter, where she is currently completing her Ph.D. thesis on the Cornish in nineteenth-century Latin America. She is also a part-time lecturer at the University's Department of Lifelong Learning, based in Truro, Director of the Cornish Global Migration Programme at Murdoch House, Redruth, and a consultant for Cornwall Archaeological Unit's construction of the bid for World Heritage Site status for Cornwall's mining districts. She is the author of several articles and the book *Lanner: A Cornish Mining Parish* (1998).

Garry Tregidga is Assistant Director of the Institute of Cornish Studies, University of Exeter. He is founder of both the Cornish History Network and the Cornish Audio Visual Archive, and has written widely on Cornish politics. His book *The Liberal Party in South-West Britain Since 1918* was published in 2000 by University of Exeter Press.

Malcolm Williams is Principal Lecturer in Sociology at the University of Plymouth and Visiting Fellow at the Institute of Education in London. He is the author of four books in social research methodology and philosophy. His latest book is *Science and Social Science* (2000). His research interests encompass migration and housing with special reference to Cornwall.

N.J.A. Williams is Lecturer in Irish at University College Dublin and a Bard of the Cornish Gorsedd. He has taught and written widely on the Celtic languages, and amongst his major works on Cornish are *Cornish Today* (1995), *Clappya Kernowek* (1997), and *English-Cornish Dictionary: Gerlyver Sawsnek-Kernowek* (2000).

12

Transfer.

62 30 53 Sort Code

03071440 A/c

Ref Payee

A/c/MI HAI ref Pay

£ ~~3080~~ 2p

2,400

Vanguard.

Jolorathan Jennings

~~Johnson~~

(0207 857 4641)

08009 88275.